Herman L. Bachne

Madison

ENGLAND IN
TUDOR AND STUART TIMES
(1485—1714)

ENGLAND IN TUDOR AND STUART TIMES

(1485—1714)

BY

ROBERT M. RAYNER, B.A.

WITH 6 MAPS AND 9 DATE CHARTS

LONGMANS, GREEN AND CO.

LONDON • NEW YORK • TORONTO

LONGMANS, GREEN AND CO LTD
6 & 7 CLIFFORD STREET LONDON W I

ALSO AT MELBOURNE AND CAPE TOWN

LONGMANS, GREEN AND CO INC
55 FIFTH AVENUE NEW YORK 3

LONGMANS, GREEN AND CO
215 VICTORIA STREET TORONTO I

ORIENT LONGMANS LTD
BOMBAY CALCUTTA MADRAS

BIBLIOGRAPHICAL NOTE

FIRST EDITION . . . . *July* 1930
NEW IMPRESSIONS . . . . *August* 1933
September 1934, *September* 1935,
October 1936, *February* 1941,
October 1952

Made and printed in Great Britain by
William Clowes and Sons, Limited, London and Beccles

PREFACE

THIS book is, like my "England in Modern Times," primarily designed for the use of classes studying for School Certificate and Matriculation Examinations.

These examinations have a great and increasing influence on the aims and methods of our Secondary Schools. It has long been customary to decry that influence as a curse to the true educationist; but as regards History, at any rate, the type of paper set has in recent years undergone a notable change for the better. So marked has been this development that the text-books of a generation ago are now almost useless. Step by step, the subject is becoming a means of bringing young people into contact with the culture-epoch into which they have been born, of giving them some insight into the interplay of character and destiny, of helping them to understand the social, political, and economic conditions in which their lives will be lived. Moreover, it is now generally recognised that most boys and girls of fifteen or sixteen have reached a stage of mental development in which the effort to group and interpret facts has become more pleasurable and more profitable than the mere comprehension of them.

This humanising of History is still in its early stages. It demands the co-operation of teacher and examiner, for in the conditions which prevail in our schools to-day, neither can move very far or very fast without the other. My ambition in writing this book has been to make such contribution to the process as lay in my power. I have not tried to make the subject seem *easy*: my aim has rather been to make it seem *worth while*—to help boys and girls to realise that the exhilaration of rising to a broader mental horizon is ample compensation for the effort involved.

v

There are two methods open to the writer of such a book as
this. On the one hand he may plough steadily through years
and reigns, sacrificing co-ordination of ideas to chronological
sequence. On the other, he may devote long passages to
particular aspects of his subject, such as " British India in the
Eighteenth Century," or " Politics and Parties between the
Reform Bills," to the dire confusion of the pupil's time-sense.
The plan of this book is an attempt to find a middle way between
these extremes. Its chapters are of approximately uniform
length—a length which experience has shown to be readily
assimilable in one lesson-period. Each chapter deals with a
definite topic, subdivided into sections with appropriate sub-
titles ; but the sequence of these topics has been contrived with
a view to maintaining the sense of onward-moving time. The
chapters are grouped into four Books, each of which is designed
to occupy the attention of the class for about half a term, leaving
the last half term of the school year for a general revision. At
the end of each chapter suggestions are made for discussion,
either orally in class, or as themes for written work ; and each
Book is furnished with a set of test-questions on the period with
which it deals. The chronological backbone of the book is
supplied by Date Charts, in which references are made to the
sections of the text which deal with the matter in question ; and
similar references are given in the course of the letter-press itself.

In matters of detail the book owes much to my friend and
pupil J. Plamenatz (Scholar of Oriel).

CONTENTS

BOOK I

THE NATIONAL MONARCHY (1485-1559)

BOOK II

THE AGE OF ELIZABETH (1558–1603)

CONTENTS

BOOK III

THE TRIUMPH OF PURITANISM (1603–1660)

BOOK IV

THE TRIUMPH OF WHIGGISM (1660–1714)

CONTENTS

CONTENTS

ENGLAND IN TUDOR AND STUART TIMES

BOOK I

The National Monarchy

(1485–1559)

LOOKING back through the history of Western Europe during the Christian Era, we can see that it falls into four epochs, each of about five hundred years. During the first of these Europe was held together by the Roman Empire. Then that empire broke up, and there began the era known as " The Dark Ages," when incursions of primitive folk broke up the settled life of Roman civilisation, absorbing some of its ideas, but turning its unity and order into a welter of confusion in which Might was Right. Out of this chaos arose a new organisation of society which we called " Feudalism," when Western Europe was held together—more closely, perhaps, in theory than in practice— by the Papacy and the Holy Roman Empire. Then, in the course of the fifteenth century, these " Middle Ages " came to an end, and there developed the conditions of life in which we live to-day—an era in which the most salient features are National Patriotism, the Power of Money, Religious Schism, and the growth of man's control over the forces of nature.

In this Book I of our history we shall study the transition to this latest epoch in our own country ; in other words, we shall see how the foundations of modern England were laid. By the end of it we shall find that Feudalism and Catholicism have been replaced by a strong centralised Monarchy and a National Church.

THE REIGN OF HENRY VII

1485	Bosworth ⚔ (§5) HENRY VII	1485
1486	King's marriage (§6) Birth of Prince Arthur (§6)	1486
1487	Stoke ⚔ (§6) Court of Star Chamber (§7)	1487
1488		1488
1489	Treaty of Medina del Campo (§8)	1489
1490		1490
1491	Birth of Prince Henry	1491
1492	Columbus reaches West Indies (§4) Peace of Etaples (§8)	1492
1493		1493
1494		1494
1495	Poyning's Laws (§9)	1495
1496	Magnus Intercursus (§9)	1496
1497	Cabot reaches Labrador (§10) Blackheath ⚔ (§9)	1497
1498	Vasco da Gama reaches India (§4)	1498
1499	Execution of Warwick & Warbeck (§9)	1499
1500		1500
1501		1501
1502	Death of Prince Arthur (§10)	1502
1503	Betrothal of Henry and Catherine (§10)	1503
1504		1504
1505		1505
1506		1506
1507		1507
1508		1508
1509	HENRY VIII	1509

CHAPTER I

The Sunset of the Middle Ages

The differences between medieval and modern times may be summed up under three heads. Firstly, the feudal system was replaced, in most of Western Europe, by nation-states, in which authority was concentrated in the hands of monarchs. Secondly, manufactures began to be produced on a larger scale, and to be bought and sold over wider areas. Thirdly, there was a resistance to the control of the Catholic Church over the beliefs and thoughts of men.

These changes were very gradual. They took place at different times, in different ways, and in different degrees in different countries ; and they were often closely connected with each other. In this chapter we shall get a glimpse of how they came about in England.

1. *The Decay of Feudalism*

In the Middle Ages the relationship between man and man depended mainly on the holding of land—then almost the sole source of wealth. Tenants paid rents not in money but in services to a feudal superior. These services might consist of fighting for him or of working for him. The King himself was little more than a supreme feudal overlord. He was expected to " live of his own "—that is to say, to carry on the government with very little in the way of taxation ; and his fighting strength consisted merely of his tenants and sub-tenants. Nobody felt any " patriotism " ; what held society together 'was loyalty between persons. As a matter of fact, feudal lords were petty sovereigns who often made private war on each other, or even on the King himself. England suffered less than Continental

3

countries from this disorder. A series of strong and able kings
—William I, Henry I and II, Edward I—were able to keep it
from going as far as it went in France and Germany ; but even
here we had anarchy under Stephen, a civil war under John,
" The Barons' Wars " under Henry III, and the " Lords
Ordainers " under Edward II.

It is easy to see the drawbacks of the Feudal System. It led
to internal disorder ; it made the great majority of the people
serfs, tied to the land they tilled and subject to the will of their
lord. Yet it must have fulfilled the needs of the time, or it
would never have grown up spontaneously all over Western
Europe as the only way out of the confusion that followed the
break-up of the Roman Empire. Whatever its shortcomings,
it was a definite organisation, in which each man had a place,
with rights dependent on the performance of duties.

Nevertheless, after the end of the thirteenth century it began
to decay. The " Barons " gradually became less independent
of the King's government, and at the same time lost their hold
over their own sub-tenants and serfs. The chief cause of
the growth of kingship was the development of national feeling
(of which we shall have more to say in the next section), which
gave increased prestige to the man who embodied it. The
invention of gunpowder tended the same way ; for the King
alone possessed artillery, and his guns could batter down the
stone walls behind which rebellious nobles had hitherto been
able to defy the sovereign. Again, the tie between baron and
knight was loosened by the prolonged war in France, in which
feudal service (limited to forty days per annum) had to be
replaced by regular professional armies. And the tie of service
between lord and serf was broken by a similar cause. To get
money with which to pay and equip these professional soldiers,
nobles were ready to let their " villeins " pay for their land in
money (gained by selling produce at a market) instead of in
goods and services ; and labourers who pay a money-rent
cannot be tied to the soil : they are in a position to make free
contracts. Moreover, the Church often encouraged lords to
" manumit," or set free, their serfs. Lastly, the acute shortage
of labour caused by the Black Death hastened the process by
improving the bargaining power of the working man.

Another important factor working in the same direction was the growth of commerce. Feudal life was lived in the country-side, on isolated, self-supplying manors, with here and there a little township in which markets were held every month or so for the exchange of goods. This town life was developing, steadily if slowly, all through the Middle Ages, owing partly to the Crusades (which enlarged men's ideas and led to foreign trade), partly to the Black Death (which broke up the old manorial life and drove many serfs to take refuge from their lords in towns); and partly to the immigration of foreign craftsmen (especially cloth-weavers) fleeing from similar oppression in Flanders and the Netherlands. Many towns gained charters from the kings, by which they were protected in return for a fixed tribute in money. Their prosperity was closely bound up with the growth of royal power, inasmuch as commerce can only flourish where the central authority is strong enough to keep order and make the roads safe for merchandise.

2. *The New Monarchies of Europe*

Amidst the chaos of the Dark Ages men had looked back longingly to the great days of Rome, when the civilised world had been an organic unit. Several attempts—the most famous being that of Charlemagne—were made to bring back peace and order by reviving the imperial authority; and the last of these attempts, " The Holy Roman Empire," survived right down to modern times. But by the close of the Middle Ages the actual authority of " The Emperor " had shrunk to a rather shadowy control over a conglomeration of states between the Rhine and the Oder. The Imperial Crown was elective. Whenever an Emperor died, half a dozen German princes known as " Electors " met and selected a successor. By the end of the fifteenth century, however, this election had become a mere fiction, for from 1432 onwards it was always the reigning Archduke of Austria that was chosen. The title conferred dignity rather than real power on its wearer, since the machinery that had to be set in motion to raise an imperial tax or army was so cumbrous as to be almost useless.

Thus " the Holy Roman Emperor " had little real authority

outside his own dominions, and none at all in England, France, and Spain.   Each of these countries had become an independent State, consisting of a compact block of territory the inhabitants of which spoke the same language and felt that they " belonged together."   These were the first countries in which nation and monarchy coincided.*   In each of them this " patriotic " feeling arose during the fifteenth century, and in each it was largely the outcome of a successful war waged by a king.

King Henry V was the first king of England to be granted the customs duties for life by Parliament.   In carrying on the war in France he relied not on knights and their squires, but on sturdy English yeomen with their cloth-yard shafts.   Agincourt was felt to be a national victory.   The ultimate expulsion of the English troops from France could not efface this patriotism, nor did the weak character of Henry VI destroy the feeling that the nation was embodied in the King.

Contemporaneously with this, the provinces of France were united into one great kingdom.   Saint Joan called into existence a national spirit which cleared the soil of France from enemies, and all the French lands which had been in the possession of the kings of England fell into the hands of the kings of France. Charles VII found himself able to impose a general *taille* or poll-tax, with the proceeds of which he maintained a regular force and kept in check his feudal chieftains.   His work of consolidation was carried on by Louis XI, who incorporated ten more provinces in the realm, and left the frontiers of France much as they are to-day.

In Spain a similar process was at work.   The nobles had for centuries carried on spasmodic struggles with the Mohammedan peoples who had conquered the country in the eighth century ; but in 1463 the marriage of Ferdinand of Aragon with Isabella of Castile formed a united government strong enough to focus a national effort which in 1492 succeeded in driving the Moors out of the peninsula altogether.   Here, again, had the monarchy

* We are to-day so accustomed to the idea of nation-states that we can hardly realise what a new thing this was ; but we can get a glimpse of the cosmopolitanism of the Middle Ages when we recall that our Henry II and our Simon de Montfort were both French by birth, upbringing, and speech, but were never felt to be " foreigners."

established its position as the symbol of unity and of success in arms.

3. *The Church also Loses its Grip*

The spiritual authority of the Church was also coming into question ; and this brought about a far more important change in men's outlook than the fading of the vision of a universal Empire. For the Popes had come much nearer than the Emperors to making good their claim to supremacy. For centuries the Church had been a sort of ecclesiastical empire, with its own capital (at Rome), its own system of laws (the Canon Law), its own revenue (from tithes, bequests, law-fees, feudal dues), and its own universal language (Latin). It had divided Christendom into provinces under archbishops, dioceses under bishops, and parishes under priests ; and all the members of this vast and complicated hierarchy owed their spiritual authority to the Pope. The Church's influence over the minds of men was immense. Her sacraments were held to be necessary for the salvation of souls from an eternity of torment. Her courts had the sole right to deal with such matters as wills and marriages. She had a complete monopoly of education ; and since nearly all educated men were in her orders, she had undisputed control over the sciences and arts, and her clergy were the only men who could act as lawyers, ministers of State, and civil servants.

But during the fifteenth century there were many signs that this dominion over the minds and actions of men was breaking up. The prime cause of the decay was the root of all evil—money. Vast wealth had been accumulated, partly from property bequeathed for Masses and prayers, and to help the work of the Church ; partly by the extortion of fees in the Church courts, especially those at Rome, where cases often dragged on for years ; partly by the traditional right of the priest to a tenth part of the annual produce of the soil. Worldly cares and worldly riches became the preoccupation of many of the higher clergy, while many monks and friars lived idle and dissolute lives, supported by wealthy foundations. Priests were beginning to be looked upon with dislike and disdain. Though very few people as yet questioned the doctrines of the Catholic faith, the Church that embodied that faith was losing, decade by decade, its old hold over men's allegiance. Hence such popular revolts as that of Wiclif in England and that of Huss in Bohemia. The Church managed to crush these movements, but not the dissatisfaction of which they were evidence.

Moreover, the Popes ruled part of Italy as temporal princes, and the growing sentiment of nationality made men resent seeing a foreign potentate exercise authority in their country, and exact tribute from it. Several national governments had openly resisted these claims. In England, for instance, was passed the Statute of Premunire (1393) which forbade the bringing into the country of papal " Bulls " (official announcements) ; while the French king had obtained (1432) a " Pragmatic Sanction " by which ecclesiastical authority in France was to be shared by himself.

Respect for the Papacy was further weakened by " The Great Schism " (1378–1447) when rival Popes, each claiming to be the sole representative of God, vituperated each other across Europe. This scandal was eventually brought to an end by a Church Council, and several attempts were made to reform the other evils and abuses which we have described ; but in the end the Papacy succeeded in maintaining its wealth and privileges intact. Nevertheless, the postponement of the day of reckoning had only made it the more inevitable. The feeling of dissatisfaction was always there, and it grew stronger than ever when, towards the end of the century, the triumph of the Papacy was followed by the election of several worldly-minded and evil-living Popes. A timely reform from within might have saved the Church from the revolt which later tore half of Europe permanently from allegiance to her.

4. *The Spirit of the Age*

Closely connected with the political, social, and religious developments of this age of transition was an increased adventurousness of mind which led men to take up all sorts of new ideas. Gunpowder, for instance, had been brought to Europe as early as 1250, by a Mongolian conqueror, but it was only now that the invention was taken and adapted for Western warfare—with the result that chivalry died a natural death. Printing, again, had long been known in China ; and Europeans would certainly have found out about it before the time of Gutenburg (*circa* 1460) if they had felt the need for books. Nor was it a mere accident that a method was now discovered of making paper : when men want such things urgently enough they can always find a way to get them. And these two inventions between them destroyed for ever the Church's monopoly of education.

An innovation of almost equal importance was the mariner's compass. This, too, had been " in the air " for centuries, but it was only now that experiments were made which led to a really serviceable instrument ; and men were impelled to make those experiments by an irresistible yearning to explore the mysteries of the western ocean. Christopher Columbus was no isolated " crank " ; many others were bent on finding a westward route to the " Indies." America would have been discovered very little later if he had never been born. As a matter of fact, he never got farther than the islands of the West Indies, and died in the belief that these were a part of Asia. The mainland of America was first reached a year or two later by John Cabot, who sailed from Bristol, and by Amerigo Vespucci, who gave his name to the whole continent. Meanwhile, Portuguese adventurers had pushed farther and farther down the coast of Africa. At about the same time that America was discovered, Vasco da Gama succeeded in opening an all-sea route to Asia round the Cape of Good Hope.

Incidentally, these voyages provide us with a good example of how the new spirit of adventure reacted on the changes already in progress in European civilisation. By proving conclusively that the earth was round, the voyagers struck a heavy blow at the credit of the Church, which maintained that Scripture implied that it was flat. Again, the fact that Europe soon began to be flooded with gold and silver from America encouraged the development of commerce, for which an abundant coinage was essential. Furthermore, these adventurers were dependent on royal support, their discoveries became royal domains, and the new wealth flowed mostly into royal coffers : hence a further increase in the power and prestige of kingship.

5. *The Tudor Usurpation*

The change from medieval to modern times was a very gradual process. So far as English history is concerned, we usually take the accession of the first of the Tudor kings in 1485 as the turning-point. Let us review the circumstances which led up to that event.

At the beginning of the century, a younger branch of the reigning Plantagenet dynasty had seized the throne. The second of these Lancastrian kings, Henry V, had sought to strengthen his doubtful position by reviving an old claim to the throne of France. For a time this renewal of the Hundred Years' War had gone entirely in favour of England, but this success had been mainly due to disunion among the French. Those dissensions once healed, the tide turned ; and there followed thirty years of accumulating disaster for the English armies, leading in the end to their expulsion from France altogether.

Then came a period of almost the same length during which England was disturbed by the " Wars of the Roses," a long-drawn-out struggle between the rival branches of the Plantagenet dynasty, each supported and abandoned in turn by various great aristocratic families. The weak-minded Henry VI was dethroned by Edward of York in 1461, restored in 1471, and finally defeated and killed a few weeks later. Edward IV continued to reign until 1483, when his death at the early age of forty-one left the throne to a twelve-year-old son, who became Edward V. This boy and his younger brother Richard, Duke of York, were murdered by their uncle, the late king's brother, who had himself crowned as Richard III.

This was the climax to half a century of disorder, crime, violence, and disaster. The feeble rule of " the royal saint," Henry VI, had allowed the country to fall a prey to self-seeking and violent nobles. The distractions of the constant faction-fighting had sorely hampered the growing commercial interests of the middle class. The repeated changes in the monarchy had robbed the royal authority of almost all its old dignity and power ; and now the throne had been seized by a heartless murderer.

It was a general longing for peace and quiet, intensified by the unpopularity of Richard III, that gave an opportunity for a fresh Lancastrian claimant to come forward, in the person of Henry, Duke of Richmond. As a matter of fact, the claims of this young man to be of the blood royal were slender in the extreme. His father was the son of Henry V's widow, by her second marriage to a Welsh courtier named Owen Tudor. His mother was one of the Beauforts, a side-branch of the Lancas-

The Claims of Henry VII

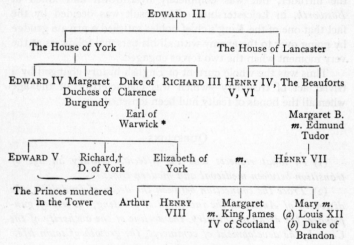

* Personated by Lambert Simnel.
† Personated by Perkin Warbeck.

trian family which had been debarred by law from the throne. Shadowy as Richmond's claim was, it had been sufficient to make his relatives feel that England was no safe place for him with a Yorkist king on the throne, and he had spent the latter part of the reign of Edward IV an exile in France.

The death of Edward IV and his sons, and the hatred inspired by Richard III, gave Richmond his chance to make a bid for the throne, with the support of a party among the English nobles. He sank all his available funds in raising a body of French troops, and set sail from Brittany for the coast of South Wales, a district which had always been devoted to Lancastrian interests. With ranks now swelled to a total of 10,000 men, he marched into Shropshire, where he was joined by the Earl of Shrewsbury with some five hundred retainers—almost the only English-speaking members of his little army.

It gives us an idea of the paralysis which had fallen upon the English monarchy since the brave days of Agincourt that this half-organised handful of men could successfully defy it. King Richard got together what forces he could muster to challenge the intruder, but was completely overthrown and killed at *Bosworth*, in Leicestershire. The result was decided by the fact that one of the King's chief nobles satisfied a private grudge by going over to the enemy with all his personal followers at the very moment when the two forces engaged.

Thus was the whole current of English history changed by a trivial act of treachery—which was characteristic of the age when all the bonds of fealty had been loosened.

QUESTIONS

(1) *In what respects was the fifteenth century an age of transition between medieval and modern times ?*

(2) *Trace the connection between the decay of feudalism, the discovery of America, the invention of printing, the use of gun-powder, the decay of chivalry, the decline of the authority of the Church, the development of commerce, the growth of town life.*

CHAPTER II

The New Monarchy

(1485–1509)

The subject of this chapter is the reign of Henry VII. We shall not find him a very attractive figure, but we shall see that he was one of the most successful of English statesmen. He had insight to see what the country needed and practical ability to supply it. At the beginning of his reign he was surrounded with danger and difficulty ; but he left to his son and successor a secure throne, efficient governmental machinery, an established position among the Powers of Europe, and a goodly supply of that first requisite of political power in our modern civilisation—money.

6. *Taking Possession*

Henry Tudor was acclaimed King by his followers on Bosworth Field, but his position was far from secure. The fact that a mere skirmish had sufficed to place him on the throne suggested that it would be equally easy to drive him off it. But he was well fitted both by character and training to cope with such a situation. He was not yet thirty years of age, but a life spent in exile, amid suspicions, plots, and intrigues had long since killed all youthful qualities in him, and in demeanour and outlook he was more like a man of forty. Wary, shrewd, and cool, he was always swayed more by calculation than by passion. The chief influence on his character as a statesman was his admiration for the great Louis XI of France, who had died a few years before, after a reign in which sagacity, unscrupulousness, and persistence had doubled both the territories and the power of the French monarchy.

Immediately after the battle, Henry led his followers on to

London, where he had himself formally proclaimed King. He was received by the civic authorities with respect but without enthusiasm. After all, what was there to give them hope that the end of the changes and chances of civil war had come at last —that this was the king who would give them the secure and orderly government for which they longed ? But from the first Henry showed that he had a clear head and a definite policy. In appointing his Council of State, he was bound to include a number of the nobles who had opposed Richard III ; but all the really responsible offices were filled by men who were at once more efficient and more subservient—plain members of the rising middle class who owed their position to his favour, " such as kept watch with him upon almost all men else." And when a few weeks later Parliament met, Henry showed himself equally adept at handling that. It hurried through a Declaratory Act which stated that " the inheritance of the crowns of England and France rest remain and abide in the most royal person of our new sovereign lord King Henry VII." The precise nature of his claims was passed over in tactful silence—to have discussed them would have exposed their weakness. The Houses then went on to grant him tunnage and poundage (*i.e.* the customs duties) for life, and to pass an Act restoring to the Crown all the lands which had belonged to Henry VI in 1455.

His next care was to make a wise and advantageous marriage. On the very day after Bosworth he had taken steps to secure the two principal Yorkist claimants to the throne. One of them, the ten-year-old Edward Duke of Warwick, the son of his predecessor, was shut up in the Tower. The other was the Lady Elizabeth, the elder child of Edward IV. In her case he designed not merely to cancel her claims, but to use them to buttress his own. By marrying her he muzzled all except the most violent of the Yorkists, and a child born of the marriage would unite the blood of both the rival Houses. The wedding took place early in 1486, as soon as the King's coronation had made clear his own prior and independent claims to the throne. Later in the year there was born a son, who was given the old Anglo-Welsh name of Arthur. It seemed that the dynastic quarrel which had rent England for thirty years was at last happily settled.

There were still some irreconcilable spirits, however, and it was not long before they made an attempt to overturn the new régime. Their great difficulty was the lack of a candidate for the throne. One Symonds, a fanatically Yorkist priest, tried to get over this by training one of his pupils, the son of an Oxford tradesman named *Simnel* to impersonate the imprisoned Earl of Warwick. The King paraded the real Warwick through the streets of London ; but supporters of the White Rose who had fled abroad sent a body of foreign mercenaries to Dublin, which was chosen as the headquarters of the enterprise. There the young Simnel was crowned " King Edward VI," and in July, 1487, he crossed the Irish Channel with some 6,000 men to renew the Wars of the Roses. But the Tudor government had already had time to take root, and very few Englishmen welcomed the idea of having a king imposed on them by Dutch and Irish soldiers. The Yorkist force grew weaker instead of stronger as it marched through the Midlands, and at the village of Stoke (near Newark) it was completely destroyed by the royal forces. The incident did Henry's position more good than harm. For one thing, it enabled him to advertise his self-confidence by contemptuously sparing Simnel's life and taking him into the royal service as a kitchen-boy. For another, most of the chief Yorkists were killed at Stoke, and their estates became forfeit to the Crown.

7. *Making Good*

Thus, within two years of Bosworth, Henry had made his position secure, and was able to develop his plans for the government of the country. He realised that what England wanted was a ruler who would crush out of existence, once for all, the elements of disorder which had so long distracted her. The task was colossal. Three kings had died violent deaths within thirty years. The habit of obedience to government seemed altogether dead. Bands of armed ruffians plundered the countryside, many of them claiming to be Yorkists. The great nobles had made themselves practically independent of the law of the land, and justice was paralysed by the fact that the judges on circuit were overawed by these local magnates.

Still, the situation was not without its more favourable aspects. The civil wars had greatly weakened the noble families. Some of the leading members of them had fallen in battle, others had perished on the scaffold ; in many cases the titles were held by mere children. Moreover, the " barons " no longer acted together as a class, as they had done under John and Henry III ; their strength was dissipated by rivalries in the race for family aggrandisement. The lesser nobility, on the other hand, the one-manor men, had taken little part in the late faction-fights. They had no ambition to act as king-makers. They were already beginning to develop into the " country gentlemen " of later times. What they wanted was a government that would give them peace and quiet in which to cultivate their estates. The growing commercial class, again, had everything to gain from firm government. For years they had been plagued by the exactions and robberies of the rival factions. These two classes, then—the gentry and the merchants—were both on Henry's side ; and it was largely through the methods of government that he now set up that they became the dominant influence in English society for the next four centuries.

Henry realised that the days of the medieval monarchy were over. The source of power was not now feudal loyalty but ready cash. He took every opportunity of extracting money from the nobles, for this operation served a double purpose : it weakened them and strengthened him. We have already mentioned that he took back into his own possession all the lands granted by his predecessors for the past thirty years. He also inflicted heavy fines on Yorkists and on magnates who disregarded his order that armed retainers should be disbanded. And this policy had the further advantage that it filled his coffers without cramping commerce with burdensome taxation. Moreover, many of the men of humble birth whom he employed in offices of state could be economically rewarded by preferment in the Church.

The power of the nobles was further crushed by the setting up of a special tribunal in London to deal with cases in which they were concerned. Hitherto, whatever violence or injustice they had committed, their local influence had sufficed to enable them to escape punishment when the judge came round. Henceforth they were compelled to appear before a special court consisting of members of the King's Council, whom they could neither frighten nor bribe. This tribunal was known as *The Court of Star Chamber* because it usually sat in a room with stars painted on the ceiling. It had already been long in existence, but it now greatly increased in importance and became a valuable instrument for building up the power of the Crown and restoring the reign of law.

8. " *Peace with Money* "

" Diplomacy," the maintenance of regular relations between rulers, was only just beginning at this time. It was at once a cause and a symptom of the development of kingship. In the Middle Ages there had been no permanent alliances between monarchs, and embassies had only been sent to arrange particular pieces of business. The fact that the conduct of this department of government was in the hands of the kings did much to enhance their power and prestige.

Henry made full use of this new instrument in pursuing his great aim of building up the English monarchy. Obviously, it would greatly strengthen his position if he could make an alliance with one or other of the rival Continental potentates who were already intriguing against each other. The opportunity soon arose. Charles VIII, the young King of France, was eager to absorb in his dominions the last of the independent provinces, Brittany, the ruler of which was a young girl, the Duchess Anne. But the King of Spain, Ferdinand, was already jealous of the growing power of France, and was particularly anxious to prevent that power from being further strengthened by the addition of the valuable sea-faring activities of Brittany. Here, then, was Henry's chance : by making an alliance with Spain to support the independence of the Duchy, he would be linking himself to the most vigorous of the Powers, and at the same time pleasing his subjects by making war on the hereditary foe across the Channel. The *Treaty of Medina del Campo* (1489) was the beginning of a close connection between England and Spain which was destined to be the backbone of English foreign policy for forty years. It was cemented by the betrothal of Prince Arthur to the Infanta Catherine. The marriage was to take place as soon as the children were of marriageable age, and a dowry of 200,000 crowns was to be paid into the thrifty Henry's hoard. The new dynasty had now fairly gained a footing among the royal houses of Europe.

Meanwhile, France resented England's interference in the matter of Brittany, and Henry asked Parliament for a special subsidy of £100,000 with which to make preparations for war. Parliament was quite ready to support a war with France, but this was an immense sum (the whole revenue of the Crown in a normal year was little more) and the King was unable to collect more than about a third of it. Still, this more than sufficed for the despatch of a force of 10,000 archers and men-at-arms to France.

Nevertheless, the war never really got going. Ferdinand did nothing in particular ; his idea was to get England to occupy the attention of France while he conquered certain Pyrenean provinces for Spain. Henry raised a further subsidy from Parliament by talking big about recovering the lost provinces of Gascony and Guienne, but he was much too cautious to squander his resources on such a visionary project ; nor had he any intention of acting as catspaw to Ferdinand. The King of France was equally unwilling to come to blows. He had contrived to gain his end with regard to Brittany by marrying the Duchess Anne, and he was now contemplating a great scheme for the invasion of Italy. He was therefore ready to buy off the hostility of England by a handsome indemnity.

This was a settlement very much to Henry's taste. He was quite a good fighting man when fighting had to be done, but he much preferred putting money in his pocket. The cause for which the war had originally been undertaken was now irretrievably lost, and it was no good crying over spilt milk. Therefore, having taken a subsidy from his subjects to prosecute a war, he now took another from the King of France to refrain from doing so. Such was the *Treaty of Etaples*.

9. *The Last Blow of the Yorkists*

Bosworth and Stoke had banished Yorkism from England, but it continued to flourish in various foreign countries where

its partizans had taken refuge. Scotland—still an independent
kingdom, of course—was always ready to strike a blow at the
old enemy across the border. France was another hereditary
foeman. Ireland was nominally subject to the King of England,
but was really semi-independent, and had been a hotbed of
Yorkism ever since a Duke of York had made himself very
popular there in the middle of the century. But the leading
spirit in all Yorkish enterprises was Margaret, Duchess of
Burgundy, the sister of Edward IV. The difficulty with these
opponents of the Tudor was still that they had no claimant of
their own to put forward. The Simnel affair had been a dismal
fiasco ; but they now raised up another impostor to serve their
turn. This time it was a young Fleming named *Peter Warbeck*.
The plot was originally hatched in Ireland, whither he had gone
on a business tour with his master, a Flemish silk-merchant. It
was agreed that Warbeck should give out that he was the
younger of the sons of Edward IV, usually supposed to have
been murdered in the Tower. When the young man was
brought back to Flanders, the Duchess eagerly recognised him
as her nephew. He then visited France, where he was received
by King Charles VIII with royal honours. When the Treaty
of Etaples was signed, a year later, it contained a clause which
banished him from French soil, but he found consolation at the
court of the Emperor Maximilian, who was offended with Henry
for making that treaty without consulting him. For several
years Warbeck and his alleged aunt busied themselves with
schemes for making a descent on England, but Henry succeeded
in making their project very difficult. He patched up his quarrel
with Maximilian, and made the commercial treaty with Flanders
known as the *Intercursus Magnus*, and in each case one of the
conditions was that all support should be withdrawn from the
Pretender.

At last, in 1495, Warbeck and his partizans managed to
scrape together enough money and men to be able to set out on
their great adventure, with half a dozen ships and some thousands
of adventurers, English and foreign. After an abortive attempt
to land in Kent, they went on to Ireland ; but Warbeck found
conditions there greatly changed since his earlier visit. The
King had determined to set the government of that country on

a sounder footing, and he had sent over one of the most trusted members of his Council, Sir Edward Poynings, as Lord Deputy. Poynings induced the Irish Parliament to pass two laws designed to make the government of Ireland entirely subservient to that of England. These famous *Poynings' Laws* enacted that the Irish Parliament could only transact such business as the King approved, and that all laws made in the English Parliament were to apply to Ireland. The leading Yorkists were also crushed, and the chief personality amongst them, the Earl of Kildare, was sent a prisoner to England. Thus, when Warbeck arrived, he found it impossible even to land, and had to continue his voyage as far as Scotland. There he found the young King James IV very ready to attack England, but with resources so limited that he could do little more than make a raid across the border.

Henry made this attack an excuse for demanding another special tax for the defence of the realm, but the attempt to collect it aroused an insurrection in Cornwall and Devon. The rebels declared themselves in favour of the Yorkist claimant, and marched right across the south of England into Kent, intending to attack London from the south-east. The King's forces barred the way at *Blackheath*, however, and totally defeated them.

A few weeks later the King of Scotland, having shot his bolt as soon as he had got as far as the Tees, made a truce with Henry which was ultimately prolonged for the lifetime of the reigning kings. Warbeck and his partizans were now desperate. They played their last card by landing in Cornwall and appealing to the traditional White Rose sentiment of the West Country. It was in vain. The last ounce of Yorkist sentiment had perished at Blackheath. On the approach of the King's army, the Pretender surrendered. He made public confession of his imposture, and was imprisoned in the Tower. Two years later both he and the unfortunate young Earl of Warwick were executed on a charge of conspiring together to escape

10. *Later Years*

As we remarked before, Henry VII was among the most successful of English kings, and laid solid foundations for the country's future greatness ; but the unpleasing coldness of his personal character increased as his reign went on. His eagerness for the wealth that was necessary for political power developed into grasping greed. In 1502 the wisest of his councillors, Archbishop Morton, died ; and the ministers who henceforth enjoyed his confidence were Empson and Dudley, whose names became a byeword for the ruthless exaction of fines and forced loans and benevolences.

Apart from this, the chief features of the last decade of the reign were the marriages which he arranged for his children and the encouragement which he gave to commercial expansion.

In 1502 Prince Arthur died, shortly after the celebration of his marriage to Catherine of Aragon as arranged twelve years before (§ 8). The King was extremely reluctant to part with the dowry he had received with the bride ; and after a good deal of bargaining with her father it was arranged that the girl-widow should be betrothed to his second son Henry, who now became Prince of Wales. It was a breach of Canon Law for a man to marry his sister-in-law, but a special dispensation was procured from the Pope to set this rule aside. In a later chapter we shall see what momentous consequences resulted from this transaction. Another marriage which was destined profoundly to affect British history was that between the King's daughter Margaret and James IV of Scotland, for the great-grandson of that match was the first king to rule over both kingdoms.

As to commercial policy, the King's achievements were not remarkable in themselves ; the noteworthy fact was that he was the first of English kings to realise the importance of the matter. To gain a share of the trade of northern Europe for English merchants he first quarrelled and then made an advantageous treaty with the Hanse Towns (a confederation of German cities) ; and to gain a share of Mediterranean trade he followed the same course with Venice (then the centre of commerce in southern Europe). To encourage shipping he passed " Navigation Laws," which forbade certain goods being brought to English ports except in English ships. He joined in the search for new markets by commissioning the Genoese explorer John Cabot to explore the northern coast of America. True, nothing very tangible resulted; but Newfoundland became the first of England's overseas possessions.

Henry was a good king, in that he gave his people what they most needed; but when he came to die in 1509 nobody was very sorry. He loved nobody, and therefore nobody loved him.

Questions

(1) *What are the claims of Henry VII to being considered a successful king?*

(2) *How far was the foreign policy of Henry VII governed by dynastic and how far by wider considerations?*

THE ASCENDANCY OF WOLSEY

Year		Year
1509	HENRY VIII. Marriage to Catherine of Aragon (§11)	1509
1510		1510
1511		1511
1512	FIRST / Guienne Campaign (§11)	1512
1513	Pope Leo X (§17) "The Prince" (§16) FRENCH The Spurs X Flodden X (§12)	1513
1514	WAR / Wolsey's 1st. Peace with France (§12)	1514
1515	Wolsey Cardinal & Chancellor (§13) Accession of Francis I (§13)	1515
1516	Erasmus New Testament (§18) More's Utopia (§18)	1516
1517	Wolsey Legate (§13) Luther attacks Indulgences (§19)	1517
1518	Cardinalis Pacificator (§13)	1518
1519	Charles V. Emperor (§14)	1519
1520	Luther burns the Bull (§19) Field of the Cloth of Gold (§15)	1520
1521	Fidei Defensor (§21) Diet of Worms (§20)	1521
1522	SECOND	1522
1523	Clement VII. Pope (§15) FRENCH	1523
1524	WAR	1524
1525	Peasants' War (§20) Pavia X (§15)	1525
1526	Diet of Spires (§20)	1526
1527	Sack of Rome (§20)	1527
1528	Divorce Negotiations with Pope (§21-22)	1528
1529	Legatine Court (§22) Premunire against Wolsey (§23)	1529
1530	Death of Wolsey (§23)	1530

CHAPTER III

The Great Cardinal

(1509–1525)

From the point of view of a student of history the reign of Henry VIII falls into three parts. This chapter is concerned with the first of these, during which the main interest lies in European politics. The rivalry between France and Spain was just beginning, and the part which England played in the early stages of that long struggle was the work of one of the most remarkable personalities of the Tudor period—Thomas Wolsey.

11. *The War with France*

Never in the whole course of English history has the accession of a sovereign been received with more universal delight than was that of Henry VIII. The new king was in his nineteenth year, a handsome, stalwart figure of a young man, full of vigour and high spirits, an expert at all manly exercises, highly intelligent, a lover of learning and the fine arts, exuding good humour and *bonhomie*. There was no rival to dispute his accession ; Yorkist and Lancastrian claims were united in him. The nation's delight turned to rapture when his first act was to cause Empson and Dudley, the hated ministers of his father's avarice, to be executed on a trumped-up charge of High Treason, and his second was to marry the lively and popular Catherine of Aragon, to whom he had for some years been betrothed.

The chief potentates of Europe were equally delighted—but from a very different point of view. Ferdinand of Spain, Louis XII of France, the Emperor Maximilian, and Pope Julius II were all wily and unscrupulous old politicians, and each

24

of them looked to treat the generous and unsuspecting youth as the potter uses his clay. Julius was absorbed in building up the temporal power of the Papacy, and he had recently formed a league with France and Spain to dismember the Republic of Venice. As might have been foreseen, the robbers fell out over the booty, and before long the Pope was looking round for a new alliance to help him to drive the too-successful French army out of Italy. Maximilian and Ferdinand were equally anxious to see France checked, but each was engaged with domestic problems at the moment. The accession of the inexperienced Henry VIII enabled them to play with more success the game that they had failed to play with his father (§ 8). They formed a Holy Alliance, and invited Henry to join in a sort of crusade to protect the Pope. Full of martial ardour, proud of his loyalty to the Church, and ambitious to cut an imposing figure in the eyes of Europe, he was very willing to listen to the suggestion that he should revive the old claim of the Plantagenets to the crown of France with the aid of Spain and the Empire. Every influence at his court impelled him in the same direction. His queen, who had great influence over him, was a powerful advocate of her father's interests ; the nobles saw in a French war an opportunity to regain some of the power and prestige to which they had long been strangers ; and the nation at large was always ready to renew the traditional feud with the French. Accordingly, an expeditionary force was sent to *Guienne*, where it was to act in conjunction with a similar force from Spain. But the campaign was a dismal failure. Ferdinand merely used the English army as a screen behind which he could over-run Navarre, a province lying between France and Spain which had long been a bone of contention between the two monarchies. The discipline of the Englishmen gave way through inaction, disease broke out among them, they missed the beef and beer to which they were accustomed, and they declared that they would not stay there beyond Michaelmas, " not for no man."

So they were brought home. Henry was bitterly humiliated, but the campaign had taught him three valuable lessons. He learnt that the promises of kings do not always correspond with their actions ; that military success can only be won by a close attention to detail ; and that he had a very able servant in one of the younger members of his Council, who had been given charge of the arrangements for the evacuation.

12. *Wolsey makes His Mark*

Thomas Wolsey (1473–1530) was a native of Ipswich, the son of a well-to-do wool-merchant, and therefore a member of that middle class which the Tudors did so much to encourage. He was educated at Magdalen College, Oxford, and took his degree at the age of fifteen ; but his real bent lay not so much with books as with men. The Church still being the royal road to advancement for ambitious young men with brains, Wolsey became a priest almost as a matter of course. The price that the Church had to pay for her monopoly of education was that men took orders who had no inclination for clerical life. There were many clergymen like Wolsey who lived wholly for this world, and never looked upon themselves as set apart for the service of religion. He attracted the notice of Lord Dorset, to whose son he acted as tutor, and by whom he was brought to the notice to Bishop Fox, the chief minister of Henry VII during the latter part of his reign. Fox made full use of his energy and ability, and soon after the beginning of the new reign Wolsey had made his mark as a subordinate member of the Council, and had been rewarded (after the custom of those times) with the deanery of Lincoln—though he never visited that city in his life.

When the King decided to follow up the ill-fated Guienne expedition by an attack on Picardy the following year, it was to Wolsey that he entrusted the arrangements for transporting and victualling the troops. Largely in consequence of the efficiency with which these matters were arranged, the expedition was completely successful. It was based on Calais, still an English possession, and was led in person by the King. So fast did the French knights retire from an engagement under the walls of Guinegate that it has ever since been known in English History as *The Battle of the Spurs* (August, 1513). Pushing on, Henry next captured Tournay, of which place Wolsey was made bishop, as a reward for his services.

While these things were happening in France, an even more

important victory was being won on British soil. The Scots carried on their traditional policy of alliance with France against England. Taking advantage of the absence of the King and most of the nobles, James IV made a great raid, captured Norham Castle, and rased it to the ground. Queen Catherine, who had been appointed Regent, acted with great vigour. Another army was raised and sent northwards under the Earl of Surrey. Surrey contrived to get between the Scots and the border, and the result of the *Battle of Flodden* (September, 1513) was the total overthrow and death of King James. Never again in Tudor times did a Scottish army invade England.

Ferdinand and Maximilian had failed their young ally as completely in 1513 as in 1512; but they now found a new brain at work against them. Wolsey persuaded his master to abandon the whole project of a war with France, and he carried through negotiations which resulted in an Anglo-French alliance cemented by a marriage between Louis XII—now an elderly widower—with Mary Tudor, the younger sister of the King.

13. *" Ego et rex meus "*

This diplomatic exploit gained Wolsey a great reputation with foreign princes and the unbounded favour of his master. Henry was still a young man, delighting in jousts and martial exercises, in music and hunting and revels, in all of which he bore his part with unfailing energy and no little skill. He was delighted at finding a servant who could carry on successfully the irksome duties of government, and his bountiful nature made him give both confidence and rewards unstintingly. Within a year or two Wolsey was the wealthiest as well as the most powerful subject in the land. " He rules both the King and the kingdom," reported the Venetian ambassador to his Senate. " He is about forty-six years old, very handsome, learned, eloquent, of vast ability, and indefatigable. He alone transacts the business which occupies all the magistracies, offices, and councils of Venice. . . . He has a very fine place where one traverses eight rooms before reaching his audience chamber. They are all hung with tapestry which is changed once a week." The extravagant splendour of his way of life became a byeword.

We learn from his secretary that he kept a household of five hundred persons, including a steward, a controller, a cofferer, sundry marshals, and (last but by no means least) a " master cook who goes daily in damask, satin, or velvet, with a chain of gold about his neck." All this magnificence was maintained out of accumulated offices in the Church. By 1520 he was enjoying the revenues of the deanery of Lincoln, the bishoprics of Winchester and of Bath and Wells, the bishopric of Tournay, two Spanish bishoprics, the archbishopric of York, and the abbacy of St. Albans (the richest in England). In 1515 he became Chancellor of the Realm and Cardinal, and in 1517 he was appointed Legate, or special representative in England of the Papal power.

His general aims, both in home and in foreign affairs, resembled in many respects those of Henry VII. His very greed for power impelled him to exclude the nobles from any share in the government, and he realised that England's lack of military resources made it necessary to keep the other Powers balanced against each other, without actually going to war on behalf of any of them.

The Anglo-French alliance of 1514 did not last very long The old Louis XII worn out, it is said, by the gaieties into which he was led by his gay young wife, died in January, 1515. He was succeeded by his nephew, Francis I, a wild, reckless and dissipated young man, who at once determined to revive the claims which had led his predecessors to invade Italy in 1494 (§ 8) and 1511 (§ 11). In September, 1515, he won the famous battle of Marignano. Pope Julius II had been succeeded by Leo X, whose great concern was the prosperity of his family, the Medicis. A victorious French army in Italy would be a serious hindrance to his plans for establishing his relatives. He therefore anxiously looked round Europe for allies, and one of his first steps was to gain the support of England by making Wolsey a Cardinal.

The next three years saw the story of 1513–14 repeated. Henry was filled with an intense personal jealousy of the King of France, and was eager to do something to check his success ; while the Emperor was again very ready to promise support but very slow to give it. English money was used to raise a force of Swiss mercenaries for service in Italy, but these achieved nothing in particular under the foreign commanders to whom they were entrusted. Finally, in 1518, Wolsey made a general peace which included all the powers of Europe.

14. *Hapsburg and Valois*

Hardly was the ink dry on these treaties, however, when the peace of Europe was once more disturbed owing to the death of the Emperor Maximilian. The heir to the Hapsburg family possessions—Austria, and the Netherlands—was Maximilian's eighteen-year-old grandson Charles. But that young man had already inherited the throne of Spain from his maternal grandfather, Ferdinand, who had died a few years before. If, in addition to this conglomeration of territories, he became head of

THE HAPSBURG INHERITANCE

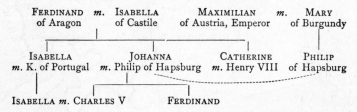

the Holy Roman Empire, he would overshadow all the other sovereigns in Europe. Henry of England and Francis of France were both extremely anxious that this should not happen. Each put forward claims to the Imperial Crown for himself, and each tried to outbid the other in bribing the Electors. But the tradition that the head of the House of Hapsburg should be Emperor (§ 2) was too strong to be resisted, and the young King of Spain became the Emperor Charles V.

For the next three centuries the politics of Europe were closely bound up with the family affairs of kings, and the greatness of the Hapsburgs is a particularly good example of this phase of history. By a series of skilfully-planned marriages and timely deaths, one and the same man had become King of Spain and of Naples, ruler of the Netherlands, Archduke of Austria, and Holy Roman Emperor, besides which the crown of

WESTERN EUROPE in the 16th. CENTURY

NORWAY

SWEDEN

DENMARK

SCOTLAND
Edinburgh
Berwick

IRELAND

Dublin

ENGLAND

London

Bristol

Plymouth

Smerwick

Gravelines
Guinegate

NETHERLANDS
Antwerp

BRANDEN-
BURG

POLAND

Wittenberg

Worms

Spires

BRITTANY

Paris

FRANCE

Augsburg

TYROL
Trent

Vienna

AUSTRIA

HUNGARY

SAVOY

Venice

Pavia

Genoa

Ferrol

Corunna

Vigo

GUIENNE

PORTUGAL

Lisbon

Cadiz

CASTILE

Madrid

ARAGON

SPAIN

Rome

SARDINIA

NAPLES

SICILY

0   100   200   300   400 Miles

Dominions of Charles V. (1519)
Papal Dominions
Boundary of The Holy Roman Empire
Route of the Armada

Emery Walker Ltd. sc.

Spain gave him claims to nearly the whole of the New World—claims which were shortly to be greatly enhanced in value by the treasures of Mexico and Peru.

In these circumstances it was inevitable that personal jealousy should lead to quarrels between the Hapsburg Emperor and the Valois King of France, who had boasted at his accession that he would bring " the monarchy of Christendom under the banner of France." Each of the young rivals was anxious to gain the support of England in the coming struggle. Wolsey did not want England definitely to take a side in the quarrel, for he well knew that he and his king could play a more effective part by acting as mediators than by involving England's very limited resources in actual warfare. But there were strong forces pulling towards war on the side of the Emperor. Firstly, the nobles always felt that in peace-time they must be subordinate to the hated cardinal, whereas in war they would have scope for ambition and a chance of glory ; nor could they get it out of their heads that it was the natural thing for England to be fighting France. Secondly, the commercial classes were anxious to keep on good terms with the Netherlands, where they found the chief market for their wool trade. Thirdly, the Queen had still a great influence over her husband's mind, and was always devoted to the interest of her native land, now ruled by her nephew.

15. *The Cardinal gets into difficulties*

As long as he could, Wolsey carried on his old game of playing the rivals off against each other. By way of whetting the Emperor's appetite for an English alliance, the connection with France was in 1520 renewed at a spectacular meeting in the meadows near Calais. All the arrangements were in the hands of the cardinal, and the very name *The Field of the Cloth of Gold* suggests the reckless profusion of pageantry which was intended to dazzle all Europe. Ornate pavilions of woodwork and plaster were set up, and tournaments were arranged in which the monarchs took part in person, arrayed in golden armour. When Wolsey honoured the proceedings by saying Mass, his sandals were put on by princes of the blood royal. But the alliance went no deeper than the gilding which glittered in the June sunshine of Picardy. Wolsey had his own reasons (including the promise of the Emperor's support the next time there was a vacancy for the papal tiara, together with the immediate enjoyment of the revenues of a couple of Spanish bishoprics) for determining that when England was compelled to make war it should be on the side of Charles. A much less ostentatious conference at Gravelines in the following year committed England to a formal alliance with the Empire, the bargain being sealed by the betrothal of Charles to the Lady Mary, the four-year-old daughter of Henry and Catherine.

Still, Wolsey could not altogether disguise from himself that events were not going as he would have wished. True, he managed to postpone the actual declaration of war until 1522, but when in that year Henry set out once more to conquer the lost French provinces, he met with very little success. By the following year there was nothing to show for the campaign except an empty treasury. The last of the hoard of Henry VII had now been squandered, and there was no option but to call a Parliament and ask for a special grant. Wolsey went down to Westminster and made his demands with the haughty insolence which had by this time become a second nature to him, but he found that the members were not in the least impressed. They sturdily refused even to discuss the matter until the prelate had left the precincts of the House, and even after he had done so the grant which they made was much less than he had asked. This was the first time that the proud cardinal had been rebuffed, and the rebuff was confirmed by the scant success which met his attempt to raise an " Amicable Loan " in the City.

By this time the alliance with the Emperor was almost at an end. Recriminations had followed Henry's unsuccessful campaigns in north-east France. A new Pope had been elected (in 1523) without Charles taking any effective steps on behalf of Wolsey. Worst of all, at *Pavia* (1525) the Imperial troops had gained an overwhelming victory and had actually taken the King of France prisoner. The balance of power in Europe was completely upset, and the Emperor had gained a preponderance which, unless it were counteracted, would be a perpetual danger to the rest of Europe. Moreover, Charles was now driven to take a step which was a personal insult to the King of England.

Being desperately in need of money—his troops in Italy were unpaid, despite their victory, and the Turks were threatening the eastern frontier of the Empire—he cancelled his betrothal to the Lady Mary, and married the Infanta of Portugal, who brought him an immediate dowry of a million crowns in ready cash.

Thus the Imperial alliance and the war with France both came to an end in 1525, and this event marks the beginning of the end of Wolsey's supremacy over the mind and policy of the King. Henry was now thirty-five years of age, and the frivolities of youth were giving way to a deeper and more sustained interest in the business of government. It was unjust but inevitable that he should blame the minister for the failure of the late war. Nor was Wolsey's quarrel with Parliament lost on his master. It reminded him that, however able a servant Wolsey was, the power of the purse lay elsewhere; it revealed the intense hatred felt for him by all classes of society, and it brought home to him that the basic principle of his own royal power was the support of public opinion.

Moreover, the breach with Charles V accelerated a revolution which was already beginning in his own family affairs; for he was becoming estranged from Queen Catherine, who was the representative at his court of the alliance with her nephew.

Coming events were casting their baleful shadows before!

QUESTIONS

(1) *How far was Wolsey's foreign policy a continuation of Henry VII's, and why was he less successful in carrying it out?*

(2) *What led Henry VIII into his wars with France?*

CHAPTER IV

Renaissance and Reformation

We have already outlined some of the changes which made the fifteenth century a sort of bridge between medieval and modern times. These changes were all a part of a great movement called the " Renaissance " or " Re-Birth." What was it that was born again ? In this chapter we shall briefly answer that question and shall see that indirectly this movement led to a great revolt against the Catholic Church.

16. *The Italian Renaissance*

The change in men's outlook which we call the Renaissance began in Italy. It was only natural that Italians should be foremost in the development of civilisation, for they lived for the most part in city-republics, and city life and republicanism make fertile soil for new ideas. Moreover, the geographical position of the peninsula gave its inhabitants the lead in trade with the East in the days before the ocean-routes had been discovered, and enabled them to widen their minds by travel. As knowledge and luxury increased among them, towards the end of the Middle Ages, there grew up an interest in the literature of ancient Greece and Rome, when men had frankly enjoyed the world and lived for it. It was somewhere about the beginning of the fifteenth century that scholars began to discover the fascination of searching out and deciphering the old manuscripts that were to be found in forgotten corners of monastery libraries. The process was hastened when Constantinople was captured by the Turks (1453), for that event caused many of the learned men who preserved the language and literature of the Greeks to seek refuge in Italy, where they were eagerly welcomed as teachers. Soon afterwards the movement received another great stimulus from the invention of printing, which enabled the new knowledge to be broadcast.

This *Revival of Learning* increased the worldly impulse that had caused it. The minds of men had for centuries been dominated by the Church, which taught that human life was a discipline to prepare the soul for another world in which it would spend eternity, and that all the truth necessary for salvation had been communicated to man through the Church. The Greeks, on the other hand, had thought of life as something to be lived to the full ; they had cared little about a future existence, and they took it for granted that truth could be attained by man by means of his own reasoning powers. We thus see why the Revival is sometimes called *Humanism*. It led to man's discovery of himself, and his assertion that the enjoyment of the world and all that it contains is the chief end of life.

Notable effects of this were seen in Art. The development of painting on canvas in oil early in the century gave the artist much more freedom to express his own individuality. He was no longer confined to decorating the walls of churches according to the accepted notions of how such things ought to be done. Natural landscape began to form the background of pictures, and portraiture to be regarded as a worthy form of art. Painters began to admire the human form, and to feel that it was their business to create beauty and not merely to inculcate holiness. The golden age of Italian painting was the first half of the sixteenth century, when Michael Angelo, Raphael, Correggio, Titian, and Leonardo da Vinci were all living.

Another outstanding figure of that time, immensely important to the understanding of modern history, was *Nicolo Machiavelli*. His book "The Prince" (1513) was a dissertation on the art of government. He assumed that the advantage of the State should be the sole object of a ruler. Questions of right and wrong had nothing to do with the relations between one State and another, or between ruler and subject ; force and cunning were the only things that counted. This doctrine may seem shockingly unprincipled, but Machiavelli did not set out to show statesmen how to be good ; his object was to show them how to be successful. The point of view he set forth led to the feeling expressed by the motto " My Country, Right or Wrong," which culminated in the World War.

To sum up, we may say that the Renaissance was made up of a number of impulses which were foreign to the spirit of the Middle Ages : (1) the idea that enjoyment is the object of life ; (2) the feeling that Beauty matters more than Goodness ; (3) the belief that man's reasoning powers are an infallible guide to the problems of life and religion ; (4) the spirit of adventure, both mental and physical ; (5) an interest in the personality and character of our fellowmen ; (6) patriotism, nationalism, imperialism.   These were the factors—taking many forms and acting in different degrees at various places and times—that have made our modern civilisation what it is—for better or worse.

17. *The Renaissance Popes*

Some of the most striking effects of Humanism were to be seen in the Church.   We have seen how the faith of Christendom had been shocked by the worldly life, the fee-snatching greed, and the undeserved privileges of many of the clergy (§ 3). Attempts at reform had often been launched, but all had come to nothing.   The monastic system and the orders of friars had been established to get back to the original unworldiness of Christianity, but in the course of time many of the monks and friars had given way to the evils around them.   Wiclif and Huss had preached a return to primitive doctrine, but their followers had been rigorously persecuted.   The attempt to subject the authority of the Papacy to the decisions of a Council had likewise been overcome.   The Popes had triumphed outwardly, but the Church could not regain her hold over the hearts and minds of men, and she was soon to find that shutting down the safety-valve of reform may be a dangerous achievement.

In Italy the humanistic movement had turned aside the current of men's thought from religious questions.   The Popes themselves went with the stream, became patrons of art and learning.   Some of them, indeed, were too enamoured of Pagan culture to make much pretence of being Christians.   The worst of them all was Alexander VI (1492–1503), the father of Lucrezia and Cæsar Borgia, who devoted his reign to making

his infamous son a great prince, who murdered all who stood in
the way of that design, and who died at last by the poison which
he had prepared for another.

It fell to this Pope to suppress the last notable attempt at
reforming the Church from within. Girolamo Savonarola was
a friar who in 1492 attracted much attention at Florence by
preaching against the immorality of the age and the worldliness
of the clergy. For a time he gained great influence over the
impressionable minds of his fellow-townsmen, but when he
grew ever more extravagant in his denunciations the Florentines
grew tired of their new sensation, and the Pope seized the
opportunity to have the enthusiast executed for blasphemy.
Once more the Papacy triumphed over the reforming spirit ;
once more the Church settled down to enjoy the good things of
this life.

After Alexander VI came Julius II, whose soul was absorbed
in designs to increase the worldly glory of the Papacy. It was
he who had formed the leagues against Venice and against
France (§ 11), who invited Raphael and Michael Angelo to
Rome, and who began the building of St. Peter's. Julius was
succeeded by Leo X, son of the famous Lorenzo de' Medici, the
merchant-prince of Florence. The wealth and influence of his
family had procured him the rank of cardinal at the age of
thirteen, and his mind was entirely occupied with maintaining
a splendid court, adorning his capital, and encouraging art and
literature. He and his cardinals thought so much more of their
culture than of their sacred office that they feared to read their
missals lest the inferior Latin should spoil their taste !

It is easy to be wise after the event, yet it cannot but amaze
us that these worldlings should have supposed that they could go
on for ever like this. But the religious spirit was not dead in
Europe, and the revival of learning was taking other forms,
besides giving men a taste for scholarship and for the fine arts.

18. *The Oxford Reformers*

The fertilising wave of the New Learning gradually over-
flowed from Italy into other parts of Europe, shaping itself in

accordance with the differing character and circumstances of the people. It found the English nation a century behind the Italians in mental development. Town life and commercial enterprise were still in their early stages in this country, and for generations it had been upset by wars, foreign and domestic. When the new movement did reach these shores it took the form of a revival of religion.

The centre of this was Oxford. In 1492 *John Colet* arrived thither from Italy where he had been studying Greek, to lecture on the Epistles of St. Paul. He abandoned the medieval method of searching for hidden meanings by which the text could be twisted into agreement with current theology, and confined himself to discovering the plain meaning of the Greek words— what they had meant to the man who wrote the letters and to the men who received them. From that date the dry-as-dust learning of the old-fashioned theologians began to lose favour, and those who still held by it were ridiculed as " dunces," from the name of the most famous of them, Duns Scotus. Colet later became Dean of St. Paul's, and in 1510 a legacy from his father enabled him to found, under the shadow of the cathedral, a school in which the pupils were to be taught the pure classical Latin and Greek of the New Learning.

The movement commenced by Colet was stimulated by *Erasmus*, a Dutchman who spent many years in England, teaching and lecturing. He was the most famous scholar of the day, and may be considered the founder of modern scientific theology. His most notable writings were an edition of the Greek text of the New Testament, and " The Praise of Folly," a satire in which the pretentious ignorance of the old-fashioned divines was mercilessly ridiculed.

Colet was the first of the Oxford Reformers in point of time, and Erasmus the most celebrated in Europe generally, but the most attractive figure among them is that of *Thomas More* (1485–1535). At Oxford More imbibed from the New Learning a delight in classical literature and a joyous interest in life, but he combined with this a firm faith in Catholic doctrine. When he came up to London to practise as a lawyer, he formed a close friendship with Erasmus and Colet, and the three men joined forces in working to promote the new spirit in religion. It was not long before More found a post in the service of the King, who delighted in the young lawyer's high intelligence, his lovable character, and his genial wit. In 1516 he published his "Utopia," which, although it was originally written in Latin, may be considered the first fruits of the English Renaissance. It begins with an account of a meeting with a traveller just back from a voyage to the New World. He is struck with the social evils which abound in Europe, and especially in England. Crime is terribly common, owing to unemployment caused by the greed of landowners who are turning arable farms into sheep-runs which require much less labour. He deplores the idleness and luxury of the rich, and the recklessness with which monarchs go to war. There follows a description of a wonderful island which the traveller has visited where none of these evils exist. "Utopia" is a pure democracy, in which there is practically no government or taxation or crime. Light labour suffices to supply the inhabitants with all that they require for health and happiness. There is no war, no private property, and no priesthood. In the business of his daily life More was a staunch upholder of the Catholic faith and of royal power, and it may seem strange that he should have glorified toleration and republicanism in this picture of the ideal state. The explanation is that the book is primarily a work of fiction in which the author is indulging his fancy ; and in any case, he could point out that the Englishmen of his day were not yet politically advanced enough to be citizens of such a State.

The Oxford Reformers were all orthodox Catholics. They attacked and ridiculed the evils of the Church, but that institution had survived far more vigorous attacks than this good-humoured criticism. If she was to be stirred up to a real reformation something much more drastic would be necessary.

19. *A Bonfire at Wittenberg*

That something was even now at hand.

In 1517 Pope Leo X, being as usual in urgent need of money, authorised a great sale of "Indulgences." The Church had long been in the habit of granting remission from penance to men who rendered her some special service, such as going on a crusade or providing funds for cathedral-building. Gradually the idea had grown up that the Pope had power to guarantee the pardon of Heaven for sins, and that this guarantee could be purchased for hard cash. The Dominicans who were entrusted with the business went on a sort of sales-tour. They would enter a city with beating drums and waving banners, and they would extol their wares from platforms in the market-place like auctioneers.

Sensible men like Colet and More might make fun of such absurdities, but if they were to be stopped some man must be found who would *do* something. The man appointed by his destiny and character for this task was *Martin Luther* (1483–1546), a monk who was acting as professor of Theology at Wittenberg. Luther had found relief from an overpowering sense of sin in the teaching of St. Augustine that man gains forgiveness less by his own deeds than by faith in the Atonement. If this doctrine were fully accepted, it would be fatal to many of the claims of the Church, and particularly to the sale of Indulgences. When in August, 1517, a particularly famous Indulgence-hawker named Tetzel visited Wittenberg, Luther drew up a list of ninety-five theses or theological arguments against the enterprise, and nailed the document to the door of the church on the night before the sale was to commence. There was nothing very startling in this : discussions on such subjects were common among perfectly loyal sons of Mother Church ; but coming just when it did Luther's action led to unforeseen consequences. The spirit of the Renaissance was seething in Germany ; and national feeling was strong against the rapacity of the Pope, now that he seemed to be more an Italian prince than a universal Father-in-God. Luther's Theses were printed, and were eagerly read and discussed all over Germany. The writer found himself immensely popular with one party and bitterly reviled by the other. His fighting spirit was aroused, and in the course of the discussions he gradually found himself driven into denying the authority of the Papacy and declaring that in the sight of God there is no distinction between priest and layman.

At first the Pope paid little attention to what appeared to him to be a rather vulgar dispute among obscure German monks and friars. But when a number of princes of the Empire accepted the new teaching, the matter began to grow serious ; and in 1520 a Papal Bull was issued declaring Luther a heretic and an outlaw. This was the crisis of the movement. Great potentates with armies at their back had sometimes defied such judgments, but they had always repented of their temerity before long. Yet plain Brother Martin had the audacity to burn the Bull outside the gates of Wittenberg !

20. *Christendom Split in Twain*

Europe was thrilled at the deed, and the next stages in the struggle were watched with eager attention. The young Emperor Charles V (§ 14) was about to hold a Diet (*i.e.* assembly) of the princes of the Empire at Worms, and the Pope sent a special Legate to exhort him to take steps to silence Luther. Charles was anxious to gain the Pope's support in his coming struggle with France, and he therefore summoned the bold monk to appear at Worms and give account of his actions. Luther's friends urged him not to go, reminding him of the fate of Huss ; but he was quite prepared to lay down his life if need be for the opportunity to bear witness before the princes and prelates of Germany to what he believed to be the truth. He went to Worms, refused to retract his attack on the papal authority, and defended himself in a long speech. Some members of the Diet wanted the Emperor to send him to the stake, in spite of the safe conduct he had received, but his great popularity made this impossible. He had become a symbol of the resistance of the German people to what they felt to be a foreign Church. When he was on his way back from the Diet he was kidnapped by one of his princely supporters to prevent his falling into the hands of his enemies ; and for nearly a year he remained secluded in a castle where he spent his time translating the Bible into German.

The excitement he had aroused led in 1525 to *The Peasants' War*, a revolt of the poorest classes against the feudal exactions of nobles and clergy. The peasants naturally looked to Luther for support and encouragement, but they were disappointed. He depended on the princes to carry into effect his plans for the formation of a national German Church, and he therefore supported them in their ruthless suppression of the rebellion.

Meanwhile, a surprising change in the political position in Europe turned in favour of Luther's movement. First of all, the Emperor quarrelled with the Pope. The astounding success of the Imperial army at Pavia (§ 15) and the capture of the French king made the new Pope, Clement VII, desperately anxious to find a counterpoise to the Hapsburg predominance in Italy. Charles released Francis from captivity on condition that he swore not to make war on the Empire again ; but the Pope hastened to absolve him from his oath, and joined with him in an anti-Imperial League. This naturally led to bitter feeling between Emperor and Pope, and Charles no longer troubled to uphold the interests of the Church in Germany. At the Diet of Spires (1526) the princes of the Empire were authorised to take what steps they chose as to the suppression of heresy—which of course implied that they need not take any steps at all.

Moreover, the attention of all Western Europe was taken up by the possibility of a Turkish invasion. The famous Sultan Soliman the Magnificent won an overwhelming victory over the Hungarians at the Battle of Mohacs (1526). It seemed for some months as if Mohammedanism might sweep right up to the Rhine, and even when the conqueror retired (driving 100,000 captives before him) the danger did not pass away for many years. It was impossible for the Emperor at such a moment to undertake to suppress heresy in Germany by armed force.

All this was very unfortunate for the Pope, but worse was to follow. We have already mentoned (§ 15) that Charles was in acute financial difficulties, even after his success at Pavia. He was unable to raise the money to pay his troops, and when he had to leave them, in order to attend to his affairs in Spain, their discipline went to pieces. In 1527 they insisted upon their commanders leading them against Rome, took the city by assault, drove out the Pope, and gave themselves up to an orgy of bloodshed, violence, robbery, and destruction.

This, then, was what had come of the territorial ambitions of the Papacy : the Diet of Spires had brought into existence a definite and permanent anti-Catholic party amongst German princes, and Pope Clement was practically a prisoner in the hands of the Emperor. Rome had ceased to be the religious capital of Western Christendom.

QUESTIONS

(1) *Explain the connection between the Renaissance and the Reformation.*

(2) *Account for the immediate success of Luther's revolt.*

THE REFORMATION IN ENGLAND

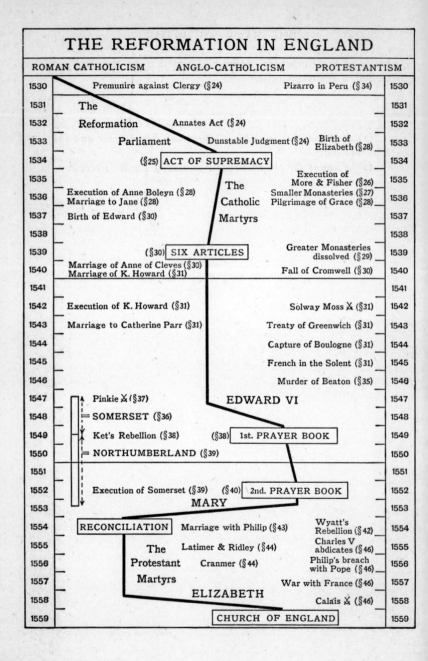

Year	ROMAN CATHOLICISM	ANGLO-CATHOLICISM	PROTESTANTISM	Year
1530	Premunire against Clergy (§24)		Pizarro in Peru (§34)	1530
1531	The			1531
1532	Reformation	Annates Act (§24)		1532
1533	Parliament	Dunstable Judgment (§24)	Birth of Elizabeth (§28)	1533
1534	(§25) ACT OF SUPREMACY			1534
1535		The	Execution of More & Fisher (§26)	1535
1536	Execution of Anne Boleyn (§28) / Marriage to Jane (§28)	Catholic	Smaller Monasteries (§27) / Pilgrimage of Grace (§28)	1536
1537	Birth of Edward (§30)	Martyrs		1537
1538				1538
1539	(§30) SIX ARTICLES		Greater Monasteries dissolved (§29)	1539
1540	Marriage of Anne of Cleves (§30) / Marriage of K. Howard (§31)		Fall of Cromwell (§30)	1540
1541				1541
1542	Execution of K. Howard (§31)		Solway Moss ✗ (§31)	1542
1543	Marriage to Catherine Parr (§31)		Treaty of Greenwich (§31)	1543
1544			Capture of Boulogne (§31)	1544
1545			French in the Solent (§31)	1545
1546			Murder of Beaton (§35)	1546
1547	Pinkie ✗ (§37)	EDWARD VI		1547
1548	SOMERSET (§36)			1548
1549	Ket's Rebellion (§38)	(§38) 1st. PRAYER BOOK		1549
1550	NORTHUMBERLAND (§39)			1550
1551				1551
1552	Execution of Somerset (§39)	(§40) 2nd. PRAYER BOOK		1552
1553	MARY			1553
1554	RECONCILIATION	Marriage with Philip (§43)	Wyatt's Rebellion (§42)	1554
1555	The	Latimer & Ridley (§44)	Charles V abdicates (§46)	1555
1556	Protestant	Cranmer (§44)	Philip's breach with Pope (§46)	1556
1557	Martyrs		War with France (§46)	1557
1558	ELIZABETH		Calais ✗ (§46)	1558
1559	CHURCH OF ENGLAND			1559

CHAPTER V

King Henry "Breaks the Bonds of Rome"

(1525-1534)

The separation of the English Church from the authority of the Pope has been described as a mere accident, brought about by the clash between the personalities and wills of a small group of individuals—notably King Henry, Queen Catherine, and Anne Boleyn. This chapter will help us to form some opinion as to how far this judgment is justified.

21. "The Christian Bachelor"

For the first few years of his reign, Henry was just an overgrown boy, exulting in his vigorous health and strength, hunting half the day and dancing half the night, prancing through lists in gilded armour, outshooting the strongest of his men-at-arms with the long-bow, or acting as pilot of the "Great Harry" and blowing his whistle "as loud as a trumpet." These were the days of Wolsey's greatness. As time went on, the King's interests became more intellectual—he would often visit Sir Thomas More at Chelsea to enjoy his wise and witty conversation; he busied himself with the expansion of York House into Whitehall Palace; he designed warships; he wrote a theological treatise to defend the Papacy from the attacks of Luther (gaining thereby from the Pope the title of " Fidei Defensor "), and still the Cardinal was able to keep the strings of policy pretty much in his own hands. But as time went on the broadening of the King's mind led to his interfering more and more directly in the government; and then Wolsey's position was complicated by the necessity for satisfying the royal will. At length these difficulties culminated in a dilemna which led to the minister's downfall.

After about 1520 the King began to grow perturbed that he had no male heir. Of the five children that had been born, all had died in infancy except the Lady Mary (born 1516). It was doubtful whether a woman could be Queen of England in her own right. Only once had such a claim been made, and the result had been the chaos of the reign of Stephen. Moreover, the marriage of such a queen would raise grave problems. If she married a subject, the jealousy of the other nobles would lead to civil war ; if she married a foreign prince there was danger that England would be absorbed in some other monarchy; while if she did not marry at all, her reign would be a welter of intrigues, and would leave the question of the succession still unsolved.

As time went on it became certain that Catherine would have no more children, and it seemed necessary in the public interest that the King should marry again. But what was he to do with his present queen ? The Canon Law does not permit divorce, and he prided himself on being a loyal son of the Church. Then a new thought arose in his mind. Why was it that his sons had all died in infancy ? Was it a sign that there was some flaw in the Papal dispensation which had allowed him to marry his brother's widow (§ 10) ? Was it, as a matter of fact, within the powers even of a Pope to suspend the sacred law laid down in Leviticus xx. 21 ? If not, then he was not really married to Catherine at all, and was still a bachelor. People can often convince themselves that what they want to do must be right, but Henry's power of doing so was exceptional. He soon became convinced that it was his religious principles that were prompting him to put away his wife.

About 1525 his doubts were hardened by other circumstances. Firstly, the battle of Pavia (§ 15) upset the balance of power, and brought to an end his alliance with Charles V.   The Queen had always been devoted to the interests of her family, and Henry's quarrel with the Emperor led naturally to differences of opinion with her. Secondly, Henry fell in love with somebody else. He seems to have felt for Anne Boleyn the one great passion of his life, to judge by the eloquent love-letters he wrote to her. She was twenty years younger than the unhappy Queen, to whom she had been a lady-in-waiting. Henry was now more convinced than ever that his conscientious scruples were justified. He ceased to treat Catherine as his wife, and instructed Wolsey to procure from the Pope (Clement VII) a pronouncement that the dispensation granted by Julius II was invalid.

The Cardinal's fear that he was becoming less necessary to the King made him all the more anxious to please him by carrying out his wishes. Of course, it never occurred to him to oppose the royal will, for on that will he depended not only for all his power and possessions, but for his very life, since he was surrounded by bitter enemies. He had a scheme for an alliance with France (as a counterpoise to the predominance of the Emperor after Pavia), and Henry allowed him to suppose that as soon as the business of the " divorce " had been put through, this alliance should be sealed by a marriage with a French princess. When Wolsey realised that he had been deceived, and that his master was determined to marry Anne Boleyn, it was a revelation to him of the decline in his position. Still, he had no option but to keep his chagrin to himself and carry out the royal will as best he could.

22. *The Legatine Court*

At first neither Henry nor the Cardinal anticipated much difficulty in getting what they wanted, for Clement had nullified several marriages in similar circumstances. But the Pope's position in the present matter was exceptionally difficult, inasmuch as he was at the mercy of the Emperor (§ 15), who was Queen Catherine's nephew. Clement was anxious not to offend Henry, but he was still more anxious not to offend Charles. He tried every conceivable device to avoid giving a judgment at all. He offered to leave the matter to Henry's own conscience, and he suggested that the case should be tried in the English ecclesiastical courts ; but the King was not satisfied that either of these expedients would give a future heir an indisputable claim to the throne. Clement always hoped that if he could waste enough time, something would turn up to ease the situation. At length he proposed to appoint a Legatine Court, to sit in London, hear evidence, and give judgment on behalf of himself. The court was to be presided over jointly by Cardinals

Wolsey and Campeggio, the latter being sent over specially from Rome.

Henry and Wolsey had hoped for a definite judgment in their favour from the Pope himself, but they accepted this proposal as the next best thing.   Campeggio, having received his final (highly confidential) instructions from Clement, set out for London, taking a good three months over the journey.   When at last he reached London (September, 1528) he spent some weeks trying to persuade the King to abandon the suit and take his wife back ; and then a few weeks more in trying to persuade the Queen to leave the case undefended and retire to a nunnery. When these pretexts for delay were exhausted, he found another one in a rumour that Pope Julius had sent a much more definite Brief of Dispensation to Catherine's father Ferdinand ; would it not be best to search for this in the Spanish archives, rather than have it turn up later to spoil a second marriage ?

Thus passed the winter of 1528–29.   At last, in April, 1529, Henry lost patience, and insisted on the Legates getting to work. Accordingly, on May 29th, the court met in the great hall of the Black Friars, and summoned the King and Queen to appear. Catherine refused to plead before it, and appealed to the Pope himself.   Here was another excuse for procrastination, and when at length the court re-assembled to hear judgment pronounced, Campeggio adjourned it on the grounds that the papal tribunals were about to close for the long vacation.   A few weeks later the case was transferred to Rome.

23. " *A Long Farewell to all My Greatness* "

This was a shattering blow to the declining fortunes of Wolsey.   His exalted position in Church and State gave him unlimited occasion for offending different classes of people, and his aggressive energy of character impelled him to use it to the full.   He could afford to disregard all opposition so long as he had the support of the King, but if that were withdrawn, he would be swept away by an avalanche of hatred.   The people loathed him as the representative of the powers and privileges of the clergy ; the clergy loathed him for the arrogance with which he used his powers as Papal Legate ; the nobles loathed him for absorbing all the offices of State. Everybody envied his ostentatious wealth and luxury—his income was about a million a year (in our values), acquired by exploiting the favour of the King and his opportunities as Legate, Chancellor, and Foreign Minister. He had incurred the dislike of the Boleyns (now a very influential family at the Court), who detested him for not putting through the " divorce," while the Queen's supporters detested him for trying to do so. Again, most people sympathised with the Queen in the stand she was taking for her rights as a wife and disliked the Boleyns for their vulgar " pushfulness " ; but the fact that the King of England had been cited to appear in the Vatican Courts at Rome stung national pride to the quick and fanned into a flame the anti-papal feeling which had so long been smouldering—and Wolsey was the embodiment in England of papal power. Henry had all the Tudor knack of " sensing " such gusts of public feeling and taking advantage of them. By throwing the Cardinal overboard he would be doing an enormously popular thing, and the action might do much to counteract the unpopularity of the " divorce." More-over, it would clear the way for a new attempt to coerce the Pope. The delight of exercising political power was growing on the King. Big ideas were floating in his head, and to have a cardinal-legate at his elbow would be a hindrance to him in the course he was now proposing to take.

It did not take Henry long to find as good a reason for getting rid of his minister as he had already found for getting rid of his wife. By acting on the Pope's authority as Legate, Wolsey had infringed the Statute of Premunire (§ 3). True, he had done so with the full approval, nay at the very orders, of the King himself, but what of that ? The King can do no wrong ; and Wolsey never even ventured to raise the point. He was deprived of the Chancellorship, and of all his offices save the Archbishopric of York. A particularly cruel blow was the check to the two colleges which he was building (at Ipswich and Oxford). He went down to York, and there for the first time in his career devoted himself to his duties as a priest. He visited every part of the diocese, confirmed hundreds of children, and endeared him-self to all. But the tireless spite of his enemies at Court was not satisfied. The Boleyns were afraid that he was getting on too well, and might be restored to favour. They brought fresh charges against him, and he was summoned to London to stand his trial for High Treason. Apparently the only evidence against him was that he had appealed to the Emperor and the King of France to intercede for him with the King ; but there is no knowing what Henry's " conscience " might have made out of this material if it had once got to work on it. Perhaps it was as well that, worn out in body, mind, and soul the great Cardinal died at Leicester Abbey on his way to London.

Was he a great statesman ? Hardly. In foreign affairs he succeeded during the first decade of his power in making foreign rulers think that England's favour was worth having, and he was an adept at the crooked politics of intrigue and counter-intrigue ; but he never established any broad line of policy. As to home affairs, he had an unexampled chance to reform the Church and regain for it the respect and affection of the people ; but he made no good use of it. His dominance was due to his amazing vigour and vitality of mind ; he lacked real intellectual power, and never saw very far ahead. Above all, he was an insatiable egoist. " Getting and spending he laid waste his powers," and such men can never leave behind them worthy monuments of great work achieved.

24. " Hacking Through "

The great figure of the Cardinal having disappeared from the scene, the King set about procuring his divorce for himself. He still looked upon the matter as a personal dispute between himself and Clement VII. Had he at this stage contemplated breaking with the Papacy altogether, he would never have appointed such a whole-hearted churchman as Sir Thomas More to succeed Wolsey as Chancellor. To his original reasons for desiring the divorce—his need for an heir and his love for Anne —there was now added a feeling of rivalry with the Emperor. He would show the Pope that Harry of England could exert pressure quite as severe as that exerted by Charles of Spain !

Just at this moment it came to the royal ear that a young Cambridge don named Cranmer had expressed the view that the Archbishop of Canterbury could legally authorise the second marriage, without reference to the Pope ; at any rate, the young man had said, it would be worth while to consult the Doctors of Canon Law at the universities (English and Foreign) on the point. The idea pleased Henry. He sent for Cranmer, discussed the matter with him, gave him an archdeaconry, and sent round a circular to the universities. Here was a threat to Papal power that would surely make an impression !

Then an even more formidable weapon was brought into play by the King. A carefully " packed " Parliament was summoned, and Henry showed himself a master of the arts of dealing with men. The members were delighted at the fall of the Cardinal, and eager to follow it up by further attacks on the powers and privileges of the clergy. The King took them into his confidence with princely condescension, explained to them his objects, and assured them that he never felt so much a king as when his faithful Parliament was sitting. A series of Acts were passed to reform the administrative abuses of the Church. The clergy were forbidden to hold more than one benefice, the fees which they could exact for administering the sacraments were reduced, and " benefit of clergy " was abolished. Then followed an Annates Act (1533) which authorised the King to withhold the fees paid to Rome by newly-appointed bishops and deans. Any resistance that the clergy might have offered was overcome by the threat that proceedings might be taken against them for recognising the Legatine authority of Wolsey—a technical breach of the Statute of Premunire.

Meanwhile, the opinions of the universities began to come in. Of course, those that were in the power of the Emperor declared against Henry's claim, but it had quite enough support to give him an excuse for regarding the general verdict as favourable. Then, at the crucial moment, the Archbishopric of Canterbury fell vacant, and Henry was able to give Cranmer the opportunity of carrying out his own scheme for the " divorce." It was highly important that the new Archbishop should receive the official sanction of the Pope ; otherwise the King's second marriage might afterwards be called in question. Of course, the cardinals at Rome knew perfectly well the real purpose of Cranmer's appointment, but Henry had a very powerful argument to induce them to expedite the necessary " bulls " ; the

Annates Act had been suspended as soon as it was passed, and it was hinted that it might never be put into force if the " bulls " came in good time. This had the desired effect, and Cranmer was duly consecrated in March. A fortnight later he held an Archiepiscopal Court at Dunstable, near where Catherine was now living. The Queen declined to appear before it, on the ground that she had appealed to Rome. Thereupon Cranmer proceeded to pronounce the judgment that she had never been legally married to the King (1533).

25. " *None Goes so Far . . .*"

The King was now in a position to publish the fact that he had been privately married to the Lady Anne some months before. This was the aspect of the affair which was least pleasing to his subjects. Everybody was glad to see the privileges of the clergy cut down and their fees reduced, and a good many were not sorry to see the English Church released from papal control ; but people were sorry for Catherine and her daughter, and some anxiety was felt lest a quarrel with the Emperor should lead to a stoppage of the Flanders wool trade. When Anne was crowned in June, 1535, the crowd looked on at the pageantry in sullen silence.

Henry's public acknowledgment of Anne, and the fact that he put the Annates Bill into force as soon as Cranmer's " bulls " had arrived safely, made a reconciliation with the Pope impossible. " None goes so far as he who knows not whither he goes," Oliver Cromwell once said. The King had not intended to travel anything like such a distance at first. After each step in Parliament's attack on the Church he had expected Clement to give way, but both his anger and his self-confidence had risen steadily through the four years of the quarrel. He had come to realise that he could defy the Papacy to do its worst. He had a high opinion of his own ability as a theologian, and was perfectly satisfied that he was in the right about his marriage.*

* " The King taketh himself to be right, not because many say it, but because he, being learned, knoweth the matter to be right," he wrote to a European potentate. " The justice of our cause is so rooted in our breast that nothing can remove it, and even the canons say that a man shall endure all the censures of the Church rather than offend his conscience."

He now began to look upon his breach with the Pope as merely the final stage in the dispute which had gone on for centuries, off and on, as to the precise limits of the papal authority in England. The very citing of Premunire was a reminder that this authority had been called in question and severely restricted by previous sovereigns. He was now going to extinguish it altogether.

The last stages in the process followed rapidly on the Dunstable judgment. In July (1533) the Pope excommunicated the King. Two months later Parliament prohibited all appeals from the English ecclesiastical courts to those of Rome. Then Acts were passed which expressly deprived the Pope of all rights and all authority whatsoever, and made the King supreme head of the Church in England. Last of all was an Act which declared that since " no man hath power to dispense with God's law," it followed that no real marriage with Catherine (" henceforth to be called and reputed the Dowager of Prince Arthur ") had ever taken place. The recent marriage with Anne was therefore valid and her children legitimate heirs to the throne. Moreover, " for the better security of the succession," any of the King's subjects might be required to take an oath " to observe the whole contents of this statute."

Then, having completed this stupendous revolution in the course of five years, the Parliament of 1529 was dissolved.

QUESTIONS

(1) *How far was the separation of the English Church from Rome an accident ?*

(2) *Estimate Wolsey's claim to be considered a great statesman.*

CHAPTER VI

The Breach Completed

(1533–1540)

The events to be described in this chapter were among the most important in the whole of sixteenth-century European history. But for them, the Church of England would probably have returned sooner or later to some sort of connection with Continental Catholicism ; and if this had happened it is very doubtful if the Protestant revolt would not have been stamped out in the rest of Northern Europe.

26. *The Catholic Martyrs*

One point must always be borne in mind with regard to Henry VIII's breach with Rome : neither the King nor his subjects regarded themselves as one wit less Catholic after it than they had been before it. The innovations taught by Luther, which the King had combated in 1520, had never made much headway in England. The people accepted all the doctrines and practices of the Church, and the King still felt himself the champion of the orthodox faith. His view, and that of Englishmen generally, was that it was quite possible to be a good Catholic without acknowledging the authority of " the Bishop of Rome or any other foreign Bishop " over the actions or moneys of Englishmen.

Nevertheless, the King was anxious that his supremacy over the Church, and—a thing which was closely connected therewith—the validity of his second marriage should be definitely and positively acknowledged. Public opinion continued to cherish Catherine as a wronged queen ousted by an ambitious upstart; and one Elizabeth Barton, " The Nun of Kent," attracted a great deal of attention by seeing visions which prophesied all sorts of evil for the King unless he took back his first wife and submitted to the Pope. A Bill of Attainder * was passed against the wretched woman and all who had supported her in any way.

Amongst the persons mentioned in the first draft of this Bill were Sir Thomas More and John Fisher, Bishop of Rochester. Their names were afterwards struck out because it was obvious that they had never done more than take a mild interest in the Nun, and that Parliament would throw out the Bill altogether rather than condemn them. Still, Henry could not let the matter rest there. No English Churchman had so high a reputation for piety and probity as Fisher, no English layman enjoyed so wide a fame for knowledge, wisdom, and culture as More. Both had felt that they could not conscientiously accept a layman as head of the Church. More, indeed, had frankly told the King so when he became Chancellor, and the King had taken his declaration in good part. But circumstances had now changed : all that Henry held most dear depended on the acknowledgment of his supremacy, for this involved the legitimacy of his future children. If it were known that the most distinguished men in England questioned it, the spirit of doubt would spread, and the whole country be divided into two camps, one in favour of Henry and Anne, and the other in favour of the Pope and Catherine. Certainly, More had resigned the Chancellorship and was living in retirement, while Fisher was an old man and an invalid ; and both were prepared to take an oath to support the succession of any children that might be born of the marriage. But this was not enough for the overbearing temper of Henry ; they must be forced to recognise him as Head of the Church in England. A new Act of Parliament was rushed through making it High Treason merely to refuse to take an oath to this effect.

This oath was first presented to some of the more important monasteries. Most of the monks submitted, but four leading

---

* *I.e.* an Act of Parliament which merely states that such and such a person has committed a crime worthy of death, and is to be executed without further trial. It was a favourite instrument of the Tudor despotism.

Carthusians were hanged, drawn, and quartered, still robed in the habits of their order, for refusing to do so. More and Fisher were beheaded a few weeks later, after steadily declining to take the oath, and calmly preparing themselves for the end which they saw to be inevitable. More's cheerful serenity has made his execution the most famous of such occurrences in all history. " I pray you, Master Lieutenant," he said, as he set foot on the rickety steps of the scaffold, " see me safely up. For my coming down I can shift for myself."

Having thus advertised his ruthless determination to have his way, Henry proceeded to demonstrate his orthodoxy by causing twelve foreign Protestants to be burnt alive. Despite the horror that such deeds arouse in these more tolerant days, we must not overlook the fact that nobody then disputed that it was the duty of rulers to enforce religious unity. More himself had persecuted heretics, and would never have claimed that men's consciences ought to be free.

27. The English Machiavellian

Beneath the surface of English politics during the momentous years of the breach with Rome there was working a mind and brain far more subtle than those of the King.

Thomas Cromwell (1485–1540) was the son of a Putney tradesman, who after sundry adventures in the Netherlands and Italy—possibly as soldier, probably as merchant, perhaps as both—returned and settled in London. He did well in the wool trade, and better in the practice of the law. Wolsey employed him in matters of detail in which his shrewd cunning, his familiarity with the seamy side of life, and his vigorous grasp of detail made him particularly useful. He became quite an important person in the administration, and when the great Cardinal fell he found an opportunity to gain a private interview with the King. What passed at that interview we can only guess, but it seems that he hinted at a bold scheme of policy which captivated Henry's mind. Broadly speaking, it amounted to this. As Legate and Chancellor Wolsey had drawn to himself all the powers of Church and State. Why should not the King make use of that concentration in order to carry through a drastic reform of the English Church, and especially of the monasteries? Everybody admitted that reform was necessary. If the King were in a position to undertake it himself, might it not be turned to the immense profit of the Crown? We know that Cromwell had studied Machiavelli's "Prince" (§ 16), and we have here the practical result of the doctrine that the power of the State is the supreme law. Henry was incapable of thinking out a large scheme of political action for himself, but he could appreciate one designed by somebody else, and he also realised that the best person to carry such a scheme out was the designer himself. He did not give Cromwell a free hand, for it was only by degrees that the quarrel with Pope Clement developed into a revolution (§ 25); but it was Cromwell who took the lead in Parliament and devised one after another the measures which destroyed the papal powers; it was Cromwell who conducted the examination and execution of the Catholic martyrs; and it was Cromwell who as "Vicar-General" now undertook a "visitation" of the lesser monasteries.

There was nothing new about this undertaking in itself. The monasteries and nunneries had long played a very valuable part in the religious, social, and intellectual life of the country, for they exercised hospitality to wayfarers, taught the children of the poor, and afforded asylums where men and women of a devotional, contemplative, or artistic turn of mind could find refuge from the rough and often lawless secular life of the Middle Ages. But many of them, especially the smaller ones, were badly managed, and had outlived their usefulness; and in some the monks took advantage of their privileges to lead idle and dissipated lives. It had often been felt that something must be done about the matter; reforms had been attempted, but had been hindered by the fact that most of the monasteries were independent of the bishops and answerable only to the Pope himself. Wolsey had been charged by Leo X with the duty of abolishing the worst of them, distributing the inmates to larger and better-conducted convents; but he had merely appropriated the funds of some of them for the benefit of his new college at Oxford and had accepted bribes from others for letting them alone. The novel feature of Cromwell's plan was the use of the newly-established Royal Supremacy for the purpose.

28. *Egotism Rampant*

Meanwhile events were moving fast in the King's domestic affairs. Every sort of pressure was put upon Queen Catherine and her daughter to make them acknowledge the justice of the "divorce," but they were unshakable. Anne's spiteful treatment of her rival made her more unpopular than ever, and even the King began to weary of her. She had borne a daughter (the Princess Elizabeth) in September, 1533, but no other children had been vouchsafed her ; and thus the main object of the second marriage seemed to be frustrated. Early in 1535 Catherine died, and Henry, with characteristic callousness, celebrated the happy release by festivities at which he appeared " dressed all in yellow satin." Anne was equally delighted ; but by the irony of fate the death of Catherine led indirectly to her own. Henry realised by this time that she would never be heartily accepted by his people, and he began to feel a grudge against the woman for whom he had squandered his popularity. A new prospect now opened before him. A third marriage would be unchallengeable—provided that Anne was dead, too. So small an obstacle was easily overcome. The wretched woman was accused of various appalling crimes, including an attempt on the King's life, and was duly beheaded, together with her brother and several of her friends. Henry, callous as ever, passed the eve of her execution in a nocturnal water-party on the Thames. The next day the invaluable Cranmer pronounced that, for certain reasons which he did not disclose, the marriage with Anne had been null and void from the first. Henry was still, therefore, a " Christian bachelor " when, a week later, he led to the altar his third bride—the Lady Jane Seymour.

At about the same time the King fixed the faith of his new independent English Catholic Church by issuing the Ten *Articles of Religion*. This was an attempt to appease the excited controversies which were arising up and down the country between Lutherans, Catholics, and people of every shade of opinion between those extremes. The Articles referred to Holy Scripture as the sole authority on matters of doctrine and practice, and denied the supremacy of the Pope ; otherwise they confirmed the old faith. The importance of the Articles was not the extent of the changes they made, but the fact that they were issued by a layman.

Small as those changes were, they led to the most serious rebellion in the whole of the Tudor period. The northern shires were out of touch with the King's government and with new ideas of all kinds, and they greatly resented the dissolution of the monasteries—of which in 1536 over fifty had been suppressed in Yorkshire alone. The insulting and insolent behaviour of Cromwell's agents led to riots in Lincolnshire which were repressed with savage violence. But the unrest had already spread to Yorkshire, where it assumed a far more formidable shape. Under the leadership of a lawyer named Robert Aske, the malcontents adopted a banner on which were depicted the Five Wounds of Christ, and called their movement *The Pilgrimage of Grace*. They declared their devoted loyalty to the King, but they petitioned him to dismiss Cromwell from his service, and to restore the monasteries. Henry had no troops beyond a few Yeomen of the Guard, and while a force was being got together he played for time. Aske was a moderate and statesmanlike leader. He urged his followers to refrain from violence and accepted the King's invitation to come up to London and talk things over. As soon as Henry was in a position to do so, he threw off the mask, dispersed the rebels by force, and ordered " such dreadful execution to be done upon a good number of the inhabitants in every town, village, and hamlet . . . as they may be a fearful spectacle to others hereafter that would practise in like manner." Amongst the victims was Aske, to whose loyalty he owed so much.

One important result of the " Pilgrimage " was the establishment of a *Council of the North*, a permanent committee of the Privy Council which met at York, and brought the authority of the King into direct contact with the people of the northern shires.

29. "*Malleus Monachorum*"

The agents sent round by Cromwell to inquire into the conduct of the monks made it their business to present such reports as would provide an excuse for suppression, and they told blood-curdling tales of the wickedness that went on. In sober truth, the monks and nuns do not seem to have been much worse —or better—than other people. The worst that can be said of monastic institutions as a whole is that they were no longer so essential to the spiritual life of the community as they had been before the Renaissance had thrown the pursuit of learning, science and art open to laymen. The wealth with which pious benefactors had endowed them were in many cases enjoyed by men living easy-going and not very useful lives. Still, the real reason for their suppression was not their shortcomings but the fact that the King coveted their wealth and regarded them as the outposts of papal power. Moreover, the rising middle class were eager to invest their savings in land—and something like a quarter of the soil of England was in the hands of monks. Certainly, the monasteries entertained travellers at a time when inns were few and far between ; and they distributed alms to the poor ; but such services as these are often only appreciated after they have been lost.

Thus the unfortunate " religious " had few defenders, and one by one the abbeys and convents were abolished, their inmates (including a large number of servants and other dependants) being turned adrift. It simplified the process for Cromwell and his agents if the victims could be induced to make a voluntary surrender, and they were often bribed into doing so by promises of pensions. Where threats and cajoleries were vain, the Vicar-General did not hesitate to act with the utmost violence. There is an interesting entry in a diary of his—" Item, the Abbot of Glaston to be tried at Glaston and also executed there "—which throws a flood of light on his methods. Finally, in 1539 a new Act of Parliament gave the force of law to all such surrenders, past and future, and vested all monastic property in the Crown.

What became of the enormous wealth that fell into the King's hands between 1536 and 1540 ? Parliament was led to believe that it would be used " that God's word might be better set forth, and that children be brought up to learning." Had this been carried out, the English would have become an educated nation centuries before any other in Europe, to the incalculable benefit of western civilisation. Cromwell, on the other hand, had intended to make the monarchy a despotism far more powerful, because far richer, than any that has been seen in Europe. Neither of these things happened. Henry was always swayed more by his passions and impulses than by any far-reaching plans, whether for good or for evil. In order to relieve his immediate necessities and to have money for his pleasures, most of the land was sold at cheap rates to courtiers, officials and Members of Parliament. The ultimate result was the building up of a landed aristocracy and squirearchy who in the next century made Parliament the supreme factor in the State.

One other result, of more immediate effect, was that it made any real reconciliation with the Roman Church henceforth impossible ; too many people had a personal interest in maintaining the royal supremacy upon which their wealth depended.

30. *Cromwell's Fall*

Cromwell's career was destined to come to a sudden end. His fall may be traced to two events which could not have been expected to have any such effect. The first of these was the death of Jane Seymour, after the birth of a son, in October, 1537. The heir so long desired had at last put in an appearance, but the little Prince Edward was a very sickly infant, and Henry soon began to look about for a fourth wife who would provide him with other children. Then, shortly after this, the Pope authorised Cardinal Pole to organise the re-conquest of England on behalf of the Roman Church. Pole was an English nobleman—connected by blood with the King himself—who had gone into exile rather than support the Royal Supremacy. He tried to induce Charles V and Francis I to cease their life-long rivalry and join in a crusade against the heretic King of England. Henry's first reply to this threat was to execute all the leading members of the Pole family on whom he could lay hands— including the cardinal's mother, the aged Countess of Salisbury. His next was to put the country in a state of defence by calling up the militia for training, and building castles along the coast *

* Among the most notable of these were Calshot and Hurst Castles in Hampshire.

He then called a Parliament which gained the nickname of " The Obsequious Parliament " by granting a special war-tax and passing an Act which gave the King's Proclamations the force of law. At the same time, Henry vindicated his claim to be considered a good Catholic by framing an " Act for Abolishing Diversities of Opinion." The very name of this indicates his claim to control even the thoughts of his subjects. It laid down *Six Articles of Religion*, all distinctly Catholic, and made it punishable with death to question them.

These events placed Cromwell in a critical position. At heart he cared little about religion of any sort, but he had made such bitter enemies among Catholics that he was forced to seek support from Protestants ; while the King, on whose support he was entirely dependent, had shown by the Six Articles that he was utterly opposed to the new doctrines. Moreover, there was a growing clique in the Council and the Court which detested him as a low-born and insolent upstart, and he had constantly to be on his guard against intrigues.

Early in 1540 Cromwell succeeded in using the danger of a Franco-Imperial alliance to force Henry into a counter-alliance with the German Lutherans, to be signalised by a marriage between the King and the daughter of the Duke of Cleves. It was this scheme which led to the minister's undoing. He had placed enormous wealth and power in the King's hands, but in doing so he had made himself extremely unpopular with almost every section of the population. By this time he had shot his bolt ; his usefulness to his master was at an end. Gratitude was a feeling utterly unknown to Henry. By casting off the servant who had served him not rightly but too well, he could gratify public hatred and private spite ; and this is what he now proceeded to do. He had never liked making friends with Lutherans, and the German alliance turned out to be unnecessary after all, since by the middle of 1540 Charles and Francis were at each other's throats once more and all danger of an anti-English combination was at an end. Moreover, *Anne of Cleves* turned out to be unattractive to the King's fastidious taste, and the royal irritation was naturally vented on the minister whose policy had involved such an unpleasant match. The Duke of Norfolk, Cromwell's chief enemy on the Council, took advantage of the royal displeasure to accuse him of mismanagement of the King's affairs. It was preposterous to accuse Cromwell of treason against Henry VIII—but not more so than his own charge against More had been. He was indeed "hoist on his own petard." Parliament passed a Bill of Attainder—his own favourite method of attack—and he was beheaded (July, 1540).

QUESTIONS

(1) *Compare the characters and careers of Cromwell and Wolsey.*

(2) *In what respects can Cromwell's political outlook be described as " Machiavellian" ?*

CHAPTER VII

King Henry's Last Phase

(1541–1547)

In this chapter we shall see how, during the last few years of his reign, King Henry ruled with no outstanding minister to influence his policy or carry it into effect. We shall also give some attention to certain developments in foreign parts which were destined to have profound effects upon our later history.

31. *The Old Story*

Cromwell had no successor as chief minister and general factotum. For the rest of the reign two parties on the Council were competing for favour, headed respectively by the Howards and the Seymours. Anne of Cleves not having come up to expectations, she was pensioned off and the marriage with her annulled by Archbishop Cranmer, who was becoming an expert in these matters. Henry was once more looking out for a bride. He had already honoured the Seymours in this way; it was now the turn of their rivals. *Katharyn Howard* was young enough to have been named after Henry's first wife, and she was only eighteen at the time of her marriage. But she had already had a love affair, and within a year or so of the wedding it came to Henry's ears that she had not broken with her former lover. He was overcome with grief, and wept tears of self-pity before his Council, that he should have been so ill-treated by the fair sex. Katharyn and her lover were duly executed; and as a final adventure in matrimony the king played for safety by marrying a middle-aged lady, already twice a widow. The mild, gentle, and pious *Katharine Parr* soothed his irritable humours, nursed him in the painful malady which

64

now began to afflict him, and proved an admirable step-mother to his children.

It was not long before Henry was involved in another war with France. His outlook upon European politics had never extended far beyond the out-of-date claim to the French provinces. In the constantly recurring struggle between Francis I and Charles V, therefore, his tendency had always been to side with the Emperor. This tendency had been interrupted from time to time for brief periods—by Wolsey's make-weight policy (§ 14), by the quarrel with Catherine (§ 22), and by Cromwell's plan for an alliance with the Lutheran princes (§ 30); but the King had always reverted at the first opportunity to his old love. And now that Wolsey, Catherine, and Cromwell were all dead, there was nothing to prevent his adhering to it indefinitely.

The connection between France and Scotland was almost as strong a tradition as the hostility of both those countries to England; and it was with Scotland that war now broke out first. The weakness of James V encouraged Henry's hopes that he might succeed in reviving Edward I's claim to supremacy over the northern part of the island. The most influential man in the Scottish government was Cardinal Beaton, a strong papalist, who had promoted the marriage of King James to a French princess. When Henry protested against the refuge given in Scotland to English fugitives after the Pilgrimage of Grace, Beaton encouraged James to resist. There followed border raids in the course of which an English party was cut to pieces at *Hadden Rig* (1543). This success turned James's head, and he tried to follow it up by an invasion of England on a large scale. But the Scottish army (18,000 strong) was utterly routed at *Solway Moss*, leaving some thousands of prisoners of war in Henry's hands, including many of the chief nobles. James V died of a broken heart when he heard of the disaster, leaving his crown to a week-old daughter.

Here was a golden opportunity for Henry. He made with his chief prisoners the bargain known as the *Treaty of Greenwich*, by which Beaton was to be driven from power, and the little Queen Mary to be sent to England until she should be of age to marry Prince Edward, and so unite Great Britain under the House of Tudor. Scottish national feeling was outraged at the proposal, the treaty was repudiated, and Beaton's pro-French party established more firmly in power than ever. Henry sent Lord Hertford (a Seymour) on a punitive expedition, in the course of which every house in Edinburgh was destroyed, and Holyrood Palace burned to the ground ; but even this argument failed to convince the Scots of the advantages of English rule.

Meanwhile, war had broken out with France also, mainly owing to the support given by Francis to the Scots. For the third time in his reign Henry made arrangements with the Emperor for a joint invasion of France, and for the third time he got the worst of the bargain. Boulogne was captured by the English, but the Imperial army did nothing in particular, and within a twelvemonth Charles had made peace behind Henry's back. In 1545 a fleet of French galleys appeared in English waters, but this was attacking England at what had already become her strongest point. Henry had lavished money and thought on the problems of coast defence, and had taken great pride in his warships. He may be considered the founder of the British Navy, and his " Great Harry " was the finest ship afloat. The Frenchmen, after some temporary success in the Solent in calm weather, were driven back home, battered and discomfited, as soon as a breeze sprang up and enabled the English sailing-vessels to get under way.

In the end, by spending money recklessly on German and Italian mercenaries, Henry managed to compel his old rival to agree to a peace which left Boulogne in English hands for eight years, after which it was to revert to France on payment of an indemnity of two million crowns.

32. *The Meaning of Protestantism*

Religious differences were the mainspring of European history for the next hundred years, and it therefore behoves us to get some understanding of the real basis of those differences.

We have seen (§§ 17–19) that the root causes of the revolution which shattered the unity of Christendom in the first half of the sixteenth century were two : the disgust felt for the worldliness of the privileged clergy and the Renaissance tendency to throw off the trammels of custom and authority. The denial of priestly claims led naturally to doubts as to the doctrines upon which those claims were based.   Thus, Luther's original protest against the abuse of Indulgences led other reformers to go on to repudiate all those teachings of the Church which tend to place the clergy in the position of a sacrosanct and privileged caste. The rejection of the clergy meant the rejection of these doctrines.

For instance, to Catholics the very pith and marrow of Christianity is the *Sacrifice of the Mass*, in which they believe that the priest by Transubstantiation changes the bread and wine into the Body and Blood of Christ.   The power to perform this miracle has, they believe, been handed down from one generation to another of the clergy by " The Apostolic Succession " since the Last Supper at Jerusalem.   Obviously, this doctrine places the priest in a category entirely apart from the layman ; and it was only natural that anti-clerical feeling should lead to a denial of such claims, and to an assertion that Holy Communion is no more than a commemoration of the Sacrifice of the Cross.

Half a dozen other developments followed logically upon this repudiation of the miraculous powers of the clergy.   (1) The fact that Catholic priests were not allowed to marry (*Celibacy of the Clergy*) helped to keep them apart from the rest of the world ; but the reformers threw off this restriction, and Luther himself married an ex-nun.   (2) The Catholic Church regards the confession of sins to a priest (*Auricular Confession*) as a necessary condition to the priest becoming the medium of divine pardon ; but the reformers declared that sin and forgiveness are matters in which nobody can intervene between the individual and God.   (3) The Catholic Church teaches that after death the souls of men undergo a period of probation in " Purgatory " before they are fit for Paradise, and that *Masses for the Dead* said by priests can shorten this period.   Much of the Church's wealth had been bequeathed to it by people who desired to gain these ministrations ; but the reformers denied both the existence of Purgatory and the power of priests to influence Divine judgment.   (4) Another aspect of this matter was the question whether men can do anything to earn salvation by good works. The reformers declared that nothing can save the souls of men from perdition save belief in the Atonement (*Justification by*

Faith). (5) If the clergy are a body of men set apart for the service of God, it is implied that they alone have authority to interpret the Scriptures ; but the reformers maintained that every man is capable of understanding them for himself, and they therefore encouraged the use of a *translated Bible.* The same principle applies to public worship ; the ritual of the Catholic Church is in Latin, whereas Protestant services are conducted in the mother-tongue of the congregation. (6) Elaborate vestments, beautiful buildings, images, and music are appropriate to a sacramental worship, but not to the simpler ministrations which were all that the reformed clergy professed to carry out ; hence Protestant enthusiasm has sometimes taken the form of destroying such things as stained-glass windows and organs.

33. *Protestantism makes good*

The very nature of Protestantism makes it liable to split into parties and sects, for when once the authority of the Church was questioned it was impossible for any one to say which of her characteristic tenets should be retained and which rejected. Luther himself grew alarmed at the lengths to which some of his followers were carrying his revolt, and tried to find a way to reunion with the Papacy. Had he stood alone his movement would probably have subsided like so many of its predecessors. But the spirit he had called up had already got out of his control. He had a bitter dispute with Zwingli, the Swiss reformer, whom he regarded as little better than an atheist, as to the real nature of the Communion service ; while the development of Protestant doctrine by Calvin filled him with horror.

Than this *John Calvin* (1509–1564) few men that ever lived had a more profound influence on our civilisation. A Frenchman who had studied theology at the University of Paris, he was driven into exile owing to his unorthodox religious views ; and at the age of twenty-six he produced in Switzerland a book called " The Institution of a Christian Life," which made Protestantism a permanent force in the modern world. Luther had been merely a destructive critic of the old faith ; Calvin built up a creed and a church-organisation to take its place.

He emphasised that nothing save faith in the Atonement can earn pardon for the sin into which all men are born. God has already determined which of His creatures shall be saved by it, and which are doomed to eternal punishment. (This doctrine is known as *Predestination*.) Those who are to be saved will be inspired by the Holy Spirit with a realisation of the fact. The power of priests to intervene between God and man he utterly denied. A minister was to be elected by his congregation. Once chosen, he was not merely to preach to his flock and to guide their public worship, but (with the counsel of a committee of " grave and pious laymen—the ' Elders of the Congregation ' ") to inquire into and control their private lives. Only thus could the Church be made worthy of God. In 1533 Calvin made his home in the independent city-republic of Geneva. There he gained such a hold over the civic authorities that the functions of Church and State became inextricably intertwined.

The split between Lutherans and Calvinists created a further complication in the religious struggle that was rending Central Europe all through this epoch. Charles V, though personally more concerned with politics than with religion, was compelled by his very position as Holy Roman Emperor to support the Holy Roman Church, and he fully realised what a source of weakness to him was this discord among his subject-princes. Yet he found it impossible to concentrate his forces against the new faith. For one thing, he was engaged in a constant struggle with the Turks, who under their great Sultan Soliman (§ 20) were pressing his eastern frontier ; for another, his attention was distracted by his life-long rivalry with Francis I. For a long time, indeed, Protestantism continued to make rapid strides in Germany. It appealed to national sentiment, it gave princes an excuse to rob the old Church, and it had now been endowed by Calvin with a definite form and a fresh wave of energy. It might well have swept all before it but for the fact that its forces were divided. At length the Emperor despaired of ever healing the breach, and at the Diet of Augsburg (1555) it was agreed that each sovereign prince of the Empire should be free to enforce whichever religion he preferred upon his subjects—" cujus regio, ejus religio."

34. *Spanish Gold*

Contemporary with these events in Europe, developments were taking place in the New World which were destined to have effects little less important.

When the Spaniards realised that their newly discovered Indies were not as a matter of fact Indies at all, they were at first disappointed. They had looked to find a direct route to the wealth of Asia, and they could make little profit out of these sparsely-inhabited islands, even when they imported negro slaves to perform the labour.

In 1513 Balboa crossed the isthmus of Panama and discovered that a mighty ocean separated Asia from America. Some years later Magellan, a Portuguese in Spanish service, sailed into this uncharted sea through the straits which were afterwards called by his name, and boldly continuing his westward route, eventually reached the Philippines. Here the intrepid commander was killed, but his no less intrepid comrades sailed on round the Cape of Good Hope, and so home to Spain— where they performed penance for the fact that they had been keeping the feasts of the Church on the wrong days, having lost a day in going round the world. Their voyage had given men for the first time a true idea of the extent and shape of the landsurfaces of the globe.

At about the same time as the circumnavigation of Magellan, Hernando Cortez, a soldier of fortune engaged in the West Indies, led a band of adventurous spirits into the interior of Mexico, where he found a highly civilised race called the Aztecs, among whom precious stones and metals were so common as to be used for common utensils. European weapons gave the invaders an overwhelming advantage, and within a couple of years hardly a trace remained of the Aztec civilisation. The courage of the Spanish *conquistadores* was only equalled by their cruelty. They excused their treachery and ruthlessness on the grounds that they were fighting the battle of the Cross against heathendom, but in many respects the civilisation of the Mexicans was a good deal higher than their own.

They had tapped what seemed to be an inexhaustible source of wealth, and a stream of gold and silver began to pour into the treasury of the King of Spain. That stream was greatly augmented a few years later when Pizarro, an adventurer quite as bold as Cortez, and twice as detestable in his treachery and greed, sailed down the Pacific coast and after incredible hardships discovered the Empire of the Incas. The Peruvian culture was much like the Mexican, though up to this time neither race had heard of the other. Regular voyages now began to convey the produce of the rich gold and silver mines up to Panama, where it was carried overland by mule-train to Nombre de Dios, and thence across the Atlantic to Cadiz.

This exploitation of the mineral wealth of the New World had important reactions upon the Old. At first it tended to foster the growth of the power of Spain, but wealth without work is as demoralising to nations as it is to individuals, and before long the Spanish national character began to decline. Furthermore, the increased amount of gold in circulation lowered its value and so raised the prices of other goods. As money became " cheaper " it became easier to borrow, and more of it was available to be invested in business. Hence a rapid development in commerce, and a stimulus to the trading classes, already feeling the stimulus of the Renaissance spirit.

35. *Closing Years*

The story of the last few years of Henry's reign is soon told.

The influence of Continental Protestantism was now beginning to be felt in England, and religious discussion was waxing hot. Even among the bishops two parties began to appear, those who inclined to the reformed doctrines being led by Cranmer, Archbishop of Canterbury, and the orthodox Catholics by Stephen Gardiner, Bishop of Winchester. Even the King himself sometimes wavered a little. The one point upon which he was always quite clear was that he would allow no dissent from what he decided at the moment to be the only true faith. On the whole he maintained the position he had taken up in the early stages of his quarrel with the Pope : the royal supremacy combined with the Catholic doctrines. The Six Articles were used so unsparingly at times as to earn the nickname of *The Whip with Six Strings*. In 1545 Anne Askewe, a lady of high birth and influential friends, was burned alive at Smithfield, together with several persons of humbler station, for denying the truth of Transubstantiation. Not even the influence of the mild and open-minded Cranmer, for whom Henry always had a warm personal regard, could rescue these victims; and the archbishop was not yet sufficiently convinced of the reformed doctrines to stand firmly against the royal will at the risk of himself becoming a martyr for them.

Henry continued to work towards his ideal of a union of the British Isles under one government; but it cannot be said that the steps he took to this end were well devised. In 1541 he assumed the title of King, instead of Lord, of Ireland. The Irish at first showed no resentment at his breach with the Pope, especially as he took care to bribe the most important nobles with the spoils of the local monasteries; but when he followed this up with a scheme to set aside local customs and introduce English laws and customs, opposition began to arise. He did not try to enforce the new system much beyond the Pale (the district immediately surrounding Dublin), but the Irish people as a whole soon began to associate the English Church with the rule of a foreign tyranny; and here began the tragic story of religious dissension and political distrust between the two nations.

In Scotland the King persisted in his efforts to overthrow the French influence. He sent Hertford on another mission of devastation, in the course of which monasteries, castles, villages, and hospitals were destroyed; and Beaton was murdered at his instigation; but neither of these crimes brought appreciably nearer the union by marriage at which he aimed.

Even more unfortunate in its immediate consequences was his *debasement of the coinage*. Finding himself heavily in debt after the French war, he caused the mint to issue coins which contained less than their face-value of gold or silver. The consequence was that nobody knew what any particular coin was really worth, prices fluctuated, and commerce was thrown out of gear.

Having too much of our own way is bad for most of us, and Henry's character deteriorated as he grew older. He became a callous egotist, ungrateful for past services and relentless in striking down all who resisted his will. Yet his misdeeds and meannesses are more apparent to us to-day than they were to his subjects. He never lost his hold over their hearts, and to them he was always " bluff King Hal," the very embodiment of the national spirit. His general popularity is evidenced from the fact that, in an age when rebellion was the common mode of expressing disapproval of a King, and with no regular troops at his disposal beyond a few score of beefeaters, he maintained internal peace throughout his reign, except for the brief episode of the Pilgrimage of Grace. When in 1547 he died, it quickly became apparent how much the nation owed to his firm grasp of the tiller of State.

Questions

(1) *Do you consider Henry VIII a great statesman ?*
(2) *Write a character-sketch of Henry VIII.*

CHAPTER VIII

The Reign of Edward VI

(1547-1553)

During the short reign of Edward VI the country was ruled at first by the futile good intentions of Protector Somerset, and then by the unscrupulous corruption of the Duke of Northumberland. Each of these noblemen, in different degrees, was animated by the worst side of Continental Protestantism, in which reformed doctrine was made a pretext for the spoliation of the Church.

36. Protector Somerset

Henry VIII had drawn up a will bequeathing the crown to his son Edward. If by any chance Edward died without issue, he was to be succeeded by his half-sister Mary, and she (in like case) by her half-sister Elizabeth. When Henry felt his end approaching, with his heir but ten years of age, he had appointed a Council of Regency in which all the parties and cliques about the Court were fairly balanced. He had hoped by this means to ensure that no individual or family should be able to seize supreme power during his son's minority. But in the last few weeks of the reign the Howards had fallen into disgrace, and this left their rivals the Seymours predominant in the Council. Within a month Lord Hertford, the head of the Seymour family, had managed to become sole guardian of his nephew the King, Lord Protector of the realm, and *Duke of Somerset*.

It was a very difficult task that he had undertaken. The governmental system of England, right down to Hanoverian times, required active control by a sovereign. Whenever this was lacking the result was intrigue and confusion. And at this particular juncture the strong hand of undisputed authority was particularly necessary, for the late King had left his successor some troublesome legacies. The new national Church had not had time to take root, and many people disliked it. Dispossessed monks swarmed everywhere. The country was committed to a war with Scotland, which might at any moment lead to an attack from France ; and there were signs that Pope and Emperor intended to combine to promote a sort of anti-English crusade. Commerce had been thrown into confusion by the debasement of the coinage (§ 35). Worst of all, there was much distress and discontent among the peasantry. This was in the main due to the working of economic forces which no government could control. The influx of American gold had raised prices all over Europe without raising wages to anything like the same extent. Furthermore, the growing demand for English wool was causing landowners to turn their farms into sheep-pastures (for which much less labour was required), and to use their position of authority to rob cottagers of their plots and to " enclose " much of the common-land which had hitherto been available for the pigs and poultry of the peasantry. Moreover, the monasteries which had formerly relieved cases of want had now been closed, just at the time when the poor were particularly in need of help.

Somerset was on the whole an enlightened and well-meaning man, and it will not be easy for us to judge whether the ill-success which dogged him throughout his career as Protector was due to faults of his own, or to difficulties which were indeed insurmountable.

37. " Well-laid schemes . . gang aft agley "

His first concern was to bring to an end the long-drawn squabble with the Scots. He had been closely connected with the late King's policy in this matter (§ 31) and he now made a further attempt to carry it out. To break up the traditional Franco-Scottish alliance and to ensure that in the next generation all Britain should be united under one sovereign—this was sound policy for an English statesman. But the Scottish nobles hated the thought of their country being absorbed by its powerful neighbour. If the sexes of the children had been reversed they would have looked on the proposed match with very different eyes. When they obstinately refused to carry out the Treaty of Greenwich, Somerset once more led an army across the border laying waste the country far and wide. But the fact that he won a decisive victory at *Pinkie* (near Musselburgh) and followed this up by sacking Edinburgh again, was worse than useless for the purpose he had in view. Scotsmen of all parties joined in indignant determination not to be forced into a connection with such an overbearing partner. The little queen was shipped off to France, where she was brought up by her mother's family, the Guises, and afterwards married the Dauphin. Somerset had no resources with which to hold Scotland down permanently by force of arms. He could only return crestfallen to England, conscious that his expedition had led to the very result it had been designed to prevent.

His next action was even more excellent in intention, and hardly less disastrous in its immediate effects. He caused Parliament to repeal at one blow all the penalties against heresy which had been enacted in the latter part of the last reign. The Six Articles, the Act that made heresy punishable with death, " and all and every other act of Parliament concerning doctrine or matters of religion," were erased from the Statute Book. Somerset showed his own enlightenment in carrying through this measure of " toleration," but the truth is that public opinion was not yet ripe for it. The result of it was that Protestants who had fled from Henry's persecution came swarming back, bringing all sorts of conflicting doctrines, Lutheran, Zwinglian, and Calvinist. All were quite sure that theirs was the only road to salvation, and it was impossible to induce them to show the same forbearance towards each other that the Government showed towards them. The conflict of the creeds became ten times worse confounded than ever before. Violent quarrels and faction-fights broke out, processions were broken up, preachers were mobbed, images and stained-glass windows were smashed, public worship was desecrated by unseemly brawling in churches.

Further confusion and distress were caused by the abolition of the " chantries." These were small foundations for the support of priests for particular objects such as the saying of masses for the souls of departed benefactors or the performance of religious duties in connection with craft-guilds. In the Middle Ages religion had been brought into contact with all the affairs of daily life, but in the new age of materialism, such observances were felt to be superstitious. The funds of the chantries were taken for the State or for the benefit of the Lord Protector and his friends. In some cases where the chantrey-priest had taught the children of the neighbourhood, provision. was made for this work to be continued. This was the origin of the *King Edward VI Grammar Schools*, many of which still flourish ; but neither the young King nor his advisers deserve much credit for them. The lands which were confiscated were daily increasing in value, whereas the income of the new schools was a fixed sum paid in a depreciating currency. Twenty pounds per annum was a good revenue in 1547, but it would not go far towards the upkeep of a school to-day ! Moreover, hundreds of such chantries were confiscated with no compensation of any sort.

38. *The Protector in Difficulties*

The year 1549 saw several events conspire to weaken Somerset's position.

First came the execution of his brother, Lord Seymour of Sudeley, on a charge of high treason. Seymour was a reckless, ambitious and unscrupulous adventurer. The Protector had raised him to the peerage and made him Lord High Admiral, but he was angry that he was not also given charge of the young King's person, and he began to plot the overthrow of his brother's government. He married Catherine Parr, King Henry's widow, who was the guardian of the Princess Elizabeth ; and on the death of the ex-Queen a year later, paid court to the princess herself. He refused to take part in the Pinkie campaign with the fleet. He maintained a small army of retainers, and started a private cannon-foundry. He tampered with the mint. He entered into a sort of sleeping partnership with a band of the Channel-pirates whom it was his business as Lord Admiral to suppress. Many a better man went to the block in Tudor times

for less serious offences than these. Nevertheless, fratricide is
an ugly word, and what made matters worse was that the
Protector had to proceed against his brother by Act of Attainder
instead of by open trial.

A month or two later another cause of ill-feeling appeared—
the *First English Prayer Book*. This was the work of Cranmer.
All through the later years of Henry VIII the archbishop had
been growing more Protestant in his views, and the Seymours
were inclined to the same way of thinking. The use of the
Latin Mass was now prohibited, and new forms of public
worship in English substituted. It was for the most part a
translation of Latin prayers and formulæ that had long been in
use in the Catholic Church, and contains some of the most
perfect examples of English prose ever written. In those passages which dealt with disputed doctrines the wording was
purposely made vague, so that people of all religious parties could
read into it their own beliefs. Nevertheless it was impossible to
avoid giving offence to the extremists on both sides. In Devon
and Cornwall many villages refused to allow the Book to be
used in their parish churches. During the summer of this
troublous year the two counties were in a state bordering on
civil war, and the malcontents got possession of Exeter. It was
only with considerable difficulty that the city was recaptured and
the disturbances quelled by the government's forces.

Meanwhile, a rebellion of far more serious dimensions broke
out in East Anglia. In this part of the country the Reformed
Church was popular, but the peasants were exasperated by the
way in which the landlord-class were buying up estates, enclosing
commons, and consolidating large areas into sheep-runs. Under
the leadership of one Robert Kett (himself a landlord of ancient
family) the dispossessed peasants formed a " commonwealth."
They encamped on Mousehold Heath, near Norwich. Here they
slaughtered and devoured some thousands of the sheep which
were the innocent cause of their troubles, but otherwise they
behaved in a perfectly orderly way, and attended open-air
services at which the new Prayer Book was used. Somerset
was a broad-minded man, and he had a good deal of sympathy
with these people. Even when they took possession of Norwich
he hesitated to do more than parley with them. The more

vigorous members of the Council were dissatisfied with these half-measures. Taking matters into their own hands they authorised one of their number, the Earl of Warwick, to go down to the disaffected district with a large force of foreign mercenaries. The rising was quickly crushed, the rebels put to the sword with ruthless severity, and Kett died a traitor's death at Norwich (September, 1549).

39. *The Fall of Somerset*

The fact that the Council had taken this action independently of the Protector made it obvious that the position of the latter was undermined. Within a month it had collapsed altogether. In the course of his two-and-a-half years of power he had given offence—as much by his good qualities as by his bad—to every class of the community except the very poorest, whose support was too unorganised to be of any practical service to him. Rigid Catholics and extreme Protestants were alike offended by the Prayer Book. His procedure against his brother had given much scandal. His action in pulling down churches to supply building materials for the stately Somerset House which was rising on Thames-side gave offence both by its sacrilege and its pride ; and it caused his efforts to restrain others from robbing the Church for their own benefit to be the more resented. The immediate cause of his downfall, however, was his sympathy for the peasantry. His attitude was inspired as much by patriotism as by the milk of human kindness. " The yeomen of England " had long been the backbone of her military strength. The conversion of arable land to pasture reduced a large proportion of this class to beggary ; while many of those who still found employment on the land were engaged in minding sheep—and " shepherds make but ill archers," as a contemporary observed. The evil was nothing new. It had been discussed in Parliament under Henry VII ; More had drawn attention to it in the " Utopia " ; Wolsey had made a half-hearted attempt to grapple with it ; Latimer, the most popular preacher of the day, often declaimed against the ruin of the class from which he himself had sprung. But decade followed decade without any steps being taken to remedy matters, for the members of Parliament were mostly of the very class which was profiting most from the new system, whereas the class which was suffering by it was not represented at all. When Somerset realised that he could expect no active support from the legislature, he took matters into his own hands. He sent a Commission round to break down illegal enclosures and to insist on a certain proportion of the new pastures being put under the plough again. Complaints against encroaching landlords were to be heard at a special " Court of Requests " set up in the Protector's private house.

The Council, which consisted largely of such landlords, grew more and more determined in their opposition to these measures, and they found a vigorous leader in the Earl of Warwick, the son of Henry VII's old extortioner Dudley. He had become a bitter foe to the Protector when the latter's commissioners had ploughed up his park as an illegal enclosure, and he had distinguished himself by his ruthlessly effective measures against Kett's rising. The quarrel quickly became acute. The Protector began to seek support amongst the citizens of London, and it looked as if a class-war might break out. This was nipped in the bud when in November (1549) the hostile majority on the Council suddenly ordered the arrest of Somerset and his supporters on a charge of treason. Warwick did not feel it safe to go to extremes against the defeated party. Somerset had to resign the Protectorship, and much of his property was confiscated ; but he was soon released from prison, and some months later he was allowed to take his place again as member of the Council.

The dominant position now fell to Warwick, a bold, self-seeking schemer. He preferred the reality of power to its outward trappings, and never took the title of Protector. He was totally devoid of religious feeling, but the failure of Somerset's easy-going toleration convinced him that he must openly favour one party or the other. Naturally, it was to the Protestant side that he leaned, for wholehearted Catholicism would have involved restoring Church property, whereas wholehearted Protestantism gave an excuse for further confiscations.

Somerset at least had a policy, even if not always a wise one ; but Warwick soon showed that beyond feathering his own nest at the expense of the Church he had no policy at all. He bought off the hostility of France by giving back Boulogne and by promising to take no further steps against the French influence in Scotland. He still further debased the coinage to the utter ruin of commerce. He caused an Act to be passed expressly authorising enclosures, and making it a crime to interfere with them.

Somerset had at first acquiesced in his humiliation, but as the new government became more and more disliked, except amongst Warwick's personal friends and supporters, he began to cherish hopes of regaining his former position. Before long there were two factions intriguing fiercely for mastery in the Council. Somerset's popularity had increased since his fall, and Warwick was hard put to it to hold his own. But the latter had a great asset in the hold he had gained over the mind of the young King. Edward was a remarkable boy. He displayed all the Tudor acuteness of brain with more than the Tudor coldness of heart. Grave and studious beyond his years, by the time he was twelve he had adopted strongly Protestant views on religion, and he now conceived a great admiration for Warwick as the " most holy instrument of the word of God." In October, 1551, Warwick took the title of Duke of Northumberland, and by December he felt strong enough to strike down the Somerset party once for all. He caused the ex-Protector and his friends to be arrested and charged with attempting to overthrow the Government. On January 14, 1552 (at an early hour of the morning, lest there should be an attempt at rescue), Somerset was beheaded on Tower Hill. His cold-hearted royal nephew merely recorded in his diary, " This morning the Duke of Somerset was executed " ; but the spectators pressed to dip their kerchiefs in his blood as mementoes of one who, with all his faults, had always an understanding heart for the woes of the under-dog.

40. *Northumberland's Conspiracy*

Northumberland's paramountcy in the Government was now undisputed. He posed as a religious reformer, and caused a more definitely Protestant form of worship to be brought into use. This *Second Prayer Book* (1552) was accompanied by an Act of Uniformity which punished by fine and imprisonment all persons who did not attend a church in which it was used. Catholic-minded bishops who had been left unmolested under Somerset were now expelled from their sees. Bonner was succeeded at London by Ridley, who replaced the stone altar at St. Paul's by a wooden communion table in the nave; while Hooper, the new Bishop of Gloucester, declined even to wear a surplice.

This principle of simplicity in public worship gave an excuse for the confiscation of valuable chalices, candlesticks, censers,

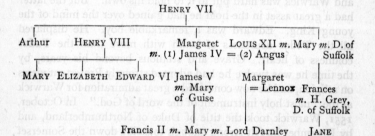

THE TUDOR SUCCESSION

HENRY VII

Arthur   HENRY VIII   Margaret LOUIS XII *m*. Mary *m*. D. of
                          m. (1) James IV = (2) Angus   Suffolk

MARY ELIZABETH EDWARD VI James V   Margaret
                            m. Mary   = Lennox Frances
                            of Guise   *m*. H. Grey,
                                              D. of Suffolk

                    Francis II *m*. Mary *m*. Lord Darnley   JANE
                    Qn. of Scots   *m*. Lord Dudley

JAMES VI & I

bells, vestments of gold and silver cloth, and so forth. Nevertheless, the Government was soon in great difficulties from lack of money. The robbery of the Church could be carried no further; the limits of possibility had been reached in the debasement of the coinage. Northumberland was too unpopular to be able to ask Parliament for subsidies; and by the end of 1552 the Government was paying 14 per cent. to foreign money-lenders for loans.

Early in the following year an appalling prospect began to loom up before the Duke's eyes. The young King's health had never been strong, and he now developed signs of rapid consumption. Northumberland's very life depended on his being able to maintain an ascendancy over a docile sovereign; but the heir to the throne under the will of Henry VIII (§ 36) was the Princess Mary, a vigorous-minded woman of thirty-five, and a devout Catholic. Bold and prompt action was necessary to prevent her accession. Northumberland determined to set aside the two daughters of Henry VIII on the ground that a queen-regnant was a danger to the State. In their place he put forward the Lady Jane Grey, the grand-daughter of Henry VIII's younger sister Mary. Lady Jane was only sixteen and a convinced Protestant. The objection to her sex was got over by marrying her forthwith to Lord Guildford Dudley, Northumberland's own son, who was to wear the "Crown Matrimonial."

The dying boy upon the throne eagerly favoured the plan, as the only possible alternative to a Catholic reaction ; but apart from him it found little support. Nobody wanted to see the Northumberland régime of robbery with violence continued indefinitely, and many people welcomed the prospect of a return to Catholic orthodoxy, after this experience of the new religion. Moreover, there was a strong feeling of loyalty to the lawful heiress, and a great deal of sympathy for her on account of her unhappy history.

Upon the death of the King in July, 1553, Northumberland at once proclaimed Jane Queen. Mary realised that it was dangerous for her to be in his reach, and she fled to the eastern counties, where he was, not unnaturally, extremely unpopular. Within a week a force of some 30,000 men had gathered round her, and Northumberland had to collect what troops he could muster and set out to deal with the menace before it grew more formidable. But his army melted away as he marched ; and the feeling in favour of Mary was so strong that she was proclaimed Queen in London as soon as his back was turned, " Queen " Jane's father taking a leading part in the ceremony. By the time he had got to Cambridge he realised that the game was up. A few days later he was lodged in the Tower, and Queen Mary entered London in triumph.

QUESTIONS

(1) *Estimate Protector Somerset as a statesman.*
(2) *Why did Northumberland's conspiracy fail ?*

CHAPTER IX

The Marian Interlude

(1553–1558)

The reign of Mary was an interruption in the development of the Tudor Monarchy. Henry VII had founded a vigorous national government; Henry VIII had given it authority even over the Church; and the tendency had been confirmed under Edward VI. But Mary gave her spiritual authority back to the Pope and made England an appanage of Spain. Moreover, she tried to force her subjects to accept her creed by burning alive those who did not do so, with the result that the Roman Catholic Church became for centuries an object of fear and hatred to Englishmen.

41. *The Daughter of Catherine*

Mary had been called to the throne by the voice of the nation, and she could afford to be lenient to the clique which had failed so ignominiously to keep her from it. For Northumberland himself pardon was out of the question, and he was forthwith beheaded, despite an ignoble attempt to gain a reprieve by recanting the Protestantism he had professed as long as it served his turn. But the puppets of his ambition, Lady Jane and her husband, were merely kept in honourable confinement in the Tower.

The new Queen was thirty-eight years of age. Since girlhood her life had been overshadowed by the wrongs inflicted by her father on her mother and herself. The only consolations of her sad existence had been her devotion to the Catholic faith, and her pride in her connection through her mother with the great House of Hapsburg. She now felt that God had frustrated her enemies, and had placed her in a position to bring England back to His Church, in which great work her natural ally would be her kinsman the Emperor Charles V.

By the advice of that cool-headed and experienced ruler, she acted with great moderation during the first few months of her reign. She went to Mass, and she expressed a hope that her subjects would do the same, but she declared that she had no intention of trying to compel them to do so. It was not long, however, before her real feelings became manifest She used the Royal Supremacy (of which in theory she disapproved) to restore to their sees the Catholic bishops—notably Gardiner of Winchester and Bonner of London—who had been deprived in the last reign. She next induced Parliament to abolish the English Prayer Book. At first there was much opposition to this, and it was with great difficulty that Gardiner (who had been made Lord Chancellor) persuaded members to take the view that the only satisfactory settlement of religion would be a return to the Anglo-Catholicism of Henry VIII—the Mass without the Pope. The debates showed that the members prized national independence above all things, and the passing of the bill restoring the Mass was accompanied by a request to the Queen that she would marry some English nobleman.

Here was the rub. Mary had already made up her mind to marry her relative Don Philip, the son and heir of Charles V. To this course she was drawn at once by her Catholic faith and her Hapsburg blood ; while to the Emperor it seemed the crowning triumph of the marriage-schemes by which his vast empire had been built up (§ 14). Mary could point out that the match would cement the traditional connection with the Netherlands ; but to her subjects the loss of national independence outweighed any possible arguments in its favour. Apart from the objection to foreign influence in the existing Government, there was the hateful prospect that a son of the marriage would inherit the vast empire of Spain, and look upon England as a mere appanage. Nevertheless, the Queen was so enamoured of the idea that she indignantly denied the right of any one to oppose her will in the matter.

42. " *Wyatt's Rebellion* "

The feeling against the Spanish marriage was so strong and so widespread that a band of nobles—many of whom had been concerned in the Northumberland conspiracy—tried to raise an armed revolt to dethrone Mary in favour of her half-sister Elizabeth. But the conspirators found that people were much readier to talk than to act. Only in the south-east, where Protestantism had its strongest hold and the prospect of a Spanish king was particularly abhorrent, did any real rising take place. The Kentish squires, under the leadership of Sir Thomas Wyatt, raised a force of some five thousand men, and advanced on London. For a day or two the position of the Queen was critical. She had no standing army, and London itself was strongly Protestant in tone. With a touch of the true Tudor courage and reliance on public opinion, she went down to the City and appealed for protection. Her speech had the desired effect. The City Fathers had no wish to see themselves at the mercy of an armed mob, and within a few days some thirty thousand men had enrolled as a defence force. Wyatt found the gates of London Bridge barred to him. Crossing the river at Hampton Court, he advanced on the city from the west, but his numbers diminished with every mile he marched. Having suffered heavy losses in fighting his way along the Strand to Ludgate Hill, he realised the hopelessness of his cause and surrendered. Before his execution he was put to the torture in the expectation that he would confess that the Princess Elizabeth was personally concerned in the plot ; but that young woman was far too astute to allow herself to be drawn into any words or actions that would place her head in danger. On the scaffold, Wyatt publicly declared that she knew nothing of the plot that was to have placed her on the throne. After that, it was impossible for the Queen to proceed any further against her, but she was kept under close watch for months.

One result of the rising was the execution of the poor young " Nine Days' Queen " and her husband. They had taken no part in the affair, and would not have gained the throne if it had succeeded, but Mary felt that they would be a perpetual source of danger to her. Lady Jane Grey has always been looked on as a model of youthful womanhood—modest, intelligent, courageous, and sincere. Without even the consolation of feeling herself a martyr, she met her death with cheerful fortitude. Just before her execution she admitted that she had done wrong in allowing herself to be made queen, but denied that she had ever desired it. She and Sir Thomas More, unlike in sex, age, and religion, will always remain the most beautiful figures among the many victims of royal justice under the Tudors.

43. *The Reunion with Rome*

Wyatt's rebellion ruined the cause which it aimed to promote : Anti-Spanish feeling was silenced, and the Queen now pressed on all the more eagerly to show her gratitude to God by restoring the Catholic Church. The only questions were how far that restoration should go, and how quickly it should take place. The Emperor urged her not to arouse hostility to the marriage by sudden and violent religious changes enforced by persecution ; for Charles V cared much more for the interests of his family than for the power of the Pope. But other advisers, especially the reinstated bishops, were burning for vigorous action. This party had an ally on the Continent in the person of *Cardinal Pole.* An exile for conscience' sake ever since Henry VIII's separation from Rome, he was a single-hearted and simple-minded enthusiast, to whom it seemed madness to talk of moderation when the souls of Englishmen were perishing daily. He induced the Pope to appoint him Legate with authority to carry out the reunion of the English Church with the Holy See, but the Emperor contrived that his arrival in England should be delayed until Mary was safely married to Philip.

In July, 1554, the Prince of Spain arrived at Southampton, and a few days later the royal wedding took place in Winchester Cathedral. Parliament insisted upon inserting in the marriage contract the most elaborate precautions to prevent Philip usurping authority over the English Government, but no precautions could counteract the wifely devotion of the Queen. Before long he was acting with as much authority as if he were a native king, and all the proceedings of the Council had to be translated into Spanish for his approval. He tried very hard to lay aside his usual haughtiness of demeanour, and it is said that on one public occasion he went so far as to drink a tankard of English ale without making a wry face. Even this condescension failed to overcome his new subjects' insular prejudice against everything foreign, however, and it was with difficulty that they could be restrained from laying violent hands on the black-bearded cavaliers and black-cowled monks who came in his train.

The Parliament which met the following autumn made little difficulty about repealing all the anti-papal legislation of Henry VIII, on one condition : that the Church would expressly surrender all right to the monastery lands which during the last two reigns had passed into the possession of laymen—many of whom were members of the two Houses. With this not very dignified compromise the Queen and the Pope had to be content, and on November 30th a solemn ceremony of reconciliation took place at Whitehall Palace. The Houses of Parliament presented a petition to Cardinal Pole in which they lamented the schism into which the country had fallen, and begged that she might be taken back into the bosom of Mother Church. The King and Queen added their prayers to the same effect. Then, after an eloquent address, the Legate pronounced the realm absolved from its sin. Mary was carried away by an ecstasy of religious joy. Her prayers had been answered. She had the husband of her choice, and her Government was purged of the taint of heresy. *Te Deums* were sung in every cathedral of Europe, and guns saluted the glad tidings at Rome.

But within a month Parliament had taken a step which led in the end to the sweeping away of all that had been said and done on that famous St. Andrew's Day. At the urgent demand of Philip and Mary, Parliament re-enacted the old Lollardy laws which empowered the Government to execute by burning all persons who obstinately maintained doctrines other than those taught by the Catholic Church (1555). Parliament had carried a step further its bargain with the Queen. Provided that the members and their friends were left in undisturbed possession of their property, the Church should have its own way as to other people's beliefs. The clergy were once more placed in a position of privilege and authority.   How long would they be able to maintain it ?   That would depend on what use they made of it.

44. *The Persecution Begins*

The Queen now set about stamping out Protestantism among the people, partly as a thank-offering to Heaven for its manifold blessings, and partly to save her subjects from sin.   The bishops were instructed to make a close inquiry into the orthodoxy of the clergy in their dioceses ; and in the meanwhile a start could be made with a number of open and notorious heretics who were already in prison.   The first victims were Canon Rogers and Bishop Hooper, who were burned at London and Gloucester respectively.   Many Catholics had prophesied that their opponents would not stand the fire, but they were speedily undeceived.   Not only these but a dozen others who followed them in the course of the next few weeks, went to their deaths with a stedfast serenity which caused thousands to look upon the reformers and their doctrines with increased interest and respect.

The summer of 1555 was the turning-point in the reign. Up to then all had gone well with the Queen, but afterwards everything went wrong.   Her hopes of having a child were not fulfilled, and the husband on whom she doted began to treat her with coldness and neglect.   Philip felt like a fish out of water in England.   His early attempts at affability faded away, and he could not disguise from himself or from others that he looked on the English as crude barbarians inhabiting a half-civilised country with an impossible climate.   Himself still on the right side of thirty, he felt no affection for his middle-aged wife, with her gruff man's voice, her greying hair, and her unattractive figure.   Keenly sensitive to ridicule beneath his impassive demeanour, he determined to quit the inhospitable island, on the pretext that he must go and take over the government of the Netherlands, the rule of which his father was about to abdicate.

Mary was overwhelmed with grief.   Why, she asked herself, had these disappointments fallen upon her ?   It must be because she was not acting vigorously enough against the heretics. Henceforward she would not be so remiss.   There were three notable victims ready for the sacrifice.   Cranmer, Latimer and Ridley had been in prison since the beginning of the reign.

They had originally been charged with complicity in Northumberland's plot, and they all upheld the reformed doctrines. Brought before an ecclesiastical court at Oxford, they made no attempt to deny their faith. Latimer and Ridley were burned forthwith ; but Cranmer's case was put back. For one thing, it was particularly important that such a conspicuous Protestant—the prelate who had pronounced the divorce of the Queen's mother and the author of the English Prayer Book—should make a public recantation. Thousands of doubters would be affected by such an event. Moreover, as Archbishop of Canterbury he had received the sacred " pallium " from the Pope, and it was but paying respect to the Holy See to wait till it had itself pronounced his degradation. Cranmer was not made of such stern stuff as Latimer and Ridley, and every means was taken to work on his sensitive mind. He was taken to witness the burning of his former comrades, learned Catholic divines were sent to argue with him, and he was given hope that he might be received back into the Catholic Church. At last he gave way under the continual pressure, and signed a recantation.

The Government had won a notable triumph. If they had now dismissed the apostate with contempt, the Protestant cause would have been disastrously discredited. But Mary found it impossible to forgive the instrument of her mother's wrongs and her own unhappy girlhood. Cranmer was told that while his change of belief would be of great service to him in the next world, it could not affect his fate in this. Thereupon a reaction began to set in within his heart. On the morning appointed for his execution he was taken to repeat in public his denial of the reformed doctrines ; but when the critical moment came he amazed the assembled multitudes by disavowing his former recantation and declaring his wholehearted Protestantism. He was hurried off to the scene of the martyrdom of Latimer and Ridley, and suffered with unflinching courage, thrusting the hand that had signed the recantation into the flames that it might be the first part of his body to be consumed. Nothing in his life became him like the leaving it. His perplexities, fears, and doubts were at an end at last, and his end shed lustre on the cause to which he had devoted his life.

45. *Character and Effects of the Marian Persecution*

From this time the persecution was carried on with increasing rigour. Apart from a few prominent ecclesiastics, such as those we have mentioned, the victims were nearly all men and women of the labouring classes. The well-to-do, many of them enriched by the spoils of the Catholic Church, were usually quite ready to conform to the Catholic faith. The general feeling amongst them was they were not theologians ; doctrine and ritual were matters for the clergy. It was the duty of the Government to enforce uniformity of worship, and it was not for laymen to question the decisions of the authorities. But humbler folk were not well enough educated to reason with such subtilty ; what they believed they were ready to die for.

There are several other noteworthy points about the Marian persecution. Firstly, it was almost limited to the south-eastern corner of the island, being severest in London and the Home Counties ; which is evidence that it was only in the more thickly populated parts, and those most accessible to refugee preachers from abroad, that the reformed doctrines had taken any firm hold. Secondly, we must always bear in mind that nobody in those days believed in toleration. Most of the martyrs would have made martyrs of others in similar circumstances. The idea that there are many roads to heaven is a modern conception. Thirdly, the Queen and Cardinal Pole (Archbishop of Canterbury in succession to Cranmer), who directed the persecution, and the bishops who carried it out, were by no means cruel or vindictive persons. They were all convinced that they were performing a sacred duty and acting in the best interests of the nation. Edmund Bonner, Bishop of London, who took a leading part in the trials for heresy, often acted in a coarse-grained and brutal way ; but he usually exerted himself to gain recantations, and was not very particular how far those recantations went. The crucial question at most of the trials was : " Do you believe that anything is taken at Holy Communion besides the bread ? " (§ 32). If the accused could answer " Yes," that was generally sufficient to save him. Fourthly, the number who suffered during those three and a half years was just under three hundred. Compared with the persecutions that took place on the Continent, such a number seems almost negligible ; but in England, where we have always been less accustomed to governmental severities than most of the Continental peoples, it was sufficient to make a profound impression. Moreover, in the years to come, the memory of the persecution was strengthened and embittered by Foxe's " Book of Martyrs," which appeared early in the next reign, giving a graphic account of the sufferings and heroism of the victims. For a century and more this was one of the most widely-read of English books. In many churches copies were kept chained on the lectern beside the Bible ; and for generations Papalism was inseparably connected in most people's minds with the fires of Smithfield.

Finally, the persecution rendered a great service to English Protestantism by purifying it. Henceforward it was clearly inspired by something loftier than the greed for Church property with which it had been so closely associated in the reign of King Edward.

QUESTIONS

(1) " *The reign of Mary was an interlude in Tudor rule.*" *Explain this statement.*

(2) *What were Mary's objects at her accession, and how far did she succeed in them ?*

CHAPTER X

The Elizabethan Settlement

(1558–1559)

The extremer form of Continental Protestantism and a restoration of Papal Catholicism had both been tried since the death of Henry VIII, and both had been found unsatisfactory. It now remained for the younger of Henry's daughters to complete his work by establishing a national Church, resembling the Roman in organisation but independent of the Papacy, which was in doctrine a compromise between the two faiths.

46. *The Unhappy Ending*

It is impossible not to pity Queen Mary amid the griefs and perplexities of the last few years of her reign. After the death of Gardiner (at the end of 1555) she had no efficient counsellor ; for Pole had been too long abroad to understand his fellow-countrymen. No child came to be a bond of union between her and her husband, or to reassure her as to the continuance of her work for the Catholic Church after her death. Her only surviving relative was the Princess Elizabeth, whose very existence was a perpetual reminder of her mother's wrongs, and whom she was beginning to hate as a heretical-minded heir-apparent to the throne. All her starved affections were centred on Philip, who refused to return to her side, and sent rude messages upbraiding her because Parliament (in spite of her tears and entreaties) refused to allow him to be crowned King of England. Her religious policy already was a manifest failure. She feverishly intensified the persecution, but she must have felt in her heart the futility of it all. " The blood of the martyrs is the seed of the faith," and instead of burning Protestantism out she was burning it in. Parliament repeatedly and emphatically refused to allow Church property to be returned, and she exhausted her already starved exchequer by re-endowing several monasteries out of the royal revenue.

Worst of all was the distressing turn that foreign affairs were beginning to take. The new Pope, Paul IV, had been engaged all his life in Italian politics, and he hated the Spanish domination over his native Naples worse than he hated Protestantism. In order to expel the Spaniards from Italy, he made a close alliance with Henry II of France (the successor of Francis I, who died at about the same time as Henry VIII). Thus the old Hapsburg-Valois vendetta was renewed. Charles V had abdicated in 1555, worn out by the struggle to rule such a vast conglomeration of territories, and had retired to spend his last days in a Spanish monastery. The Holy Roman Empire fell to his brother Ferdinand, but the dominion of Spain, Milan and the Americas was inherited by his son Philip, who was already King of England and of Naples, and supreme lord of the Netherlands.

Philip expected all the resources of England to be placed at his disposal for his war with the Franco-Papal alliance ; and so completely had Mary surrendered her rights into his hands that all England's foreign affairs were conducted by Spanish ambassadors. But the war placed the Queen in an agonising dilemma : she must either quarrel with her beloved husband, or fight against her Father in God. Even Henry VIII had never gone so far as to make war on the Holy See. And the matter was complicated by the fact that the Pope had already started a quarrel with her ; for he insisted that Church property must be restored, and refused to accept her protestations that this was impossible without the consent of Parliament. Most unkindest cut of all, the Pope was very angry with Pole because England was siding with Spain ; the Cardinal was deprived of his legatine authority and was actually summoned to Rome to stand his trial for heresy !

The last drop in Queen Mary's cup of woe was the disastrous result of the war, when at last the Council had been bullied and cajoled by Philip's envoys into taking part in it. At first some successes were won in Flanders, but all the advantage of these fell to the Spanish Netherlands, whereas the French counter-stroke resulted in their capturing Calais, the last foothold of England on the Continent. It is easy for us to see to-day that the apparent loss was really a gain, inasmuch as the possession was more dangerous than useful to this country; but at the time it seemed a crushing blow to the national pride. Even more humiliating was the fact that the forces of the Crown were in such an impoverished and disorganised state that it was impossible to make even an attempt to retrieve the loss. It was not surprising that people openly asked what use was the alliance with Spain for which they had sacrificed so much, if it led to such disasters.

The unhappy woman on the throne fell sick in the summer of 1558, as much from grief as from disease. In November she sank into her grave, bewildered at the inscrutable ways of Providence. The reign which had begun with such high hopes and pious resolutions had turned into a tragic failure. She knew that the hearts of the English people were further from Catholicism than at her accession, and that the hatred of Spain had become a ruling passion with them. Cruellest of all was the knowledge that her icy-hearted husband was already anticipating her death and paying court to her sister.

47. A " Mere English " Queen

Elizabeth's reign was destined to be one of the longest and most glorious in our history; but nobody could have anticipated this at her accession. Her right to the throne was disputed by an able and powerful rival; her treasury was empty and her people dispirited; commerce had been crippled by the debase-ment of the coinage. Religion was in a state of chaos, while Hapsburg and Valois seemed to be about to make the country a battlefield for their contending claims. Yet this remarkable young woman grappled with each of these manifold difficulties in turn and overcame them all.

She was indeed one of the most remarkable women in history. Her young days had been blighted by her mother's disgrace and execution; and during her sister's reign the slightest indiscretion on her part would have been fatal to her—even as it was she went in fear of the headsman's axe for weeks at a time.   But adversity and anxiety had not broken her spirit ; they had made her cool-headed, cold-hearted, impervious to all sentimental or generous feelings.   Above all, they had made her cautious.   She had learnt the lesson that masterly inactivity is often the wisest as well as the safest policy.   She was always very reluctant to take any definite action unless she could see a safe way of withdrawing from it if things went amiss ; and the arts of deception became a second nature to her.

Still, we must bear in mind that a hard heart and a cunning brain were necessary to guide her through the labyrinth of dangers in which she found herself, not merely at her accession, but for the greater part of her long reign.   Nor must we overlook the fact that it was for her country that she intrigued and prevaricated, rather than for any personal ends.   She boasted to her first Council that she was " mere English " ; not a drop of foreign blood flowed in her veins.   Here we have the keynote of her whole reign : patriotism.   She had inherited from her father that sixth sense by which he always understood the passions and prejudices of his people, and that obstinate insularity by which he made England independent of all foreign influences.   And to these qualities she added a far-sightedness and self-control which were altogether beyond his reach.

48. *A Momentous Decision*

Within a month of her accession, Elizabeth had to make one of the most vital decisions of her reign.   Her right to the throne was disputed by her cousin Mary Stuart, who as a Catholic denied that Anne Boleyn had ever been lawfully married to Henry VIII, and claimed the inheritance through her grandmother, the daughter of Henry VII.   (See diagram, p. 82.) We saw in an earlier chapter how this Mary Stuart had become Queen of Scotland while still in the cradle, how she had been taken to France as a small girl of six (§ 37), had been brought up there and had married the heir to the French throne. The military strength of France was three times that of Engalnd, and the threat to Elizabeth's position was formidable indeed. It seemed that her only chance of resisting it would be the support of Spain. This, fortunately, had been promised her by Philip, even before the late queen's death. What made this champion of the Catholic Church undertake to support the claims of a heretic against those of a Catholic? Simply the bitter feud between Hapsburg and Valois. If Mary Stuart were to obtain the throne of England, her husband would eventually command the resources of England as well as those of France and Scotland; and the Channel—that high-road between Spain and the Spanish Netherlands—would become French waters.

Philip was prepared to go a long way to prevent such a blow to his own position; and within two months of his wife's death he made a formal offer of marriage to her sister. He made it clear that he was conferring a great favour, that she must not expect him to spend much of his valuable time with her, and that he would expect her to confirm the establishment of the Catholic Church in England. The young queen hesitated, for she and England had much to gain from an alliance with the greatest monarchy in the world. Nevertheless, to Philip's great astonishment, she returned a polite refusal. She realised that the Spanish marriage had been the ruin of her sister, and that the people thought more of their national independence than of the most advantageous foreign alliance. Nor could she overlook the fact that a papal dispensation would be necessary for Philip to marry his deceased wife's sister (§ 21). How could she, the daughter of Anne Boleyn, admit the validity of such a dispensation? Moreover, she foresaw that Philip would be bound to support her against her rival, whether she married him or no. Even when the quarrel with France was temporarily patched up by the Treaty of Cateau-Cambrésis (April, 1559), she was confident that he would never allow a French princess to be placed on the throne of England, and that the deep-seated jealousy between France and Spain would make each of them most anxious to prevent the other from acting against her. Her forecast proved to be correct; and in thus preserving her independence she laid the foundations of that " mere English " policy which was to be the guiding principle of her whole reign.

49. " *After the Manner of her Father* "

Closely connected with this marriage question was the religious problem which had distracted the country for the past twenty years; and the solution which she contrived for this showed the same general principle of national independence. Nobody quite knew what were her own personal views on the subject; but it gradually became apparent that, in direct contrast to her sister, she was far more concerned for the political welfare of England than for its religious orthodoxy. She told the Spanish ambassador soon after her accession that she intended to rule *more patris sui* (after the manner of her father). This implied that she was going to break with the Papacy once more, and build up a national Church over which the sovereign would hold the supreme authority. There were, indeed, many reasons prompting her to take this course. The general trend of feeling in England was all in this direction. At the accession of Mary the greed and hypocrisy of such " Protestants " as Northumberland had made the return of the old worship popular for a time; but since then Catholicism had become associated in people's minds with the rule of priests and the fires of Smithfield, with dependence on Spain and national humiliation. And while the poorer and more sparsely-populated northern counties (where the old-fashioned nobles still held almost feudal sway) remained true to the old faith, Protestantism was making strides in the more populous and civilised south; especially in those parts which were in close touch with the Continent, such as Kent, through which the chief roads to the Continent ran, and London, the centre of the country's commerce and shipping. The reformed religion was fashionable, too, among the younger members of the educated classes, who had grown up to manhood and womanhood since the original breach with Rome.

As a matter of personal taste, Elizabeth had a fondness for Catholic ritual, and she preserved as much of it as she could in the English Church; but Papalism was as impossible for her as it had become for the England which she embodied. To admit the authority of the Pope was to admit that her father was the husband of Catherine of Aragon at the time of her birth, and therefore that she had no legitimate claim to the throne.

50. *Via Media Anglicana*

The main idea which Queen and Parliament kept in view in making their settlement of religion was *comprehension*. Membership of the national Church was to be compulsory, but its creeds and forms of worship were to be made acceptable to all moderate-minded Christian people, whether their personal leanings were to the Catholic or to the Protestant point of view in these matters.

For instance, the sovereign was no longer, as under Henry VIII, to be styled *Head* of the Church. By the *Act of Supremacy* (February, 1559) she was styled " Supreme Governor as well of things spiritual as temporal." Nor was the acceptance of even this comparatively modest claim to be enforced on all citizens. Only officials in Church and State could be required to take an oath acknowledging it ; and even then those who refused to do so were merely deprived of office. The same general principle was observed in the *Act of Uniformity* passed a few weeks later. The Second English Prayer Book—the more Protestant one of 1552 (§ 40)—was adopted as a general basis ; but the wording of the Communion Service was altered so that any member of the congregation could believe what he liked as to Transubstantiation ; and a phrase about " the detestable enormities of the Bishop of Rome " was deleted, so as not to give needless offence to Catholics.

The polity of the Anglican Church became a compromise between the autocratic Church of Rome in which all authority flowed from the Pope, and the democratic Genevan Church which was under the control of laymen. The priestly office was to be conferred by bishops who claimed to be possessed of spiritual powers handed down to them by the Apostolical Succession (§ 32) ; but the supreme control was to be in the hands of the State. The forms of worship were prescribed by Parliament (as we have been reminded by recent events) ; no clergyman could alter them, or punish any one for not accepting them.

This system, by which an endowed and established Church is subject to the authority of the Government, is often known as *Erastianism.*

A Church constructed for political purposes—as part of a scheme for building up an all-embracing national monarchy—could not be expected to arouse much devotion or affection at first; but in the middle of the sixteenth century religious enthusiasm everywhere led to religious strife, and this was just what Elizabeth most desired to avoid. At first there was a feeling of despondent indifference, both among the priesthood and among the laity. There had been four changes of religion during the past fourteen years, and there seemed to be little reason to suppose that this would be the last. But, as we shall see, the reign of Elizabeth was long enough to allow this Church of England to take root, and the stirring events of the latter half of that reign made it become a symbol of national sentiment.

Questions

(1) *Why did Queen Mary's reign end in failure?*

(2) *How far is it true to say that the Church of England was " constructed for political purposes " ?*

GENERAL QUESTIONS ON BOOK I

(1) *What changes in the character of the monarchy marked the reign of Henry VII?*

(2) *" No English King left so large a personal mark upon the nation as Henry VIII." Examine this statement.*

(3) *Compare the Religious Reformation under Henry VIII with that under Edward VI.*

(4) *How was England affected by the discovery of America?*

(5) *Compare what happened to the wealth of the monasteries with what* might *have been done with it.*

(6) *How far were the marriages of Henry VIII related to his policy, domestic and foreign?*

(7) *Explain and illustrate the position of Parliament under Henry VII and Henry VIII.*

(8) *Trace the relations between England and Scotland under the three Tudor kings.*

(9) *Illustrate and explain the statement that the reigns of Edward VI and Mary were exceptional in comparison with the rest of the Tudor period.*

(10) *Trace the relationship of Henry VIII to* (a) *Francis I,* and (b) *Charles V.*

(11) *Distinguish the causes of the several armed insurrections which took place in the reigns of Henry VII, Henry VIII, Edward VI, and Mary.*

(12) *Account for the unsettled religious position during the last ten years of Henry VIII.*

(13) *How far was the Reformation in England political and how far religious in its causes?*

(14) *Sketch the characters and outline the careers of More and Cranmer.*

(15) *Compare the positions and opportunities of Henry VII and Henry VIII on their accession.*

(16) *What difference would it have made to English history if Catherine of Aragon had had a son who lived to maturity?*

(17) *What were the effects of the dissolution of the monasteries?*

BOOK II

The Age of Elizabeth

(1558–1603)

THE great features of the latter half of the sixteenth century were the growth of national self-confidence and the development of the national character. Queen Elizabeth renewed the building up of a vigorous and efficient Government, which had been begun by her grandfather and father, but allowed to fall into decay under her brother and sister. At the beginning of her reign she was faced with appalling dangers and difficulties; yet in the end she lived them all down, owing partly to her own political sagacity, partly to a temperament peculiarly suited to the needs of the time, and partly to the mistakes of her enemies.

The religious settlement which we have already described led in the course of the reign to a general acceptance of a national Church which retained much of the doctrine and organisation of Catholicism, but acknowledged the sovereign as supreme head and governor.

The nation began to realise that its future lay upon the water. Making the most of the advantages afforded by the geographical situation of the island for the new age of oceanic commerce, English seamen laid the foundation of a maritime supremacy which has lasted down to our own day.

Finally, the last phase of the Renaissance now appeared in England, in the form of a burst of literary activity—the beginning of a literature which will always be a symbol of national greatness and an object of national pride.

ELIZABETH AT PEACE

1558	ELIZABETH	1558
1559	Church Settlement (§50) Peace of Cambrésis (§51)	1559
1560	Treaties of Berwick & Edinburgh (§52)	1560
1561	Mary returns to Scotland (§53)	1561
1562	English at Havre (§56)	1562
1563	"Thirty-nine Articles" (§76)	1563
1564	Shakespeare born (§84)	1564
1565	Mary Stewart marries Darnley (§54)	1565
1566	Parker's "Advertisements" (§76)	1566
1567	Murder of Darnley (§54) Revolt of Netherlands (§58)	1567
1568	Mary flees to England (§54) St. Juan de Ulloa ⚔ (§63)	1568
1569	Rising of Northern Earls (§55)	1569
1570	Excommunication of Elizabeth (§59) French Alliance (§60)	1570
1571	Ridolfi Plot (§59) Lepanto ⚔ (§62)	1571
1572	St. Bartholomew (§60)	1572
1573		1573
1574		1574
1575		1575
1576		1576
1577	Drake starts Circumnavigation Voyage (§65)	1577
1578		1578
1579	French Marriage Scheme revived (§67)	1579
1580	Smerwick ⚔ (§66) Arrival of Jesuits (§66)	1580
1581	Execution of Campion (§66)	1581
1582	Ruthven Raid (§66)	1582
1583	Throgmorton's Plot (§68)	1583

CHAPTER XI

The Scottish Revolution

(1559–1568)

The difficulties which Queen Elizabeth had to face in the first years of her reign were aggravated by the fact that the Queen of Scotland claimed the English throne. At first it appeared that Mary Stuart would have the support of the traditional Franco-Scottish alliance; but an unexpected death in France and a religious revolution in Scotland changed the whole situation, and paved the way for a permanent connection between the two parts of Great Britain.

51. *The Reformation in Scotland*

We have already described (§ 50) how within a year of her accession Elizabeth established the Church of England in much the same form as we know it to-day, and thus settled the religious confusion created by her predecessors. That year, 1559, was in several other respects the turning-point in the history of the sixteenth century. It saw the election of Pius IV, the first of a series of popes who made it the main object of their policy to win back the ground lost to the Roman Church by the Protestant revolt. It saw also the Treaty of Cateau-Cambrésis, which settled the long Franco-Spanish struggle for Southern Italy in favour of Spain. It saw the accession of Mary Queen of Scots to the throne of France, owing to Henry II being accidentally killed in a tournament. But none of these events was of greater historical significance than the swift and sudden revolution by which the Scottish people threw off the Catholic Church and adopted the extremest form of Protestantism.

To understand the events that follow, we must be clear as to the political situation in Scotland. As a result of the blundering violence of Henry VIII and Protector Somerset, the Scots had come to prefer the traditional connection with France to any proposed alliance with England (§ 37). Their young Queen had been brought up in France, and was married to the Dauphin; and her kingdom was ruled in her name by her mother, Mary of Guise. Thus French influences and the Catholic faith were in the ascendant. Moreover, Mary (the younger) was not only the actual Queen-Regnant of Scotland and the prospective Queen-Consort of France; she also put forward claims to the throne of England. As we have already seen (§ 48), she declined to recognise the " divorce " of Catherine of Aragon, and claimed that when Elizabeth was born, Anne Boleyn was not legally married to Henry VIII (§ 25). If this were the case, Elizabeth was illegitimate and Mary was the heir, as the grandchild of the elder daughter of Henry VII.

Obviously, this was a very formidable threat to Elizabeth, for Mary was no obscure adventuress; she had at her back all the resources of France (quite three times as great as England's) and Scotland, and the sympathy of Catholics in all countries—including England.

The situation came to a head in the summer of 1559, when Henry II met his death as the result of an accident in the lists at a tournament held to celebrate the Peace of Cateau-Cambrésis, and his son Francis (Mary's husband) became King of France at the age of seventeen. All the power in the government of France fell into the hands of the girl-queen's uncles, the Duke of Guise and the Cardinal of Lorraine. The Guise family had two ruling passions—the Catholic religion and the advancement of their own family. Both these motives impelled them to make the most of their niece's claim to the English throne; and they proceeded at once to assert it by quartering the royal arms of England on those of France.

51. *Twixt Cup and Lip*

But two unforeseeable events now dashed these hopes to the ground.

The first was a religious and political revolution in Scotland. Nowhere was the Catholic Church in more urgent need of a drastic reformation. Scotland was a poor country, and its national life was still in a very primitive state. Even in the comparatively civilised Lowlands factious feudal nobles were as ready to fight against their kings as for them, while the Highlands had hardly advanced beyond the age of the Norse pirates. Something like half the national wealth was in the hands of the Church, and of this the greater part formed a revenue for bishops and abbots of aristocratic family, who spent their lives in fighting and plundering like their relatives. But Protestant doctrines had long been spreading among the lower classes, and during the 'fifties two circumstances combined to give added momentum to this movement. The first was the preaching of *John Knox* (1505–1572), who had imbibed the doctrines and temper of Calvinism while in exile at Geneva, and was one of the most inspiring and impressive preachers that ever lived ; and the second was the formation of a band of nobles who called themselves the " Lords of the Congregation of Jesus Christ." These claimed to be ardent Protestants scandalised at the corruptions among the " Congregation of Satan," as they called the Catholics ; but most of them seem to have been attracted to the cause mainly by the prospect of enriching themselves at the expense of the Church.

In the summer of 1559 the Queen-Mother-Regent, acting on instructions from France, made an attempt to stamp the movement out ; but the only result was a violent explosion which brought about the end of the French influence in Scottish affairs altogether. Knox went on a preaching tour which aroused all southern Scotland against the Catholic Church and the foreign government with which it was associated. Wherever he went abbeys were sacked, monks expelled, churches stripped of images and the Mass abolished. The Lords of the Congregation gathered their retainers about them and gained possession of Perth and Stirling. The Regent was deposed, and had to send to France for men and money with which to regain her authority. The position of the two parties in Scotland was reversed. Hitherto it had been the pro-French Catholics who had enjoyed the advantage of posing as Scottish patriots resisting English interference ; now it was the pro-English Protestants who were resisting French interference. Knox headed a deputation to Queen Elizabeth to ask her to come to the aid of Scottish fellow-Protestants. She did not at all like the idea of encouraging rebellion, or of doing anything that might provoke a war with France ; but the opportunity of overthrowing French influence across the border was too precious to be lost. In February, 1560, she made the *Treaty of Berwick* with the Lords of the Congregation ; and a month or two later an English force was besieging Leith with the aid of an English fleet in the Firth of Forth. By the end of May the French garrison was at the point of starvation; the gallant Queen-Mother died in June, and in July Queen Mary had to send an envoy from France to make terms with Elizabeth. By the *Treaty of Edinburgh* (July, 1560) all French troops were to leave Scotland, no Frenchman was to take any further part in Scottish affairs, and Elizabeth was recognised as lawful Queen of England.

This intervention was one of the boldest strokes of Elizabeth's reign, and one of the most successful. For the first time in history an English army marched out of Scotland leaving good will behind it. Knox now organised the Scottish Kirk on the Presbyterian principles he had learnt at Geneva (§ 33). The inhabitants of each parish henceforth elected their own minister, who supervised all the public and private life of the little community with the aid of a body of elected lay " elders " ; and each of these local " Kirk Sessions " sent representatives to a national General Assembly which gained far more influence on the nation than any Scottish Parliament ever had. The Presbyterian Church was handicapped by the fact that the nobles managed to get possession of most of the wealth of the old Church. Nevertheless, it contrived to make some provision for village schools, and the lowland Scots began to develop into what they have become in modern times—the best-educated and most thoughtful peasantry in Europe, their whole outlook coloured by the Calvinistic theology which they imbibed in earliest childhood. Thus the English and the Scotch were henceforward united by the fact that each nation had a national Protestant Church which was in some danger from a foreign Catholic Power. Elizabeth had succeeded where her predecessors had failed, and the enemies of England could no longer hope to stir up trouble for her at her back door, as it were.

53. *Mary returns to Scotland*

The second misfortune which overtook Mary Stuart at this juncture was the sudden death of her young husband, Francis II, after a reign of a year and a half. An instructive parallel may be drawn between her position in the history of Scotland and that of Mary Tudor in the history of England. Each of these Queens was foreign on her mother's side. Each of them married into her mother's family. A son born to either of them by these marriages would have led to the absorption of their respective countries in a great foreign monarchy, and to the rehabilitation of the Catholic Church. To complete the coincidence, in neither case was the son born.

Mary was now a childless widow of eighteen. The crown of France was inherited by Charles IX, the ten-year-old brother of the late King ; and the paramount position in the Government now fell to the Queen-Mother, Catherine de Medicis, who had long been jealous of the Guises. Mary did not relish her position at a court ruled by a hostile mother-in-law ; and in 1561 she returned to her native land after an absence of twelve years. The situation in which she found herself at Edinburgh must have seemed a cruel contrast to her happy girlhood in the most cultured and luxurious court in Europe. Within the last two years French ideas had been swept out of Scotland, and the most aggressive form of Protestantism had been embraced by the bulk of the nation. The nobles were for the most part boorish and factious chieftains, and the most influential man in the country was John Knox, an eloquent and fervid hater of the Queen's sex, nationality, and religion. Nevertheless, for some years she played her difficult part with coolness, courage, and skill. She showed that intellectually she was a match even for Elizabeth, while she had far more enterprise and willingness to take risks ; and she possessed a womanly charm which was altogether lacking in her rival.

Her political schemes, like Elizabeth's, were closely bound up with the question of marriage. Despite the Treaty of

Edinburgh, she was determined to gain the English throne, and to rule over a united and Catholic Great Britain. Of course, she did not avow this openly. She repeatedly protested to Elizabeth that her ambition were merely to be recognised as her heir-apparent. But Elizabeth was far too shrewd a politician not to see the true value of these protestations ; and she used every artifice of her diplomacy to prevent Mary from contracting a marriage with a foreign prince who could support her in making good her claims. At last the Queen of Scots set all these doubts and anxieties to rest by marrying her cousin, Lord Darnley. Certainly, this marriage really strengthened Mary's position, for Darnley was related both to Stuarts and to Tudors ; but at least it removed the possibility of a Hapsburg " King of Scotland."

54. " *The Queen's Quhair* "

The events of the next few years have been the theme of countless romances and dramas, but they belong rather to the domain of biography than to that of history. Mary was emboldened by her marriage with the leader of the Scottish Catholics to strike at the Lords of the Congregation, and drive the leaders of them into exile. But Darnley turned out a weak and worthless rascal, utterly unfit for any authority, yet petulant because he was not given more. In the circumstances, the Queen turned for counsel to an Italian named Rizzio, originally a singer in her chapel choir, but now raised to the position of confidential secretary. The exiled lords regarded him as responsible for the anti-Protestant policy, and they made a pact with the jealous husband to "remove" the low-born foreign favourite. Rizzio was dragged from the very presence of the Queen and brutally murdered on the stairs outside her chamber.

With cool duplicity Mary broke up the opposition by cajoling the abject Darnley back to her side ; but she was already plotting to get rid of him altogether, for she had fallen in love with a bold, bad man named Hepburn. Swept away by the passions of love and hate, she encouraged her lover * to murder her husband by blowing up with gunpowder the house in which he was sleeping

* There is no positive proof of her complicity, but the circumstantial evidence is very strong.

(February, 1567). This was bad, but worse was to follow.
She openly supported the assassin, made him *Earl of Bothwell*,
and as soon as he had divorced his wife, married him. This was
" more than a crime—it was a blunder." Catholic Europe was
aghast at her indiscretion. Moreover, the Scottish nobles
were disgusted to find that they had got rid of Darnley only to
make room for Bothwell, as their lord and master. They

THE BORDER COUNTRY IN TUDOR TIMES

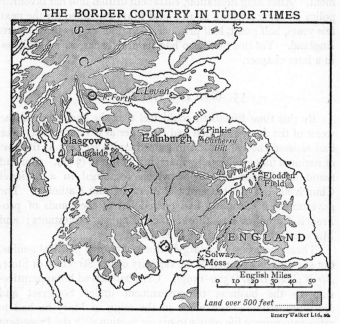

Emery Walker Ltd. sc.

raised an armed rebellion, captured the Queen at *Carberry Hill*
(June, 1567), and imprisoned her in Loch Leven Castle (Bothwell left her to her fate, and disappears from history). She was
now compelled to abdicate in favour of the little son who had
been born to her and Darnley just after the murder of Rizzio.
A year later she managed to escape from Loch Leven, and made
a gallant attempt to win back her crown; but her supporters
were scattered at *Langside*, and she only escaped capture by a
desperate ride for the English border.

Elizabeth could not but feel some satisfaction at the discomfiture of her rival ; but this latest turn of events was not a little embarrassing to her. What was she to do with Mary ? It was contrary to all Elizabeth's principles to hand her back to her rebellious subjects as a prisoner ; but to force the Scots to accept her again as Queen would make an end of the Anglo-Scottish *entente* which was such an asset to the English Government. After long hesitation, Elizabeth drifted into her favourite policy of doing nothing at all ; and Mary remained for the next few years, half guest, half prisoner, in various castles in Northern England. Yet this plan also had its drawbacks, as we shall see in a later chapter.

55. *Cecil and His Enemies*

By this time Elizabeth could feel that she had survived the worst of the dangers which had beset her at her accession. She had resisted the temptation to gain Spanish support at the cost of national independence by marrying Philip II (§ 51). She had made a religious settlement which combined in a national Church all but the extremist Protestants and Catholics. The government of Scotland had passed out of the hands of pro-French Catholics into those of pro-English Protestants ; and Mary herself was a fugitive in England.

These successes were largely due to her own political genius, but she also owed much to the sagacity of her Secretary of State, *Sir William Cecil* (1520–1598). Cecil had served his apprenticeship to the business of government under Somerset and Northumberland ; and when in the reign of Mary he had to retire into private life owing to his connection with the Protestant party, he had attached himself to the fortunes of the Princess Elizabeth. Upon the accession of the Princess to the throne, he reaped the reward of his foresight by becoming her chief minister. " This judgment I have of you," she told him, " that you will not be corrupted by any manner of gifts, and that you will be faithful to the State."

Cecil justified her confidence. No English sovereign was ever served with riper wisdom, more single-hearted devotion or more unwearied diligence. In many respects he carried on the tradition of Thomas Cromwell, for the main object of his policy was to build up the strength of a national monarchy, and to concentrate in its hands all the powers of Church and State, with the support of the classes enriched by commerce and the spoils of the monasteries.

Just as Cromwell had been opposed by the parties that felt themselves pushed into the background by this centralising policy, so now was Cecil. The conspiracy against the latter culminated in the *Rising of the Northern Earls* (1569), which was in many respects a counterpart of the Pilgrimage of Grace (§ 28). It was confined to the northern counties, still the most feudal and Catholic part of the country. The leading spirits were the Duke of Norfolk, and the Earls of Westmorland and North-umberland. Discontent with Elizabeth's government had long been brewing, and in 1568 it was focussed by the arrival in northern England of Mary Stuart. There was no very definite agreement among the malcontents as to their objects, but in general they aimed at expelling Cecil from the Queen's Council, at overthrowing the Anglican Church, at compelling the Queen to consent to the marriage of Mary to Norfolk, and at gaining the recognition of Mary as heir-apparent. Information reached Elizabeth and Cecil of what was going on, and Norfolk was summoned to London to give an account of his doings. An angry interview with the Queen destroyed the Duke's nerve. He fled from the court, as if to start the rebellion ; then changed his mind, and sent messages to his fellow-conspirators advising them to proceed no further with the business. The Earls were surprised by this tame surrender, but they felt they had gone too far to turn back. They assembled their supporters at Durham, where they caused High Mass to be said in the cathedral, and then turned southwards to rescue Mary from her semi-confinement at a castle in Derbyshire. But the Govern-ment anticipated this move, and had the ex-Queen of Scots removed to safer keeping at Coventry. When the rebels found what had happened, they halted to consider what they should do next. This was a very difficult question, and they finally gave it up and marched back to the north, their forces melting away all the time. It was soon obvious that the game was up. Northumberland fled across the border, while Westmorland escaped to the Continent. Norfolk was imprisoned for a time in the Tower, but was released the following year. The vengeance of the Government fell most heavily on the misguided peasants who had followed these noblemen in the belief that they were fighting to restore the true religion, and eight hundred of them were hanged.

Thus ended the last effort of the old régime to resist the Tudor dictatorship.

QUESTIONS

(1) *Make a comparison between the Pilgrimage of Grace and the Rising of the Northern Earls.*

(2) *What dangers threatened Elizabeth at her accession, and how did she overcome them?*

CHAPTER XII

The Counter-Reformation

(1560–1580)

The Protestant movement, which had torn half Europe from the Roman Church, was followed by a reaction in which the Papacy recovered a considerable part of these losses. In this chapter we shall see how the struggle affected England.

56. Elizabeth and the Huguenots

The religious revolution in Scotland was a part of the second or Calvinistic Reformation (§ 33). Lutheranism had won its way through the support of governments. It had been Luther's aim to create a national German Church through a union of German princes, and the compromise reached at Augsburg had been an agreement between rulers. It was King Gustavus Vasa, again, who had established Protestantism in Scandinavia ; while in England the revolt from the Papacy had been carried out in the personal interests and by the personal will of Henry VIII. In Scotland, on the other hand, the Reformation was in the main a popular insurrection against a Catholic government.

Nor was this the only case of the newer form of Protestantism being associated with rebellion. It was but natural that in France the Reformation should be Calvinist rather than Lutheran, for there was something essentially Teutonic about Luther's movement, whereas Calvin was himself a Frenchman and had all that logical clearness of thought so characteristic of the French mind. Nevertheless, Protestantism made very slow progress there, and even by 1560 not a tenth part of the population belonged to the Reformed Church. Still, that tenth included a large proportion of the wealth and intelligence of the country, being particularly strong in the industrial towns and amongst the nobility ; and in 1560 these were able to extort from the Government an Edict of Toleration, by which the two religions were to exist side by side in peace. This was highly offensive to the extreme Catholic Party headed by the Guises, and in the following year there broke out the first of those terrible *Wars of Religion* which devastated the country intermittently for the next thirty years.

In this first war the Huguenots, as the French Protestants were called, won some success in Normandy, and invited Elizabeth to come to their aid, offering her the possession of Havre as a pledge for the ultimate restoration of Calais. Elizabeth took the bait, and sent a force to occupy Havre. But the Queen-Mother, Catherine de Medicis, succeeded in patching up a reconciliation between the warring parties, based on a new Edict of Toleration. This enabled the Government to concentrate all its forces on expelling the English garrison from Havre, and Elizabeth's first attempt to support Continental Protestantism ended ingloriously. Nevertheless, as we shall see, events were at hand which made such support a permanent part of her foreign policy for a quarter of a century.

57. *The Great Reaction*

Just at this juncture it really appeared that the Catholic Church was doomed to extinction. England, Scotland, Scandinavia, Poland, and most of Germany had thrown off allegiance to her, while Protestantism was making strides in France and the Netherlands, and had appeared even in Italy. But a great change was at hand. During the next decade the tide turned and set strongly the other way ; and by the end of the century Catholicism had regained its hold over Italy, Poland, the Southern Netherlands, much of Germany, and nearly all France. The Church of Rome had taken a new lease of life.

This process of rejuvenation is generally known as " The Counter-Reformation." It was based on a purification of the Church from the worst of the evils which had caused the Protestant revolt. The improvement began with a change in the character of the popes themselves. All through the latter half of the sixteenth century there was a succession of popes who devoted themselves to winning back the ground that had been lost to the Church owing to the vices and follies of their predecessors. It was Pius IV (1559–1565) who first determined that the worldly interests of the Papacy must be sacrificed to a relentless crusade against heresy, and who first realised that the success of that crusade could be won only by a close alliance with Spain, however distasteful such an alliance might be to an Italian ecclesiastic.

The first step in the new direction was the summoning of the Council of Trent. This assembly of Church dignitaries from all countries had sat off and on for seven years, vainly trying to find some compromise that would bring the Lutherans back into the fold. In 1563 Pius IV brought the members together for a final session with a very different object in view. What was sought now was not an agreement with the enemy, but a policy by which he could be destroyed. This last session of the Council of Trent made it clear that Catholicism was to be no tolerant *via media :* it decided that no concessions whatever were to be made to the reformed doctrines : the celibacy of the clergy, transubstantiation, the supremacy of the Pope— all were declared to be *sine qua non* of Catholic orthodoxy. Had the purification of the Church taken place fifty years earlier, the Protestant movement might never have begun ; as matters were, not even the tremendous effort of the Counter-Reformation could put the clock right back to 1517.

Nevertheless, the reaction that took place during the last third of the century was one of the most remarkable phenomena in modern history. It owed much to two famous institutions— *The Holy Inquisition* and *The Society of Jesus.* The former was a system of tribunals and officials which existed for the sole purpose of inquiring into and punishing cases of heresy, independently of the ordinary courts of justice. The latter was an order of priests founded by one *Ignatius Loyola* in 1540. As a young Spanish knight, Loyola had been severely wounded at a siege, and on his sick-bed his chivalry had taken a religious turn. He vowed to devote his life to the service of the Catholic Church, and particularly to stamping out the Protestant heresy

which had become such a serious menace to her. The members
of his Society vowed unquestioning obedience to the General of
the Order, they severed all ties of family and friendship, they
never accepted clerical offices. They specialised in those
priestly functions which gave them most influence over the minds
of individual men—as confessors, preachers, and schoolmasters.
Their organisation was most systematic and rigid. Elaborate
rules were drawn up as to the management of confessions, and
as to the hours, lessons, and methods of teaching in school;
and the framers of these regulations showed a profound insight
into the working of human nature. The Order spread rapidly,
and played a great part in the reaction, by its combination of
burning zeal with cool intelligence.

58. *The Revolt of the Netherlands*

Perhaps the most notable arena of the conflict between
Protestantism and the Catholic Reaction was the Netherlands.
This was the most prosperous of the dominions of the Hapsburgs,
and provided a substantial part of their revenues, but discontent
with their rule had long been growing there. The people
resented (*a*) taxation to pay for wars with which they had no
concern; (*b*) the Emperor's severe decrees against Protestantism; and (*c*) the centralising policy which robbed them of their
cherished privileges of choosing their own magistrates. Charles V
was a native of those parts; he understood the people, and he had
a genial way with him which did much to keep this resentment in
check; but when he abdicated in favour of his son Philip (§ 44)
a great change took place in the position. For Philip, despite
the Flemish blood evidenced by his fair hair and complexion,
was a pure Spaniard at heart. He could not speak a word of
Flemish, and his haughty demeanour repelled all with whom he
came into contact. In 1559 he left the Netherlands for good, and
returned to Spain.

Philip was the very embodiment of the Catholic Reaction.
He felt himself called by God to purify the world in general and
his own dominions in particular from the taint of heresy.
Towards that object he laboured all his life long with solemn and
dull-witted persistency. He trusted nobody; he never opened

his heart to a friend or explained his policy to his ministers. The one thing of which those who served him might be certain was that to show the smallest favour to heretics would be to forfeit his favour for ever.

The leading nobles of the Netherlands—notably Count Egmont, who had won for Philip the great victory of Gravelines against France, and William of Orange, a wealthy Prince of the Empire—found themselves ignored in the government of the country, while the burghers were exasperated by the severity of Philip's taxation and his persecution of heresy. To resist this oppression the lesser nobility and merchants formed a sort of league, the members of which called themselves " The Beggars." This movement grew so formidable that Philip had to promise that the grievances should be redressed ; but he was only biding his time—he assured the Pope that he would rather exterminate his subjects than rule over heretics. In 1567 he sent the Duke of Alva and a force of 12,000 picked Spanish troops with definite instructions to stop at nothing to stamp out all religious and political liberty. Alva's name has become a byeword for callous and ruthless severity. After beginning with fair words, he arrested Egmont and had him executed on an utterly baseless charge of fomenting the disturbances ; and his " Council of Blood " followed this up by creating a reign of terror throughout the provinces, thousands being executed in the course of a few months. William of Orange would have been among the first victims but that he had foreseen what was coming and fled the country. A great change of heart now took place in that remarkable man. Hitherto his discreet self-possession towards the Government had earned him the nickname of " The Silent " ; but the abominable cruelties he had recently witnessed made him embrace the reformed religion and devote himself to winning the freedom of the Netherlands from oppression. From his various places of exile he organised the famous revolt which continued for thirty years to be a grievous source of weakness to the Spanish monarchy and to the Catholic Reaction. And we see here, as in Scotland and France, another example of the second or Calvinistic Reformation bound up with rebellion against a Government.

59. *The First Attack on England*

But when the Counter-Reformation began—about 1560—
these developments were still in the future. The most serious
breach in the Catholic unity of Christendom was England, and
it was certain that Philip II, as protagonist of the reaction, would
sooner or later attack Elizabeth. Indeed, we may say that
he had already done so—by the traditional Hapsburg method of
an offer of marriage (§ 48). Why, when this matrimonial
onslaught was repulsed, did he not at once follow it up by more
direct methods ? Partly, as we have seen, because the Catholic
heir to the throne was a French princess ; and partly because
he felt that he must allay the unrest in the Netherlands before
he could effectively give his attention to external undertakings.

Meanwhile, he continued to support with advice and
encouragement the English Catholics in their plots against the
Queen. The Rising of the Northern Earls (§ 55) had collapsed
ignominiously, but the general plan was by no means abandoned ;
and in the following year Pope Pius V took a step which greatly
encouraged the plotters. He issued a *Bull of Excommunication*
against Elizabeth, absolving her subjects from their allegiance to
her, and calling upon them to dethrone her (1570). The effect
was to give English Catholics an assurance that rebellion was
authorised by their religion ; and we may look upon the *Ridolfi
Plot* of 1571 as the first blow of the Reaction at England.

Ridolfi was an Italian banker in London who acted as secret
agent of the Pope. He entered into correspondence with Norfolk
and the other peers who had for the past two years been dabbling
in treason. The objective was no longer merely the recognition
of Mary Stuart's right to the succession ; their aim was now to
get rid of Elizabeth altogether and to make Mary Queen of a
Catholic Great Britain, with Norfolk as her husband. Philip
and Alva gave verbal encouragement to the scheme, but
explained that they could spare no troops from the Netherlands
until the English Catholics had taken the all-important first step
of getting Elizabeth into their hands, alive or dead.

Meanwhile Cecil (now Lord Burghley) had been on the
scent of the conspiracy almost from the beginning : spies had
been employed, hints had come from ambassadors, suspected

persons had been watched.   At last a lucky arrest led to the unearthing of evidence which implicated Norfolk and several other peers, as well as the Pope, the Spanish Ambassador, and the ex-Queen of Scots herself.   Even the threat of assassination could not break down Elizabeth's determination not to drive any section of her subjects to despair by stern measures.   Norfolk himself was the only peer to be brought to trial, and the Queen hesitated for a long time to sign the death-warrant even of this double-dyed traitor.   It was only when her Council began to press for the execution of Mary herself that she gave way about Norfolk as a sort of compromise.   The scaffold on Tower Green which had been kept in such constant use by her predecessors had fallen to pieces during the thirteen years of her reign, and had to be specially rebuilt.

60. *A Diplomatic Revolution*

We have seen that the governments of France and Spain might be expected sooner or later to attack England on behalf of the Counter-Reformation; and that each of these governments was troubled by internal religious dissensions of its own.   From this situation Elizabeth and her advisers deduced an obvious line of foreign policy : to foment the disturbances and so keep the hostile Powers occupied.   Burghley and his colleague Walsingham would have liked to see the Queen put herself openly at the head of the Protestant cause in Europe, but Elizabeth would not go so far as this.   She never liked adopting a decisive line of policy about anything ; she hated spending money ; she disliked encouraging rebels ; and she dreaded lest she should bring down upon herself an attack from France and Spain together.   She therefore limited herself to giving secretly just enough help to the foreign Protestants to prevent their movements from collapsing, and she revelled in the course of shifts, protestations, and denials in which this two-faced policy involved her.

Of the two Powers concerned, Elizabeth for the first decade of her reign carried on the traditional Tudor policy of leaning to Hapsburg rather than to Valois (§ 31) ;   but about 1570 circumstances caused a reversal of the position. For one thing, the Netherlands were now in revolt; their wool-trade was no longer under the control of their Hapsburg sovereigns. For another, Mary Stuart had practically severed her connection with France, now that the Queen-Mother was the dominant personality in the French Court. Lastly, English seamen were making piratical attacks, as we shall see in the next chapter, on Spanish ships plying to and from the Netherlands.

It was obvious that the bad relations between England and Spain would sooner or later lead to open war, and it was clearly advisable for Elizabeth to guard against the possibility of having to meet an attack from Spain while relations with France were still strained. Walsingham was therefore sent to Paris in 1572 to negotiate a treaty of alliance to be sealed by a marriage between the Queen and the Duke d'Anjou, the brother of the French king.

These negotiations were interrupted for a time by the *Massacre of St. Bartholomew.* Charles IX had tried to bring about a reconciliation between the religious parties, and a marriage had been arranged between his sister Marguerite de Valois and Henry of Navarre, the leader of the Huguenots. But when all the chief men of both faiths were gathered in Paris for the wedding, the Queen-Mother persuaded her weak-willed son to end the Wars of Religion by a very different method— the massacre of the unsuspecting Protestant nobles. This project was carried through with appalling completeness, within twenty-four hours of its inception. It helps us to realise the character of the Catholic Reaction when we learn that Pope Gregory XIII had a medal struck to celebrate the event, and that Philip II when he heard of it actually laughed in public for the first and last time in his career.

Queen Elizabeth professed to be horrified at the deed, but she did not allow any sentimental concern for fellow-Protestants to deflect the course of her policy. To be sure, Anjou now declared that he could not bring himself to marry a heretic, but it was decided to transfer the honour to the youngest of the Valois brothers, the Duke d' Alençon, who was not so particular. For the next ten years there was played the ghastly comedy of a courtship between a sickly boy in his twenties with a woman old

enough to be his mother.   But Elizabeth had no real intention
of marrying him or anybody else.   She was merely using the
fact that she was unmarried as an instrument in her diplomatic
game.

QUESTIONS

(1) *What was the Counter-Reformation ?*
(2) *Give an account of Elizabeth's method of keeping the
Catholic Reaction at bay.*

CHAPTER XIII

Young England takes to the Sea

(1560–1580)

We have now to trace the beginnings of British sea-power. We shall find that it was the outcome of the Renaissance thirst for adventure and exploration, coupled with the growth of the commercial instinct which marked the break-up of the Middle Ages. These motives were greatly stimulated in the reign of Elizabeth by the fear of a foreign tyranny, and hatred of the religion which that tyranny represented.

61. *The Merchant Adventurers*

The urge to adventure overseas must always have been in Englishmen's blood from the days of their Viking forbears; but for centuries it was suppressed by geographical circumstances. Until the end of the fifteenth century England was on the outside edge of the world, and her merchants had confined themselves to traffic across the narrow seas. But the discovery of America and of the route to India *via* the Cape altered the whole position. Hitherto international commerce had been centred in the Mediterranean; now it began to range all over the world, and England shared with France and Spain the advantage of directly facing the ocean which henceforth became its highway.

Still, England was by far the smallest and most backward of these three countries; how came it that by the end of the century she was already gaining a lead over the other two, and had laid the foundation for her later world-supremacy in commercial, maritime, and colonial enterprise?

Firstly, because she is an island, with an irregular coastline ; whereas her rivals were solid masses of land with comparatively few natural harbours.   No part of England is more than seventy miles from the sea.

Secondly, because her capital being itself a port, maritime interests have always been in direct contact with the Government ; whereas Paris and Madrid are quite out of touch with the sea.

Thirdly, because France and Spain were absorbed in European interests, whereas English governments had learned the lessons of the Hundred Years' War, and, except for spasmodic and shortlived efforts, had kept aloof from Continental adventures.

Lastly, because the persecution of the Huguenots deprived France of many of the best of her seafaring population ; while Spain murdered the prosperity of the Netherlands, where the seafaring element was also particularly strong.   Elizabeth, on the other hand, kept England free from the blight of religious strife, and her policy of " not opening windows into man's soul " left her people free to pursue their own commercial interests.

These advantages were exploited to the full.   All through the Tudor age English merchants had been constantly seeking new markets.   Pope Alexander VI had divided the newly discovered lands between Spain and Portugal, and the governments of those countries jealously excluded the ships of other countries from these possessions.   For a time Englishmen interested themselves in other regions, and sought new routes to Asia round the northern coasts of Europe and America.   In 1533 Chancellor found his way to Archangel and returned home *via* Moscow, while a year later Jenkins succeeded in reaching the Volga and sailed down into the Caspian.   Repeated efforts were made—especially by Frobisher and Davis—to find a north-west passage, but all in vain.   As time went on it was realised that these routes were impracticable,—and also that the Iberian Powers could not effectively preserve their monopoly. There was no Law of Nations to which they could appeal, and no submarine cables over which international complaints could be made ; nor had either Power a naval organisation capable of " policing " such far-flung trade routes.   Great profits could be made by men of bold and self-reliant spirit who were prepared to take great risks. Trading voyages became adventures in which honest trading, smuggling, marine exploration, and something very like piracy became mixed up in a glorious medley immensely attractive to Young England.

62. *Pirates in the Channel*

British sea-power began by a combination of piracy with commerce; it developed through a combination of piracy with warfare. The animosity aroused by the Spanish policy of exclusion was, after the middle of the century, intensified by religious hatred. Philip felt that he was doing God's work by preventing his subjects from having intercourse with heretics. He installed the Inquisition at his ports on both sides of the Atlantic, and horrible tales began to reach England of English sailors being flogged, tortured, and burnt alive by Spaniards merely for being Protestants. It was not long before the joyful discovery was made that retaliation was both easy and profitable. The English Channel was the highway between Philip's homeland and the richest of his outlying European dominions. The men of Cornwall, Devon, and Dorset found that the Spanish ships were an easy prey, for they were not designed either for speed or for fighting. The deeply indented south-west coast of England was admirably adapted for such adventures, and young men of all classes were attracted by a career which combined sport with gain. The two countries were not at war, and it is impossible to justify these lawless proceedings, especially as they were often accompanied by savage cruelty; but it is also impossible not to admire the daring shown in this defiance of the greatest naval and military power in the world. Nor can it be doubted that these attacks greatly hampered the King of Spain in his efforts to subdue the Netherlands, and so gave England many years of precious respite from the long-contemplated attack of the Catholic Reaction.

An equally important result of this privateering was that it gave rise to a method of sea-fighting which was destined in the long run to enable Britain to oust Spain altogether from the supremacy of the sea. The Spanish navy had developed in the Mediterranean, where oared galleys were used, and the fighting consisted mainly of hand-to-hand conflicts between boarding parties. As late as 1572 it won a brilliant victory by these methods over the Turkish fleet at *Lepanto*—a victory which made an end of the danger that Western Europe would be conquered by the Sultan. But oared galleys were quite unsuited to the more violent wind and weather encountered in the ocean, nor was it possible to provide sleeping accommodation and stores for hundreds of galley-slaves for a long voyage ; and the Spaniards had long learned to rely on sail alone for their trans-Atlantic voyages. Still, they could never get rid of the galley idea in designing their ships, and they never learnt the use of any but square sails which involved constant tacking in unfavourable winds. Nor could they get out of their heads the notion that mariners were persons of inferior status whose duty was merely to put the ships alongside the enemy for the soldiers to do the fighting. The English adventurers, on the other hand, had not the financial resources to build large ships, nor had they enough men to meet the enemy with cutlass and pike ; and they had to evolve tactics by which these disadvantages could be overcome. They found that a combination of square sails on the foremast with fore-and-aft rig on the main enabled them to sail much nearer to the wind, and made their ships much easier to handle in all sorts of weather conditions. They used this superior mobility to avoid coming to close quarters, and battered their unwieldy opponents into submission at a comparatively long range with artillery fired through port-holes. Moreover, as they had no room on board for one set of men to sail the ship and another set to fight her, they contrived to combine these functions ; and this plan had the advantage that there were fewer claims to a share in the booty, when the hapless Spaniard was towed captive into some rocky inlet.

63. " *Unofficial War* "

The Queen's Councillors were anxious lest these proceedings should be carried so far as to goad Philip into declaring war, for they felt that the country would be utterly unable to cope with the overwhelming resources of Spain ; but this was the sort of diplomatic game at which Elizabeth was supremely skilful.

She gave secret encouragement to the sea-dogs who were weakening her enemy at no cost to her exchequer; but when Philip's protests grew dangerously heated she declared that she was as horrified as he at such misdeeds, and would see what could be done to bring them to an end. Thus matters drifted on from year to year, with Philip often at the point of making war, but always postponing this until he had mastered the trouble in the Netherlands. And all the time England was becoming better prepared to defend herself when the crisis should come.

We may divide this unofficial warfare into two chief categories—piracy in the Channel and smuggling in the Caribbean. The most famous of the men engaged in the latter occupation was *Sir John Hawkins*, who has also the doubtful honour of being the chief founder of the Slave Trade upon which so much of Britain's later commercial prosperity was based. The Spanish colonists having found that the natives of America died off like flies when compelled to work in mines and plantations, Hawkins devised a scheme for turning this demand for labour to his own profit. The African negro is made of tougher stuff than the Caribbean Indian, and Hawkins began to carry English manufactures to the West Coast of Africa, where he traded them with the native chiefs for their prisoners of war, and even their own subjects. He then conveyed these unhappy creatures across the Atlantic, and sold them at enormous profit to the Spanish colonists. This was infringing the trade monopoly claimed by King Philip, and he ordered stringent precautions to be taken to prevent it. On Hawkins' third voyage, for which the Queen lent him two royal ships with a view to a share in the proceeds, his little fleet was treacherously attacked, while re-fitting at San Juan de Ulloa, by some Spanish war vessels which he had allowed to shelter in the harbour from a gale. Of his five ships only two escaped, and all the profits of the voyage were lost. Elizabeth was very indignant, but a splendid opportunity for revenge came her way a few weeks later.

Alva had ruined the Netherlands with his persecution, and Philip had to borrow money from Genoese bankers to pay the Spanish troops there. The ships conveying the coin were chased by Huguenot privateers into Plymouth Sound; and the Queen announced that the only way to prevent the money from falling into wrong hands would be to borrow it herself. The Genoese were quite ready to ratify the transfer, but Philip (not unnaturally) was extremely angry. The indirect results of the transaction were more disastrous to him than the actual loss of the money, for Alva was compelled to raise money for his veterans (who were on the verge of mutiny) by a new and impossibly severe tax upon the Netherlanders, which goaded them into open rebellion against Spanish rule.

One of the most effective ways in which they could strike at their tyrants was by piratical attacks upon Spanish shipping in the narrow seas, very similar to those carried out by English seamen farther down the Channel. These *Beggars of the Sea* (§ 58) at first used the ports of Kent and Sussex for disposing of their booty and refitting their ships ; but Philip protested so emphatically against his rebellious subjects being thus harboured and encouraged that the Queen felt that the time had come to give way. Yet even this little diplomatic victory for the King of Spain did his cause more harm than good in the end ; for the Sea-beggars, excluded by an Order of the Council from English harbours, were driven by sheer necessity to take the bold step of capturing Brill, a port in Flanders, while the Spanish garrison was temporarily absent. They maintained possession of it, and it became the starting-point of an independent Dutch Republic.

64. *Drake goes West*

One of the more fortunate members of Sir John Hawkins' party who returned with him from the disaster of San Juan was a young relative of his named *Francis Drake* (1540–1596). If the King of Spain could have foreseen the future, his regret at this escape would have greatly dashed the joy with which he heard of the incident. For the rest of Drake's life was spent in waging war—at first on his own account and later in the Queen's service —against the Spanish empire, and a terrible foe he proved himself. This sturdy thick-set Devon man with steel-blue eyes and reddish beard was the very personification of the spirit that inspired the Elizabethan seamen. His audacity in sailing his

cockleshell of a ship into uncharted seas infested with fierce
enemies, the glorious insolence with which he would capture
vessels ten times the size of his own under the very guns of
Spanish fortresses, the half-humorous, half-contemptuous ruses
he invented to deceive his enemy, the humanity which he,
almost alone among his contemporaries, displayed towards
non-combatants : all this established the traditions which have
been preserved in the sea-service of Britain right down to our own
day.

He began his career as an independent commander by a
determination to recoup himself for his losses at San Juan, and
very thoroughly did he do it.   One of the most famous of these
earlier exploits was a bold piece of highway robbery ashore.
He learnt that the Spaniards were in the habit of taking the
annual tribute of Peru by sea to Panama, transporting it on the
backs of mules across the isthmus, and placing it aboard galleons
at Nombre de Dios Bay to be carried to Spain.   After a vain
attempt to take Nombre de Dios itself (a good-sized town held
by a strong garrison) with a party of thirty-seven men and boys,
he went up country, laid an ambush for the mule-train, and
carried off the treasure to his own ship.   This exploit made him
famous, and led to others setting out on similar quests—mostly
with indifferent success.

65. *" Round the World if need be "*

During his sojourn at Panama, Drake had caught a glimpse
of the Pacific Ocean, and the sight had inspired him with a new
ambition, bolder than anything he had yet conceived.   The
ships which carried the produce of the Peruvian mines to
Panama were built on the spot, and no vessel had ever sailed into
the Pacific from Europe since Magellan's voyage fifty years
before.   The west coast of South America and the ships which
plied along it were therefore left quite unprotected.   Here was
a booty of fabulous richness lying waiting for anybody bold
enough to undertake the long and perilous voyage.   It was this
that Drake now determined to do.   He had to make his preparations in secret, for there was a strong party in the Council—
headed by Burghley himself—who feared that such an enterprise
would provoke Philip to make a direct attack upon England.

THE VOYAGES

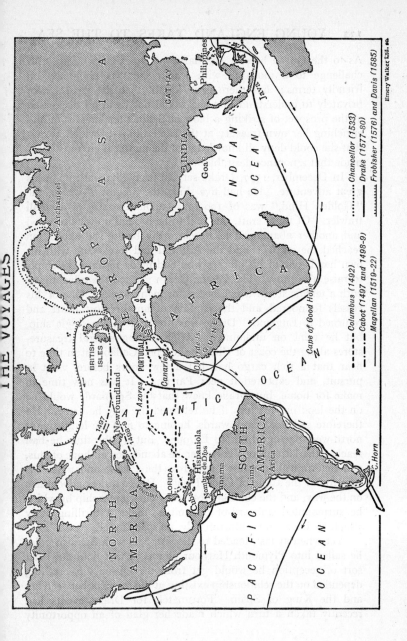

Columbus (1492)
Cabot (1497 and 1498-9)
Magellan (1519-22)
Chancellor (1533)
Drake (1577-80)
Frobisher (1576) and Davis (1585)

Emery Walker Ltd. sc.

As to the Queen herself, she dared not openly encourage this challenge to a monarch with whom she was nominally on friendly terms ; but there is no doubt that she gave Drake privately to understand that she would not be at all displeased at the prospect of striking a blow at Spain's tenderest spot and enriching her own treasury at the same time—provided always that she could deny all knowledge of the matter if circumstances made that ignorance desirable.

In December, 1577, Drake set sail from Plymouth upon his great adventure. He had five ships, the biggest of which, the " Golden Hind," was of 100 tons—about the size of a small trawler. Of these craft, one had to be broken up for fire-wood and another abandoned as unseaworthy before the expedition reached the straits ; and the Admiral had to execute with his own hands one of his officers who had made repeated attempts to raise a mutiny. The Pacific Ocean greeted the adventurers with a terrific storm which lasted for many weeks. One of his vessels foundered, and the captain of another lost heart and returned to England. Drake was now left with a single ship, but he went on undaunted. After raiding several treasure-stores along the coast of Chili, he reached Callao just in time to hear that a rich cargo had left a few hours before, went in pursuit, and captured it near Panama. It was now time to make for home, but Drake knew that the Spaniards would be on the look out for him if he returned the way he came. He therefore sailed on northwards, hoping to find the long-sought north-west passage back to Europe. But by the time he had reached the latitude of Vancouver he abandoned all hope of this, and determined to strike out across the Pacific and make his way round the Cape of Good Hope. His countless adventures on the way, and the courage, resource, and seamanship by which he surmounted unheard-of difficulties, make a thrilling story which we have here, unfortunately, no space to tell.

Yet when at last, loaded to the scuppers with Spanish gold, he sailed into Plymouth Harbour, it was at first doubtful what sort of reception he would get from the Queen. Everything depended on the relationship existing at the moment between her and the King of Spain. Fortunately for Drake, events had recently taken a turn which made her glad of an opportunity to snub Philip ; and after a delay of some weeks Drake received orders to sail the " Golden Hind " round to Greenwich, where the Queen paid a visit to the historic little vessel and knighted her intrepid commander on his own quarter-deck.

We may look upon this act of the Queen's as one of the decisive events of her reign, for it indicated that she had made up her mind that war with Spain was inevitable sooner or later, and that she could not withhold her support from the men who would be her main defence in it.

Questions

(1) *How did England become a sea-power ?*
(2) *Was Drake a pirate ?*

ELIZABETH AT WAR

1583	Throgmorton's Plot (§68) — First Settlement of Newfoundland (§80)	1583
1584	Death of Anjou (§68) Murder of Orange (§68)	1584
1585	English Army in Netherlands (§69)	1585
1586	Babington Plot (§70) — Zutphen ⚔ (§69)	1586
1587	Execution of Mary (§70) — Drake in Cadiz Harbour (§71)	1587
1588	"Dr. Faustus" (§83) — The Spanish Armada (§73)	1588
1589	"Martin Marprelate" (§77) — Henry IV of France (§74)	1589
1590	"The Faery Queene" (§82)	1590
1591	*The Revenge* (§74)	1591
1592	"Romeo and Juliet" (§84)	1592
1593		1593
1594		1594
1595	"A Midsummer Night's Dream" (§84)	1595
1596	Essex at Cadiz (§87) Death of Drake & Hawkins (§87)	1596
1597	The Islands Voyage (§87)	1597
1598	Death of Burghley (§87) Irish Rebellion : Blackwater ⚔ (§88) Edict of Nantes (§87)	1598
1599		1599
1600	East India Company founded (§80)	1600
1601	New Poor Law (§80) "The Triumphs of Oriana" (§85) Execution of Essex (§89)	1601
1602	"Hamlet" (§84)	1602
1603	Death of Elizabeth (§90)	1603

CHAPTER XIV

From Peace to War

(1580-1587)

For twenty-five years Elizabeth and her trusty counsellors had succeeded in warding off the threatened attack of the Catholic Reaction personified by Philip II. They managed to stir up trouble for him in his own possessions without ever going so far as to provoke him to open warfare. In this chapter we shall deal with a series of untoward events which at last compelled them to take more open steps and which brought the country within measurable distance of the cataclysm.

66. *The Papal Attack*

The excommunication of the Queen pronounced by Pope Pius V (§ 59) had not been followed by any definite action, for the Kings of France and Spain were not prepared to admit that any one—even a Pope—had the right to dethrone an anointed sovereign. As a matter of fact, the Bull did more harm than good to the cause it was intended to serve, for many English Catholics, forced to choose between loyalty to their Queen and loyalty to their Pope, began to attend their parish churches as a proof of their patriotism. This drift towards Anglicanism caused much anxiety to the leading spirits of the Catholic Reaction. A seminary to train young English priests to act as missionaries to their native land had already been started at Douai in France, but the movement did not really get under weigh until the election to the Papacy of Gregory XIII in 1572. This Pope made the re-conversion of England his particular aim. He established a special Jesuit College for the purpose in Rome itself, and in 1580 the first batch of priests was sent over into England with the knowledge that the best service they could render their Church would be to die for it as martyrs, and so re-awaken the religious enthusiasm which was dying down into an easy-going acceptance of the *via media anglicana*. The most famous of these Jesuit missionaries was *Thomas Campion*. He wandered about the country for over a year, sometimes preaching openly in the market-places of midland towns, sometimes taking shelter in the country houses of Catholic gentlemen. Then he was captured, horribly tortured, and put to death as a traitor, despite the fact that there was no scrap of evidence that he had ever uttered a disloyal word or harboured a disloyal thought. His execution was the first of many such. For the first half of her reign Elizabeth had prided herself that her Government had never inflicted the death penalty for offences connected with religion ; but after the " Papal campaign " began nearly two hundred Catholics were executed. This is shocking to our modern ideas of toleration, but in judging such matters we must bear in mind the standards of the age. We must remember, too, that the forty-four years of Elizabeth's reign saw only half as many sufferers for conscience' sake as the six years of her sister's ; nor must we forget that even the Marian persecution was mild compared with the butchery that went on in Continental countries in the name of religion. Moreover, the Queen and her Council always maintained that the penalties were inflicted for treason, not for religion. The prosecutions were under an Act of 1352, passed by a Catholic King and Parliament, and the fact that papal pronouncements made it a merit to contrive the death of the Queen, placed all sincere Catholics under suspicion.

Nor did Pope Gregory limit his efforts to missionary endeavours and vague denunciations. He promised great rewards both in this world and the next to any one who would assassinate the heretic queen, and he repeatedly urged the King of Spain to undertake a " crusade " against her. But the murder-plots all fell through, and Philip still hesitated ; so at last the Pope got together a force which, though not strong enough to invade England, might, he calculated, cause a lot of trouble in Ireland, where the people were staunchly Catholic. The Papal troops landed at *Smerwick* in June, 1580. There they dug themselves in and held their own for over a year, being reinforced early in the following year by some Spaniards sent secretly by Philip. But very little active support came from the Irish, and in November they were surrounded by the Queen's forces and compelled to surrender. Philip denied all knowledge of the affair, and the prisoners were put to death as pirates.

The Pope then contrived an embarrassment for Elizabeth in Scotland. James VI, the son of Mary, had in 1578 taken over the Government from his guardians. To him was sent one Esme Stuart, a Catholic kinsman of his own, who had long been an exile in France. Stuart captivated the young king, and half persuaded him to join the Church of Rome. An excuse was found for executing Lord Morton, who had long held the leading place in the Government in the Protestant interest (§ 54) ; and his position was taken by Stuart, who became Earl of Lennox. Thus the old Franco-Catholic influence in Scotland was renewed. It was not long, however, before the Protestant leaders among the nobility contrived the overthrow of the newcomer. By the *Raid of Ruthven* (1582) they kidnapped the young King, regained their hold over his mind, and frightened Lennox back into exile.

67. *A Bridegroom as Catspaw*

For fifteen years Philip II had shrunk from facing the fact that Elizabeth was giving underhand help to his revolted subjects in the Netherlands ; but events were now making it impossible for her to go on working underground, or for him to ignore the damage she was doing him.

Alva had failed to crush the revolt with his " Council of Blood " (§ 58) ; nor were his successors able to do so by other methods. In 1576 the Spanish garrison, whose pay was a twelvemonth in arrears, broke out into a riot in which they sought to recoup themselves at the expense of the citizens of Antwerp. This " Spanish Fury " did so much damage to the city that it was never again able to challenge the supremacy of London among North Sea ports. Two years later yet another Governor was appointed—the *Duke of Parma*, one of the ablest soldiers and statesmen of the day. Parma succeeded in persuading the southern provinces to return to their allegiance to the Spanish throne and the Catholic faith on condition that their political liberties were guaranteed ; but nothing would shake the determination of the northern provinces to maintain their independence and their Protestantism.   William of Orange, the leading spirit of the rebellion, realised that the " United Provinces " needed active support from an external Power, and that some sort of monarchy was necessary to hold them together. The sovereignty was first offered to Elizabeth, but she declined with thanks.   She had no territorial ambitions, and she dared not openly defy the King of Spain.   The choice of the Netherlanders then fell upon the former Duke of Alençon, who had become Duke of Anjou on the accession of his brother as Henry III.   This move gave Elizabeth some alarm, for she did not want to see the new State fall into the hands of France. She therefore re-opened the old negotiations for a marriage between herself and Anjou (§ 60), hoping by this means to keep a hold over the situation, and to use the prince as a catspaw.

In 1580 her position became more critical than ever owing to the annexation of Portugal by Philip.   This not merely made him master of the whole Iberian Peninsula, including two splendid harbours on the Atlantic seaboard ; it also gave him all the Portuguese possessions in South America, Africa, and Asia.   It now became more necessary than ever that France and England should draw together (§ 60).   The weedy, pock-marked young prince came over to England and began once more the mockery of a courtship with a woman of forty-seven.   Rings were exchanged and the betrothal publicly announced.   The idea of a French marriage for Elizabeth was as unpopular in England as her sister's Spanish marriage had been, and for a similar reason, Anjou being heir-apparent to the French throne.   But, of course, the whole courtship was a mere political device on the Queen's part.   When Anjou departed to take up the government of the Netherlands, his fiancée accompanied him as far as Canterbury, and made a touching display of grief at losing his society ; but when a year or so later his subjects drove him back to France for trying to destroy their liberties, and he had ceased to be a useful tool, she broke off the match.

Nevertheless the episode marked a distinct advance along the road to open war between England and Spain, for Elizabeth

had not been able to disguise the fact that she was supporting
Anjou with English money.

68. *The Plot Thickens*

Between October, 1583, and the July of the following year
three events occurred which made the situation more acute
than ever. The first was the exposure of what is known as
Throgmorton's Plot. After the first batch of Catholic con-
spiracies (1569–1571) (§§ 55, 59) there had been a lull; but the
Jesuit missions inspired by Gregory had fulfilled their main
purpose by infusing fresh ardour into the English Catholics, and
the next fifteen years were full of schemes for " removing "
the Queen and putting Mary Stuart in her place. Cecil and
Walsingham had innumerable spies at work, and in 1583 they
came upon traces of a plot in which a Catholic gentleman
named Throgmorton was playing a principal part. Throgmorton was arrested, and his lodgings searched. Amongst his
papers were found letters involving the Pope, Mary Stuart, and
the Spanish Ambassador. Elizabeth still could not be induced
to bring her sister-queen to trial, but she expelled the ambassador from the country. Philip protested that he himself had
no knowledge of his representative's doings. Elizabeth knew
better ; but as she still felt herself in no position to go to war with
Spain, she let the matter drop. Nevertheless, the dismissal
of an ambassador came dangerously near to open warfare.

The second untoward event of this fateful half-year was the
death of Anjou (July, 1584). The importance of this lay in
the fact that the heir to the French throne was now Henry of
Navarre, a Huguenot The prospect of a Protestant king in
the seat of St. Louis drove the Duke of Guise and the other
leading Catholic nobles of France to form a " Holy League "
with the King of Spain, the watchword of which was " No
heretics on thrones." Another " War of Religion " (the fifth)
broke out. If the League won, it would be in a position to apply
its principle to England as well as to France.

An even more epoch-making death followed a few weeks
later—the *murder of William the Silent* at the instigation of
Philip II. Orange was one of the outstanding figures of six-

teenth-century history. The loss of his wise statesmanship and his inspiring personality was a severe blow to the Netherlanders, and it seemed as if their rebellion must now be crushed. If Philip were successful in the Netherlands, he would be able to devote the whole of his resources to the long-threatened conquest of England.

69. *Open Warfare at last*

To delay the inevitable attack as long as possible, Elizabeth was now forced to make open efforts to keep her adversary's attention engaged elsewhere. In the autumn of 1585 she sent Drake to strike at the source whence Philip drew the wealth with which he waged war. This time there was nothing of buccaneering about the expedition. Sir Francis held the Queen's Commission and commanded a fleet of some thirty vessels. He called in turn at the port of Vigo in Spain, at the Cape Verde Islands in the Atlantic, at San Domingo in the Indies, and at Cartagena on the Main, and wherever he went took whatever spoils he could come by and destroyed all the stores and shipping. When he returned (in July, 1586) his booty was small compared with the immense treasure he had brought home from his earlier voyages, but this was of minor importance compared with the confusion and terror he had left behind him.

The Revolt of the Netherlands had also to be kept going by hook or by crook. On the death of Orange, the United Provinces renewed their petition that Elizabeth would become their " Protector." She now accepted, on condition that all her expenses were paid, and that certain towns were handed over to her as a pledge for the payment of the money. These hard terms having been reluctantly accepted, a body of 6,000 men was sent over in the autumn of 1585 under the command of the *Earl of Leicester*. This nobleman—the son of Edward VI's Northumberland and grandson of Henry VII's Dudley—was a vain, handsome, unprincipled courtier, of mediocre abilities both as soldier and as statesman. He had long cherished hopes that the Queen would marry him, and it was said that he had murdered his young wife so that he might be in a position to gain the " crown matrimonial." For twenty-five years he had lived on the hope which maketh the heart sick, sometimes in high favour with his capricious mistress, sometimes banished from the Court in disgrace, and he was now getting grey and elderly. In the Netherlands he soon showed that he was utterly incapable, both in character and in ability, of tackling a task which had baffled even the wise and heroic William of Orange. He quarrelled with his English subordinates ; he took part in the party squabbles of the Netherlanders ; he accepted from them the title of Governor-General without consulting the Queen— to her intense indignation. In any case his campaign was fore-doomed to failure through the fact that the Queen, parsimonious as ever, could not bring herself to spend money on it. The ill-equipped and starving troops gave but a poor account of themselves, and the important town of *Zutphen* fell into the hands of the enemy through the incapacity and pusillanimity of an English commander.

In August, 1587, Leicester returned home, broken in health, spirits, and fortune, and he died in the following year. The campaign had been a dismal failure, but it had been a definite and undeniable act of war against Spain. How long would Philip continue to hold his hand ?

70. *The end of " The Daughter of Discord "*

Meanwhile, the closing scenes in the tragedy of Mary Stuart were being enacted.

Until the first plots on her behalf began, very little restraint had been put upon her movements. Even during the 'seventies she had been able to hunt, take the waters at Buxton, to receive and correspond with whom she chose. It was only after the Throgmorton conspiracy that Queen and Council fully realised how dangerous she was. Thenceforward she was kept in a castle where her liberties were more narrowly restricted.

It was obvious that as long as she lived she would be a source of danger. The only hope of the Catholic plotters lay in the death of Elizabeth. Probably something like two-thirds of the English nation were still Catholic at heart, but few of them would take part in a rebellion against a sovereign who repre-sented the national unity. Only when she was dead would they

welcome the reinstatement of the Catholic Church and recognise
Mary's claims to the succession. On the other hand, the
Protestant minority (which included most of the members of the
Council) looked on the prospect of the Queen's death with grave
anxiety. It was their desire to ensure a Protestant succession
that made them urge her to marry a Protestant while she was
not yet too old to have children ; and after the Throgmorton
Plot and the murder of William the Silent had brought home the
danger of assassination they formed a *Bond of Association*, of
which the members undertook to stand together in defence of
the Queen's life, and to avenge her murder not only on the
contrivers of it, but also on the person on whose behalf it had
been committed.

The leading spirit in all this was *Sir Francis Walsingham*
(1536–1590). Long practice had made him a supremely skilful
unraveller of plots. His spies were everywhere—even in the
Jesuit College at Rome ; he was an expert at unsealing and
resealing correspondence ; he often employed the rack to extract
evidence from suspected persons. He now determined that the
death of Mary was essential to the safety of the Queen, of the
country, and of the Protestant faith.

Meanwhile, Mary herself was becoming desperate. She learnt
that her son was now a convinced Protestant, that he was drawing
a pension from Elizabeth, and that it was becoming an understood thing that he was to succeed to the English throne. Nothing but a violent revolution could rescue her from the obscurity
and neglect which was a greater affliction to her proud spirit
than death itself. She therefore fell readily into the trap which
Walsingham set for her. Her correspondence in cypher with a
Catholic gentleman named *Babington* revealed an elaborate plot
to dethrone Elizabeth with help from Spain. Walsingham
allowed the plans to develop until he had got indisputable proof
of her complicity. The Queen was then induced to appoint a
special commission to go down to Fotheringay Castle, where
Mary was now lodged, and try her. She could not deny her
connection with the plot, though she would never admit that she
had consented to the actual assassination of Elizabeth. The
court condemned her to death ; but Elizabeth underwent a
long and agonising hesitation before she could bring herself to

sign the warrant for the execution. Apart from her chronic dislike of coming to an irrevocable decision about anything whatever, she was very unwilling to break through " the divinity that doth hedge a king " by cutting off a head that had once worn a crown.   At last she was forced to admit that it was essential to the peace and happiness of her people that they should be protected from the woman who had repeatedly planned to curse them with the horrors of a civil war.   The delighted Council could hardly wait for the ink of her signature to dry before they hastened off to execute the warrant.   Two days later Mary met her death in the great hall of Fotheringay Castle with a dignity worthy of a queen.   London was delighted at the news, and bonfires were burned in the streets ; but the worst side of the Queen's character now came to the surface.   With contemptible hypocrisy she pretended that she had never intended the execution to be carried out.   In the hope of convincing the world of her innocence she ruthlessly sacrificed her unfortunate secretary, Davison, who had merely obeyed her orders.   She would have had him executed for treason if she could ; as it was, she had to be satisfied with inflicting a fine that ruined his family, and an imprisonment that lasted for the rest of her reign.   And all this was in vain, for nobody was deceived by her protestations, while the execution made Philip more determined than ever to avenge the cause of Kings by invading the territories of the Jezebel of the West.

QUESTIONS

(1) *Explain the steps by which Elizabeth was driven to open warfare with Spain.*

(2) *Give an account of the life of Mary Queen of Scots.*

CHAPTER XV

The Invincible Armada

(1587–1590)

*The defeat of the Armada was one of the most noteworthy
landmarks in our history, for it raised the national self-confidence to a higher pitch than it had ever reached before, and it
made Englishmen realise that it was their destiny to rule the
waves.*

71. *Planning a Crusade*

Philip of Spain was as incorrigible a procrastinator as
Elizabeth of England. Each of them resisted the forces that
were making for war as long as they possibly could, and each
preferred to attack the other by underhand methods, despite
counsellors who favoured more open and decisive action. But,
as we have seen, circumstances had now arisen which made it
impossible to postpone the crisis any longer. The death of
Orange and of Anjou had compelled Elizabeth to intervene
openly in the Netherlands ; and this had forced Philip to the
conclusion that instead of postponing the invasion of England
until he had subjugated the Netherlands, he must reverse the
process. Moreover, the attacks of Drake and his like had convinced him that until England was crushed his Empire would
never enjoy peace and security. Again, the new Pope, Sixtus V,
was prepared to go further than his predecessors, and contribute
in hard cash towards the cost of a Spanish invasion of England.
Lastly, the execution of Mary Stuart had not only raised the
anger of Catholic Europe to a white heat, it had also removed a
hampering obstacle from Philip's path. Hitherto he had always
hesitated about making such a great venture on behalf of a
princess unconnected with his own family ; but now that Mary

was dead and had bequeathed her claims to the English throne to himself, he found himself in a much stronger position.

All through 1587 great preparations went on in the ports and arsenals of Spain and Portugal. Philip was, as usual, short of money, for his resources were nothing like as great in fact as they were in theory. The Netherlands had long been a source of expense instead of revenue, the English corsairs constantly intercepted the treasure-ships of the Indies, and the governmental system of Spain was honeycombed with corruption. Still, the enterprise was looked upon as a sort of crusade against the infidel. Scarcely a noble family of Spain but sent one or more of its members to take part in it, attended by a suitable retinue of men-at-arms. The general design was as follows. The whole naval force of the peninsula should be concentrated on breaking through the defences of England. Then an army of 50,000 of the finest troops in the world—some already in the Netherlands under Parma, the rest to be transported in the fleet itself—was to be thrown upon the island, where the only regular army consisted of a few score Yeomen of the Guard. The Duke of Santa Cruz, an experienced and able officer, and the designer of the plan of campaign, was put in command.

But misfortunes dogged the undertaking from the start. Drake succeeded in gaining the reluctant consent of the Queen to an attack on the ships and stores that were being concentrated at Cadiz. With thirty ships he set sail from Plymouth in April, 1587 (hastening out to sea before the Queen could change her mind), and within two months he had wrought such havoc that the Armada had to be postponed till the following year. In his own characteristic phrase, he had " singed the King of Spain's beard." Then, in order that his men should not return empty-handed, he slipped down to the Azores, and picked up the " San Felipe," the greatest ship afloat, crammed with gold and jewels. Early in the following year the preparations were further disarranged by the death of Santa Cruz, and the appointment of the Duke of Medina Sidonia, an hidalgo of bluest blood but completely ignorant of the business of fighting, whether by sea or land.

At last, in April the fleet weighed anchor. It consisted of 132 ships (including six of the largest ever seen) manned by 10,000 mariners and carrying 20,000 soldiers, together with some 300 priests and inquisitors to undertake the conversion of the population as soon as the conquest had been completed.   The sacred character of the enterprise had been marked by the fact that every man had confessed and taken the sacrament before going on board ; but less pains had been taken about the commissariat, and the fleet had not been at sea two days before the men began to fall sick, owing to putrid meat and sour water.   Moreover, the crews had been largely recruited among Mediterranean peoples who had no experience of navigation in the ocean.   As soon as a fresh wind sprang up the sick and bewildered crews ran for safety into Ferrol, and their unhappy commander besought his King to excuse him from a task for which he felt himself to be altogether unfit.   But Philip reassured him, and on July 12th the Invincible Armada made a second start.

72. England's Defences

And what was going on in England by way of counter-preparation ?

Very little indeed.   We often think of Elizabeth as a heroic figure, the embodiment of the national pride which overthrew " the Inquisition dogs and the devildoms of Spain " ; but as a matter of fact, the qualities by which she served her country were by no means heroic.   It is true that she had postponed the Catholic attack for twenty years by her cold-blooded cautiousness and deceit, and that she had used the respite to build up the national resources ; but she now showed herself unable to expend those resources wisely.   When the crisis of her reign came it found England with a Royal Navy no stronger than it had been in her father's time.   This was not such a serious weakness then as it would be to-day, for in those days there was little difference between warships and merchantmen, either in equipment or crews ; and when it became known that the Armada was preparing, the merchants of London, Southampton, Poole and Plymouth armed and equipped dozens of ships at their own expense—which was just what the thrifty Queen had counted on their doing.   What was far more serious was that the royal ships—naturally, the most important part of the fleet—were stinted of supplies, both of food and of ammunition. Economy is a fine thing, and England was in sore need of it at the beginning of the reign ; but this was hardly the moment to cut down rations or to forbid the purchase of more than two days' supply of powder.

In the end the rival fleets were not ill-matched in point either of ships or of sailors. Certainly, the Spaniards were bigger and carried more soldiers, but we shall presently see that these were disadvantages rather than otherwise. Lord Howard of Effingham was given the command of the English fleet. He owed this position rather to his rank than to his ability as an admiral, but he was an upright and clear-sighted man, and had the good sense to give due weight to the views of Drake and Hawkins, who were members of his Council of War. It is interesting to see in the list of ships engaged in this memorable campaign the names which have become traditional in the Royal Navy— Triumph, Victory, Swiftsure and Dreadnought.

An even more important factor in England's favour was that the nation presented a united front to meet the danger. The King of Spain had been informed that the Catholic majority would rise in rebellion against the Queen as soon as the Armada appeared in the Channel ; but the claim of Philip to the English throne turned the expedition which he intended to be a crusade into a mere piece of foreign aggression. There were very few Englishmen indeed, whatever their views on religion, who wanted to be ruled by Philip II, or by any prince appointed by him. Catholic gentlemen were proud to accept the Queen's commission to serve in her ships or in the county militias that were now assiduously training to meet the famous Spanish infantry.

73. " Flavit Deus et dissipati sunt "

Owing to the shortage of provisions, the English fleet could never move far from its base ; and at the moment when the Armada hove in sight of the Cornish coast it was in Plymouth harbour re-victualling. A fresh south-westerly breeze was blowing, and had the Spaniards attacked the port they would have had the English ships at a disadvantage. But the King had given definite instructions that the fleet, maintaining a crescent formation, was to proceed directly to the Foreland where the Admiral was to get into touch with Parma, and make arrangements with him for the invasion. As soon as the Spaniards had passed the Sound, Howard and his captains warped their vessels out, and a running fight ensued all down the Channel, the English having the advantage of the windward position. By the time the Armada reached Calais, the disadvantages under which it fought became apparent. High-built " castles " fore and aft were useful for boarding enemy ships, but they made the vessels top-heavy and caused them to heel over in a beam wind. This being the case, the shot from their cannon either passed harmlessly over the heads of the English or plumped into the water, for they had no means of elevating or depressing their guns. Moreover, the Englishmen took advantage of their superior mobility to keep clear of all attempts to board. It was a duel between artillery and infantry at a range selected by the artillerymen. The serried ranks of pikemen drawn up on the Spanish decks impeded the working of the ships, and were mown down in hundreds without being able to strike a blow. No wonder the fleet had lost so much of its proud self-confidence by the time it had reached the Calais Roads ! There Medina Sidonia besought Parma to come out and help him, but the latter said that his only craft were flat-bottomed transports, which would all be sunk in a few minutes by the Dutch ships which were watching the ports ; it was the business of the Admiral to get command of the sea before the land forces could stir.

Then the equanimity of the Spanish crews was further disturbed by some hastily-devised fire-ships sent down upon them with wind and tide. In a panic the masters cut their cables and drifted on towards *Gravelines*. The English fleet followed them up, and the decisive battle of the campaign took place on July 28th. Medina Sidonia was utterly unable to control his fleet, and the battle soon split up into a number of isolated ship-actions in which all the advantage lay with the English. The following night the south-westerly wind freshened into a gale. The Spanish ships were not in a condition, as regards either rigging or crews, to do anything but run before it up the North Sea. Drake pursued them until he had made sure that they had gone too far to get in touch with Parma again ; then he was compelled to give up the chase owing to lack of supplies, especially of powder. Throughout that tremendous fortnight the English lost not a single ship and only sixty men.

The Spaniards suffered the most tremendous disaster in the whole of modern history. The storm completed what the sea-dogs had begun. All round the iron coast of western Scotland and Ireland were piled up the wrecks of the splendid vessels which had set out, the wonder of the world and the pride of every Spanish heart, only a few weeks before. Only a few score battered hulks, manned by exhausted spectres, crept back to Spain one by one during the autumn. We can but guess what Philip must have felt at that blastment of his hopes, how puzzled he must have been at the mysterious ways of the Almighty. Yet nothing could shake his faith in his mission : " It is Thy cause, O Lord. If in Thy infinite Wisdom defeat be best, Thy will be done ! "

74. *The Aftermath*

The defeat of the Spanish Armada was a turning-point in the history not only of England and Spain, but of the Catholic Reaction in Europe as a whole. Had it been successful, Protestantism would have been crushed into a mere persecuted sect in England, Scotland, Germany and the Netherlands ; Philip II would have been able to make good his claim to the throne of France against Henry of Navarre, and the leading part in the era of oceanic commerce which was now opening would have fallen to Catholic Spain and Portugal rather than to Protestant England and Holland.

Still, these results were not apparent at the time, and it was only with great difficulty that the Queen and her Council were induced to authorise a sort of counter-Armada against Philip in the following year. Preparations were made on a very large scale. A hundred and fifty ships were gathered in Plymouth Sound—a greater number than had ever been seen there before. Yet the plans for the conduct of the expedition showed that very little had been learnt from the experience of the last few years. Ignoring the fact that it was in sea-fighting that England held the advantage over Spain, the ships were crowded with soldiers who were to operate on land. It was intended that they should act as a nucleus for a national rising in Portugal in favour of a pretender to the throne of that country, one Don Antonio, who had long been exiled in England.

The whole affair was mismanaged. To begin with, the start was long delayed by the Queen's hesitancy to give either supplies or instructions ; and when the fleet at last reached the peninsula there were misunderstandings between Drake, who commanded the sailors, and Norris who commanded the soldiers. Corunna was destroyed, but an attempt to take Lisbon was a dismal failure, and the Portuguese proved to be wholly indifferent to the claims of Don Antonio. Hundreds of the men died of sickness and hundreds more deserted. To make matters worse, the weather was so unfavourable that Drake had to abandon all hope of capturing the Spanish treasure-ships at the Azores ; and the fleet returned ingloriously with the loss of half its personnel and the whole of the money that had been invested in it.

Thereafter the relationship between England and Spain returned to much what it had been before the sailing of the Armada had precipitated a crisis. After twenty years of pin-pricks and indirect proceedings, Philip and Elizabeth had each launched a great attack on the other. Both had failed, and Elizabeth now resumed her old policy of supporting " The Common Cause of the Protestant Religion " partly by giving half-hearted help to the Dutch rebels and the French Huguenots, and partly by attacking the ships and overseas possessions of Spain—attacks in which legitimate operations of naval war were mingled with sheer piracy conducted for profit.

The Queen's connection with the Huguenots was for some years drawn closer than ever by the remarkable events which took place in France in 1589. Henry III hated the domination of the Duke of Guise and the League (§ 68) and supported the claim of Henry of Navarre to be recognised as heir-apparent. Early in this fateful year he resorted to a common political device of those days—he caused his enemy to be murdered ; but he him-self fell victim to the same device a few months later when he was assassinated by a zealous monk who resented his support of the heretic. Navarre now assumed the title of Henry IV, but the League redoubled its efforts to prevent his entering Paris, the seat of government. The French Catholic leaders urged Philip II to give them active support, while Henry appealed to Elizabeth for men and money with which to maintain "the common cause" against the League. The English subsidies came at a critical moment, and enabled him to win a brilliant victory at Ivry, near Paris; but he was still unable to gain possession of the capital, where Catholicism was tremendously strong. The struggle continued with varying fortunes for the next three years, until at last Henry was forced to realise that the French people would never, as a whole, submit to a Protestant king. Like Elizabeth herself, he was far more interested in politics than in religion, and he now decided that (as he himself put it) Paris was worth a Mass. He was received into the Catholic Church in July, 1593, and became one of the ablest and most famous of all the kings of France. Elizabeth professed to be very shocked at his defection from Protestantism; but as she was still at war with Philip II (who persisted in his claim to the French throne), the Anglo-French alliance continued for some years more.

The most memorable of the naval expeditions of the early 'nineties was the attempt of Lord Thomas Howard to waylay the Spanish treasure-fleet in 1592. He had only four ships, and when he arrived at the Azores news was brought that the galleons were convoyed by a whole fleet of war-vessels. He had to beat a hasty retreat, but one of his captains, Sir Richard Grenville, refused to give way before Spaniards even in these circumstances, and insisted upon staying to face them alone. The last fight of the " Revenge " was a useless sacrifice of ship and crew; but it was a heroic gesture the story of which will never be forgotten as long as men cherish the fighting spirit.

75. Raleigh and Virginia

It may seem strange that the Englishmen of Elizabeth's day should have contented themselves with destroying and plundering the overseas possessions of Spain, instead of trying to take and keep them permanently for themselves. As a matter of fact, several attempts to do this were made; but the country was neither rich enough to be able to carry through such a great undertaking, nor crowded enough to need an outlet for surplus population.

The idea of an overseas settlement of Englishmen seems to have first occurred to Sir Humphrey Gilbert, a Devonshire gentleman who obtained a charter from the Queen in 1578 " to inhabit and possess such remote and heathen lands as are not in the actual possession of any Christian prince." Unfortunately, Gilbert was lost at sea on his way back from an attempt to start a settlement in Newfoundland. His project was taken up by his kinsman, *Sir Walter Raleigh* (1552–1618), another Devon man who had in the year 1580 come up to London to win his way at Court. He had many valuable assets in the fierce competition that was always going on for the Queen's favour—a handsome face and figure, fascinating manners, keen intelligence and an enterprising spirit. It was not long before he gained enough posts of honour and profit to make himself one of the most prominent and wealthy men in the realm. Much of his wealth he spent on schemes for trans-oceanic settlement. In 1583 he sent Sir Richard Grenville to claim possession in the Queen's name of the whole American seaboard from Florida to Newfoundland. It was to be called " Virginia " in honour of the Virgin Queen. A small party of settlers was established at Roanoke ; but the conditions of success in such enterprises were not yet understood. The pioneers quarrelled with the natives and with each other instead of producing food ; and a year or two later Drake had to bring the survivors home on his return from his famous expedition to the West Indies (§ 69). Undiscouraged by this failure, Raleigh sent out another party, consisting of 150 men, women and children, in 1589 ; but lack of experience was again evident in the preparations and equipment. In the following year several members of the party came back to England to make good these deficiencies. When they returned all trace of the settlement had vanished, and the fate of that little band of pioneers remains a mystery to this day. One serious hindrance to the success of these schemes was that Raleigh, though he spent something like a quarter of a million sterling (in present-day values) on them, was never able to take command of the expeditions himself. Despite his earnest entreaties, the Queen would never spare him from the Court, for she loved to have a number of handsome young cavaliers vying for her favours, even now when she was approaching sixty years of age.

Apart from this, the fundamental reason for the failure was that the time was not yet ripe for colonial enterprise. Still, these early attempts will always have a particular interest for us, for they were the first driblets of that mighty stream of emigration which soon began to flow from these shores to all quarters of the globe.

QUESTIONS

(1) *Why did the Armada come when it did?*
(2) *Why was the Armada defeated?*

CHAPTER XVI

The Government and the Nation

In this chapter we shall discuss several aspects of the social and political life of the Elizabethan age which we have so far neglected ; particularly the development of the national Church and the measures taken by Parliament to deal with the change which had taken place during the century in the economic life of the people.

76. *The National Church*

None of the internal developments of the reign was more important than the steady development of the Anglican Church. The greatest danger to internal peace came from religious animosities ; and it is fortunate that the Queen had no violent prejudices of her own on the subject. Unlike her brother and sister, she had no strong religious feelings ; the main interest of her life was in politics. She wanted all her subjects to sink their theological differences and join in a national Church under the control of a national government embodied by herself. The doctrines and ritual of that Church were purposely made such that people could see in them whatever they themselves believed, whether they were Catholic or Protestant. Of course, it was impossible to please everybody. A certain proportion of Catholics found themselves unable to accept a Church which did not acknowledge the authority of the Pope or the full doctrine of the Mass (§ 32). And many Protestants (especially among those who had fled from the Marian persecution to Switzerland or Germany) felt that the Church established by the Act of Uniformity (1559), required a good deal more purification from the " corruptions of Popery." These ultra-Protestants came to be known as " Puritans," but it must not be supposed that they had as yet any thought of *leaving* the Church—their aim was to *alter* it. They formed a strong leaven even among the clergy; and when Convocation met in 1563 to define the faith and practice of the Church they only failed by one vote to abolish the Sign of the Cross in Baptism, kneeling at Holy Communion, and other practices which they associated with the Church of Rome. When the Thirty-nine Articles were first issued (1564) they omitted all reference to the doctrine of Transubstantiation. Elizabeth was still hoping to keep friendly with the Papacy; and it was only in 1571, after Pius V had launched his excommunication, that a categorical repudiation of the doctrine was incorporated in the Articles.

For the first twenty years of her reign the Queen refrained almost entirely from persecuting the extremists on either side. Her favourite policy of letting well alone served her in this matter as in other departments of statecraft. She hoped that if she did nothing to exasperate Romanists or Puritans they would gradually grow accustomed to the worship prescribed in the Prayer Book. Prosecutions under the Act of Uniformity, to compel people to attend their parish churches, were few, and fines for " recusancy " were light. Only in one matter was there any definite attempt to tighten up Church discipline. We have seen that Protestantism tended to minimise the authority of the priesthood (§ 32) and that this tendency led them to dislike the special sacramental robes worn by Catholic priests. For some years a " Vestiarian Controversy " went on, pamphlets being published by learned divines of both parties. When at last Archbishop Parker issued his " Advertisements " (1564), requiring officiating clergy to wear surplice and stole, some hundreds gave up their livings rather than don " the rags of Popery "; but the great majority submitted.

As a matter of fact, the Queen's personal feelings were less sympathetic towards Puritanism than towards Catholicism, partly because she had been brought up according to her father's Anglo-Catholic ideas, and partly because she realised that she need make no concession to gain the goodwill of Protestants— they were bound to be loyal to her so long as the alternative was the Catholic Mary Stuart. On the other hand, the drift towards Protestantism was strongest among the seafaring folk (as was but natural, seeing that many of them were making great profits by waging private war on the ships and ports of his Most Catholic Majesty of Spain) ; and it was impossible for her to be harsh towards those on whom she was largely dependent for the defence of her throne and kingdom.

77. *Schism in English Protestantism*

After about 1580, however, circumstances changed, and the Queen began to be driven to take sterner measures against the extremists of either side. Her Council always maintained that they only took those measures when religious unorthodoxy took such forms as made it dangerous to the unity and safety of the nation as a whole.

First as to the Catholics. It was not until the Jesuit missionaries sent over by Pope Gregory XIII (§ 66) became concerned in plots to place Mary Stuart on the throne that the Government began to make the fines for recusancy severe, or to inflict them rigorously. Catholics had henceforward to choose between loyalty to Queen and country (which was so much in the air in the sixteenth century) and loyalty to the Church which had excommunicated the one and was planning a foreign invasion of the other. The pressure put upon them from two directions at once had the effect of sifting them out. Some of them felt themselves compelled to sever their connection with Romanism, while those that remained faithful to it became a distinct and persecuted minority whose patriotism was under grave suspicion.

We can see the same political principle at work in the treatment of the Puritans. Persecution did not begin until some of them began to advocate Calvin's system of Church government (§ 33) which later became known as *Presbyterianism*. As head of the Church the Queen appointed the bishops, who were responsible for the appointment and discipline of the lower ranks of the clergy. The presbyterian system of Calvin would shatter that national unity which it was her life business to foster. " At the beginning," complained Archbishop Parker, " it was but a cap or a surplice and a tippet ; now it is grown to the overthrow of the established order and the Queen's authority in causes ecclesiastical. These reformers would take the supreme authority in ecclesiastical matters from the prince and give it to themselves with the grave seignory in every parish." To Parker succeeded the mild and broad-minded Grindal, who was half a Puritan himself; but when the latter died in 1583 the position fell to Archbishop Whitgift, who made it his special mission to stamp out all Puritan tendencies within the Church, by means of a *Court of High Commission*, of which he himself was president. Several leading Puritans, including Cartwright, the Professor of Divinity at Cambridge University (who had started Church councils on the presbyterian model in several parts of the country), were brought before the Court and compelled to apologise. These activities provoked some of the leading Puritans to write a series of tracts, under the assumed name of "*Martin Marprelate*," attacking the whole system of Episcopacy. Orthodox divines attempted to reply, but they were no match for the vigorous, racy English of the Tracts, which consisted largely of satires on the conduct and spiritual worth of individual bishops. Whitgift had therefore to fall back on a general censorship of the Press. He obtained a proclamation from the Star Chamber forbidding the printing of any manuscript until it had been approved either by himself or by the Bishop of London. When this order proved ineffective, a further proclamation was issued forbidding printing altogether except at London, Oxford and Cambridge. Furthermore, several of the most prominent controversialists, including Penry (the reputed author of the Marprelate Tracts) and Barrow (who proposed to abolish Church government altogether), were executed for attacking the Royal Supremacy.

78. *The Elizabethan Parliament*

We have heard very little about the doings of Parliament during the reign, for the simple reason that there was very little to record. The country was ruled not by Parliament or ministers responsible to Parliament, but by the Queen and her Privy Council. The present-day control of Parliament over the Executive is due to the fact that the House of Commons has the power to grant or withhold the taxes without which the government of the country cannot be carried on ; but in the sixteenth century the sovereign was still supposed to provide for all the ordinary expenses of government out of his own hereditary revenue from Crown lands, *plus* certain customs duties granted him for life at his accession. The Tudor sovereigns only summoned Parliament when they wanted a subsidy (a special tax for a specified purpose, such as preparations for some threatened war) ; or when they wanted some definite piece of legislation put through (such as penal laws against religious or political opponents of the Government). The idea that it is the duty of Parliament to spend six or eight months of every year in passing " reforms " has only sprung up within the last century. During the forty-four years of Elizabeth's reign there were only fourteen sessions of Parliament ; nor would the nation at large have grumbled if there had been fewer still ; for no parliaments meant no taxes. The Queen's ideas of government were those of a " benevolent despot." She was entirely devoted to the welfare of her people ; but she much disliked having an assembly of knights and burgesses at Westminster, criticising her policy and petitioning her to marry. One of the chief reasons for her cheeseparing economy and for the niggardly support she gave to the Netherlanders and the Huguenots was that she wanted to avoid having to ask Parliament for money. Most of the fourteen sessions took place during the latter part of her reign, when the need of increased revenue began to grow acute, owing partly to the war with Spain, and partly to the fall in the value of money due to the continued influx into Europe of American gold and silver. The members now took advantage of her necessities to do a good deal of grumbling. One famous occasion of this was when in 1601 the Commons complained of the *Monopolies* which the Queen had granted to certain favoured courtiers. These monopolies gave the holders the exclusive right of manufacturing or selling some particular class of goods ; and they naturally led to the goods in question becoming dear, or bad, or both. Elizabeth had the truly princely attribute of knowing when to give way, and how to do so gracefully. When she saw that the Commons were in earnest, she withdrew the monopolies that were objected to, and assured the Speaker that " if her kingly bounty had been abused, and the grants turned to the hurt of her people, it was contrary to her will and meaning."

The incident thus happily closed was the cloud no bigger than a man's hand that presaged a great storm—the quarrels between Crown and Parliament, of the following century.

79. *The Justices of the Peace*

One other department of government remains to be mentioned—the administration of local affairs. In most countries this was carried out by Government officials, appointed by the King, paid out of his treasury and under his control, but in England the Government was too poor to be able to afford this and such matters were left in the hands of country gentlemen who lived in the districts concerned, and were not paid for their services. It fell to these " magistrates " or " Justices of the Peace " to arrange for the upkeep of roads and bridges, to make provision for the poor, to punish petty crime and to see that more serious offences were brought before the Judges at the Assizes, to hunt out recusants, and generally to carry the decisions of the Queen's Government into effect. This characteristically English institution had been developing all through the Tudor period, but it was not until the reign of Elizabeth that it became a regular and essential part of the national life. It had a most important effect on the development of our social and political system during the next two centuries. A Government which is dependent on the goodwill of hundreds of independent citizens to carry out its decrees must always be based on the consent of the governed. Moreover, it made the country gentlemen a most important and influential element in the community. No other country had had a class corresponding to our English "squires" ; and we shall see later how important was the part which they played in the religious and political upheavals of the next century.

80. *Economic Developments*

The changes in agriculture and manufactures which we mentioned in an earlier chapter (§ 39) were going on all through the Tudor period. By the end of Elizabeth's reign the process had gone far. There were now far more landless labourers working for wages on farms owned by others than there had been under her grandfather; the gilds which had formerly regulated prices, wages and workmanship in the towns had almost disappeared in favour of individual employers of labour; gone were the monks who had helped the poor through times of trouble; and there were hundreds of vagrants on the roads looking in vain for employment.

The efforts of the Government under Henry VIII, Edward VI, and Mary to find a remedy had consisted mainly in attempts to cure the disease by suppressing the symptoms. Elizabeth and Burghley were more enlightened in their aims and more successful in their achievements. Instead of trying to compel landowners by statute to return to arable farming, they encouraged manufactures; and the consequent growth of town-populations caused a steady increase in the demand for foodstuffs from the countryside.

This development of English manufactures was greatly assisted by the religious persecutions in France and the Netherlands. In both countries the Protestants were for the most part town-populations engaged in industry, and these skilled workers were now driven into exile by persecution. A great many sought refuge in England, where Burghley gave them every encouragement to settle down, set up their looms, and become the nucleus of manufacturing districts. England soon ceased altogether to export her raw wool. The produce of the sheep-farms was now used to make woollen cloth in the neighbouring villages. Soon this woollen cloth became a staple article of export, wherever the enterprise of merchants and seamen could find markets for it. The ships brought back other forms of wealth in exchange, and by the end of the reign British predominance in oceanic commerce was already foreshadowed.

Another notable achievement of Burghley's in this direction was the restoration of the coinage to its face value, after the successive debasements it had suffered during the preceding reigns (§ 35). In this work he was aided by the financial genius of *Sir Thomas Gresham*, the founder of the Royal Exchange. It was Gresham who first clearly realised that the purchasing power of gold coins is limited to their intrinsic value. If this is less than their nominal value, the prices of goods will rise and fluctuate to the great hindrance of business. He further realised that " bad money drives out good "—that is to say, if there is base coin about, people will hoard their good coin, and soon it is only the base that will be in circulation. This principle is known to this day as " Gresham's Law." Burghley and his mistress determined on the bold course of calling in all the base coin and giving out good in exchange for it. This was a severe strain on the Treasury ; but courage and determination had their reward, and within ten years of the Queen's accession the credit of her Government was so good that it could borrow money at less than half the rate of interest that bankers had charged under Queen Mary.

An equally striking example of Elizabethan commercial policy was the granting of a charter in 1600 to the *East India Company*. This was a combination of merchants who clubbed together for protection from pirates and for negotiating with native princes for commercial privileges. The Queen gave the Company the sole right to trade in the East Indies, so that the members should be protected from the competition of outsiders who might seek to profit by their pioneer work without sharing in its cost. But it is noteworthy that the Government did not attempt to interfere with the actual conduct of the business : that was left entirely to the individuals concerned. In this way English merchants were saved from that demoralising governmental control which paralysed the commercial development of France, Spain, and Portugal. English commerce has always been a matter of private enterprise.

In social matters, on the other hand, the tendency of the age was for the national government to undertake the duties which in the Middle Ages had been performed by independent organisations. For instance, the Gilds had formerly controlled the taking of apprentices by master craftsmen ; but these bodies were no longer strong enough to do this efficiently ; and in 1563 an *Act of Artificers* was passed to set up a uniform system for the whole country. Nobody could set up as a master craftsman or take wages as a journeyman until he had served a seven years' apprenticeship. English lads thus gained a technical education and a social discipline which did something to make up for the lack of schooling, and the apprenticeship system remained one of the most characteristic features of English social life for two or three centuries.

Again, the loss of the charity dispensed by the monasteries was to some extent made good by a series of measures which culminated in the famous *Elizabethan Poor Law* of 1601. Since the monastery lands had passed into the possession of individual laymen, it was but fair that the obligation to maintain the destitute poor should be undertaken by those laymen also. In each parish a " Poor Rate " was to be levied, collected and distributed by unpaid " overseers " elected by the parishioners ; and in practice this rate was assessed on the annual value of the land.

QUESTIONS

(1) *How did Parliament deal with changing conditions of economic life during Elizabeth's reign?*

(2) *Describe and account for the change in Elizabeth's policy towards those who dissented from her religious settlement.*

CHAPTER XVII

The Spacious Days of Great Elizabeth

It was not until the latter part of the sixteenth century that the spiritual rejuvenation which we call the Renaissance took full effect in England. When once the movement had begun it developed rapidly into one of the great epochs in the history of European art. It was in Music and the Drama that the English Renaissance was particularly manifested. We must now give some attention to this most important aspect of the period we are studying.

81. *The Renaissance in England*

That great, many-sided movement which we call the Renaissance was flourishing in its native Italy a century before its effects were felt in northern Europe. As we have seen, it took different forms in different countries, according to the character and circumstances of the various peoples. We can trace its influence in such dissimilar phenomena as the study of ancient philosophy and literature, the growth of the feeling for nationality, the adoption of classical models in architecture, the birth of modern scientific method, the development of printing, increased activity in overseas commerce, the spread of education, the pictures of Raphael and the sculptures of Michael Angelo, the Protestant Reformation, and the discovery of America. For however much these activities differed on the surface of things, they all sprang from the same source—the revival of interest in human personality and the world in which it is environed.

It is not surprising that of all the countries of Western Europe England was the last to feel the full effects of the new spirit. Geographically she had been on the outside edge of civilisation all through the Middle Ages; and during the heydey of the Italian Renaissance she was devastated by the sordid faction-

fights of the Roses. It was but natural, again, that the rejuve-
nating flood of ideas, when at last it reached these distant shores,
should be coloured by its passage through France and Germany.
We have seen that the first form it took here was the movement
of the " Oxford Reformers " (§ 18) towards (*a*) a renewed interest
in the Greek and Latin classics as a subject of education ; and
(*b*) a simpler and sincerer Christianity based on a plain interpretation of the Bible. Not until Elizabeth had given the
country religious peace, the assurance of orderly government,
and a high sense of self-confidence in facing foreign enemies,
were the true, original impulses of the Renaissance movement
released. It was only during the latter part of her reign that the
feeling that the world is a place to be enjoyed, and man's nature
a thing to be expressed in words and deeds took possession of
Englishmen's minds. Thus the movement burst into vigour in
this north-eastern corner of Europe long after it had burnt itself
out in the land where it first arose. We see it in the passion for
fine clothes ; in the spread of luxury in food and comfort in
dwellings ; in the joyous adventures of voyagers into unknown
seas ; above all in a new-found and widespread delight in the
fine arts—especially in the various forms of literature.

82. " *A Nest of Singing Birds* "

Since the death of Chaucer (1400) scarcely a single work of
note had been produced in the English language ; but during
the latter half of Elizabeth's reign were laid the foundations of
our national literature as we know it to-day. So eager were the
Englishmen of that generation to get into touch with the finest
minds of past ages and of other lands that translations poured
from the printing presses. Some of these, such as Lord North's
rendering of Plutarch's " Lives " and Florio's version of the
" Essays of Montaigne," have had a profound influence on
English thought and literature right down to our own times. Sir
Philip Sidney (1554–1586) produced the first prose romance
(the " Arcadia ") and the first critical work (the " Defense of
Poetrie ") in the language. Hooker's " Ecclesiastical Polity,"
a learned and eloquent exposition of the historical position of
the Church of England, established English as a medium for

argumentation; while Bacon's "Essays" showed that the language was equally serviceable to convey worldly wisdom with the pithiest and acutest vigour.

But it is in verse rather than in prose that we find the characteristic expression of the age. To the Elizabethans the world was too full of interest and delight for prose, and the poetical activity which now suddenly burst forth was prodigious. It is perhaps significant that the first notable poem of the era— Spenser's "Shepheardes Calendar"—appeared in 1579, the central year of Drake's voyage round the world, for this brings home to us that Elizabethan literature was the expression in art of that exuberant vitality which the seamen expressed in action. In the course of the reign there appeared in print over two hundred volumes of verse, most of them during the 'eighties and 'nineties, when the national heart was beating high over the successful struggle with the mighty empire of Spain.

A notable feature of the Italian Renaissance had been versatility: Michael Angelo excelled as painter, poet, sculptor and architect; Leonardo da Vinci as painter, poet, engineer and scientist. The same is true of many of the men of the English Renaissance. Much of the finest poetry of the age was produced as a pastime by men whose chief thoughts and endeavours were engaged in other fields. Sir Philip Sidney, for instance, was Member of Parliament for Kent, and spent most of his short life in seeking some post in Court or Government from his uncle the Earl of Leicester; and we remember him to-day rather as the fine flower of English chivalry who gave the cup of water to the dying soldier while himself lying mortally wounded at Zutphen (§ 69), than as the author of the "Arcadia."

Even more noteworthy is the case of *Edmund Spenser* (1552– 1599), for Spenser holds a place among the half-dozen very greatest English poets. His enormous allegorical poem, "The Faery Queene" (although only a quarter of the original design was carried out, it is longer than the Odyssey, the Iliad and the Æneid put together), laid for English poetry the foundations of metre and rhyme upon which all subsequent poets have built. Indeed, so much have they admired his glowing imagery and his musical diction, that he has been called "the Poet's Poet." Yet to Spenser the writing of "The Faery Queene" was the mere bye-product of enforced and unwelcome leisure. After several years of seeking some congenial employment he accepted an administrative post in Ireland, then as remote and uncivilised a country as Central Africa would be to-day ; and it was there, in a country house in County Cork, that he produced his great poem.

83. *The Art of the People*

Still, the writings of Spenser and Sidney appealed only to the cultured few who could read and could afford to buy books. The form of literature which appealed most strongly to the mass of Elizabethan Englishmen was the Drama. The development of this was extraordinarily rapid. It was only in the reign of Henry VIII that medieval " tumblers " and jesters and speakers of " interludes " began to be replaced in the entertainment of the great by regular plays adapted from Latin authors. These translations were gradually ousted by original dramas specially written to suit the taste of the general public ; and by the accession of Elizabeth this form of entertainment was already becoming a passion with all classes of the nation.

It was an important fact about the Elizabethan Drama that it thus came to rely more on general popularity than on the patronage of the Court. The livelihood of the actors depended on their ability to please mixed audiences, and the English drama was a native art which developed spontaneously to suit our national character and speech. The demand for it was strongest among the classes which felt the Renaissance impulse in the air, but could not read for themselves. (Illiterate people are often the best listeners.) These simple folk cared nothing for elaborate rules of dramatic art ; what they wanted was to see men of like passions with themselves acting in circumstances more varied and exciting than those of everyday life ; and they loved to hear high-sounding verse spouted from the platform. The Elizabethan drama was therefore marked by sensational action, the portrayal of character, and a complete freedom from artificial restrictions as to the scenes represented, the lapse of time, and the form of the plot.

Originally the companies had travelled from place to place, playing for the most part on portable stages set up in the courtyards of inns ; but by the middle of the reign their increasing prosperity enabled them to build theatres for themselves just outside the walls of London. The design of these theatres was suggested by the inn-yards to which the players were accustomed. They had no roofs, no artificial lighting, and no scenery. The stage projected into the " pit " (so called because the building was sometimes used for bear-baiting and cock-fighting), and the audience stood on three sides of it ; while round the walls were built balconies corresponding to those that led to the upstairs rooms in Tudor hostelries.

As to the plays that were put on, we should nowadays think most of them very crude affairs ; but everything must have a beginning, and the development of the English drama from these primitive experiments up to its full flower under Shakespeare took but a quarter of a century. During the 'eighties the most notable playwrights were a group of young students of the revived classical learning, known as " The University Wits," Greene, Kyd, and Lyly being the best known. Then these were all eclipsed by the meteoric career of *Christopher Marlowe*, who carried the public by storm with the magniloquent heroics of " Tamurlane the Tartar," and the heart-clutching thrills of " Doctor Faustus." Marlowe's four plays (he was only twenty-nine when he was killed in a tavern brawl) have high merits of their own, but their chief importance for us to-day is that in them he established that form of " blank verse " which his great successor used with such power and flexibility, and which has since become the most characteristic form of English prosody.

84. *The Greatest of Englishmen*

Somewhere between 1585 and 1590 the company known as " The Lord Chamberlain's Players " were joined by a young man named William Shakespeare. Of his early life we know little save that he was born at Stratford-on-Avon, in April, 1564, of a respectable middle-class family ; that he married young, and came up to London to seek his fortune. He began as an actor, but the company soon found that he could be more useful to them as a writer and adapter of plays. For the greatest need of these companies was always dramas that would attract the public.

There was no law of copyright in those days. If a particular type of play or a particular subject had proved successful elsewhere, there was nothing to prevent another company from getting something similar " knocked up " for their own use—perhaps based on an actual existing model. It was upon this hack-work that Shakespeare served his apprenticeship to the craft of play-wright ; but as time went on and his powers developed, he began to clothe with flesh and blood the dry bones which he took over from other men, so that the characters came to life and have moved to pity, fear and laughter every generation of civilised men since. His earliest plays were fantastic comedies such as "Love's Labour's Lost" and "A Midsummer Night's Dream"; historical plays such as "Richard II" and " Henry V " (the burn-ing patriotism of which seems to reflect the spirit which was carry-ing England through the war with Spain) ; and his romantic tragedy " Romeo and Juliet." As he gained in experience his work became more original in conception and more mature in workmanship ; and this first period of his career came to an end with his most glorious comedies, " Twelfth Night " and " As You Like It." Then, at the beginning of the new century a great change came over his spirit. Whether it was the result of some personal experience, or of maturing age and reflection, we know not ; but he became more and more absorbed with the darker aspects of the human soul, and with the deeper problems of life and destiny. During the next eight years he poured forth a series of great tragedies : " Julius Cæsar," " Hamlet," " Timon," " Macbeth," " Othello," " Antony and Cleopatra," " King Lear." At length those mighty passions burnt them-selves out. Somewhere about 1610 he gave up his active con-nection with the theatre and retired to live in the home of his boyhood, where he had invested his very considerable savings in buying house-property. For the next six years he lived the life of a country gentleman, though he found time to write two or three more plays, all of which breathe a spirit of high serenity and peace of mind. Then, in 1616, he died, on his fifty-second birthday.

There are three respects in which Shakespeare is supreme among dramatists. The first is his gift for stage-craft, for playing upon the feelings of an audience by the very structure of a scene.

The second is his capacity for portraying character in action—a capacity based upon an almost superhuman insight into the secret places of the human mind and heart. Third, and greatest of all, is his genius as a poet. His powers of expression were unparalleled in any age or tongue. When an idea took possession of his mind, he could put it into words that thrill us by their beauty and startle us by their truth.

This delight in expression is characteristic of his place in history as the exponent in literature of the whole Renaissance movement. That position is likewise evidenced by his absorbing interest in the world and the people that inhabit it. To take but one example of this, it would have been utterly impossible for Hamlet's glorification of humanity * to have been written in the Middle Ages.

We have made this digression from the beaten track of history because Shakespeare's position among his countrymen is unique. He was by common consent one of the two or three greatest writers of all time ; of all our national possessions he is that in which we have the best reason to be proud ; and his fame is wider spread over the world at large than that of any other Englishman that ever lived.

85. *Elizabethan Music*

As in literature, so in music, the English of the later sixteenth century could hold their own with any other nation in Europe. Indeed, the love of song was even more general than the love of play-acting, for it could be indulged wherever two or three were gathered together. Shakespeare's plays abound in musical allusions which could only have been appreciated by audiences familiar with the art ; and he lost no opportunity of embellishing his plays with songs and instrumental pieces.

Elizabethan music took three chief forms. Firstly, many of our traditional folk-songs and country dances, afterwards handed down from generation to generation of the English peasantry, seem to have had their origin during this period ; and nothing shows the vitality of a race or an age more than creative energy in these directions. Secondly, the adoption of the Book of Common Prayer gave a fresh field for composers to write music

* Act II, Scene 2.

to be sung in churches to the English words of the services. The fathers of English church music were Thomas Tallis and his pupil William Byrd. Both were cathedral organists, though both seem to have remained Roman Catholics at heart; and both wrote music which is still used in the Anglican Church to-day. Thirdly, there was what would to-day be called " Chamber Music," both vocal and instrumental. To be able to sing a part in a madrigal was an almost essential mark of good breeding in a lady or gentleman, and no country house of any pretensions was complete without " a chest of viols "—a set of stringed instruments of various sizes which were the ancestors of the modern violin family. One of the most notable musical productions of the day was " The Triumphs of Oriana " (1601), a book of part-songs, praising the glory, beauty and virtue of the Queen. No fewer than twenty-six of the leading composers of the day contributed to it, the most famous being Thomas Morley, Willbye, and Weelkes. Another similar collection was that known as the Fitzwilliam Virginal Book. This consisted of pieces to be played on the virginal, the very primitive forerunner of the modern pianoforte, and are said to have been originally brought together for the use of the Queen herself. Both of these collections show that a very high level of skill had been reached, both in composition and in performance.

It is not easily explained how a country in which music and drama were so highly developed should have been so backward in the plastic arts; but England produced no painter or sculptor of even second rank throughout the whole of the century. The great Flemish painter, Hans Holbein (1499-1542), came over at the invitation of Henry VIII and made magnificent portraits of all the most prominent men of the day, including More, Wolsey, Cromwell, and the King himself; but he had no successful imitators, and so little was his own greatness appreciated that when he died in the course of one of the recurrent epidemics of the plague in London, his body was flung into a common grave the situation of which was forgotten.

QUESTIONS

(1) *How was the Renaissance manifested in England ?*
(2) *How far was Shakespeare the outcome of his era ?*

CHAPTER XVIII

The Last Decade

(1593–1603)

The last ten years of Elizabeth's reign saw the country safe from the dangers which had threatened it almost from her accession. The most important events which diversified this last decade— apart from the production of Shakespeare's plays, and the passing of the Poor Law, both of which matters we have dealt with in earlier chapters—were various attempts at counter-attack against Spain, and a formidable rebellion in Ireland.

86. *New Times, New Faces*

The defeat of the Armada divided the reign of Elizabeth into two unequal parts. During the first the task of the Queen and her ministers had been to prepare for the inevitable struggle with the Counter-Reformation. The victory of 1588 set the seal on their labours by proving to all the world (and to Englishmen themselves) that the English had become one of the leading nations of the world, able to carry on a war on level terms even with the mighty Spanish Empire. The last third of the reign was a period of fruition ; these were the truly " spacious days of great Elizabeth " when the spring of Elizabethan culture and self-confidence burst forth.

During this period a new generation of statesmen and court-iers was arising. Leicester, the magnificent personage who had dominated the Court ever since the beginning of the reign, and had more than once seemed a likely suitor for the Queen's hand in marriage, had died in the year of the Armada. For some time before his death he had found a serious rival for the Queen's favour in Sir Walter Raleigh, who was equally handsome, far abler, and twenty years younger. By way of counterpoise to Raleigh, Leicester had brought forward his stepson, Robert Devereux, *Earl of Essex*. Essex was a member of one of the few families who traced their lineage back to feudal times before the new nobility had been created by the Tudors and endowed from the monastery lands. He had inherited the earldom at the age of nine, been educated in all the airs and graces of a cultured gentleman of the time, and had won a reputation as a dashing cavalry leader in the Netherlands under Leicester. Returning to England, his youthful, high-spirited impetuosity of disposition had fascinated the ageing Queen, and he became the most favoured of the band of brilliant young men about her Court.

Just as Leicester was succeeded in the Queen's affections by Essex, so Walsingham's death in 1590 opened the way for young Robert Cecil. True, Lord Burghley, the father of the latter young man, was still alive ; but he was growing old and was very glad to see the chief burdens of state falling on the son whom he had trained for the Queen's service.

The position was complicated, however, by the fact that Burghley had also a nephew, an extremely able young lawyer named Francis Bacon, who was also looking to him for political advancement. Naturally, paternal affection made the old statesman use all his influence to push the fortunes of his own son. Equally naturally, young Bacon began to look elsewhere for patronage when he came to realise that his uncle would do nothing for him. The obvious person from whom to seek such support was the Queen's favourite. Henceforth Essex, supplied with political brains by Bacon, began to take an active part in the proceedings of the House of Lords and of the Privy Council. Soon there was open rivalry for the direction of the Queen's affairs between the prim, assiduous little hunchback Cecil, and the ardent, brilliant and dashing Essex.

87. *The End of an Epoch*

Meanwhile, the Spanish War was dragging its slow length along. From time to time the " men of war," such as Raleigh and Essex, who dominated the Court, got the better of the men of peace, such as the Cecils, who dominated the Council ; and when this happened the result was some semi-official expedition against Spain ; but the preparations were always hampered by the constant changes in the old Queen's mind and purpose. The three most noteworthy of these enterprises were (*a*) the last voyage of Hawkins and Drake to the West Indies in 1594 ; (*b*) the attack on Cadiz in 1596 ; and (*c*) " The Islands Voyage " of 1597. All of these were rendered ineffective by delay in setting out, by haziness in design, and by personal quarrels in the execution.

In 1593 it became known that Philip was contemplating another attack on England, and counter-preparations began in the Queen's dockyards. Drake had been in disgrace ever since the failure of the expedition to Portugal in 1589 (§ 79), but he and Hawkins now managed to gain permission to go to Panama to destroy Spanish strength at its very source. When at last, after many difficulties, their little fleet arrived on the other side of the Atlantic, it met with a much stouter resistance than had been expected, and was repeatedly repulsed. Disagreements broke out between the commanders, while enteric fever decimated the crews. First Hawkins and then Drake fell victims to the disease, and the survivors sailed for England, leaving Drake " slung atween the round shot, in Nombre Dios Bay " within sight of the coast where his name had struck terror for so many years.

Had he lived, he was in the following year to have led another " beard-singeing " expedition to Cadiz. When that expedition did set sail, the command was divided betweeen Lord Admiral Howard and the Earl of Essex. Their primary object was " to burn the king's ships of war in his havens, before they should come forth to the seas, therewith destroying also the magazines of victuals and munitions for arming of his navy " ; and as a secondary object the ports themselves might be pillaged and destroyed. When the fleet reached Cadiz the vanity of Essex made him insist upon the latter part of the plan being under-taken first. This enabled the Spaniards to get their most important stores and shipping up the river out of reach, and the original purpose of the voyage could not be carried out. Still, much damage was done to the principal Spanish arsenal ; and the fact that the threatened second Armada never sailed suggests that the expedition was not such a complete failure as has generally been supposed.

"The Islands Voyage" was an attempt by Essex to do on a large scale what had been attempted on a small scale by Howard in 1592 (§ 79)—namely, to intercept the Spanish treasure-fleet in the neighbourhood of the Azores or the Canaries. The adventure was dogged by misfortune from the start ; a quarrel broke out between Essex and Raleigh because the latter had ventured to carry out a successful exploit without orders ; they missed their quarry by a combination of bad luck and bad judgment, and eventually returned home empty-handed, to the high displeasure of the Queen.

The year 1598 may be said to mark the close of the epoch. Burghley, the last survivor of the earlier generation of Elizabethan statesmen, died during that year. Henry IV brought to an end the French Wars of Religion by the *Edict of Nantes*, which enabled Catholic and Protestant to live peaceably side by side for nearly a century. Philip II himself, now grown old and smitten by mortal disease, was compelled to renounce his claim to the throne of France by the Treaty of Vervins, and to give the Netherlands a separate government under an Austrian archduke. Before the year was out he himself had died, a disappointed man. England continued to be nominally at war with Spain for another six years, but no active operations were undertaken by either side, and the political conditions of the Elizabethan age were fast melting away.

88. *The Irish Rebellion*

During the last five years of the reign the attention of the Government was occupied less by the war with Spain than by a rebellion in Ireland. The " Irish Problems " which have baffled English governments for centuries had already emerged. The root cause of the difficulty lay in the fact that the Irish had always been outside the main stream of European civilisation ; they had never come under the influence of the Roman Empire or of medieval feudalism. Repeated efforts to bridge the gap had all failed, and at the end of the sixteenth century the country still remained for the most part a chaos of septs or clans ruled by chieftains in accordance with primitive systems of tribal law. English governments almost down to our own day have generally acted on the principle that these peculiarities ought to be ignored, and the country be ruled in the interests of England and according to English ideas. This mistaken line of policy had already begun under the Tudor sovereigns. To them there seemed to be only two alternative methods of governing Ireland. One was to establish a strong system of despotic rule, and the other was to settle an English ruling class there on lands confiscated from native tribes. The former plan was too expensive, and it was upon the latter that English governments chiefly relied both in this century and the next. But these high-handed methods naturally aroused the bitterest resentment, and rebellion against the English Government was already beginning to be a normal state of things for the Irish. Under Edward VI and Mary they looked to France and Scotland for sympathy and support; under Elizabeth to Spain and the Pope. Moreover, the injuries they suffered from the English Government made them detest the Church which that Government supported, and confirmed them in their devotion to Catholicism.

Elizabeth's first dealings with the country were an attempt to settle a family quarrel amongst the O'Neills which had long disturbed the peace of northern Ireland. The head of the clan had been made Earl of Tyrone by Henry VIII, and one of his sons had been specially nominated to succeed both to the title and to the chieftainship. When the first Earl died, however, most of the clan supported the claims of another member of the family, Shane O'Neill. In the long run the latter gained the day and Elizabeth was forced to recognise him as Earl.

Ten years later there broke out in Munster a rising of a totally different character. This was the rebellion of the Earl of Desmond, a descendant of the Fitzgeralds who had settled there in the time of Henry II. He attempted to make himself independent of the English Government, and the movement was fomented by the emissaries of Spain—indeed, for the next twenty years the position of Philip II towards the Irish was very like that of Elizabeth towards the Netherlanders. Before long the Desmond rebellion became merged in the papal attack on Elizabeth which came to a head in 1580 and led to the Massacre of Smerwick (§ 66). After that event the embers of the rebellion were stamped out with savage ferocity, and most of the Desmond land was confiscated.

Fortunately for the Government, jealousies prevented the various clans from making common cause, and these disturbances were all confined to particular localities. It was not until 1598 that anything like a national rising took place. This began with a personal quarrel between Hugh O'Neill, the new Earl of Tyrone, and an English official named Bagenal; but the movement soon spread. Tyrone had spent several years at Elizabeth's court; he possessed remarkable personal magnetism and powers of organisation. Moreover, the agents of the Catholic Reaction had now had twenty years in which to inflame the minds of the people against the Government. Within a few months Tyrone was at the head of a formidable confederation of clans. The authorities had very limited resources with which to cope with the situation, and in August, 1598, they suffered a severe check at *Yellow Ford* near the Blackwater, in County Armagh.

89. *The Tragedy of Essex*

The Earl of Essex had long had his eye upon Ireland as a promising field for his energies and ambitions. The influence he had gained over the Queen by his handsome presence and high-mettled demeanour had turned his head. It seemed to him an intolerable grievance that any favour should be shown to his rivals, or any power entrusted to them; and this jealousy led to more than one open quarrel with the Queen. The young man's mind began to be haunted by large and shadowy schemes for driving the Cecils and their like away from the Court and taking his position as master of the Government by main force. When the disaster of Yellow Ford made it obvious that a punitive expedition on a large scale would have to be sent to Ireland, he urged his own claims to be put in command of it. The Queen hesitated, but as his demand was supported by Cecil (who may have foreseen that his rival's ruin would be the result) she gave way.

Essex was appointed Governor-General, and was given an army of 20,000 men, the largest that had ever crossed the Irish

Sea. The Queen was much perturbed at the expense, and gave strict orders that the campaign was to be cut as short as possible. But instead of seeking out Tyrone at once in his Ulster fastness, Essex decided on a preliminary campaign in Munster. This part of the country was still suffering from the Desmond rebellion, and there was no sustenance there for an army. Within a month or two the royal forces had dwindled, owing to disease, desertion, and the necessity for garrisoning occupied districts, to five or six thousand. The Queen understood nothing of the difficulties with which Essex had to contend, and wrote him upbraiding letters. Essex replied by complaining of the favours she was showing to Raleigh and Cecil in his absence, and hinted that he might return to London to explain the situation in Ireland, trusting to his old power over Elizabeth's heart and mind to win back her confidence and affection. The Queen forbade him to do any such thing, sending him some reinforcements and re-iterating her injunctions that he should carry through the con-quest of Ulster without delay. Thereupon Essex marched northwards ; but as soon as the two forces came into contact, Tyrone suggested a parley at Louth, where he completely twisted the unwary Essex round his finger, and induced him to agree to an armistice which postponed further action for six months. A day or two later a letter came from the Queen for-bidding him to make any agreement with the rebels without her express approval. Headstrong and " spoilt," smarting from a sense of failure, angry with Tyrone, with his enemies at Court, with the Queen, and with himself, Essex impetuously hastened back to Dublin, took boat for England and rode post-haste to London, where he rushed travel-stained and unannounced into the Queen's presence. Elizabeth treated him more kindly than he had any right to expect, but she could never forgive him for his flagrant disobedience, and she would neither receive him again at Court nor send him back to his command in Ireland.

Any ordinary man would have been thankful to have escaped so lightly from the consequences of his own conceited folly ; but to Essex success, favour and power were the breath of life. When after some months the Queen showed no sign of restoring him to favour, he lost patience. With the support of a little band of young fools like himself, he entered into a plot to coerce the

Queen into dismissing her counsellors. Summoned before the Council to give an account of his actions, he and his friends rushed to arms and defied the Government. Essex was always a popular figure, but he represented no cause that could rally a large following to his side, and his movement was suppressed within twenty-four hours.

Bacon had the misfortune to be compelled, as Attorney General, to prepare the case against the man to whom he owed his own position; but the Earl's condemnation and execution would in any event have been almost a matter of course. It is impossible not to sympathise with his warm-hearted generosity and high-spirited courage, but it is equally impossible to deny that, according to the ideas of the time, he thoroughly deserved his fate, for his wanton attack on the public peace of the realm.

The end of the Irish rebellion served to emphasise the incompetence of Essex as a general; for his successor in the command, Lord Mountjoy, with less than half the forces, succeeded in subduing Ireland completely for the first time in history. He received the final surrender of Tyrone a few days before the Queen's death

90. *Reflections*

This tragic episode cast a gloom over the last years of Elizabeth. Old age was a desolate time for her. As a Queen she had never had any near relatives, and all her old friends and ministers were now dead. The very enemy with whom she had contended for so many years was gone, and the situation in European affairs, in which she had played such an active and skilful part, was changing into something new and strange. She had lived for this world and for the game of politics, and as her physical health and strength faded away she felt forlorn indeed. She refused to discuss the question of the succession; but it had long been obvious that the only possible candidate was James VI of Scotland. He was a direct descendant of Henry VIII, he was a firm Protestant, he had shown considerable grasp of the business of government, and his accession would strengthen the Kingdom of England by uniting it with that of Scotland. When, in March, 1603, the old Queen felt her end to be at hand she at last signified her approval, and several of the leading members of the Council hastened northwards to be the first to greet the new sovereign.

Why is it that we always look on Queen Elizabeth as one of the heroic figures of history? Certainly she had courage— nobody ever saw her look anxious or perturbed, whatever dangers might be threatening; but the main features of her policy were the very reverse of heroic. They were a lack of deep sincerity in religion, underhand trickery towards friend and foe, cheese-paring economy, and shiftless procrastination. Yet these were the very qualities to which she owed her success. If she had at the outset boldly put herself at the head of the Protestant move-ment in Europe, she would have brought down upon England the whole force of the Catholic Reaction long before the country was strong enough for such a struggle. If she had spent her subjects' money freely in supporting the revolt of the Nether-lands and in preparing a great fleet, she would have prevented the growth of that national prosperity upon which the triumphant resistance to Spain ultimately depended.

Doubtless, the real reason why Englishmen from her own day down to ours have been proud of " Good Queen Bess " is that with all her shortcomings, she succeeded in carrying through one of the most difficult tasks that have fallen to the lot of a sovereign. She not only beat off the threatened attack of the Counter-Reformation; she actually turned it into a source of strength, and made it an instrument by which the nation was made proudly confident of its ability to hold its own against the greatest of world-powers. In her the Tudor dictatorship reached its climax. When we contrast the national spirit at the moment of her death with what it had been when her grandfather had gained the crown with a handful of foreign mercenaries, we can realise what that dictatorship had done for England. And we can realise how great was the Queen's own contribution towards this raising of the national spirit when we remember how her sister lost Calais for lack of the spirit to raise a few thousand men.

QUESTIONS

(1) *Estimate Elizabeth's claims to be considered a great queen.*
(2) *Ireland under the Tudors.*

GENERAL QUESTIONS ON BOOK II

(1) *To what extent does Elizabeth's home and foreign policy entitle her to be considered the Champion of Protestantism?*

(2) *" The Spacious Times of Great Elizabeth ": what did Tennyson mean by the word " spacious " in this connection? How far is its use justified?*

(3) *Examine the statement that in Tudor times changes in religion depended on the will of the sovereign.*

(4) *What reasons had Elizabeth for* (a) *keeping Mary, Queen of Scots, a prisoner ;* (b) *beheading her ?*

(5) *Outline the relations of England and France during the reign of Elizabeth.*

(6) *What attempts did England make under the Tudors to gain a share in the colonial and commercial expansion of Europe?*

(7) *Trace the course of Tudor policy in Scotland.*

(8) *What causes depressed the condition of the poorer classes in the sixteenth century ? What attempts were made to meet the difficulties ?*

(9) *When, where, and why were there serious risings in England during the sixteenth century ?*

(10) *Compare Elizabeth's position in relation to France, Spain, and Scotland at the beginning and at the end of her reign.*

(11) *Describe the economic condition of England, in the middle of the century.*

(12) *How do you account for the great power of the Crown during the sixteenth century ? Illustrate* (a) *its extent, and* (b) *its limitations.*

(13) *How far is it true to describe Elizabeth's foreign policy as one of makeshifts and vacillation ?*

(14) *How far was the history of Elizabeth's reign the history of England's resistance to the Counter-Reformation ?*

(15) *What factors combined to promote the growth of the spirit of nationality and patriotism during Elizabeth's reign ?*

(16) *Compare the position occupied by England among the Powers of Europe at the beginning and at the end of the reign.*

BOOK A

The Triumph of Puritanism

(1603–1660)

WITH the accession of the Stuart dynasty our national history takes a new turn. Hitherto it has always more or less followed the stream that is flowing on the Continent—the Reformation and the consolidation of Monarchy. Henceforth it goes down a road of its own, impelled partly by national character, partly by political circumstance. That road was the development of parliamentary government.

The seeds of this had been sown during the later Middle Ages all over Europe. Everywhere except in England they had been trampled out of existence by the Renaissance monarchies of the sixteenth century ; but in England they had merely lain dormant. As soon as the conditions that led to the Tudor dictatorship disappeared, they germinated vigorously. Circumstances caused political freedom to be associated with ultra-Protestantism in religion. The " Puritans " were strongly represented in Parliament; in order to prevent the King from enforcing an unwelcome interpretation of the doctrines of the Church of England they were obliged to hold him in check by maintaining the parliamentary monopoly of taxation. This was the root cause of the Civil War.

War led to the supremacy of a knot of extremists who controlled the victorious Puritan Army. These extremists were driven to maintain their supremacy by acts of tyranny which led to violent reaction in favour of kingship. Yet the foundations of constitutional monarchy had by this time been so firmly laid that no Restoration could move them.

PURITANISM SUPPRESSED

1603		JAMES I	Trial of Raleigh (§94)	1603
1604	Hampton Court Conference (§92)		Peace with Spain (§94)	1604
1605	Gunpowder Plot (§93)			1605
1606				1606
1607	Plantation of Ulster (§109)		Foundation of Virginia (§108)	1607
1608				1608
1609				1609
1610	Debate on Impositions & Gr. Contract (§95)			1610
1611	Dissolution of 1st. Parliament (§95)		The Bible (§98)	1611
1612	Death of Salisbury & Pr. Henry (§96)		Carr E. of Somerset (§97)	1612
1613				1613
1614	The Addled Parliament (§87)			1614
1615				1615
1616	Death of Shakespeare (§98)			1616
1617		Raleigh's Voyage (§97)	Villiers E. of Buckingham (§97)	1617
1618		Execution of Raleigh (§97)	The Thirty Years War begins (§99)	1618
1619				1619
1620	Pilgrim Fathers (§108) The "Novum Organum"(§98)		White Mountain X (§99)	1620
1621	Fall of Bacon (§99)	3rd. Parliament (§99)		1621
1622				1622
1623			Visit to Spain (§100)	1623
1624	Mansfeld's Expedition (§101)		War with Spain (§101) French Marriage Treaty (§100)	1624
1625	1st. Parliament (§101)	CHARLES I	Expedition to Cadiz (§102)	1625
1626	2nd. Parlt (§102) Impeachment of Buckingham (§103)		War with France (§103)	1626
1627	Forced Loan (§103)		Expedition to Rhé (§103)	1627
1628	3rd. Parlt (§104) Petition of Right (§104)		Murder of Buckingham (§105)	1628
1629	Wentworth in the North (§109)		Peace with France (§106)	1629
1630	Distraint of Knighthood (§106)		Peace with Spain (§106)	1630
1631				1631
1632				1632
1633	Laud Archbishop (§107)		Wentworth in Ireland (§109)	1633
1634	1st. Writ of Ship Money (§106)		Enlargement of Forests (§106)	1634
1635				1635
1636	Hampden's Case (§110)			1636
1637	Edinburgh Riots (§111)			1637
1638	Scottish National Covenant (§111)			1638
1639	First Bishops' War (§111)			1639

CHAPTER XIX

Shadows Before

(1601–1611)

The first of the Stuarts was in many respects a wise and well-meaning king ; he was warmly welcomed by his new subjects, and he enjoyed the advantage of uniting England and Scotland by a personal bond. Yet within six or seven years of his accession, partly by bad luck but more by bad judgment, he found himself involved in disputes which led in the end—long after his own disappearance from the scene—to disaster for his family and for his ideas of government.

91. " *James Sixt and First* "

During six weeks of spring weather King James made his leisurely way from Edinburgh to London, and the people of England crowded into the country towns through which he passed to get a glimpse of their new sovereign. They were so glad to be relieved of their fears of disputed succession that they were not disposed to be very critical. This was fortunate, for James did not present a very kingly figure. A tallish, shambling, weak-kneed person, with a good-natured, talkative, conceited disposition, he was in many ways more like a crotchety professor than a great king. A man of intelligence far above the average, particularly well read in theology and history, and with a sound theoretical knowledge of European politics, he was intensely proud of his learning, and nothing delighted him more than an opportunity to display it. He hated war and fighting men of all kinds, which was an excellent thing ; but it was less excellent that he should have been pitiably afraid of the very sight of cold steel. Altogether, a man whom it was difficult to dislike, but more difficult to respect.

For a great part of his life he had been under the tutelage of overbearing Scottish nobles, badgered by ministers of the Presbyterian Kirk, and chronically short of money. He had long looked forward to the moment when his accession to the English throne would set him free from these restrictions. He knew little or nothing about his new subjects or their institutions; but he never realised his ignorance—nor would he have thought such matters worth his attention, in any case. He regarded himself as an expert in " kingcraft," as he called it, and he was a great believer in the political theory known as *The Divine Right of Kings*. This was still somewhat of a novelty. We have seen that the development of monarchical power was an outcome of the Renaissance—indeed, it seemed the only thing that could save civilisation from falling into chaos after the decay of the medieval order of society. Towards the end of the sixteenth century men began to invent a theory to justify the sanctity of kingship. Naturally, James was much taken with the doctrine, for it accorded well with his personal vanity, with his taste for history and theology, and with his love of logical argument. He had gone so far as to write a book to expound it—" The True Law of Free Monarchies." Hereditary monarchy, he declares, has been ordained by God; and a king is accountable to God alone for his actions. Since he is the author of the law, he is above it. All other authorities in the State derive their power from him and owe him absolute obedience. To be sure, a good king will keep the welfare of his subjects in mind, but rebellion against him is always an abominable crime. A wicked king is the instrument of God, sent to scourge people for their sins : " patience, earnest prayer and amendment of their lives is the only lawful means to move God to relieve them of that heavy curse." It seems very difficult nowadays to find any justification for the theory, either in Scripture or in common sense. Moreover, if the Divine Right could be handed on by a woman, half the rulers of Europe were usurpers; and if it could not be so handed on, the other half were. Yet this dogma was the mainspring of European politics for centuries; it was held by many of the finest intellects of the age, and it had a profound effect upon English history.

On the whole, King James approved of the policy of his predecessor; and he not only confirmed the position of Sir Robert Cecil as Lord Treasurer, but made him Earl of Salisbury. But he felt confident that he was far better qualified by wisdom and learning to bring the blessings of peace and good government to the people of England than the late Queen—who after all was only a woman and had never made such a profound study of " kingcraft " as he had.

We shall now see how his ignorance of human nature more than counterbalanced his theoretical knowledge of politics, and led him into a series of blunders which more than nullified all his good intentions.

92. *The Rebuff to the Puritans*

The first of these blunders was his treatment of those clergymen who desired that the national Church should be more distinctly Protestant in its doctrines and practices than it had been made by the Elizabethan settlement (§ 77). This " Puritan " way of thinking and living was commonest among the trading classes in the towns and the yeoman farmers in the country. It was marked by a sense of personal relationship with God, as revealed by a constant study of the Bible, and by a sober, earnest and duty-doing outlook on life. " My father never scrupled about common prayer or ceremonies, nor spake against bishops," wrote a famous Puritan preacher. " But only for reading Scripture when the rest were dancing on the Lord's Day . . . and for reproving drunkards and swearers and for talking sometimes a few words of Scripture and the life to come, he was reviled by the name of Puritan, Precisian and Hypocrite : and so were the godly conformable ministers that lived anywhere in the country near us." During the latter part of the late Queen's reign Puritanism had been discredited by an extremist minority who wanted to abolish the episcopal system of Church government in favour of independent congregations choosing their own ministers, and this had given the Government an excuse to repress all demands for reform. But great hopes had been aroused by the accession of a king who had been brought up in an atmosphere of Presbyterianism. A petition (said to represent the views of a thousand clergymen, and therefore called *The Millenary Petition*) was presented to James in the course of his journey southwards. It asked that clergymen should be allowed at their discretion to dispense with vestments and with certain other regulations laid down in the Book of Common Prayer. The King determined to summon a conference to consider the petition. He was delighted at such an opportunity to display his ability in theological argument before a fresh audience. Fourteen of the High Church party (including six bishops) were summoned to *The Hampton Court Conference* (1604) to argue out the points at issue with four of the Puritan divines, headed by Reynolds, Dean of Lincoln. The disproportion in numbers suggests that the King had queer notions of fair play, and in the discussions which followed he sided openly against the Puritans. He had suffered more than enough at the hands of ultra-Protestantism in Scotland ; he was determined not to let it get the upper hand of him in England. In some respects he was well-disposed towards Puritanism : he was more interested in preaching than in ritual, for instance ; but the Anglican form of Church government, with the King exercising control through the bishops, was exactly suited to his political ideas, and he was determined to uphold it at all costs. For several days the debate went on, with James revelling in his privileges as a royal chairman, and treating the Puritans with genial contempt. But at last a chance phrase of Reynolds about bishops consulting their Presbyteries caused an explosion of wrath. " If you aim at a Scottish Presbytery," he cried, " it agreeth as well with a monarchy as God with the Devil." And then, seizing his hat as a sign of dismissal to the assembly, " How they used the poor lady, my mother, is not unknown, and how they dealt with me in my minority. I thus apply it : No Bishop, no King. . . . Well, Doctor, have you anything more to say ? " " No more, if it please your majesty." " Then if this be all your party hath to say, I will make them conform themselves, or else will harry them out of the land."

This brusque dismissal was the first step towards bringing into existence a permanent and powerful party of opposition to Divine Right and the State Church. About six months later some three hundred parsons were expelled from their livings for not conforming to the Prayer Book. Amongst these " non-conformists " were many of the ablest and most high-minded of the clergy, while the congregations which continued to support them included some of the soundest and most respectable elements of the nation.

93. *Gunpowder Treason*

Roman Catholicism had been driven underground during the last twenty years of Elizabeth, and nobody could guess what proportion of the nation still adhered to the old faith. Mostly it centred round the households of isolated country gentlemen, especially in the North and Midlands. There were penal laws of three kinds in force : a ban on priests, fines for " recusancy " (*i.e.* not attending the Anglican Church), and exclusion from public offices ; but the penalties were not inflicted with any regularity. Much depended on the character and opinions of the local magistrates. James was confident that this was one of the problems of government for which his wisdom would readily find a solution; for " The British Solomon " felt himself poised high above the narrow-minded and angry passions of common folk. One of his first promises after crossing the border was that so long as Catholics remained loyal they should not be molested in the exercise of their religion. But the result of this relaxation was startling. Such large numbers took advantage of it that the real strength of the Catholic Church in England stood revealed for the first time in half a century. King, Council and Parliament were alike struck with panic, and the penal laws were again put into active operation. The disappointment of the Catholics was acute, and some of the leading spirits among them entered into the most famous conspiracy in English history.

The scheme was devised by one Catesby. A group of fanatical Catholics felt that nothing less would serve their turn than the destruction at one blow of all the leading men in the kingdom. It was decided that when King, Lords and Commons were assembled for the opening of the third session of Parliament in November, 1605, they should be blown to destruction by gunpowder concealed in a cellar beneath the Parliament house, and in the resultant confusion a general Catholic rising was to take place.   The practical details were entrusted to one Guy Fawkes, a Yorkshire gentleman who had sold his family estates and joined the English Legion in the service of Spain in the Netherlands, and was an expert in such matters as sapping and mining.   Unfortunately for the conspirators, one of their number lost his nerve as the critical moment drew near, and tried to prevent the deed without betraying his comrades, by sending an anonymous warning to a nobleman who (he knew) would show it to the Council.   He did not distinctly state that gunpowder was to be used, but his words seemed to imply something of the sort.   It became known to the conspirators that the Government had been warned ; but nothing could shake the iron nerve of Fawkes.   When, on the night before the meeting of Parliament, the cellars were searched, he was arrested in the act of making his final preparations.   He was executed, after undergoing horrible tortures with signal fortitude, and all the other chief conspirators were captured or killed.

The attempt and not the deed confounded the English Catholics.   Naturally, it led to a fresh outburst of persecution against them, but the heaviest blow which it inflicted on their cause was moral.   *The Gunpowder Plot* had a profound and lasting effect on public opinion.   For three centuries afterwards, Catholicism was associated in the mind of the average Englishman with murder-plots.   The hatred and fear of " Popery " has been kept alive right down to our own day by the annual burning of an effigy of Fawkes in almost every town and village in the land.   And we shall see that this passion was destined to be closely connected with decline and fall of the Stuart dynasty.

94. *James the Peacemaker*

Since Edward the Confessor, no such thorough-going pacifist had sat upon the throne of England as James I.   He had already formed elaborate plans to bring about a close union between England and Scotland and a permanent pacification of Europe. In these matters he was far more enlightened than most men of his age; yet even here his good intentions were frustrated largely by his own tactlessness and inability to see the point of view of other people.

As to the connection between England and Scotland, the fact that he was king of both countries was of great advantage for his purpose. Border warfare had practically ceased under Elizabeth : henceforth it became impossible. James wanted to bring about a complete political union by which the two peoples would be members of one Church, subject to one Law and one Government. " I am the husband and all the isle is my wife," he said. " I hope therefore that no man will be so unreasonable as to think that I, that am a Christian King, should be the Polygamist and husband to two wives." But Parliament was not to be cajoled by his facetious figures of speech. The prejudice against Scotsmen was very great, their competition in trade was much feared, and the jealousy was increased by the lavish way in which James had bestowed English places and titles and pensions on his fellow-countrymen. Nothing would induce the Houses to pass an Act of Union. In 1604 a decision of the Law Courts laid it down that the *Post Nati—i.e.* Scotsmen born after the King's accession to the English throne—were to have the same rights and privileges as his English subjects. With this James had to be content. A century and more was to elapse before a real union between the two countries could be carried through.

With regard to European peace, one of James's first cares on coming to the throne was to bring to an end the war between England and Spain which had been dragging on since the Armada. By the terms of the treaty English merchants were to be allowed to trade with all the Spanish possessions in Europe, but nothing was said about the far more important markets across the Atlantic. The Spanish War had been a source of profit and glory to many, and the King's anxiety to be on good terms with foreign powers aroused much ill feeling among the seafaring elements of the population. Furthermore, several of the most notable of the Elizabethan " men of war " were put under lock and key during the first few months of the reign, in connection with an alleged plot—it seems not to have gone farther than indiscreet talk—to put James off the English throne in favour of his cousin Arabella Stuart. The most famous of these victims was Sir Walter Raleigh. Condemned to death on very insufficient evidence, his execution was postponed indefinitely, and he was kept a prisoner in the Tower, where during the next few years he beguiled his enforced leisure by writing his famous " History of the World."

95. *The King Quarrels with his First Parliament*

Even more serious was the conflict which developed between the King and his first Parliament. This sprang from two distinct causes.

The first to arise was the question of parliamentary powers and privileges. This had been kept in the background under Elizabeth, for the great Queen was too practical-minded to demand a formal recognition of her supremacy so long as she was left to govern in her own way ; and Parliament was equally ready to let the subject sleep, so long as she carried on the government cheaply and effectively, and kept the Spanish danger at bay. But circumstances were now changed. The classes from which Parliament was mostly drawn—country gentlemen and prosperous merchants—had been growing rapidly in importance and self-confidence throughout the latter half of the last century ; all fears of invasion were now past, and the new King had none of the claims to the nation's respect and affection possessed by his predecessor. Moreover, James started his reign by setting forth in explicit terms his claims to the Right Divine, which if they were once admitted would cause the English Parliament to fall into the decay that had overtaken the States-General of France and the Cortes of Spain. When, therefore, James declared to his first Parliament that all its powers depended on his good will, and that it was sedition for the members even to discuss the limits of his prerogative, the House of Commons made a respectful but firm protest : " We hold it an ancient and undoubted right of Parliament to debate freely all matters which properly concern the subject." The King retorted with an angry denial of this claim, and the dispute continued intermittently all through the six years of the Parliament's life.

But the most serious bone of contention was the revenue. Within a year or two of his accession, the King found his expenditure almost double his revenue, and bankruptcy was staring him in the face. He therefore issued a new " Book of Rates " by which the customs duties were increased on many classes of goods. A London merchant named Bates refused to pay one of these new " impositions " on the ground that they had not been authorised by Parliament, but when the Government brought him before the Law Courts to enforce payment, the Judges decided that the new taxes were lawful. At the time Parliament took no notice of the matter, but a year or two later the members began to realise that with the growth of foreign trade there would be an end of all parliamentary control over taxation if the King were allowed to increase the duties at his own will and pleasure. In the session of 1610 the *Bates' Case* was hotly debated. As in most such disputes, there was a good deal to be said on both sides. James was certainly extravagant. Compared with Scotland, England seemed to him to have inexhaustible supplies of wealth, and when he came to London he had flung about presents and pensions with a lavish hand. Yet it was not entirely his fault that he found himself unable to make ends meet. A drastic reform of the royal revenue was long overdue. For a hundred years or more the expenses of government had been constantly increasing and the value of money diminishing. Even the parsimonious Elizabeth had been unable to pay her way during the later years of her reign, and James had inherited a considerable debt. Then again, as a married man with a family to provide for, he found his personal expenses far greater than those of the Virgin Queen.

He now showed himself quite ready to meet Parliament half way, by agreeing to give up all right to impose any further duties in consideration of a definite and permanent increase in the old duties being authorised by Parliament. Meanwhile another dispute had broken out. This was in connection with a bargain known as *The Great Contract*, whereby the King was to receive a lump sum to pay off his debts and an annual income of £200,000 in exchange for certain vexatious feudal dues which had hitherto been paid to the Crown. At the close of the session of 1610 it appeared as if an agreement had been reached on both these matters; but during the recess both King and Parliament decided that they were making a bad bargain. When the Houses re-assembled the bickering began again, and the King dissolved Parliament in a fit of temper, leaving the whole question still " in the air."

The dispute with Parliament was perhaps the most threatening of the omens of trouble to come for the Stuart dynasty; but it was not the only one. The Law Courts which were directly under the King's control, such as the Star Chamber and the Court of High Commission, which controlled Church matters, came into conflict with the ordinary Courts which administered the " Common Law," the " Law of the Land." Some of the judges in the latter Courts, headed by the Chief Justice, Sir Edward Coke, maintained that the Common Law was above the King, and could not be altered save by Parliament. Coke was not only an acute and learned lawyer, but a fearless, self-assertive, and pugnacious man. In 1616 James brought the dispute to a summary conclusion by dismissing him from his post. Coke received little support from his colleagues on the Bench; but the controversy had focussed the professional pride of the younger generation of lawyers; and when the constitutional struggle came to a head in the following reign their powerful influence was thrown almost entirely against the Crown.

QUESTIONS

(1) *Why was Parliament less amenable to James than it had been to Elizabeth ?*

(2) *Illustrate James's disregard of human nature.*

CHAPTER XX

The Spanish Marriage

(1611–1624)

In the last chapter we saw that within a few years of his accession King James gave offence to some of the most respectable elements of the nation by his treatment of Parliament and Puritans. We shall now see that during the latter part of his reign he also flouted public opinion by pursuing a foreign policy that disregarded the national and religious prejudices of his subjects.

96. *Peace through Marriage*

Self-satisfied as James was as to his " kingcraft " in home affairs, it was in his grasp of European politics that he took the greatest pride.

So far as Western Europe was concerned, the struggle between Protestantism and the Catholic Reaction had by this time been fought out. It had ended in a draw: France, Flanders, and Poland were now definitely Catholic, while Britain, Holland, and Scandinavia were as definitely Protestant. In Germany, on the other hand, the contest had been postponed by the Treaty of Augsburg (§ 33), which allowed the princes of the Empire to impose whichever faith they preferred upon their subjects. But there were signs that this truce was now coming to an end. Once more it was the Hapsburg family that was to take the lead on the Catholic side ; but this time the protagonist was to be the Emperor Ferdinand, with his cousin the King of Spain in support. In the light of later events, we can see that Spain was already weakened by corruption, misgovernment and the lethargy that comes of living on unearned wealth ; but to contemporaries she still appeared by far the greatest power in the world, and her resources seemed likely to be the decisive factor in the coming struggle. Moreover, the Catholic party had the further advantage that the Protestant princes of Germany were divided into two bitterly hostile sections, Calvinist and Lutheran. Thus there was a prospect that within a few years the Emperor would gain control over the whole of Central Europe, and that all the civilised world except France and Britain would be subject to the House of Hapsburg. To prevent such a catastrophe, Henry IV of France planned a coalition between France and the Protestant elements in Germany ; but in 1610 he was murdered by a Catholic fanatic.

The stage was now cleared for King James to come forward as the arbiter of Europe. Henry's method of attacking the problem would have involved a great war, but James's was the way of peace. He would marry his eldest son to a Spanish Infanta, and his eldest daughter to the Elector Palatine ; Catholic and Protestant rulers would thus be united by family ties, and the lion would lie down with the lamb under his fatherly persuasion. It was a capital plan on paper, but like so many of the worthy king's plans it was impracticable. For one thing, his own subjects would have none of it. The prospect of a Queen who would bring up the future King of England in an atmosphere of Spanish Catholicism was appalling to the nation, and particularly to the class which dominated Parliament. James had not yet found out that he could not act effectively in foreign affairs without the support of public opinion ; but he was hampered for some years by the fact that the two most important people at his Court were opposed to the scheme : Lord Salisbury, his chief minister, and Prince Henry, the proposed bridegroom. It was only after both Cecil and the Prince of Wales had died (in 1612) that the King was in a position to push forward negotiations for a marriage between the Infanta and his second son, Charles. Here, however, he encountered an even more formidable obstacle—the fact that the King of Spain had a better match in view for his daughter, who was betrothed soon after to the young King Louis XIII of France. Half of James's scheme had now to be abandoned, but he carried through the other half by marrying the Princess Elizabeth to the Elector Frederick amid extravagant festivities at the beginning of 1613.

97. *The Personal Rule of James I*

After the death of Cecil, the King determined that his own genius as a ruler should have unrestricted sway. He would be his own Prime Minister, like Philip II. The members of the Council found themselves treated as mere executive officers All the affairs of state were settled by the King himself at odd times, such as the luncheon hour in some great hunt in Windsor forest, and the only men consulted were personal favourites. James might have had the counsel of one of the wisest of English statesmen, Francis Bacon; and Bacon was so ambitious of power and place that he stooped to unworthy compliance and flattery to gain his master's favour. But James was not seeking wisdom in his *entourage*—was he not himself " The British Solomon " ? What he wanted was pleasant company, especially in the form of attractive young men. The first of these favourites was a good-looking but worthless young Scotsman named *Robert Carr*, whom James raised to the Peerage (the first Scotsman to sit in the English House of Lords) as Earl of Somerset. Soon this vain and empty-headed youth was dispensing all the royal patronage, and making enormous profit out of it. No petition had any chance of being noticed unless it was accompanied by a handsome bribe to Somerset. His only rival in the King's favour was a man even less loved by the public—the Spanish Ambassador, Count Gondomar. James's anxiety to induce the King of Spain to fall in with his marriage schemes made him abjectly subservient to all the demands, official and unofficial, of this haughty hidalgo. The Penal Laws were once more relaxed at his behest, and his dwelling became the centre of English Catholic society.

If James wanted to do without Parliament, he should have cut down his expenditure ; but this was just what he could never do. He certainly spent little on the navy, or any other national cause ; but in personal matters his extravagance knew no bounds. He lavished £60,000 on the wedding of his daughter Elizabeth, and he could never say " No " to applicants for places and pensions. He tried all sorts of expedients for raising money, including selling baronetcies on the easy payment system (the price was £1,080 in three instalments) ; but at last the deficit reached such alarming proportions that there was no alternative but to summon another Parliament. This proved as intractable as its predecessor, however. The members objected to the unauthorised " impositions " which the King had continued to collect (§ 95) ; and they denounced the bribery and corruption that were so rife at the Court. Within a few weeks, and before it had been able to achieve anything in the way of legislation, the King went down in dudgeon and dissolved what has ever since been known as " *The Addled Parliament.*"

The Somerset régime continued for another two years, but it then came to an end in dramatic fashion. The Earl and his wife were accused of having caused a personal enemy to be murdered. Somerset relied on the King intervening to prevent justice from taking its course ; but James was getting tired of the overbearing manners of his protégé. The Somersets were brought to trial, found guilty and condemned to death. They were subsequently reprieved, but were permanently banished from the Court.

The place thus left empty in the King's affections was soon taken by one *George Villiers*, who became Earl (later *Duke*) *of Buckingham*. This was a much more ambitious, courageous, and capable person than his predecessor. His handsome face and figure and his fascinating insolence of demeanour quite captivated the King. We get a glimpse of the unseemly lengths to which James carried his infatuation when we learn that he said to the Privy Council, " I will not have it to be thought a defect that I love the Earl of Buckingham, for Jesus Christ did the same. He had his John and I have my George."

When Buckingham first came to Court, he had been pushed forward by an anti-Spanish clique. Hence an immediate result of his rise to power was that Raleigh was released from the Tower and given a commission to go in search of a gold mine in Guiana of which he had told the King. While the preparations for the voyage were going forward, however, the favourite changed his mind and went over to the supporters of the Spanish marriage project. Sir Walter was allowed to set out, but was given strict injunctions that he was not to interfere with the territories or the subjects of the King of Spain. As that monarch claimed the whole of America as his private preserve, any sensible person must have realised that these were impossible conditions, but Raleigh was doubtless too glad to be free and adventuring again to make much demur. Meanwhile, the King had weakly gossiped to Gondomar about the expedition, and when Raleigh arrived at the mouth of the Orinoco, he found the Spaniards prepared and waiting for him. After the inevitable but forbidden conflict, the Englishmen succeeded in forcing their way up the river ; but they found no gold, and they were driven back to the coast by an attack from overwhelming numbers, Raleigh's own son being among the slain. The survivors insisted on sailing for home. Meanwhile, the King of Spain had protested very angrily at these depredations, and James, almost grovelling before Gondomar, had promised that condign punishment should follow the culprit's return. As soon as Raleigh landed at Plymouth, he was hurried up to London, and brought to trial for High Treason. It was found impossible to twist his actions into this shape, however, so the King simply had the sentence of 1604 carried out—fourteen years after it had been pronounced. This may not have been a wicked deed, but it was a deed which most wicked men would blush to commit.

98. *Literature and Science*

Here let us pause a moment to consider certain matters which, though they attracted much less attention at the time, were of far greater importance for the development of the British race than any Addled Parliaments or Spanish Marriages.

As we have already mentioned, the earlier years of the reign saw the production of the tragedies of Shakespeare, and in 1616 he died.* His thoughts and words have had a profound effect on every succeeding generation of Englishmen, but there was another literary masterpiece coming into existence at about the same time which had an even profounder influence on Anglo-Saxon speech and character. Of all the suggestions put forward by the Puritans at the Hampton Court Conference, the only one which King James accepted wholeheartedly was a request for

---

* It is interesting to note that his last play of all, "The Tempest," was written (or at any rate re-written) for the betrothal ceremonies of the Princess Elizabeth and the Elector Palatine.

an improved translation of the Bible. Three committees of learned divines were set to work, and in 1610 the famous *Authorised Version* appeared. It was based on already existing translations, of course, but in the new form it became accessible to almost every home in the land. For every person who saw " Hamlet " there were hundreds who read the Bible day by day, or listened to it on Sundays with rapt attention as the inspired word of God. And this was a special privilege of the English-speaking peoples, for no others possess in their mother tongue a version of the Scriptures so pure, vigorous and eloquent.

In 1620 appeared Bacon's *Novum Organum*. This was one of the last, and one of the most important, achievements of the Renaissance in England. It set forth the principles on which all modern scientific investigation rests. Bacon argued that the only roads to knowledge are investigation and experiment ; he urged that such studies are of little worth unless they can be harnessed to the practical needs of mankind, he claimed that all knowledge might be mastered by any one who would make patient and persistent use of these methods, and he warned men of the errors in reasoning to which the investigator is liable. He was himself too much pre-occupied with politics, the law, and place-hunting to be able to travel very far along the road that he thus pointed out to others. Indeed, he did not even keep abreast of the scientific progress that was being made in his own day. Harvey had just revolutionised physiology by demonstrating the circulation of the blood ; Napier had recently invented logarithms, one of the most useful tools of the modern mathematician ; Gilbert was taking the first steps in the investigation of magnetism and electricity ; but of all these matters Bacon remained in complete ignorance. Nor did he accept Galileo's recent confirmation of the Copernican system of astronomy : to the end of his days he adhered to the belief that the sun goes round the earth. Nevertheless, his work was of profound importance for that development of man's command over the forces of nature which has been such a characteristic feature of modern times. As he himself said, " he rang the bell which called the other wits to work " by indicating the powers of inductive reasoning.

99. *The Thirty Years' War Breaks Out*

In 1618 the long-threatened religious war broke out in Germany. So far from the cherished marriage schemes of James availing to preserve peace, it was his own son-in-law who actually provoked the outbreak. The inhabitants of Bohemia had been Protestants ever since the days of the Hussite Wars, and when in 1618 their royal house became extinct, they declined to accept the Catholic sovereign appointed for them by the Emperor, and invited the Elector Palatine to be their king. Frederick accepted the invitation, but he was crushingly defeated by the forces of the Emperor at the Battle of the White Mountain (1620) near Prague, and was driven headlong out of Bohemia. What was worse, a Spanish army was sent up the Rhine from the Netherlands to occupy the Palatinate.

James had not supported the Elector in his efforts to gain the throne of Bohemia, but he could not stand by while his daughter and grandchildren were thus robbed of their own hereditary dominions. But he was now to discover how fatal to his own peace policy his neglect of the national forces had been. To his chagrin, he found that his fellow-sovereigns took little notice of a king who could do nothing but talk. Yet he still clung to the delusion that the Catholic movement could be kept in check by a family alliance ; and he now tried to procure the restoration of the Palatinate by re-opening negotiations for a marriage between Prince Charles and the Infanta Maria.

When the Spanish troops pushed on relentlessly with their operations on the Rhine, James felt that he must at all costs raise funds for an army with which to support his son-in-law. For this purpose he was compelled to summon Parliament once more. The members were sympathetic about the Palatinate, and were disposed to do something on behalf of the Protestant cause in the European War ; but they postponed these matters to a great onslaught upon the corruption and profligacy of the Court. They began by attacking the practice of granting monopolies which enriched courtiers at the expense of the public (§ 78). The King gave way on the question of principle, but contrived to screen from punishment the highly-placed personages who had been most concerned in the traffic. The next victim of parliamentary indignation was Bacon, who had become Lord Chancellor and Viscount St. Albans in 1618. He was accused of taking bribes in the administration of justice. There is no doubt that he had allowed suitors to make him presents in a way that would be considered highly improper nowadays, but in that age the transaction of official business was often sealed by gifts from the favoured party, and Bacon was no more corrupt than most other men in public life. But the King eagerly threw him to the wolves in order to shield others who were nearer and dearer to himself. The great statesman-philosopher was driven from office and condemned to pay a heavy fine. He spent the few remaining years of his life in the quiet pursuit of his scientific studies.

The King was of one mind with his Parliament over the misdeeds of Bacon; but the members then got on to more debateable ground. Intensely patriotic and intensely Protestant, they were bitterly opposed to the whole policy of the Spanish marriage, and to the influence of Gondomar, with which that policy was closely connected. They were convinced that the best way for England to support the Protestant cause in Europe would be to renew the naval war with Spain. The members of these Stuart Parliaments were for the most part high-minded and public-spirited men, but very few of them had any grasp of the business of government. They spent most of their lives in the pursuits of country gentlemen, and there were no newspapers from which they could learn what was going on in the great world. James therefore had some reason to be indignant at their presumption in debating foreign affairs, which he regarded as peculiarly his own province; and when the Commons made a solemn "Protestation" of their right to debate all matters that affected the Commonwealth, he went down to the House and angrily tore out with his own hands the page of the records on which the Protestation was written. A day or two later Buckingham was able to give Gondomar the delightful information that a dissolution had been decided on (Jan. 1622). Thus James had parted in anger with each of his first three Parliaments.

100. *Castles in Spain*

Adverse criticism being thus silenced, the King returned eagerly to his own plans for settling the problems of Europe. Since his quarrel with Parliament left him with no funds with which to raise an army for the Palatinate, all that he could do was to send a volunteer force, which was immediately destroyed, and his luckless daughter and her family were exiles all the rest of their lives. Nor was he more fortunate as regards the Spanish marriage plan. The discussions dragged wearily on for months, until at last Buckingham (who had gained as complete an ascendancy over the Prince of Wales as over the King) lost patience, and proposed that he and Charles should cut matters short by travelling *incognito* to Madrid, carry through the match by a personal wooing, and return in triumph with the Infanta. James was delighted to see his " twa boys sally forth like dear adventurous knights worthy to be put in a new romanso "; but the whole scheme turned out a ludicrous failure. The dignified courtiers at the Escurial were deeply shocked at such unconventional proceedings, their etiquette forbade that the Prince should even see the Infanta; Buckingham's pretentious manners disgusted everybody with whom he came in contact, and King Philip demanded what amounted to a restoration of the Catholic Church in England. After six months of bickering, the young men returned home with their mission unaccomplished.

Meanwhile, the enterprise had aroused great anxiety in England; and the return of the Prince, still unmarried and still a Protestant, was the occasion of great public rejoicing. Popularity was a new experience for Buckingham, and he found it very pleasant. Carried away by the current of public opinion, he declared himself disgusted at the arrogance of the Spaniards, and demanded that the whole project should be dropped. A fourth Parliament had just been elected, and when the abrupt change of front strained relations with Spain to breaking-point, the members welcomed the prospect of a war with that country. But this ardour cooled when the Houses heard rumours of other manœuvres that were going on behind the scenes. Cardinal Richelieu, who was ruling France in the name of the young Louis XIII, had revived Henry IV's plan for an anti-Hapsburg alliance ; and it was an obvious step for King James to join this alliance, since one of its immediate aims would be to win back the Palatinate for the Elector Frederick. But Parliament and the class it represented had no inclination for a land war in Germany, as we have already seen ; and they objected to a French marriage almost as strongly as to a Spanish.

As for the King, he was somewhat bewildered at this sudden revolution in policy, but he could deny nothing to his " Steenie " (as he affectionately called the Duke of Buckingham)—not even the abandonment of his cherished plan for a Spanish marriage. He was now falling into premature old age, and in March, 1625, he died. One can but wonder whether when his end drew near he realised how far the monarchy for which he claimed the Right Divine had declined in power and popularity during his reign owing to his own defects of judgment and character.

QUESTIONS

(1) *Explain the conflict between James I and his Parliaments on the subject of Foreign Policy.*

(2) *James I has been called " The wisest fool in Christendom." How far was this view just ?*

CHAPTER XXI

The Rule of Buckingham

(1625–1629)

For the first four years of his reign Charles I was under the influence of the Duke of Buckingham. The disagreements between King and Parliament which had arisen during the reign of King James were now focused into a clearly defined issue. Parliament felt that it could not trust the King to preserve the Protestantism of the Church of England or to carry on the government of the country efficiently. It therefore struggled to preserve that monopoly of taxing-power which was its sole means of bringing pressure to bear on him. Charles, on the other hand, denied its right to interfere with his policy in Church or State, and was determined to free himself from its control, by hook or by crook.

101. *The First Quarrel*

The young king made a notable contrast to his father, both in character and in demeanour. Whereas James had been good-humoured, quick-tempered and expansive, Charles was grave, dignified and shy. With no claims to his father's acuteness and learning, he had some literary talent, was a connoisseur of painting, and excelled in all manly exercises. In his private life he was everything that a gentleman should be, but as a king his faults were many and grievous. He had imbibed the Divine Right theory from the cradle, and clung to it with dull obstinacy. He was convinced that people who resisted his will were either fools or knaves, whom it was lawful to outwit by any trickery. He was always dependent on some livelier intelligence than his own ; nor did he possess the real ruler's capacity for choosing the right people to trust.

At the outset of his reign his heart and mind were enslaved by the vain, fickle, headstrong Buckingham. Within the last twelvemonth or so this reckless adventurer had broken with Spain, joined Richelieu's anti-Hapsburg alliance, sent a force of 12,000 under a German general named Mansfeld to rescue the Palatinate from the clutches of the greatest power in the world, promised large annual subsidies to Denmark, and arranged a French marriage for Charles. The first business of the new reign was to carry this last scheme into effect. The Pope exacted great concessions for English Catholics before he would give permission for a marriage between a Catholic princess and a Protestant king ; but Charles was very ready to pledge his royal word on this or any other subject to please his friend.

The royal wedding safely over, the next thing was to summon Parliament to procure supplies for the forthcoming war with Spain. Neither Charles nor the Duke expected any serious opposition, for the last Parliament had acclaimed the new policy (§ 100). They were therefore somewhat taken aback when discordant notes were sounded at the very first meeting. Members approved in a general way of plans to recover the Protestant Palatinate from a Catholic Power, but they knew so little about European affairs as to suppose that this could be done by putting pressure on the other branch of the House of Hapsburg. They were quite ready to support a naval war with Spain, for the tradition of Elizabethan glories still lingered, but they had no confidence in Buckingham, and no mind to endow him with vast sums with which to finance a war in Germany, especially as Mansfeld's expedition had been a disastrous failure. They made a niggardly grant of £140,000 for the general purposes of the war, and then began to discuss grievances.

The first of these was the King's marriage. A French queen was just as objectionable in their eyes as a Spanish one would have been—either alternative seemed to portend favours to Catholics in the present, and a line of Catholic kings in the future. The King now showed for the first time that trait of character which afterwards did more than anything else to lead him to destruction—his lack of straightforwardness. Having readily promised freedom of worship for Catholics under pressure from France, he was equally ready to withdraw that promise under pressure from Parliament ; and the Penal Laws were once more put into operation.

Nor was this Parliament's only cause for anxiety on the score of Protestantism. Suspicions were aroused that the King himself was turning Catholic. A Dutch theologian named Arminius had recently attracted much attention by breaking away from the Calvinist doctrines which prevailed both in the Dutch and in the English Churches. He maintained that the traditional usages, ceremonies and festivals of the Roman Church ought to be kept up, and he adopted the doctrine of the Real Presence. To ultra-Protestants " *Arminianism* " seemed to be the thin edge of Popery, and the fact that the King encouraged it among the clergy aroused deep suspicions as to his orthodoxy.

The House showed its distrust of the Government by proposing to grant the Customs Duties (commonly known as *Tunnage and Poundage*) for one year only. For centuries it had been the invariable custom that a king should be granted these at his accession for the whole of his reign, and this innovation was little short of an insult. Moreover, the special subsidy of £140,000 granted for the war was ludicrously inadequate—it would not pay the cost of it for a month. Indeed, a much larger sum had been promised as a subsidy to the King of Denmark. But Parliament made it clear that no more was to be expected so long as the Duke of Buckingham was in control. The King felt that if he gave way and dismissed the favourite, he would be admitting that Parliament had the right to control the conduct of the war and the appointment of ministers. Not for a moment would he allow such a claim. Had Parliament dictated on such matters to Henry VIII, or Elizabeth, or his father ? Never would he permit such unconstitutional proceedings. He dissolved Parliament abruptly before even the one year's Tunnage and Poundage had been formally granted.

102. *A Second Attempt*

The King and his favourite had no intention of trying to do without a Parliament. Their hope was that, war having now actually broken out with Spain, they would within a few months be able to meet a new Parliament after winning a resounding victory that would silence all opposition. Every penny they could lay their hands on was invested in a fleet and army to make an *attack on Cadiz* in the grand Elizabethan manner. But a quarter of a century of neglect had told its tale on the fighting forces. For fleet they had to press merchant vessels and their crews into the royal service, equipped with supplies that had been rotting in Plymouth warehouses ever since the days of Drake and Hawkins. As for their army, it consisted of ploughmen torn from their cottages and footpads released from gaols, armed with rusty cutlasses and firearms more dangerous to themselves than to the enemy. After a false start, Lord Wimbledon, the commander, at last got his motley force into Cadiz Bay; but he found that the shipmasters concentrated most of their attention on keeping out of harm's way. He then disembarked his " army," marched a dozen miles into the country in search of an enemy that was not there, realised too late that he ought to have brought some rations, but found unlimited quantities of wine. The result may be better imagined than described, and Wimbledon was lucky to get away at all. When the fleet arrived back in Plymouth Sound with tattered sails, sick crews and mutinous troops, it became obvious that military prestige was the last thing to be looked for in this quarter. Meanwhile, the Duke had been busy in the Netherlands organising a confederacy against the Emperor, to be financed with English money. Clearly, the summoning of a new Parliament could not be delayed. This time the King took the precaution of nominating the most troublesome members of the last House of Commons to be sheriffs of their counties, which made them ineligible for Parliament. But this trick brought him no advantage. A new and more forceful personality now came forward to lead the opposition—a Cornish gentleman named *Sir John Eliot*. He formerly been a close friend of Buckingham's, but recent events had convinced him that that young man was quite unfit to have control of the Government.

Charles had assumed that the granting of Tunnage and Poundage by Parliament was a mere formality, and he had gone on collecting the duties. Indeed, great confusion would have

resulted in business circles if he had not done so.   But the House
of Commons made an emphatic protest against this illegal pro-
ceeding, and then passed a vote authorising Eliot to prepare
articles of impeachment against the Duke of Buckingham.   In
the course of the debate, Eliot compared the Duke to Sejanus,
the wicked associate of the tyrant Tiberius.   For this insult to
the King he was sent to the Tower, but the Commons refused to
transact any further business until he was released.   They let it
be known that they did not want to press the charges against
Buckingham, so long as he was dismissed from office.   This
brought up once more the question of the responsibility of
ministers, however, and rather than give way on that subject
the King again dissolved Parliament before a penny of taxation
had been granted him.

103. *The Forced Loan*

The King and the Duke now sought some way of financing
their war independently of Parliament.   The position was desperate indeed.   The King of Denmark had been severely defeated
by the Imperial army at Lutter (1626) for lack of the subsidies
he had been promised.   Moreover, as if the unsuccessful war
with Spain was not enough to have on their hands, they had now
blundered into one with France.   The steps towards this con-
summate piece of folly were three.   Firstly, Buckingham felt a
personal grievance against Richelieu because the great cardinal
would not fall in with his ill-conceived plans for an attack on
Germany.   Secondly, Charles had weakly promised to send a
fleet to help the French Government to put down a rebellion of
the Huguenots at Rochelle, and then, ashamed of aiding the
persecution of Protestants, had delayed sending the ships until
they were too late to be of use.   Thirdly, the young Queen
much resented the renewal of the Penal Laws against the English
Catholics, contrary to her marriage contract, and the King
replied by angrily sending all her French attendants back to
France, accusing them of inciting these family jars.

With two wars to wage at once, the King decided to have
recourse to a Forced Loan.   Commissioners were appointed for
each county to collect the money and to send before the Privy

Council all who refused to pay the sum required from them. Dozens of gentlemen were imprisoned, and hundreds of poor men " pressed " for the army, which meant destitution for their families, and (not infrequently) starvation and death for themselves. Districts where resistance was general were punished by being placed under Martial Law, and by having troops billeted on the inhabitants without payment.

By these methods a certain amount of money was raised, and an expedition sent to the relief of Rochelle under the command of Buckingham himself. He and Charles always felt that a great victory, which would place Parliament at their feet, was just round the corner. It continued to elude their grasp, however. Buckingham showed considerable energy, courage and military capacity in occupying the Isle of Rhé, just off Rochelle ; but the bankruptcy of the Government made real success impossible. In quality the forces were little superior to those which had been sent to Cadiz the year before, and no supplies or reinforcements were available from home. Having lost more than half his strength by starvation and disease, the Duke brought the expedition home without having accomplished anything.

What was to be done now ? The unsatisfactory results of the Forced Loan made it obvious that an English government could not raise money for war by methods of Continental despotism. Richelieu could rule France with a rod of iron by means of his " Intendants " (officials sent round by the central government) ; but Charles had to rely on local magistrates—country gentlemen whose sympathies were with the people they were called upon to persecute. Some of the Commissioners for the Loan refused to act, or even to subscribe to it themselves.

With considerable misgiving, therefore, the King was forced to summon a third Parliament.

104. *The Petition of Right*

His forebodings were speedily justified. His attempt to collect taxes without parliamentary sanction (for that was what the " Forced Loan " really amounted to) seemed to the Houses a threat to rights which Englishmen had cherished for centuries. If the King could raise revenues without consulting the representatives of the nation, he would be able to set up a despotic government like those of France and Spain. The Commons therefore determined to postpone such comparatively minor matters as the impeachment of Buckingham, the danger to Protestantism, and the conduct of the war, until they had made good this foundation of English liberties. We cannot but admire the courage and public spirit of these Puritan squires. Nowadays a Member of Parliament may talk himself into office by attacking the Government, but in those times he was more likely to talk himself into gaol. So long as Parliament was sitting members were immune from arrest, but the minute the King chose to dissolve it they would be at his mercy—as some of them later found to their cost.

After some debate, the House decided to present to the King a *Petition of Right*—a kind of memorandum, drawing attention to the fact that certain laws had been broken, and requesting that they be duly observed for the future. The two chief laws referred to were (*a*) the clause of Magna Charta (1215) which said that no free man could be imprisoned without trial ; and (*b*) the " Statuta de Tallagio non Concedendo " (1297), according to which no " gift, loan or benevolence " could be exacted without consent of Parliament. This appeal to old laws and customs is very characteristic of the innate convervatism of Englishmen. Both King and Parliament always strenuously denied that they desired to make innovations ; in all the disputes that followed, the question always was : What used to be ?

In its final form the Petition declared that the four following practices were, and always had been, illegal : Martial Law, the Billeting of Troops, Arbitrary Taxation, and Arbitrary Imprisonment.* An ample supply of money was promised, as soon as the King should have signified his acquiescence.

For a week Charles hesitated, torn between his annoyance at being thus tied down, and his dire need of money. Then he sent an evasive answer, assuring the House that he would do his duty by his subjects as he had always done it : but the Commons would not accept this. At last he surrendered, and

---

* It will be observed that Arbitrary Taxation was really the crux of the whole matter, for the other three practices were all methods by which taxation could be enforced or the need for it evaded.

gave his assent in the traditional terms : Soit droict fait, comme il est desiré.

Great was the rejoicing throughout the land : it seemed a complete triumph over Buckingham and all that he stood for. But the House knew better. They could not rest satisfied while the favourite was directing the war, and they presented a remonstrance to the King asking that he should be dismissed from office. Thereupon the King angrily prorogued (*i.e.* adjourned) the session.

105. *The End of Buckingham*

It was fated, however, that the country should speedily be delivered of its bugbear. With the money just granted by Parliament, a new expedition was fitted out to go to the relief of Rochelle. Buckingham was once more placed in command ; but while he was at Portsmouth, superintending the embarkation, he was murdered by a man named Felton, who had been an officer on the last expedition, and had some personal grievance against him. The deed aroused wild enthusiasm throughout the country : the murderer's health was publicly drunk, poems were written in his honour, the bells were rung in the steeples, and bonfires lit in market squares. When Buckingham's funeral procession passed to Westminster Abbey, it was accompanied by cheering crowds as if it were a wedding. The sounds of rejoicing reached the King in Whitehall Palace, where he was overwhelmed with grief at the loss of his friend. With impassive dignity he hid his feelings from the outside world, but the harsh and brutal cheers of this London mob raised a fatal and permanent barrier between himself and his people.

The second Rochelle Expedition was as disastrous as the first, and early in the following year Parliament had once more to be summoned. The members re-opened at once the discussions which had been suspended while the Petition of Right was being prepared. The chief grievances now brought forward were : (*a*) that the King was altering the character of the Church of England by appointing as deans and bishops only High Church or Arminian clergymen ; and (*b*) that he was continuing to collect Tunnage and Poundage without Parliamentary authority. Bitter argumentation went on between Palace and Parliament House, especially when the Commons summoned before them clergymen who had introduced Catholic ceremonies and officers who had enforced payment of the unauthorised customs duties.

Eventually the King decided once more to cut the dispute short by a dissolution. The Commons learned of his intention, and determined to anticipate his action by passing resolutions that would lay down definitely the principles for which they were contending. Time pressed—word was brought that the King's messengers were actually on their way to the House to announce the dissolution. The Speaker tried to leave the Chair, so as to prevent anything being done contrary to the King's wishes ; but two members held him in his place while Eliot read the resolutions. Whoever brought in innovations in religion, whoever advised the unauthorised levying of Tunnage and Poundage, whoever voluntarily paid those duties : all such were to be accounted enemies of the Kingdom and betrayers of its liberties. The resolutions were carried amid frenzied cheers. Then the doors were flung open and the members poured forth in an excited throng. Those doors then closed behind them and were destined not to be opened again for eleven years.

The King followed up the dissolution with a Statement to His People, setting forth his point of view with regard to the recent disputes. He complained that Parliament had first induced him to go to war, and had then made use of his need for money to extract unheard-of concessions from him. Moreover, it had tried to interfere with the undoubted constitutional rights of the sovereign. Queen Elizabeth, for instance, had often imprisoned people without trial, she had done what she liked about religion, she had employed whom she chose as ministers, and neither Parliament nor anybody else had ever presumed to interfere. He, Charles, would be scrupulously careful to preserve all the traditional rights of his beloved subjects, but he would be equally careful to preserve his own.

All this was true enough ; but the real cause of the disagreement lay much deeper. It lay in the fact that Parliament could not trust the King, as it had trusted Elizabeth, to carry on the war successfully and economically, or to keep in touch with public opinion, or to make a wise choice of ministers and officers. Moreover, it soon became apparent that he could not be trusted even to keep his royal word, for within a few days of the dissolution nine members of Parliament were imprisoned in the Tower, despite the provisions of the Petition of Right.

QUESTIONS

(1) *Sketch the career of Buckingham.*

(2) *To what extent were these quarrels between King and Parliament a continuation of those under James I ?*

CHAPTER XXII

Personal Rule

(1629–1638)

The King was determined to prove to Parliament that he could do without it, and so reduce it to a more modest and respectful frame of mind. The difficulties of carrying on the government without parliamentary grants could be overcome only by his cutting down expenditure to the lowest possible level, and stretching his existing rights of taxation to their utmost limits. For ten years he succeeded in carrying on an autocratic government by means of this two-fold policy, and he endeavoured to use his independent position to re-model the national Church.

106. *Raising the Wind*

King Charles had no intention of abolishing Parliament: his object was to show that it was not indispensable. But the events of the past few years had shown him all too clearly that he could not carry on a war even for a year without the support of the Houses. Obviously, then, the first necessity was peace. The quarrel with France was made up by the Treaty of Susa (1629), and there was no more fighting with Spain, though the actual Peace of Madrid was not signed until the following year. The Thirty Years' War went on its devastating and sanguinary way without any further intervention by Britain. Charles was still very anxious to see his sister and nephews restored to the Palatinate. He negotiated ceaselessly with the warring Powers; but Gustavus Adolphus and Cardinal Richelieu, the Emperor and the King of Spain, all knew that his position prevented him from taking any warlike action, and they treated his communications with scarcely-veiled contempt.

In his fiscal policy the King owed much to his Lord Treasurer, *Weston*. Within four or five years this able but unscrupulous minister had liquidated a war-debt of £1,000,000, and had placed the finances of the Government on a sound basis. As to devices for raising money, the King and his Treasurer prided themselves on doing nothing illegal ; but in contriving to keep within the law they had to distort it into some very queer shapes. For instance, Weston discovered that Edward I had compelled all men holding lands worth £40 a year to come up to Court and be knighted. By imposing heavy fines on all who had unwittingly ignored this " *Distraint of Knighthood* " quite a useful sum was raised for the Treasury. Again, in the feudal times all waste spaces (technically known as " forests ") were supposed to belong to the King. In the course of centuries much of this land had been brought under cultivation, with thriving villages and stately manor-houses, by the enterprise of individual landowners. Fines of £5,000 or £10,000 were now imposed on their descendants or successors, for these " encroachments " on the royal domain. Yet again, *monopolies* were revived. By a law passed under James I (§ 99), they could no longer be granted to individuals ; but that law was now evaded by granting them to trading companies—who were willing to pay for the privilege by a good round sum, which they eventually extracted from the consumer by enhanced prices.

But the most famous of these revenue-raising expedients was *Ship Money*. It had formerly been a recognised right of the sovereign to call upon the sea-ports to provide ships for the defence of the realm, whenever danger threatened. This was the means by which most of the fleet which defeated the Armada had been raised, for instance. The Royal Navy had been utterly neglected since the accession of James I, and Algerian pirates were preying upon English shipping within sight of the cliffs of Dover. Charles determined to put a stop to these depredations, but he could not afford to build a fleet out of his ordinary revenues. He therefore (1634) called upon the maritime counties to supply him either with ships or with money where-with to build them, and they nearly all chose the latter alternative. The next year the inland counties were also called upon to pay : after all, the national defence was the concern of all alike.

These imposts were enforced by law courts under the direct control of the King, particularly the *Court of Star Chamber* (§ 7), which consisted of certain members of the Privy Council *plus* two judges. Such tribunals were not guided by any recognised law of the land, nor by the ordinary rules of evidence. They simply existed to carry into effect the royal will. They could summon any person before them, and inflict fines, imprisonment or mutilation.

107   *The Laudian Persecution*

Still, these proceedings did not directly affect a large proportion of the population, and there were no newspapers to focus public opinion on grievances. What did come home to everybody throughout the length and breadth of the land was the alteration in the character of the Church of England ; for in those days people went to church as a matter of course, and religion played a vital part in their lives. The dominant feeling in the country was Puritan. As we have already seen (§ 92), this does not mean that most Englishmen wanted to abolish the Prayer Book and the the Bishops, or that they went about in sombre clothes with upturned eyes, or that they looked upon singing and dancing as wicked. It means that people on the whole thought more of the Bible than of Sacraments, and felt a direct responsibility for their lives to " the Great Taskmaster." But the inclinations of the King were entirely in the opposite direction. The man whom he took as his chief adviser in ecclesiastical matters was what would to-day be called a High Churchman. William Laud (1573-1644), who became Archbishop of Canterbury in 1633, was a ritualist and disciplinarian. He was a great supporter of the Royal supremacy and of the authority of the Bishops. He insisted upon the sacred character of the clergy and of Church buildings ; he required elaborate vestments to be worn ; he discouraged unauthorised preaching ; he had Communion Tables moved to the east end of churches, and railed off. To many people all this seemed like introducing the Mass into the Anglican Church. It is hardly to be wondered at that an increasing number of earnest Protestants began to stay away from the parish churches in which they saw these innovations carried out, and began to attend Puritan " conventicles," despite the severe penalties to which they thereby rendered themselves liable.

Laud was a man of upright character, of immense industry, and of genuine zeal. Amongst other activities, he organised a *Metropolitan Visitation :* that is to say, every parish in his Province was visited by himself or by some Church dignitary appointed by him, to see that the incumbent was carrying out his regulations. He was also president of the *Court of High Commission*, which enforced uniformity and silenced criticism by fines and imprisonment. He even went so far as to insist upon the right of parish clergy to inquire into and punish immorality amongst their flock. It really seemed as if the clergy were about to resume their pre-Reformation position of privilege.

What made matters worse from the Puritan's point of view was that while men were punished for being too Protestant, Roman Catholics were getting off scot free. This was chiefly owing to the influence of the Queen. Since the death of Buckingham, Henrietta Maria had won the chief place in her husband's affections, and he could deny her nothing. To please her he allowed a papal agent to appear at her Court, and Mass to be celebrated publicly in her chapel. The archbishop, who, to do him justice, was no respecter of persons, tried more than once to stop this sort of thing and to put the anti-Catholic laws in motion, but he was prevented by the King. We know to-day that Charles and his archbishop were both sincere Protestants, but it is not surprising that rumours spread that they were paving the way for a reconciliation of the Anglican Church with Rome.

108. *A New England for Puritans*

The greatest and most lasting result of Laud's crusade against Puritanism was one which never entered his head : nothing less than the supremacy of the Anglo-Saxon race in North America.

In the reign of James I two distinct types of settlement had already been established there. (1) Despite the failure of all Raleigh's attempts to colonise Virginia, a third Virginia Company was formed in 1606. The new enterprise might well have failed like its predecessors had it not been for the energy and personal magnetism of a romantic adventurer named John Smith. The first critical years safely passed, the important discovery was made that a great demand was growing up in Europe for tobacco, and that the soil and climate of Virginia were ideal for the cultivation of this crop. The younger sons of English country gentlemen with a taste for adventure took up grants of land for tobacco-plantations, built themselves spacious manor-houses and transported into the New World the habits and outlook of the English " squire." In 1624 the first colonial government was set up at Richmond, with a Governor appointed by the King and a Legislative Assembly elected by the " freeholders."

(2) Farther north a contrasting type of civilisation was established in 1620. That small minority of Puritans who wished to set up separate congregations, independent of the authority of the national Church, had been persecuted into exile in the later days of Elizabeth. These " Brownists " had mostly taken refuge in Holland, where a Protestant Republic had now been set up as the outcome of the Revolt of the Netherlands. The numbers of the little band increased when James I showed that he was determined " to harry Puritanism out of the land " (§ 92). As time went on, the leading spirits among the exiles began to fear that if they remained in Holland their younger generation would become absorbed in the Dutch nation. They therefore determined to transport the whole party, men, women and children, across the Atlantic, to start life afresh in the New World. The " Pilgrim Fathers " sailed first of all to Plymouth, where they made their final preparations. Thence they set out in the " Mayflower " in August, 1620. They had intended to settle in Virginia, but the winds carried them farther to the north, and it was on the less hospitable shores of Cape Cod that they eventually landed. Terrible hardships were endured during the first few years, but the staunch spirit of English Puritanism enabled the survivors to wrest a precarious living from the soil.

Still, the tiny settlement at New Plymouth would have made very slow progress if it had not been reinforced during the 'thirties by a new wave of emigration. When the Laudian persecution began to make life in England very difficult for earnest Puritans, a number of them got together and decided to follow the example of the Pilgrim Fathers. A " Company of Massachusetts Bay " was organised, and in 1630 a carefully selected band of 2,000 settlers was sent out. They built a township which they called Boston, in the neighbourhood of which most of them settled down to agriculture. In the course of the next ten years they were followed by 20,000 more, and by 1640 this " New England " was doing a thriving trade with the Old. A large proportion of the new settlers were men of education and substance, whose emigration was impelled solely by religious zeal. They set up a sort of Bible Commonwealth in which their own particular type of worship was enforced quite as intolerantly as Laud was enforcing at home the Anglo-Catholicism from which they fled. The King placed no obstacle in their way. Perhaps he was glad to be rid of such troublesome people. The emigration certainly removed some of the most obstinate opponents of the campaign for uniformity of worship. But the real significance of the movement was that it established in America a solid nucleus of Englishmen fitted by numbers, character and traditions to resist the encroachments of France during the conflicts of the next hundred years.

109. Wentworth and his "Thorough"

We have not yet mentioned the name which is always most closely associated with the absolutist experiment of King Charles. It is that of *Thomas Wentworth* (1593–1641). He was a Yorkshire gentleman who, shocked at the misgovernment of Buckingham, had supported Eliot in the agitation to bring the ascendancy of the favourite to an end. But, unlike Eliot, he had no faith in parliamentary government. He did not believe that five hundred squires and merchants could have the necessary knowledge and experience of affairs to govern a country. That was the business of the King, assisted by expert ministers. Therefore, when Parliament made an attempt to keep a permanent hold over the Executive, he had gone over to the King's side in the dispute, and soon after this Buckingham was murdered.

In 1629 Charles made him President of the Council of the North (§ 28). In the position of a pro-consul ruling in the name of the King half a dozen counties still in a state of semi-civilisation, Wentworth displayed a remarkable genius for administration. His was a quick, clear, definite type of mind. He had unlimited self-confidence, and showed neither fear nor favour. Magistrates were called to strict account for their proceedings ; abuses, slackness and irregularity were put down with a firm hand.

In 1633 he was sent to Ireland, to re-organise the government of that unhappy country. The Irish had already been embittered by attacks on their religion and the confiscation of their land. The most extensive and systematic of these " plantations " had been made by James I, who had established a colony of his thrifty fellow-countrymen in Ulster. This added yet another element of confusion, for these Scots were staunch Presbyterians, who had as little use for the Church of England as they had for the Church of Rome. Wentworth set out to make the country a source of wealth for the King's treasury and of soldiers for his army. He started the linen industry, established fisheries, and improved the breed of the native cattle. As at York, so in Dublin he showed himself no respecter of persons. He bullied juries into giving verdicts for the Crown, he harried the Scottish dissenters, he haled great landlords before the Castle Court. He put the interests of the State far above those of any individual—far above even those of personal honour. A parliament summoned in 1634 was promised the redress of certain grievances in return for a subsidy. The subsidy granted, the redress was only half carried out, and the Irish found, not for the first or the last time, that English governments were not to be trusted to deal fairly by Ireland.

This was the conception of government which Wentworth, in writing to his friend Laud, called by the name of " Thorough ": an autocratic government that is ruthless, independent of public opinion—but efficient. It was much the same policy that Richelieu was carrying into effect with such success in France at about the same time. It is probable that if Wentworth had been given the position of authority in the English Government that Richelieu enjoyed in the French he might have prolonged the personal rule of the King indefinitely. Fortunately for English liberties, however, Charles was too poor a judge of men to realise the minister's abilities until it was too late—as we shall see.

110. *A Rising Tide*

It must not be supposed that during this decade the English were a nation groaning under oppression. On the contrary, the country had never been so prosperous. Peace, with the rest of Europe torn by war, meant a steady growth of material wealth, while taxation was lighter than in any other country of the civilised world. Many people disliked the changes in the Church, some were harried for stopping away from it, but nobody was in danger of his life for conscience' sake. There were no rebellions such as had repeatedly broken out in the previous century. Sir John Eliot died in the Tower rather than apologise for his conduct in the last Parliament, and two of his comrades remained there for the whole period of Personal Rule; but nobody seemed to mind, or to sympathise with these men as martyrs for the national liberties. It was not until 1638 that any demonstration of resentment was made against the savage punishments inflicted by the Star Chamber on perfectly respectable citizens for the crime of criticising the Government. In that year Prynne, a lawyer, Bastwick, a physician, and Burton, a clergyman, were sentenced to have their ears cut off in the pillory, to pay fines of £5,000, and to solitary confinement for life, for an attack on the High Church bishops. When the mutilation was carried out the crowd round the scaffold manifested its sympathies in no uncertain fashion, and the Government had to hurry the victims off to remote prisons in Jersey, Guernsey and Scilly Isles.

This was almost the only instance of a public demonstration of hostility to the Government, but much anxious discussion of public affairs was going on among the educated classes, who alone realised the gravity of the situation. The traditional rights of the nation seemed to be fading away as the years went by. For instance, it had long been the Englishman's boast that he was entitled to trial in a public court, by the known law of the land, with a jury of his fellow-citizens to decide as to his guilt; but the Government was bringing more and more cases before such courts as the Star Chamber and the High Commission, in which accused persons had none of these safeguards. For in these " Prerogative Courts " the King was regarded as the author of all Law, and therefore above it , whereas it was the English tradition that the Law was independent of the King, and alterable only by Parliament.

Even more serious was the fact that the King seemed to be making himself financially free from parliamentary control.   It was to hinder this disaster that in 1637 a Buckinghamshire gentleman named *John Hampden* determined to resist the collection of Ship Money.   He did not deny that the money was well spent—the Navy had been rebuilt and the pirates chased out of the Channel ; he did not complain that the tax bore heavily on individuals—even a well-to-do man like himself was only assessed at 20s.   Neither of these circumstances affected the fundamental issue.   What Hampden was challenging was the lawfulness of unparliamentary taxation.   The King allowed the matter to be brought before the ordinary law courts, for at that time any judge could be dismissed who incurred the royal displeasure, and Charles was confident that he could get the decision he wanted.   He was right.   Of the twelve judges, only four decided in Hampden's favour.   One of the majority went so far as to lay it down that any Act of Parliament which restricted the King's right to defend the realm by any means he chose and at whatever cost to any of his subjects, was null and void.

So John Hampden was called upon to pay his twenty shillings (with costs), and the King took care that the victory of the Treasury should be well advertised.   Yet in the end it did his cause more harm than good.   In a thousand manor-houses and merchants' parlours men asked each other, " What has become of Magna Charta and the Petition of Right, if the King can levy taxes at his own will and pleasure, under pretext—even at a time of profound peace—that it is for the defence of the realm ?   Won't he next raise an army by the same means, to keep his people in subjection like the King of France ?   If this decision is good law there need never be another Parliament at Westminster ! "

Still, it was difficult to see what was to be done about it ; and it is quite possible that years might have passed with nothing done at all, if the King had not now committed a signal act of folly which caused his hardly-won position to collapse like a house of cards.

QUESTIONS

(1) *How did the King set about the establishment of his " Personal Rule " ?*

(2) *Explain Wentworth's views on government.*

CHAPTER XXIII

The Day of Reckoning

(1638–1642)

The King's reckless resolve to force episcopacy on the Scots led to his being compelled to call a Parliament again, after eleven years of autocratic rule. This Parliament took advantage of his necessities to compel him to consent to measures designed to prevent any repetition of that rule. The High Church system of Laud was also swept away, but there was no agreement as to how far Puritanism was to be established in its place ; nor could members agree as to whether the King was to be entrusted with the control of the armed forces of the Crown. It was upon these issues that the Civil War broke out.

III. *The First Bishops' War*

In those days the national life of Scotland was separated from that of England by two hundred miles of barren moorland, and the Scottish people had a very distinct national character of their own. For one thing, they were intensely attached to the extremest sort of democratic Calvinism. James I, being himself a Scotsman, had understood this. Eagerly as he supported the Episcopal Church in England (" No Bishop, no King ! "), he had not ventured to interfere with the presbyterian form of Church government in Scotland, beyond appointing a few bishops who were often ignored by their clergy. His son, on the other hand, knew little and cared less about the Scottish national temperament. Laud paid a visit to Edinburgh in 1633, and reported to the King that the Scots had " no religion." This, of course, was an absurd thing to say. The Scots were the most intensely religious people in the world ; but to men like

223

PURITANISM VICTORIOUS

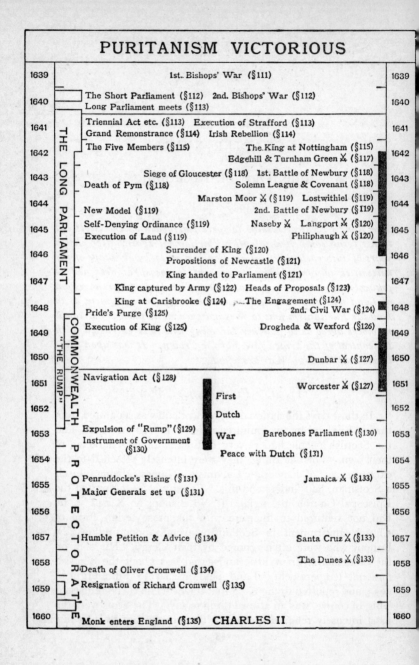

1639	1st. Bishops' War (§111)	**1639**
1640	The Short Parliament (§112) 2nd. Bishops' War (§112) Long Parliament meets (§113)	**1640**
1641	Triennial Act etc. (§113) Execution of Strafford (§113) Grand Remonstrance (§114) Irish Rebellion (§114)	**1641**
1642	The Five Members (§115) The King at Nottingham (§115) Edgehill & Turnham Green ⚔ (§117)	**1642**
1643	Siege of Gloucester (§118) 1st. Battle of Newbury (§118) Death of Pym (§118) Solemn League & Covenant (§118)	**1643**
1644	Marston Moor ⚔ (§119) Lostwithiel (§119) New Model (§119) 2nd. Battle of Newbury (§119)	**1644**
1645	Self-Denying Ordinance (§119) Naseby ⚔ Langport ⚔ (§120) Execution of Laud (§119) Philiphaugh ⚔ (§120)	**1645**
1646	Surrender of King (§120) Propositions of Newcastle (§121)	**1646**
1647	King handed to Parliament (§121) King captured by Army (§122) Heads of Proposals (§123)	**1647**
1648	King at Carisbrooke (§124) The Engagement (§124) Pride's Purge (§125) 2nd. Civil War (§124)	**1648**
1649	Execution of King (§125) Drogheda & Wexford (§126)	**1649**
1650	Dunbar ⚔ (§127)	**1650**
1651	Navigation Act (§128) Worcester ⚔ (§127)	**1651**
1652	First Dutch	**1652**
1653	Expulsion of "Rump" (§129) War Barebones Parliament (§130) Instrument of Government (§130)	**1653**
1654	Peace with Dutch (§131)	**1654**
1655	Penruddocke's Rising (§131) Jamaica ⚔ (§133) Major Generals set up (§131)	**1655**
1656		**1656**
1657	Humble Petition & Advice (§134) Santa Cruz ⚔ (§133)	**1657**
1658	The Dunes ⚔ (§133) Death of Oliver Cromwell (§134)	**1658**
1659	Resignation of Richard Cromwell (§135)	**1659**
1660	Monk enters England (§135) **CHARLES II**	**1660**

THE LONG PARLIAMENT · COMMONWEALTH · "THE RUMP" · PROTECTOR ... ATE

Laud and his master, " religion " was bound up with the Prayer Book, altars and vestments, and a hierarchy of Bishops, Deans and Canons. Within the next few years they introduced several reforms to bring the Scottish Church more into line with the English. These aroused fierce opposition, and any sensible ruler would have seen the red light ahead. But Charles had no sense when it came to dealing with his fellow men. In 1637 a special edition of the English Prayer Book was sent down, all ready printed, for the Scottish churches. The first attempt to use it in St. Giles', Edinburgh, caused a riot in which a woman threw a stool at the Dean's head, and the building had to be cleared by the Town Guard. Similar disturbances occurred all over the country : the Scottish people simply would not have that Prayer Book. Nobles, townsfolk, clergy, peasants, all pressed forward to sign a *National Covenant*, pledging themselves " to labour by all means lawful to recover the purity of the Gospel as it was established before the recent innovations."

The King had no means of coping with the situation, and was forced to gain time by summoning a General Assembly of the Kirk to meet at Glasgow. That Assembly expressed profound respect for him, but ignored all his wishes. It abolished every vestige of episcopacy from Scotland. To accept this decision seemed to Charles to be an abdication of powers which had been entrusted to him by God. After spending nearly a year in fruitless negotiations with the covenanters, he determined that they must be brought to their senses by force of arms.

Yet it was not easy to see how this was to be done. There was no army, and no money with which to raise one. The King at last determined to revive long-forgotten feudal rights and summon all landowners in the north of England to come to his aid with their tenants. But it was a ludicrous array that assembled in response to his call. The officers—that is to say, the nobles and gentry—did not want to beat the Scots, for they realised that this would encourage the King in his personal rule ; while the rank and file neither understood nor cared anything about the quarrel they were engaged in—they simply wanted to get back home. There was no money, no commissariat, no organisation.

The " enemy," on the other hand, were in fine fettle. For

centuries it had been the custom for young Scotsmen to become soldiers of fortune in foreign service, and the Thirty Years' War was just at this time offering unlimited scope for such careers. Thousands now flocked back, highly trained soldiers, eager to fight for their religion. As the two forces lay side by side at Berwick the disparity in efficiency and discipline made all thought of coming to blows impossible. The Scottish commander, one Alexander Leslie, a veteran who had fought campaigns under the great Gustavus Adolphus, was too shrewd to arouse English national feeling by "making up for Flodden." He readily agreed to the King's proposal that the questions at issue should be referred to another General Assembly (*Treaty of Berwick*, 1639).

112. *Strafford to the Rescue*

Of course, Charles was not sincere in making this "treaty." He merely wanted to gain time to coerce the Scots more effectively. Now—all too late, as it proved—he sent for Wentworth, made him Earl of Strafford, and put him in charge of affairs. Obviously, the first thing to do was to get money, and Strafford advised the King to take the bull by the horns and summon Parliament. He anticipated that the general dislike of Scotsmen would rally the nation to the support of the King ; and, accustomed in Ireland to quelling parliamentary opposition by sheer force of character, he did not see why he should not do the same thing in England.

He quickly found that he was mistaken, however. The classes represented in the two Houses of Parliament were just the people who had suffered most from the King's irregular taxation, and who best realised the threat to the constitution that was involved in his proceedings. When they met, it was at once apparent that their indignation at the past eleven years of unconstitutional government blotted every other consideration out of their minds. They utterly declined to grant any money until their grievances had been redressed, and within three weeks "*The Short Parliament*" had been dissolved in anger by the King. But the situation could never again be what it had been before it had met. Men from all parts of the country had come together

for the first time since 1629. They discovered that their resentment was shared by the whole nation ; and they went back
home to discuss their grievances more eagerly than ever with
their neighbours. The Scots, moreover, were greatly encouraged
to find that the English people were as hostile to the King's
policy as they were themselves.

What was Charles to do now ? He tried all sorts of wild
schemes for raising money. The City refused to lend him a
penny, and so did the East India Company. With an utter
lack of self-respect, this Protestant king applied both to the
Pope and to the King of Spain for assistance in suppressing his
own too-Protestant subjects ; but neither of these potentates
would do anything for him. His only success was in Ireland.
Strafford crossed thither, summoned a Parliament, and by hinting
to the Catholics that they should be let loose on the Scottish
Ulstermen, obtained a subsidy with which to raise an Irish army.

Still, a year or more might elapse before this would be fit for
service, and the King made an attempt to raise another
militia-force in England. This time they were scraped together
in the southern counties, by means of the press-gang. The
farther north this wretched rabble marched, the more disorganised it became ; and when the re-assembled Scottish army
crossed the Tweed into England (August, 1640), it was unable to
offer the smallest resistance. Even Strafford was compelled
to advise that an armistice be accepted, By the *Treaty of Ripon*
the Scots were to be paid for their time and trouble in invading
England, at the rate of £850 a day, and they were to remain in
possession of Northumberland and Durham at the King's
expense until the money was paid. So ended *The Second
Bishops' War*.

The King's position was now desperate indeed. As a last
hope of avoiding the ruin that the assembling of another Parliament would bring to all his policy, he summoned a Great
Council of the Peers (yet another medieval expedient) to meet
at York ; but the peers could or would do nothing beyond
advising him to call Parliament forthwith.

113. *The End of "Thorough"*

Almost the whole of the last Parliament was re-elected, and the members came back to Westminster (November, 1640) in an angry and determined mood. The most experienced parliamentarian in the Commons was *John Pym* (1584–1643), and the House quickly learned to look to him for leadership in the struggle that lay before them. Pym was not a great constructive statesman, but the circumstances did not call for such. What was wanted was a clear-headed, resolute, courageous man, who could inspire others with a determination to do their duty ; and all this Pym was.

The King requested an immediate grant to relieve his most urgent needs ; but the House realised that they had him at their mercy until the Scots were paid off, and they were determined to use their advantage not merely to gain redress for their immediate grievances, but to root out the causes of them.

Their first task of all was to strike down Strafford. It was a compliment to the force of the man's personality that Parliament did not feel safe so long as he was alive. He had been very reluctant to put his head into the lion's mouth by coming to London ; but Charles needed his support and (always very ready to make promises when he wanted anything) had guaranteed his safety. He at once advised the King to put the leading members of the Commons under lock and key, in defiance of their parliamentary privileges ; but his enemies were too quick for him. The day after Parliament met, Pym moved that he should be impeached, the message was at once carried to the Lords, and the Lords ordered his arrest pending his trial. Laud was also imprisoned, while several other ministers of the Personal Rule fled abroad.

In March (1641) Strafford's trial for High Treason took place, with the House of Lords acting as judges, in Westminster Hall. Pym was the chief spokesman for the prosecution, but it soon became obvious that he had a very weak case. High Treason means conspiring against the King, and everybody knew that the prisoner had served the King not wisely but too well. Pym urged that treason was an offence not against the King's person, but against the King as representative of the commonwealth ; and he argued that by making Charles too powerful, Strafford had made him unpopular. But much as the Lords hated the prisoner for his high-handed dealings with them, they realised that they were there to say whether an accusation had been made out ; and it was evidently impossible for them to condemn him on such specious arguments as these. The King and his court, seated behind a grid, were delighted at the discomfiture of their opponents, and even the prisoner's haughty face relaxed into a grim smile. They little knew the temper of the Commons. A majority of the House determined to make sure of destroying their enemy by dropping the impeachment in favour of a Bill of Attainder (§ 25). This tyrannical evasion of the Englishman's right to a fair and open trial had been invented at the time of the Wars of the Roses and had been much used by Henry VIII. Pym and Hampden were entirely opposed to its being brought into use in this case ; they were convinced that they could get a condemnation on the impeachment. But the House would take no risks. The Attainder was rushed through and sent up to the Upper House. The Lords had much less objection to passing an Act of Attainder as one of the Houses of Parliament than they had to bringing in a false verdict when they were acting as a Court of Justice. And whatever hesitation they may have felt was brought to an end by news of a plot, said to have been instigated by the Queen herself, among the officers of the King's army at York, by which they were to march to London and bring Parliament to its senses by force of arms. This was the last straw, and the Bill was passed forthwith. It still required the royal assent, and Strafford was confident that, after all that had passed, the King would never give it. But Charles had always left public opinion out of his calculations, and it now swept him away. Howling mobs gathered round Whitehall Palace demanding the blood of the condemned man, and after a day and a night of anguish the King gave way. " Put not your trust in princes," said Strafford, when he heard the news. He was beheaded on Tower Hill (May, 1641) before a tremendous crowd of people exulting in the end of " Black Tom the Tyrant."

With him fell the whole system of government that he stood for. The Houses began with an Act which said that they could not be dissolved without their own consent.   By the Triennial Act, Parliament was in future to meet at least once in three years. If the King did not summon it, the Lord Chancellor was to do so, and if that officer failed in his duty, the sheriffs of the counties were to hold the elections on their own initiative.   Distraint of Knighthood, Enlargement of Forest Rights, Ship Money, were all declared illegal.   The Prerogative Courts were all abolished. Parliament was practically unanimous in passing all these reforms, and the King accepted them without demur.   What else could he do ?   And besides, what did it matter ?   A time would come . . .

Thus, in July Parliament could feel that English liberties were saved.   They paid off the Scots and sent them home, and adjourned until the autumn.

114. *A Breach Opens*

If Parliament had been as unanimous upon all subjects as it was upon those just described, there would have been no Civil War. Unfortunately, signs of division had already appeared when the question of a Church settlement came up for discussion.   All were agreed that the High Church practices of Laud must be swept away ;   but whereas some wished that in future the authority of bishops should be limited by an assembly of their clergy, others were for a purely presbyterian form of Church government. The latter party brought in what was called *The Root and Branch Bill* for " the utter abolition of Archbishops, Bishops, Archdeacons, Deans, Prebendaries and Canons."   This was supported by most of the leading men, such as Pym and Hampden, but was opposed by a minority which included Falkland and Hyde.   It was never actually brought to a division, but in the debate on it the two sides in the coming contest began to take shape.

The struggle was postponed by the adjournment of the Houses and the departure of the King on a visit to Scotland (August, 1641).   This visit was a shrewd move.   Charles pacified opposition in his northern kingdom by giving way on all matters of Church organisation, and soon succeeded in forming a strong party, especially among the nobles who, when once they were satisfied on these points, were full of devotion to their Stuart king. A reaction in his favour began to take place in England, too. When once grievances have been removed, people soon forget them, and old loyalties quickly reassert themselves. As Charles journeyed back through the country, he was warmly greeted everywhere, and his reception in the City of London was enthusiastic. On the re-assembly of Parliament, Pym and his friends felt that if they were not very careful all the safeguards that they had erected might be swept away. Then a terrible event in Ireland brought about a crisis. The religious animosities which Strafford's recent visit had re-awakened culminated in the Catholics breaking out into rebellion and massacring thousands of English and Scottish Protestants. Bad as the deed was, it was much exaggerated by rumour. Indefinite but enormous numbers of men, women and children were said to have been done to death with every sort of atrocity. All parties in Parliament were agreed that an army must be raised to put the revolt down, and money was promptly voted for the purpose. But the question at once arose : who was to control the forces thus raised ? That had always been the duty and the privilege of the King ; but was Charles to be trusted with such power ? His minister was known to have been in close touch with these very Irish Catholics only a year before, and the leaders of the rebellion claimed that they were acting by royal authority. Moreover, there was no guarantee that the King would not use the army to disperse the Parliament by force, sweep away all concessions and establish a despotism ten times worse than before. Once more a sharp division appeared in the Commons. Those who were for moderate measures in Church government were for trusting the King : such men as Hyde and Falkland were convinced that he had now seen the error of his former ways. In any case, they asked, who ever heard of an army under the control of a Parliament ?

By a small majority a Bill was passed which provided that the forces were to be commanded by " persons in whom the House had confidence " ; but even Pym felt that such a novel measure must be justified by a statement of the reasons for it. He therefore drew up the *Grand Remonstrance* from the Commons to the King, in which all the misdeeds of the Government since the beginning of the reign were recalled in exaggerated and sometimes misleading words. The debate on this document was one of the most famous in the history of Parliament. All day long and for half the night it went on, and much bitter language was used. When at last a vote was taken, the Remonstrance was approved by a majority of eleven. The division into parties was now clear-cut, definite and undeniable.

115. *Cavalier and Roundhead*

The last half of 1641 had seen a marked improvement in the King's position. He had made a strong party in Scotland, London had greeted him with acclamation, and the vote on the Grand Remonstrance had shown that half the members even of the House of Commons believed him worthy of confidence. He had only to show by deed as well as word that he was worthy of that confidence, and he would have paralysed the opposition altogether. But he now took a step which seemed to prove that his enemies were right and his friends wrong as to his character. He resolved to charge five leading members of Parliament (including Pym and Hampden) with attempting to overthrow the constitution and with carrying on treasonable negotiations with the Scots. Accompanied by a disorderly mob of officers from the army which had been recently disbanded at York, he came down to the Parliament to arrest them in person. The House had heard what he intended and had sent the threatened members down the river to take refuge in the City. Leaving his followers at the door, Charles strode up the floor of the Commons and asked where the culprits were. Finding that, as he said, "the birds had flown," and that their fellow-members were determined not to give them up, he returned baffled to the Palace.

Once more had Charles grievously injured his cause by carelessness of public opinion. There was a good deal of justification for his charges against the five members; they had certainly gone much nearer the general idea of "treason" than Strafford ever had, and they were now thinking of impeaching the Queen herself. But by attempting to take the law into his own hands, surrounded by swaggering bullies with drawn swords and cocked pistols, he had given a hint of the violent measures he would take if he got the chance. The City of London turned definitely against him. It treated the five members as honoured guests, and two days later they were taken back to Westminster in triumph, escorted by the train-bands, while 4,000 freeholders came up from Buckinghamshire to protect their beloved Hampden from harm.

Rather than witness the triumph of his enemies the King had already set out for Windsor. Open war was now in sight. The next eight months were spent in an exchange of angry documents on the subjects in dispute ; but the fundamental question was : Who was to rule England ? Neither side could give way without sacrificing all that it held sacred. Simultaneously, each party began to collect fighting forces. Despite the King's mistakes, quite two-thirds of the House of Lords and at least one-third of the Commons left London rather than join in levying war against him, and many of these volunteered to serve him in the coming contest. The most notable of these recruits was Edward Hyde, who all through the troubles that followed acted as his chief counsellor. The Queen crossed to the Continent with the Crown Jewels, on the security of which she obtained a supply of arms and ammunition. Parliament raised an army of 10,000 men " for the defence of both Houses of Parliament, and of those who have obeyed their commands, and preserving the true religion, the laws, liberty and peace of the kingdom." On August 22, 1642, the King raised his standard at Nottingham, and the Civil War had begun.

QUESTIONS

(1) *How far was the Civil War due to* (a) *weaknesses in character, and* (b) *errors in judgment, on the part of the King ?*

(2) *Which side would you have taken in the war, and why ?*

CHAPTER XXIV

War

(1642–1646)

The King began the war with every prospect of speedy victory, and for a long time it appeared as if an ultimate success for his cause was inevitable. Then the scale was turned against him, partly by the intervention of the Scots, but chiefly by Parliament's superior resources in " the sinews of war."

116. Some General Ideas

Our English Civil War was in several respects unique among such contests.

For one thing, only a very small proportion of the nation took part in it. Only once was an army of as many as 25,000 assembled, and then only for a few days ; nor were there at any time more than about two per cent. of the nation under arms. The bulk of the population did not take sufficient interest in the causes at stake to be willing to risk life and limb for them, and regarded the whole thing as a nuisance. Still, all the men of light and leading in the nation were engaged on one side or the other, and there was therefore nobody to focus any " stop-the-war " demand from the less enterprising.

It was not a war between sharply-divided districts. On the whole, the north and west were for the King, and the south and east for the Parliament, but in almost every county there was a considerable minority that favoured the less popular side.

Nor was it a war between distinct social classes. Certainly, most of the nobility and gentry were royalists ; for although the King's political and ecclesiastical ideas had offended many of them, yet all this seemed now a thing of the past ; and many, even of those who tended to Puritanism, were unwilling to submit to the rule of the extremists in the Commons who talked of abolishing the Church of England altogether. Moreover, loyalty to the Crown—expressed by the motto, " Fear God and Honour the King "—was bred in the bone of the country families.* The business men, on the other hand, and the yeomen farmers were mostly for the Parliament ; for these classes contained the bulk of the ultra-Protestants who had been offended by Laud's innovations and persecutions. Yet there were always plenty of exceptions to the general rule, and members of the same family were often engaged on different sides. The only section of the community that was unanimous was the Catholics, who knew well enough what they had to expect if the Puritans gained control over the State.

On the whole, it was a humane war. Quarter was almost invariably given to the beaten side in an encounter. A good deal of plundering went on, but there was little of the wanton destruction and outrage such as was devastating wide districts in Germany. After all, the combatants were men of one blood and speech ; families and friendships were divided ; and both sides were struggling, not to destroy England, but to make their views prevail in English hearts.

A great deal of the fighting was carried on, not by organised armies engaged in large plans of campaign, but by small parties acting as mounted infantry, who were concerned with purely local objects. Such " troops of horse " were often raised by public-spirited " gentlemen-colonels " and taught to fight by professional " lieutenants " who had learnt their business in the foreign wars.

In the early stages of the war, the King had several notable advantages over his opponents. Cavalry was much more important than infantry in those days of unenclosed fields, when foot-soldiers were armed either with clumsy pikes or with

---

* The feelings of the Puritan country gentleman at the crisis were well expressed by Sir Edmund Verney, in a letter written just as the war broke out. " I have eaten the King's bread and served him near 30 years, and will not do so base a thing as to desert him ; and choose rather to lose my life—which I am sure I shall do—to defend those things which are against my conscience to defend. For . . . I have no reverence for Bishops, for whom this quarrel subsists." The writer was killed defending the Royal Standard at the first battle of Newbury.

muskets that required several minutes to load ; and the gentle-men who flocked to the royal standard, followed by their grooms and gamekeepers, were ready-made horsemen and swordsmen. Moreover, the family plate which they sent in to be melted down for the King's service was more immediately available than the commercial assets of the parliamentarian classes.

But Parliament had several countervailing advantages of its own, which became increasingly valuable as time went on. Firstly, it had the support of London and the south-east— always the centre of ultra-Protestantism (§ 45). London was already one of the most important financial centres of the world, and the south-eastern counties the most populous and prosperous parts of the country. Thus the Houses were able to collect regular taxes ; whereas the wealth of the cavaliers consisted mostly of agricultural rents which almost ceased during the war. Secondly, the seafaring classes were still sturdily Puritan, and they never forgave the neglect of the navy during the first thirty years of Stuart rule. Sea-power was from the first in the hands of the Parliament ; and the commerce of London (seven-eighths of that of all England) went on undis-turbed, while the King's communications with the Continent were precarious in the extreme.

117. 1642 : *Edgehill and Turnham Green*

Parliament chose the Earl of Essex to command its forces. Essex was a high-minded, faithful-hearted Puritan, who had gained some practical experience of warfare on the Continent ; but he lacked the fighter's instinct for attack, and his actions were always hampered by his instinctive loyalty to the throne. If he had led his 20,000 men promptly to Nottingham, he could have dispersed the King's slowly-gathering forces at a blow, and the war would have been over almost before it had begun. But he dallied on the way, and was probably relieved when Charles moved off into the West Country. There Puritanism was almost unknown, and the royalist army swelled in numbers daily. An effective body of cavalry had already been got together by Prince Rupert, son of the Electress Palatine, who had come over to take up arms for his uncle. Rupert was only twenty-three years of age, and had seen but one campaign in Germany; but his high rank, his quick intelligence, and his spirited temperament made him an ideal leader of gentlemen-cavaliers in days when battles were often decided by headlong charges of gallant horsemen.

The King now felt strong enough to make a move on London, and Essex was compelled to make a counter-move to cut him off. Near *Edgehill*, on the borders of Warwickshire, the two armies came into conflict. Rupert's charge was irresistible, and he chased the forces opposed to him for miles across country. The Parliamentarian infantry stood firm, however, and Charles decided not to renew the attack on the morrow. He pushed on to Oxford, which remained his headquarters for the rest of the war. It was an advanced point, far in front of his three main recruiting-grounds (Devon and Cornwall, the Welsh border, and the north country); but it was an excellent spot from which to launch an attack on London, which was always his main objective. He now stayed there just long enough to reorganise his forces, and then moved forward on the capital. Essex had already returned thither with his men, but the City Fathers were not a little panic-stricken at the approach of the royal army. The train-bands were mustered, and thousands of journeymen and apprentices seized what weapons they could come by, and poured out to *Turnham Green*. The King stopped short when he came in sight of the defence force. What might have happened if battle had been joined it is impossible to say; but Charles felt a dilemma similar to that which had earlier in the campaign stayed the hand of Essex : he could not bring himself to order an attack on his capital defended by his own subjects. After hesitating for twenty-four hours, he retired into winter-quarters at Oxford, and the university town was the scene of much gallantry and gaiety, some duels, and a good deal of discussion as to what was to be done with the Parliament dogs as soon as the spring made campaigning again possible.

118. 1643 : *Newbury and The Covenant*

It was an excellent " general idea " that Charles and his advisers hit upon for the campaign of 1643. The three centres of royalism were to combine in a triple advance on London. The King himself, based upon the West Country and drawing levies from Wales, was to hold the attention of Lord Essex, while Sir Ralph Hopton marched from Cornwall right through the southern counties into Kent, and the Earl of Newcastle brought the northern royalists down from York. Then the three forces were to close in simultaneously upon the doomed city. There were difficulties, however. In each of these centres Parliament still held an important city, and the royalists would not march for London so long as their homes were in danger of raids from these strongholds. Lord Newcastle had shut Sir Thomas Fairfax up in Hull, but could not dislodge him therefrom; Plymouth, another parliamentarian seaport, held out obstinately against Hopton; nor did the King feel safe to move forward until he had captured Gloucester. He pressed on the siege of this city with considerable vigour, and Pym realised that if he were successful London would be in grave danger. The Londoners responded gallantly to an appeal for a special force to be sent to the *relief of Gloucester*. Shops were shut and the train-bands were mobilised under Essex and sent on a long march down the Bath Road. Their arrival compelled the King to raise the siege; but on their way back home they were attacked by the royal forces near *Newbury*. The fighting took place in enclosed country where Rupert had no room for his wild charges; and the London pikemen held their ground so firmly that the King decided to draw off and let them go their way.

During these months a force was coming into existence which was destined in the end to have a decisive effect on the fortunes of the war. *Oliver Cromwell* (1599–1658) was a Puritan country gentleman of Huntingdonshire. He had been a member of the last three parliaments, but had taken no very prominent part in their proceedings. When the war broke out he had reached his forty-third year without having heard a shot fired in anger or exerted any authority over his fellow-men beyond that of a magistrate. But from that moment he began to display genius of the highest class, both in organisation and in warfare. His resolute energy and promptitude quickly brought him to the front on the Parliamentary side in his own district; and when the House decided to group together the

THE CIVIL WARS, 1642-1651

English Miles
0 20 40 60 80 100

Land over 500 feet

Killiecrankie
Stirling
Kilsyth
Bothwell
Brig
Edinburgh
Dunbar
Philiphaugh

IRELAND

Drogheda
Dublin
Wexford

Preston
Marston
Moor
York
Warrington
Nottingham
Naseby
Worcester Edge Hill
Cropredy Bridge
Gloucester
Oxford Chalgrove
Field
London
Bristol
Newbury
Turnham Green
Langport
Winchester
Taunton
Hurst
Castle
Lostwithiel
Carisbrooke
I. of Wight

Emery Walker Ltd. sc.

eastern counties for purposes of raising troops and supplies, he soon became the leading figure in that larger field of activities. He had commanded a troop of horse (about sixty men) at Edgehill, and his experience in that one battle enabled him to put his finger on the secret of success. He realised that, in warfare as in most other matters, " it is the spirit that quickeneth the flesh profiteth nothing." Self-respecting men, who believed in pure gospel religion and loved it, would always make the best soldiers to fight for it. This was the spirit that his infectious enthusiasm breathed into the regiment of cavalry (most of them farmers' sons who provided their own horses and equipment) which he now commanded; and before long it pervaded all the fifteen thousand men of the army of the *Eastern Association.*

But the effect of all this was not yet apparent. The campaign of 1643 had seen many local successes for the King, fully two-thirds of the country was now under his control, and London was very nervous at the prospect of a sack as the result of the next year's fighting. Pym feared that if success did not come quickly to the parliamentary cause, it would be impossible to prevent the House from accepting disadvantageous terms to bring the conflict to an end. Moreover, it was suspected that Charles was negotiating right and left for foreign support—with the Pope, with the kings of France and Denmark, and even with the Irish Catholic rebels. In the circumstances it seemed advisable to accept an offer of help which had recently come from the Scots. The covenanting chiefs who had seized control of the government there had become alarmed at the turn things had taken in England. If the King won this war he would be in a position to force his detested episcopal system upon his Scottish subjects. They therefore offered to send an army to the support of Parliament, provided that the latter would agree to set up in England a Presbyterian Church " according to the word of God and the model of the best reformed churches." This under-taking was embodied in a *Solemn League and Covenant* which they laid before the House. Parliament, now that most of the supporters of the Anglican Church had joined the King, was well disposed towards a presbyterian system. It had abolished episcopacy, and had set up a council of Puritan divines (*The*

Committee of Westminster) to advise it as to a reform of the national Church.   But members were very reluctant to bind themselves to set up a Church after the Scottish model, completely free from State control, and given to interference with men's private lives (§ 52).   Nevertheless, they felt that their danger was so acute that there was nothing for it but to swallow their objections and the Covenant, and hope for the best.

This year 1643 saw the deaths of three of the most prominent figures of the early stages of the revolution.   In June, in the course of a skirmish at Chalgrove Field (not far from Oxford), John Hampden received a wound of which he died a week later, leaving a name which will always stand in history for high-souled resistance to tyranny.   Two months later the noble Falkland, torn with grief at the sight of his beloved country at war with herself, sought death in vain in the trenches before Gloucester, but found it at Newbury.   Lastly, in December died John Pym, worn out by overwork and anxiety—happily in time to be spared from seeing the degradation of the institution he had loved and served.

119. 1644: *Marston Moor and the New Model*

The immediate result of the Scottish intervention was that the King lost the advantage he had hitherto held in the northern counties.   Fairfax and his men were released from Hull, while Newcastle was himself shut up in York.   Rupert hastened up to his relief.   The parliamentary forces raised the siege at his approach ; but they had themselves been reinforced by the army of the Eastern Association under Lord Manchester (with Cromwell in command of the horse), and by the Scots under Leslie.   With these combined forces they gave battle to the Prince's army on *Marston Moor*, about eight miles from York. This was, in point of numbers, the biggest battle of the war : about 40,000 were engaged altogether.   The result was a sweeping victory for Parliament, owing chiefly to the sheer fighting quality of Cromwell's horse, and to the skill and coolness with which they were handled while the fighting was in progress. It was in this battle that Prince Rupert, with the half-affectionate familiarity of a doughty foe, coined for Cromwell the nickname which was afterwards transferred to his troopers—" Old Ironsides."

In spite of this victory, the campaign of 1644 was on the whole hardly more successful from Parliament's point of view than that of 1643. At *Copredy Bridge* the King beat off in decisive fashion an attack by Sir William Waller on Oxford. Essex made the mistake so common in this war of trying to overrun territory rather than coming to grips with the enemy's main force. He penetrated too far into the royalist south-west, was cut off at *Lostwithiel* in Cornwall, and lost his entire force. Later in the year, as the King was returning from this little campaign, Lord Manchester was sent with the Eastern Association army to cut him off; but the only result was the half-hearted engagement known as the *Second Battle of Newbury*, which allowed Charles to get safely back to Oxford.

When the fighting was over for the year, Cromwell did some very plain speaking in Parliament about the conduct of the war. " If the army be not put into another method and the war more vigorously prosecuted," he said, " the people can bear it no longer, and will enforce you to a dishonourable peace." He complained that generals like Manchester and Essex were not wholehearted about winning, and were thinking all the time about coming to terms with the King. The House listened with divided feelings. They realised that Cromwell and his men had alone stood between them and defeat in the recent campaign; but they distrusted his religious views. He had taken the Covenant, but he was far from being an orthodox Presbyterian. He was inclined to the idea that all enforcement by the State of a fixed pattern of belief was a mistake, and he encouraged his men—to the great scandal of their Presbyterian chaplains—to pray and preach according to their own notions. Up to the outbreak of the war such *Independents* (as they now came to be called) had been but a small and unpopular minority, but their ideas were now spreading rapidly among the soldiers of the Eastern Association.

Still, Parliament realised that it could not afford to break with Cromwell, and it authorised him to consult with the Committee of Both Kingdoms (a sort of Anglo-Scottish war cabinet which had recently been set up) as to the best way of reforming the army. It was decided that the least unkind way of shelving " the old gang " would be to pass a *Self-denying Ordinance* to the effect that all Members of Parliament were to resign their commissions. This would at once get rid of Essex and Manchester, since they were peers ; Cromwell would also have to resign, but there was nothing to prevent his being reappointed after a decent interval. The Committee then decided to raise a *New Model Army*, to consist of professional soldiers, regularly paid, armed and equipped ; a field-force which, unlike the train-bands and country militiamen and private troops of horse, could go anywhere and do anything. To pay for it, a new system was devised for collecting taxes monthly from all the counties under control of Parliament. The command was given to Sir Thomas Fairfax, a first-class fighting-man and the idol of his men. It was only some months later that Cromwell was appointed second-in-command ; but it was his Eastern Association troops who formed the nucleus of the new force, and their example and influence soon permeated the whole body.

The Presbyterian majority in Parliament had been forced by circumstances to give this much rope to Independency ; but they made up for it by carrying an Act of Attainder against poor old Archbishop Laud, and having him beheaded (January, 1645).

120. 1645: *Naseby and Langport*

The New Model was still in the early stages of its organisation when it was called upon to face the King's army, which, having captured Leicester, began to threaten the headquarters of the Eastern Association itself. Fairfax hastily gathered his half-trained forces and challenged the King's further progress at *Naseby*. The story of the battle was much like that of Marston Moor. Rupert's horse on one side and Cromwell's on the other swept all before them, but the superior discipline of the Ironsides enabled their commander to bring them back promptly to assist the struggling infantry.* The royalist army was

---

* Nothing gives a better idea of the spirit that won the war than Cromwell's famous letter after this battle : " When I saw the enemy draw up in gallant order towards us, and we a company of poor ignorant men, to seek

utterly destroyed, and the loss in officers was irreparable. Above all, the King's private papers fell into the hands of his enemies. They did his cause more harm than the battle itself, for they proved that he had been intriguing with foreign powers for an invasion of England.

This disaster was the beginning of the end for the King ; and some months later the New Model inflicted an equally decisive defeat on the royalists of the south-west at *Langport* in Somerset. Nevertheless, Charles was still confident that help would come from somewhere.   For some time his hopes were centred on Scotland, where the Earl of Montrose had, by supreme skill in the arts of leadership, built up an army out of the Highland clansmen by promising them a chance to harry the detested Campbells.   In August, 1645, he broke into the Lowlands and defeated the Covenanters at *Kilsyth*. But before he could rally his wild followers for an invasion of England he found to his dismay that they dispersed to carry their plunder back to their mountain fastnesses.   When the Scottish army in England sent a detachment against him, the remnants of his force were annihilated at *Philiphaugh*, and he fled abroad.

The King also cherished hopes of help from Ireland.   He sent the Earl of Glamorgan to make terms with the rebels ; but their leaders, under the influence of a papal legate named Rinuncinni, made excessive demands of independence as the price of their support.   In any case Parliament's command of the sea would have made it impossible to transport any considerable body of Irish troops to England.

All through the winter and spring detachments of the New Army were occupied in reducing isolated cities which still held out.   Fairfax took Bristol, for instance, and Cromwell took Winchester. There were several famous sieges of private houses belonging to stout-hearted royalist noblemen, such as that of Basing House, the seat of the Marquis of Winchester. But on the whole the cavaliers were not in a mood to throw away their lives and what remained of their fortunes in useless

how to order our battle—the General having commanded me to order all the horse—I could not, riding about my business, but smile out to God in praises, in assurance of victory, because God would, by things that are not, bring to naught things that are.   Of which I had great assurance, and God did it."

resistance, especially after the revelations that followed Naseby ; nor were the Roundheads disposed to refuse them honourable terms.

In April, 1646, Charles at last realised that the game was up, so far as active resistance in the field was concerned. He rode off to Southwell in Nottinghamshire and surrendered to the Scottish army there encamped.

QUESTIONS

(1) *Why did Parliament win the war ?*

(2) *Write notes on* (a) *The Scottish National Covenant ;* (b) *The Solemn League and Covenant ;* (c) *The Self-denying Ordinance ;* (d) *The New Model Army.*

CHAPTER XXV

Army versus Parliament

(1646–1649)

Scots, Parliament, and New Model had combined to bring about the defeat of the King, but these parties had conflicting aims, and such coalitions usually fall to pieces, and to loggerheads, as soon as they have achieved their immediate objects. The King was confident that he could win back all that he had lost by dexterously playing them off against each other ; but he was too clever by half. The Army became convinced that he was not to be trusted, and they used their superiority in brute force to bring about his execution.

121. *The King in the hands of the Scots*

The King had joined the Scots because he believed that they would support him in bargaining with the Parliament. He was still supremely confident that he would come out on top in the end. His belief in the righteousness of his cause was unshaken by his defeat in the war. He felt that he stood for two things divinely ordained : Kingship and Episcopacy. God had punished him (possibly for his desertion of Strafford), but would not really desert one who was fighting in His cause. In any case, he had two irresistible advantages on his side : his consent would be required for any permanent settlement, and if he held out long enough his enemies would certainly fall out amongst themselves. When, therefore, the Scots assumed that he would now admit defeat and agree to become a Presbyterian king, he merely said that was prepared to discuss the matter with them and with the Parliament. Somewhat disappointed, the Scots moved him up to Newcastle, where there would be

246

less chance of his falling into other hands while the negotiations went on.

Meanwhile, Pym and Hampden being both dead, Parliament was suffering from a lack of capable and statesman-like leadership. The Presbyterian majority were jealous of the generals of the New Army, suspicious of their support of the Independent sects, and angry at the favourable terms they had granted to individual cavalier noblemen. The fact is that the members had, suddenly and without any merit of their own, become the supreme political power in the land, and it is not surprising that they did not make wise or magnanimous use of their position. They confiscated a considerable part of the estates of all who had fought for the King; they abolished the Prayer Book and turned out thousands of Anglican clergy to make way for Presbyterian ministers. They were even more intolerant than Laud had been, for they passed ordinances threatening Unitarians with death and Baptists with imprisonment for life, and forbidding laymen to preach or expound the Scriptures.

They were anxious to come to such terms with the King as would ensure their continuance in power, and they sent him a list of proposals which are known as *The Newcastle Propositions*. The Covenant was to be enforced on the three kingdoms, Parliament was to keep control of all armed forces, and a number of royalists were to be excluded from pardon. Charles kept up a pretence of considering these conditions all through the autumn and winter of 1646. At last the Scots grew weary of the business. They were getting anxious about their arrears of pay, and they wanted to be home again. The main object of their intervention in the war had been attained, for Parliament had set up a Presbyterian Church. It was but a " lame Erastian Presbytery," they said, for the supreme control over it was to be in the hands of the Government; but it was good enough to be going on with. As for the King, they gave up all hope of bringing him to a frank and definite acceptance of their Covenant. They therefore suggested that if Parliament would pay them their arrears, they would hand him over and depart. The bargain was struck, and Charles was brought under a parliamentary guard to Holmby House in Northamptonshire. His journey thither was a triumphal procession, for the memory of his misdeeds was fading, his captivity excited sympathy, and the route lay for the most part through districts in which the royalist tradition had always been very strong. Charles was more than ever convinced that he held the winning cards in his hand.

122. *The King in the hands of Parliament*

Now that the Scots had left the country the war seemed to be really over. All that remained was for Parliament to send a part of the New Model Army to quell the Catholic Rebellion in Ireland, to disband the remainder, and to come to a definite agreement with the King (now in its own custody) for the future government of the kingdom. But here a hitch occurred. The pay of the army was several months in arrears, and the soldiers refused either to disperse or to volunteer for Ireland until they had been paid in full. It seems strange that Parliament should have expected them to do so; but the members' heads were turned by their sudden accession to power; and the fact that they were sitting in London—always strongly Presbyterian—caused them to exaggerate the amount of support they could look for, and made them feel that they could do what they liked with the other elements in the nation.

They soon found their mistake. Led by the cavalry, who were men of better standing and education than the infantry, the soldiers elected " agitators " (*i.e.* agents) to a sort of parliament of their own; and this body presented a petition to the generals to see that justice was done them. Fairfax and Cromwell endeavoured to pacify them, and pleaded with Parliament to act fairly by the men who had given it victory.

Meanwhile a new complication was arising. While these discussions were going on, the more active spirits in the Army had an opportunity to spread the gospel of Independency in the ranks. The men began to feel that the war for religious freedom would have been fought and won in vain if rigid Presbyterianism was to be its outcome. It is true that when these men spoke of religious freedom they merely meant toleration for the various types of Puritanism; nevertheless, their aim was the first step towards that liberty of opinion which is to-day one of the most cherished of our birthrights as Britons. To the orthodox Presbyterian this seemed a mixture of wickedness and madness : " If the devil had his choice whether the hierarchy, ceremonies and liturgy should be established in the kingdom, or a toleration granted, he would choose a toleration," declared a meeting of London ministers.

For a long time Cromwell tried to act as mediator between the Parliament of which he was a member and the Army of which he was a general. But he had always been a supporter of Toleration, and he was now coming to believe that the Presbyterian majority in the Houses was too narrow-minded ever to make a satisfactory settlement. Then it came to his knowledge that the parliamentary leaders were planning a sort of *coup d'état* to end the controversy with the Army at a blow. The Scots undertook to send another army into England to enforce their Covenant ; the City militia (many of whom had seen much fighting in the late war) was to be embodied ; royalist feeling was to be aroused. By these three forces the mutinous New Model was to be crushed, and a Presbyterian Monarchy was then to be set up. A necessary preliminary would be to bring the King to London, where he would be amenable to moral pressure from City and Parliament.

These revelations brought Cromwell's hesitation to an end ; he now determined that he must throw in his lot with the Army and Independency. When he had once come to this decision, he acted with characteristic promptitude and efficiency. He punctured the whole plot by suddenly sending a troop of horse (under one Cornet Joyce, never heard of before or after) to remove the King from the possession of the Parliamentary guard at Holmby House and bring him to the Army headquarters at Newmarket.

123. *The King in the hands of the Army*

The Army felt itself to be maintaining the cause of the nation at large against a usurping assembly. The possession of the King was a great advantage, and the officers now began to put stronger pressure on Parliament to obtain a broad and tolerant settlement. The " agitators " sent a demand that eleven leading

Presbyterian M.P.s (including Holles of the " Five Members " and Waller, one of the ablest Parliamentarian generals in the early part of the war) should be excluded from the House on the ground that they were making trouble. Cromwell strove to keep the soldiers' demands within moderation. " The best you can gain by consent," he warned them, " is far better than the very best gained by force." But he realised that if his resistance went too far they would break out into a revolution which might lead to appalling bloodshed and chaos. He and Fairfax (who, though nominally his superior, was wholly under his influence) therefore led their men slowly towards London. At first the City tried to adopt a defiant attitude in support of Parliament, called out the train-bands, and prepared for a siege ; but when the terrible New Model cavalry trotted in along the West Road and encamped in Hyde Park, the courage of the militiamen oozed out. Parliament gave way, and the Army retired to the neighbourhood of Putney ; but the episode had shown every one that the country was now under the shadow of a military dictatorship.

All this time Charles was thoroughly enjoying himself at Hampton Court. He found the generals much pleasanter hosts than either Scots or Parliament had been—especially as they allowed him his own Anglican chaplain. Moreover, his enemies were fulfilling his fondest expectations by coming to blows. The poor gentleman was as bad a judge of facts as he was of men. Because people stood bareheaded before him and called him " Your Majesty," he thought he was in the same position as ten years before ; and he could see little difference between the generals of the New Model Army and the Presbyterian members of Parliament : to him they were all paltry rogues whom it was positively meritorious to deceive.

The Army chiefs now brought forward their own scheme for a settlement. *The Heads of the Proposals* set forth a scheme for a constitutional monarchy with a Council of State responsible to Parliament. The Anglican Church might be re-established, but there was to be complete freedom of worship (except, of course, for Catholics). The armed forces of the realm were to be controlled by Parliament for the next ten years. These were the best terms ever offered to Charles, but he still haggled and argued. He felt that he had a better card up his sleeve, for he was in secret negotiation with the Scots, who were offering to reinstate him in his old position by force of arms, provided that he would give satisfactory assurances about the Covenant.

Meanwhile a sect of out-and-out " radicals " was growing up in the Army. " Honest John " Lilburne, who, though a gentleman born, had been flogged through the streets of London in Laud's time for refusing to acknowledge the authority of Star Chamber, had raised the question whether kings were necessary at all. He found many followers, especially in certain regiments ; and the *Levellers*, as they were called, presented a petition to the generals demanding a republic, votes for all and universal toleration. They called this *The Agreement of the People*, but it is quite certain that " the people " as a whole were still devoted to the Monarchy, and that the idea of toleration was not really popular outside the army. Here was more trouble for Cromwell—a schism within the Army itself ; and his task in dealing with it was all the more difficult because the Levellers were already very angry with him for having any dealings with the King. They said that he was betraying the Cause, and accused him of self-seeking.

At the height of the agitation, all parties were dumbfounded to learn that the King had escaped from Hampton Court and had taken refuge in the Isle of Wight. Here he was received by the Governor, who lodged him in Carisbrook Castle, hardly knowing whether to treat him as a prisoner or a guest.

124. *The King at Carisbrook*

Some have thought that Cromwell purposely allowed Charles to escape with a view to luring him to his doom, but of this there is no real evidence. As a matter of fact, the incident led to an open mutiny by the Levellers, which was only quelled by the general's matchless courage and presence of mind. Nor was there any reason why the move should have led to disaster for the King. A strong reaction in his favour had set in all over the country. People were sick of the jealous wrangling between Parliament and Army, and felt that there was no hope of a return to settled government and the pleasant customary routine of life until the King was once more head of the State. Much sympathy was felt for a captive monarch and for cavalier gentlemen fallen on evil days, and much love for the English Church whose services were now forbidden. If Charles had from this point acted with a modicum of statesmanship, or common sense, or even straightforward sincerity, he might have recovered nearly all that he had lost. But blundering deceit was still his only notion of " policy," and within a year of his arrival at Carisbrook he had completed his own ruin.

From his new retreat he began a fresh negotiation with the Scots. Preliminaries of this had begun at Hampton Court, and one of the reasons for his flight had been that his new friends required that he should be out of the hands of the Army before they would stir any further in the matter. By *The Engagement* they undertook to send an army to restore his authority, provided that he would promise to establish rigid Presbyterianism in both kingdoms for three years. Meanwhile, his emissaries were everywhere stirring up revolts against the rule of the Army. All who had supported either King or Parliament in the late war must unite to overthrow this new power that was usurping the authority of both. In the summer of 1648 revolts broke out in Wales, in Kent, and in Essex, while the Scots crossed the border, captured Carlisle, and began to march slowly through the Lake Country into Lancashire, waiting for expected reinforcements.

The Army was full of bitter wrath. The Council of Officers which met at Windsor to form a plan of campaign felt that this new disaster was the punishment of Providence upon them for having held parley with " that man of blood, Charles Stuart." Their conference opened with prayer and closed with a determination that if God allowed them to return in peace they would not rest until they had called the King to account for the bloodshed caused by his wicked plots against the peace and happiness of his people.

The campaign that followed is sometimes called *The Second Civil War*, but it seems hardly to deserve such a high-sounding name. Wherever a detachment of the New Army appeared it proved very much more than a match for the half-organised enthusiasm of the royalists. Fairfax pulverised the Kentish rising, and then swept East Anglia clear, except for Colchester, which he besieged. Cromwell made short work of the trouble in South Wales, then marched up through the midlands into Yorkshire, and threw his army across the Pennines on the Scots who were still making their way in a straggling line of march through Lancashire. The so-called battle of Preston resulted in a complete overthrow for the invaders, and it was only a miserable handful that struggled on to Warrington, where they were finally rounded up. The news of this was sufficient to compel the garrison of Colchester to surrender, and the " war " was over.

The Army chiefs now proceeded to make sure that Charles should have no further opportunity of raising trouble. As a preliminary measure, they took him from his easy confinement at Carisbrook and shut him up in Hurst Castle, a lonely fortress on a spit of land running out into the Solent, while they thought matters out.

125. *Judgment of Death*

The King half expected to be murdered at Hurst, but the men into whose hands he had fallen were not assassins. What they designed they did in the sight of Heaven, convinced that they were acting for the glory of God and to promote His Kingdom on earth. Any lingering doubts they may have felt were dispelled by the discovery that, after the defeat of the Scots, the King had turned once more to Parliament and had made yet another compact by which Independency was to be crushed out of existence. Of course, Charles was not sincere over this *Treaty of Newport*—he had merely made it, as he wrote privately to the Queen, " in order to my escape " ; but this made it all the worse. Cromwell himself had now made up his mind that the recent victories of the Army were a sign that God approved of its determination that the King must die ; and once convinced of this, he was not the man to shrink from responsibility. It was determined that Charles should be brought to trial on a charge of Treason against Parliament and People in connection with the Second Civil War. The first obstacle to be overcome was Parliament itself. Despite the fact that the Army was now in possession of London and Westminster, the

Commons passed by a large majority a resolution that the Treaty of Newport was a sound basis for a permanent settlement. The next morning one Colonel Pride went to the House with a regiment of soldiers, arrested forty-five members and prevented a hundred more from entering the building. " *Pride's Purge* " left the supporters of the Army supreme in the Commons, and they now proceeded to pass a declaration that a special court of justice should be set up to try the King. The House of Lords—now reduced to a score or so of Presbyterians like Manchester and Essex—declined to accept this. Thereupon the " House of Commons " decided to abolish the Upper House altogether, on the grounds that all political power resided in the people, and had been delegated by them to their elected representatives.

One hundred and thirty-five prominent persons—officers, M.P.s and lawyers—were nominated to the special High Court ; but less than half of these attended its sittings in Westminster Hall—even Fairfax declined to take part in the proceedings. When the King was brought before it, he behaved with perfect dignity and composure. He refused to defend himself against the charges. He simply declined to admit that the Court had any jurisdiction over him. No hereditary King could be judged by his own subjects, he maintained ; and if the law of the land could be set aside by main force, there would be an end of justice, constitution, liberty—everything that made life worth living for the nation.

His serene self-confidence somewhat shook the complacency of some of his " judges," and Cromwell had great difficulty in obtaining the fifty-eight signatures that were ultimately affixed to the Death Warrant. When, in the early morning of January 29, he was brought across St. James Park between two hedges of soldiers for execution, he walked so fast that his guards could scarcely keep up. He was kept waiting until two in the afternoon before they brought him out on the scaffold that had been erected in front of the Palace windows. The vast crowd was held at a distance by brigades of soldiers, but when the deed was done their suppressed feelings found vent in a mighty groan of horror.

If Charles had been playing a part, he could not have done it more artistically ; but he was not acting in the least. He was

utterly convinced that he was a martyr for the idea of kingship
(which he believed could alone save men from chaos), for the
laws and liberties of England, and for the national Church.
In truth, it was a good deal easier for him to die bravely like a
fine gentleman than to rule wisely like a good king.   Nor must
we forget that the men who brought him to his death were
equally convinced of their righteousness ; and that however
disastrous were the immediate consequences of their deed, it did
ultimately bring into the world the conception of the Sovereignty
of the People upon which our modern political system rests.

QUESTIONS

(1) *How far was King Charles entitled to regard himself as a
martyr for the Church of England ?*

(2) *Write four speeches (two on each side) to open a debate on :
Whether the execution of Charles I was justified.*

CHAPTER XXVI

The Commonwealth

(1649–1653)

We shall now see that the jealousy between Parliament and Army had by no means been extinguished when " Pride's Purge " excluded the members most opposed to the rule of the Army chiefs. When once those Army chiefs had annihilated the dangers that threatened the Commonwealth from Ireland and Scotland, the quarrel broke out afresh ; nor was it brought to an end until Cromwell used his soldiers to destroy every vestige of parliamentary authority. Henceforth military rule was undisguised.

126. " The Curse of Crummell "

The Army seems to have thought that when once the King's head was off, peace, liberty, and justice would come of themselves. It was mistaken. A republican government, more even than a monarchy, depends on the consent of the governed ; and the vast majority of the English nation were firmly attached to their old constitution. To object to the absolutist innovations of Charles I was one thing ; but for most Englishmen the net result of his execution was that their King was now Charles II— a young man against whom nothing was known, and who was certainly innocent of his father's misdeeds. Therefore, what followed, however much it might be disguised, was rule by force. The government was in the hands of a fragment of a House of Commons elected ten years before, and winnowed down to eighty members by the exclusion first of royalists and then of Presbyterians ; and this so-called " Parliament " was dependent for its authority on the swords and muskets of the New Model Army.

That Army had been welded into the most formidable fighting force in the world. Its numbers were kept up to 50,000 by a steady flow of recruits attracted by its generous rates of pay (say £4 a week for a cavalryman, at present-day values), and newcomers to its ranks quickly caught the general tone prevailing there—Puritanism, Toleration, Democracy.

The Rump (as the residue of the Commons was facetiously called) now elected a Council of State to carry on the actual business of government. This Council consisted of forty-one persons, of whom the majority were members of the " Parliament " as well. The Army chiefs were dissatisfied with this as a " Commonwealth Government " ; but what could they do ? A general election at that moment would have resulted in chaos, for the new régime was threatened both at home and abroad. Their ideal constitution would have to wait for quieter times.

The most pressing business was to " pacify Ireland." Ever since the massacre of 1641 that country had been torn by anarchy, but the execution of the King had now united the diverse elements—Catholic peasantry, Anglican landlords, Presbyterian Ulstermen—in opposition to the Roundheads. A small parliamentary army was beleaguered in Dublin, and all the rest of the country was under the authority of the cavalier Duke of Ormonde. If Dublin fell, Ireland would become an entirely independent country, and an excellent jumping-off ground for royalist attacks on England.

In August (1649) Cromwell landed at Dublin with 15,000 men. The slaughter that followed has always been, and always must be, the greatest reproach against his name. When he stormed *Drogheda* all quarter was refused, the whole garrison put to the sword, and five hundred priests were butchered in cold blood. Similar scenes were enacted a few weeks later at Wexford. Cromwell appears to have felt that he was avenging the massacre of eight years before ; but vengeance is no work for a Christian warrior, and in any case it is very unlikely that any of his victims had been concerned in the massacre. It is perhaps a better excuse that he felt that he had to be cruel to be kind ; he was there to do a piece of work, and the quickest way may have been the most merciful in the end. One result of his ruthless efficiency was that the coalition of forces against the republic broke up. The Protestant elements rallied to the winning side, and the struggle once more became racial and religious. By the following spring he had made good his hold over the whole of eastern and northern Ireland. In May he was recalled by the Government, and the clearing up was left to his lieutenants. These were less efficient though quite as harsh, and it took them two years to subdue the rest of the island.

127. *The " Crowning Mercy "*

The reason for Cromwell's recall was the threatening aspect that things were taking in Scotland.

The Scottish people were indignant at the execution of Charles I. They owed no allegiance to the Commonwealth Government, and they invited the Prince of Wales to come and be their King—upon terms. The Earl of Argyll and the Covenanters, who had carried on the government of Scotland ever since the Bishops' Wars, were still hoping to set up a Presbyterian monarchy. The Prince was torn between his desire to regain his throne and his dislike of this extreme form of Protestantism. For some months he flitted between Holland and the Channel Isles, bargaining with Scots' Commissioners and hoping that something would turn up to save him from their demands. At first he thought of making Ireland his starting-point, but he could not forget that one of the chief causes of his father's downfall had been his connection with the Catholic Irish ; and in any case, Cromwell's activities soon obliterated his hopes from that quarter. Then the heroic *Earl of Montrose* undertook to return from exile and raise the old cavalier spirit in the Highlands, despite the fact that he had failed in a similar enterprise five years before (§ 120), when the government of the Covenanters had been nothing like as strong as it was now. On this occasion he stood no chance at all. He was quickly hunted down and hanged in Edinburgh amid every degrading insult that his spiteful foes could devise—insults which he endured with a scornful pride which helped to make him the most famous of martyrs for the Cavalier cause.

The Prince now decided that he must swallow the Covenant ; and in June, 1650, he was permitted to land at Leith. It makes us smile to-day to think of Charles II as a covenanted king ; but he was young, his character was unformed, and the Scots ministers of religion thought they could mould him to their will. They made him listen to long sermons, they would not let him walk in the fields on the Sabbath, they compelled him publicly to bewail his father's errors and his mother's idolatries.

Here was another danger to the English Commonwealth ; for if the monarchy were re-established in one part of the island, there would be nothing to prevent the King from coming to subdue the other part—in fact, the Scottish government was already planning an expedition against the men who had killed their King and repudiated their Covenant. A force must be sent to nip this movement in the bud ; but Fairfax declined to take command—he did not see why the Scots should not settle their own affairs in their own way. Cromwell was appointed in his place, and he now became for the first time commander-in-chief of the Army which his spirit and his military genius had created.

He proceeded by the east-coast route, so that his army might draw supplies from the fleet which accompanied it. He found the Scottish forces (under David Leslie, son of his old comrade-in-arms of Marston Moor) entrenched in front of Edinburgh. Their position was too strong to be attacked, and before long the English army was in danger of starvation. It therefore retired to Dunbar, to get in touch with its fleet again, the Scots following at a respectful distance. Cromwell's lack of regular military training prevented him from ever becoming a far-sighted strategist—it was in tactics on the field of battle that he was supreme. The *Battle of Dunbar* was an example of both these characteristics. He blundered into an impossible position, between the Lammermuir Hills (now covered by the Scottish army) and the sea, with the enemy in possession of the narrow pass in front and starvation behind. But the council of Presbyterian ministers who controlled Leslie's movements (and had weakened his army by expelling soldiers whom they considered unworthy of the honour of fighting for the Covenant) was impatient to make an end of " the Godless sectaries," and they induced him to make an immediate attack. " The Lord hath delivered them into our hands ! " exclaimed Cromwell when he saw his enemy move down towards him on the morning of September 3 (1650). He used his cavalry with such devastating effect that the Scots' army was utterly destroyed at a loss of not more than a score of the Ironsides.

The following winter Cromwell spent in Edinburgh, trying to bring the Covenanters to reason, and arguing that the recent battle was a witness of the judgment of God against them. But there was another Scottish army forming behind Stirling. The defeat of Dunbar robbed the Kirk of much of its influence amongst the fighting men, and Charles now found himself in a more congenial cavalier atmosphere. While Cromwell was engaged on an expedition in the Highlands, the leaders of this second army decided to invade England, hoping that the presence of the young King would call forth latent royalist feeling there. They marched by the western route through royalist Lancashire, but they found that the fear of Cromwell kept people at home, and that Scottish invaders were even less popular than the Rump and its Army. Cromwell dashed down through Yorkshire and the Midlands, and overtook the Scots at *Worcester*. The victory that followed he afterwards spoke of as " a crowning mercy." It was the end of armed resistance to the republic (Sept. 3, 1651).

After the battle, notices were posted offering a reward for the capture of " a tall, dark, young man above two yards high " ; but after incredible adventures, which helped to throw a halo of romance about the cause he represented, the young King made his way back to the Continent.

128. *The Dutch War*

It may seem strange that none of the Continental Powers intervened on behalf of a brother monarch in distress. The main reason was that until 1648 Europe was distracted by the Thirty Years' War, while even when the Peace of Westphalia brought that bloody chaos to an end France and Spain continued to fight, and each feared lest the powerful fleet and army of the English Republic should be employed on behalf of the other.

We are already familiar with the strength of the Common-wealth Army ; it remains to say something of the Fleet. The late King had expended his ship-money to good purpose in increasing the number and improving the quality of the ships. At his death about a third of the crews revolted against the regicides and sailed their ships to Holland, where they placed themselves under the command of Prince Rupert. The Council of State, however, soon repaired the loss. The member particularly concerned with naval policy was *Sir Henry Vane*. By calling in the assistance of experts both in the designing of ships and in the organisation of fleets, he laid the foundation of the modern Admiralty ; and he discovered a first-rate com-mander in *Robert Blake* (1599–1657). Though Blake had distinguished himself as a general in the defence of Taunton against the royal forces, he had never been to sea till he was over fifty. Yet in the course of the next ten years he did enough to earn a place not far behind Nelson and Drake amongst the sea-kings of Britain. Rupert (equally inexperienced but almost equally adaptable) took his squadron out to prey on the merchant-ships of the Commonwealth from a base-port in south-west Ireland. Blake soon drove him away and compelled him to take refuge in Lisbon. Outside that port the admiral maintained the first blockade in our naval history ; and when a Portuguese fleet came to attack him he smashed it to pieces in a terrific battle fought in a gale. Rupert had meanwhile slipped into the Mediterranean, but Blake followed him up and finally scattered his fleet—the first appearance of English warships in these waters.

These successes turned the heads of the Council of State, and their next exploit was a stupid war with the other Protestant republican naval Power. Commercial rivalry with the Dutch had been growing in intensity all through the century, and in 1651 the Rump passed a *Navigation Act*, to the effect that foreign goods could only be brought to English ports in ships built, owned, and manned by Englishmen, or in ships of the country whence the goods came. This measure aimed at encouraging English shipping and sailors (especially with a view to the navy), and it was a severe blow to the Dutch, who at this time had almost a monopoly of the carrying trade of the world. It naturally caused friction between the two governments, and other grievances had been developing—the English claim to exclusive fishing-rights in certain parts of the North Sea, and the demand that the English flag should be saluted by foreign vessels in English waters. A chance encounter between some ships in the Thames estuary was the immediate cause of the war, which raged in the narrow seas for two years. It was a conflict of giants, for Van Tromp was an even greater admiral than Blake. Eight big battles were fought in the course of the war, the most famous being Tromp's victory off Dungeness, and Blake's off Portland. But economic and geographical factors acted inexorably in England's favour. The Dutch were dependent for their very existence on their overseas trade, which was at the mercy of the English navy as it passed up and down the Channel ; whereas England was still, comparatively speaking, self-contained, and her ships had direct access to the ocean. In 1654, therefore, the Dutch were compelled to make peace on terms favourable to England.

But in the meantime the form of the English government had undergone a remarkable development.

129. " Take away that Bauble ! "

Many of the members of the Commonwealth Government were men of the highest ability and character. " They are economical in their private affairs," reported a foreign envoy to his government, " and prodigal in their devotion to public affairs. They handle large sums of money, which they administer honestly." Vane's work for the Navy we have already mentioned. The great Milton was foreign correspondent, and sacrificed his eyesight to his labours in its service. Cromwell, after all his military triumphs, dropped back into civil life as an ordinary member of the Council. Nevertheless, the Government was very unpopular with the country at large. The cost of the huge army and navy compelled it to raise a revenue three times that of Charles I. It continued to wring money out of the unfortunate cavaliers, by the sequestration of their estates ; but the ordinary taxes had also to be greatly increased. To the bulk of the population, Charles II was the rightful King of England ; on the other hand, many of the most active-minded republicans belonged to the " Levellers " who disliked the Commonwealth Government as not being truly democratic. " Freeborn " John Lilburne flooded the country with pamphlets stigmatising it as a tyrannical usurpation ; and when he was brought to trial for sedition, he was acquitted by the jury amid frantic rejoicings.

So long as the republic was in danger, Army and Rump had stuck together ; but as soon as the crisis was past the soldiers themselves began to clamour for a general election and a free Parliament. The Rump claimed to be still the Parliament elected in 1640, and therefore only dissolvable by its own consent (§ 113). The members enjoyed exercising their power ; and they knew, better than their critics, that in the disturbed state of national feeling, an election would lead not to an ideal republic, but to chaos—perhaps to a renewed civil war. Cromwell, owing to his military reputation, his force of character, and his massive common sense, was already looked to by all the supporters of the Commonwealth for leadership and guidance. He strove to keep the peace between the contending forces, but in the end he was carried away by the irresistible current of events. The Rump prepared a Bill to perpetuate its own power by providing that vacancies in Parliament should be filled by persons of whom the existing members approved. The Army chiefs were furious at this, and Cromwell induced the parliamentary leaders to postpone the measure, pending further discussion. When, next morning, he learnt that they were pushing on with it in spite of this undertaking, he lost his temper. He strode down to the House with a company of troopers to disperse Parliament by force. Hat on head, and with a red and angry face, he stamped up and down the floor of the House, scolding the members individually and collectively. He told them that the Lord had done with them, and had chosen other instruments for carrying on His work that were more worthy. " You are no Parliament ! " he shouted. " I say you are no Parliament. I will put an end to your sitting ! " Then, catching sight of the Mace, he cried, " What shall we do with that bauble ? Here," calling to a soldier, " take it away."

" That bauble " was the emblem of parliamentary authority,

and in removing it he was destroying the last shred of legality possessed by the republic.

130. *Experiments*

What was to be done now? First King, then Lords, and now Commons had disappeared, and in each case it was the Army that had passed judgment. Under the presidency of Cromwell, the Council of Officers now debated two alternative schemes of government. General Lambert proposed an unalterable written constitution, with a free Parliament and a small Executive Council. General Harrison, on the other hand, suggested an Assembly selected from among the most godly citizens. He belonged to the Independent sect known as the " Fifth Monarchy Men," who believed that, the empires of Assyria, Persia, Macedonia, and Rome having all fallen, that of Christ was now about to begin. Cromwell was a combination of practical statesman and mystic : he distrusted written constitutions, and he was attracted by the idea of the " Rule of the Saints." Thus it was the second scheme that was now put into practice.

The *Barebone's Parliament*—so called from the name that stood first on the alphabetical list of members—was not really a parliament at all. It was a convention of Puritan notables, some elected by Independent and Baptist congregations, others nominated by the Officers' Council. Cromwell opened its first session with a speech full of religious rapture. The members were called, he said, by reason of their godliness. " I never thought to see such a thing as this. . . . This may be the dawn to usher in the things that God promised and prophesied."

Unfortunately, the Saints were not so practical as they were well-meaning. They did not go so far as the Fifth Monarchy Men proposed, and substitute the Mosaic Code for the Laws of England, but they upset everybody and everything by their rash meddling. Many of their views were very enlightened, and indeed far ahead of the time—as to the care of lunatics, for instance ; as to the simplification and cheapening of law-procedure ; as to the abolition of tithes ; but the practical remedies they proposed betrayed their utter lack of practical experience. Confusion and uncertainty reigned in every class of society, and the new Assembly was soon even more unpopular than the Rump had been. Once more all eyes were turned on Cromwell, who had quickly lost his enthusiasm for government by the godly when he found that the godly were not all as sensible as himself. With his approval a group of members who were out of sympathy with the majority got up early one morning, and before the others arrived passed a vote that the Assembly should resign its powers into the Lord-General's hands.

The Army Council now fell back on Lambert's idea, and evolved from it *The Instrument of Government* The executive power was henceforth to be vested in a Lord Protector, assisted by a small Council of State which was itself to fill up vacancies in its own numbers. Law-making was to be entrusted to a Parliament consisting of one House elected by well-to-do voters, such as had a stake in the country. The Protector was to have a fixed income with which to carry on the ordinary business of government, but for any extra expenditure he was to apply to Parliament ; and he was to have only a suspensory veto for twenty days over the laws it passed. Before the Parliament met, the Protector and his Council could rule by means of Ordinances ; but these were to be submitted for approval to the Parliament as soon as it met. The constitution thus laid down was to be independent of any factious parliamentary majority ; it was to be fixed and unalterable.

Of course, there was only one possible Lord Protector, and Oliver Cromwell was solemnly inducted (dressed in black, so as to indicate that the rule of the sword was over) in January, 1654.

Questions

(1) *Write a short history of England under the Commonwealth.*

(2) *It has been said that Cromwell's dismissal of the Rump justified Strafford. Explain this statement.*

CHAPTER XXVII

The Protectorate

(1653–1660)

It is one of the strangest ironies of history that the Protector found himself driven step by step into doing most of the things which had cost the late King his crown. He quarrelled with his parliaments, imprisoned people without trial, raised unauthorised taxes, and restrained opposition by martial law. All this was ultimately due to the fact that he was ruling without the consent of the nation ; and after his iron hand had been removed by death it speedily became apparent that this consent would be given to no form of government except a restored monarchy.

131. " *Cromwell, our Chief of Men* "

The Protector was in no hurry to call his first Parliament, and trouble began as soon as it met. On the very first day members began to criticise the Instrument of Government. The Protector excluded by force all who would not accept the fundamental provisions of the new constitution—a more drastic step than Charles I had ever dreamt of ; but even then the residue went on arguing. It was not that they objected to Oliver's conduct as Lord Protector—they made no difficulty about passing into law nearly all the ordinances he had issued before they met. What they resented was that any individual should base political authority upon mere military support. They pointed out that the Civil War had been fought to gain parliamentary control over the government. Cromwell replied that the House owed its very existence to the Instrument, and that if that constitution was to be open to amendment by successive parliaments the

266

country would have no fixed form of government at all. To this the House replied that they drew their authority direct from the votes of the people, whereas the Instrument and the Protectorship had been created by a mere self-appointed committee of officers which had no legal existence whatever. Thus the wrangle went on, and on the very first day that the constitution allowed him to do so, Cromwell dissolved the Parliament in disgust.

This evidence that the Protectorate was not supported by any considerable body of public opinion led to a general feeling of unrest. Scots, Cavaliers, Levellers, Fifth Monarchy Men—all nursed grievances against it. At Salisbury in March (1655) a royalist rising actually broke out under one Colonel Penruddocke. It was quickly suppressed, the leaders executed, and others transported (without trial) to work as slaves at Barbados. Nevertheless, Cromwell was determined to guard against such movements for the future. He divided the country into ten districts, and placed over each a *Major-General*, supported by a special military force. These officers had power to supervise the local magistrates, and to compel the people of England to live sober and godly lives. They suppressed horse-racing, bear-baiting, and cock-fighting; they repressed such frivolous amusements as play-acting and country-dancing; they forbade Sabbath-breaking; they abolished many ale-houses and compelled the others to close at sunset. As a police system nothing could have been more effective; but twelve months of it gave England a horror of rule by either " saints " or soldiers that has persisted down to our own day. Moreover, it was quite illegal; for the Protector's power to issue Ordinances had expired with the meeting of his first Parliament, while the cost of the system was met by an equally unauthorised income-tax of 10 per cent. on former royalists.

Nor was this the end of Cromwell's illegalities. A merchant named Cony refused to pay Customs Duties not imposed by Parliament, and when the law courts decided in his favour, the judges were dismissed from the bench and his counsel thrown into prison. And this was the result of a revolution begun to assert the supremacy of law over arbitrary rule !

132. *Toleration*

Cromwell was greatly distressed by the turn things were taking. " What is it that you would have ? " he asked one of his critics. " That which we fought for," was the reply, " government by consent." " I am as much for government by consent as any man," answered the Protector, " but where will you find it ? " That was the root of the trouble. When once the customary system of government by King, Lords, and Commons had disappeared, innumerable groups and parties sprang up, each quite sure that it alone knew the cure for all the public ills. Oliver realised that his first duty as a ruler was to keep order, and he had great practical capacity for tackling administrative problems ; these two facts led him to take many steps which he felt to be disagreeable necessities. For instance, he was not in sympathy with much of the harsh Puritanism of the Major-Generals, but he felt that the tight hand they kept over people was, at the moment, the only way to carry on the government. There was little of the tyrant about his own nature. Amongst his ordinances were wise reforms of the legal system—making justice cheap, reducing penalties for crime, and regulating imprisonment for debt—which, if they had not been swept away at the Restoration, would have put England centuries ahead of any other country in the world.

His settlement of religion, again, was far more broad and tolerant than anything that existed before his time or for a long time after it. He established a comprehensive Puritan Church. Commissions of *Triers* were set up in different parts of the country to test the qualifications of candidates for the ministry, making no distinction between Independent, Baptist, or Presbyterian, or even moderate Anglican. It was universally admitted that the endowments of the Church were never enjoyed by such a worthy set of men as those thus appointed. Certainly the open use of the Prayer Book was forbidden, for this had become associated in people's minds with the monarchy ; but if an individual clergyman introduced part of it into his services, he was not usually interfered with. As to Catholicism, it was essential to Cromwell's political position that his government should be distinctively Protestant—it was the suspicion of

" Romanising " tendencies that had united the nation against the King at the beginning of the revolution ; but even Catholics were generally unmolested during the Protectorate, so long as they did not attempt to make converts, or celebrate Mass in public. Even the Jews who had been excluded from the country ever since the thirteenth century were now allowed to return and settle here.

Naturally this policy of toleration led to the rapid spread of unorthodox sects. Of these, the most famous was the *Society of Friends* established by George Fox. These folk adopted the purest and simplest form of Christianity, cut adrift from all the ritual and organisation that had grown up round the gospel preached in Palestine. Following the words of the Sermon on the Mount, Fox and his followers denounced resistance to evil, and taught that religious inspiration comes from within the individual rather than from outward signs and ceremonies. Every man was his own priest. *The Quakers*, as they were nicknamed, have had a profound influence on the national life and character.

133. *Oliver the Imperialist*

Cromwell was the most thorough-going imperialist that ever ruled England.

In the first place, he united the British Islands under one government for the first time in history. He deprived Scotland of her national independence, and Edinburgh of her position as a capital city. The country was represented in each of his Parliaments. The Kirk was maintained in honour and dignity, but robbed of the privilege of persecuting other sects. Order and unity were preserved in Highlands and Lowlands alike by an English Army of Occupation under General Monk.

Cromwell's treatment of Ireland was (for the moment) equally effective, though a good deal less enlightened. Like most of his contemporaries, he had exaggerated ideas about the massacre of 1641, and he looked upon Irish Catholics as savages who could have no more right to the soil of their country than the wolves on the Kerry hills. He completed the transfer of the land to English proprietors which had been begun under Mary and Elizabeth and continued under James and Charles. Over three-quarters of the land now confiscated was granted to men of the New Model Army, with the three-fold object of rewarding those who had taken part in the conquest, of providing a permanent Protestant garrison, and of extirpating Catholicism. In the long run the policy was a failure, for within the next fifty years the officers (who had been granted large estates) bought up most of the smaller holdings of the troopers, and the latter became absorbed in the Catholic peasantry. The Province of Connaught was reserved for the Irish, and the fact that the humbler classes in the rest of the country had been deprived of the leadership of their own gentry had the result of leaving them subject to the unlimited influence of their persecuted priests. Still, these ill effects did not show themselves in Oliver's lifetime. In this, as in other matters, what he sought and found was a practical solution of an immediate problem.

As to European politics, his education and early life had not brought him into contact with such affairs ; yet it must be admitted that his conduct of them was both more enlightened and more patriotic than that of his predecessors. James I had made himself the laughing-stock of Europe with his Spanish-marriage projects, and Charles I had made feebly futile efforts to regain the Palatinate for his sister ; but genuine national interests now took the place of dynastic ambitions. Oliver's first action on becoming Protector was to end the Dutch War as a preliminary step towards the formation of a great League of the Protestant Powers—England, Sweden, Denmark, and Holland. This scheme never came to anything, but it was a big idea. His second step was to organise an attack on the Spanish West Indies in the interests of British seamen and merchants. This was quite in the old Elizabethan spirit. Cromwell was determined to punish the Spaniards for their ill-treatment of English sailors who fell into their hands, and to compel them to allow English merchandise to be imported into their American territories. Perhaps he was also desirous of keeping his great fleet busy in some enterprise that might bring in a dividend of Spanish gold. His belief in the divine right of victory received rather a shock, however, for the attack on San Domingo, though unprovoked and unexpected, resulted in a disgraceful defeat. The commanders withdrew and sailed off to *Jamaica* to retrieve their humiliation. Here they were successful, and the island has ever since been the most important of our West Indian possessions.

Cromwell had supposed that Spain would allow hostilities to be confined to the western side of the Atlantic ; but the days when wars could be thus localised were gone by. A formal declaration of war by the Spanish government compelled him to accept an alliance with France. By the terms of this a joint attack was to be made on the Spanish Netherlands. Six thousand of the famous Ironsides were sent over to Flanders. There they proved themselves as invincible as in England, and the fighting qualities they displayed on the sandy flats round Dunkirk (*Battle of the Dunes*, 1658) aroused the admiration of both friend and foe. That port now became an English possession.

The only other memorable event of the war was the exploit of Blake at *Santa Cruz*, in the Canary Islands. A treasure fleet which he was pursuing took refuge under the guns of a fortress there. Hitherto, no fleet had ever attempted to silence guns mounted on shore-batteries ; but Blake showed all subsequent British naval commanders how to deal with such a situation.

134. *Revision of the Protectorate*

Meanwhile, the Protector was struggling on, conscious that his rule was becoming increasingly unpopular, but unable to bring it to an end without the loss of all that he held most sacred. He could only prevent royalist risings by unceasing vigilance, and he was in constant danger of assassination. The republicans regarded him as a traitor to their cause ; to the Presbyterians he was a fomentor of strange sects ; the Fifth Monarchy Men likened him to the Beast mentioned in the Apocalypse. Moreover, his imperialism was a very expensive luxury. The Spanish War cost a great deal more than it produced in the way of spoils, and it crippled foreign trade. Despite the sale of Crown and Church lands and the sequestration of the estates of " malignants," taxation was far heavier than ever before in our history.

It was the need for war-subsidies that compelled Cromwell to call another Parliament in the autumn of 1657. He hoped that the Major-Generals would be able to see to it that the opponents of the Government were not elected, but their efforts were so unsuccessful that a hundred disaffected members had to be turned away at the doors, and even then the remainder began at once to attack rule by martial law and the tax on royalists. The Protector gave way at once on both points; but still the House was not satisfied. As with the first Parliament, it was not a personal feeling against Cromwell so much as a desire to get back to the old traditional way of government that everybody understood. The members were not prepared to go so far as to recall the Stuarts, but they wanted a king of some sort; and despite the frantic opposition of the republican members, the House voted in favour of a revision of the constitution to this effect. By the *Humble Petition and Advice* Cromwell was requested to change the title of Protector for that of King, and to nominate an Upper House to take the place of the old House of Lords. Cromwell was tempted. It really seemed that this was his best chance of getting that " government by consent " of the majority that he had always aimed at. But the Levellers were still the backbone of the Army, on the good will of which the Government was dependent for its very existence. He therefore declined the invidious title, but was re-installed in something like regal splendour, with a sceptre and heralds in tabards and silver trumpets and robes of purple and ermine.

When old Oliver spent that Christmas of 1657 with his family at Hampton Court Palace he had good reason to hope that the position was at last assured; for he could now feel that he was the chosen of Parliament as well as the nominee of his brother officers. But he was once more doomed to disappointment. The moment Parliament met for its second session (Jan. 1658) fresh troubles broke out. The *personnel* of the Commons had greatly altered during the recess, for the opposition members could no longer be excluded, and many of the staunchest of the Protector's supporters had been nominated to the new House of Lords. There was now a republican majority, and this began at once to attack the revised constitution. Oliver summoned the House to the Palace and protested against their indulging in these wrangles instead of getting on with the public business for which they had been summoned. All was in vain. The republicans began to organise a petition for a new Parliament, and in order to prevent this from going any further, the Protector hurried down to Westminster and dissolved the Houses in anger. A few months later he was dead. Worn out by incessant labours and anxieties he sank to his rest on Sept. 3 (1658), the anniversary of Dunbar and Worcester.

Cromwell was one of the greatest Englishmen that ever lived. In his greatness and in his weakness alike, his disposition was in many ways typical of our nation. He was no brilliant, intellectual schemer. Both as soldier and as a statesman his greatest gift was his strong common sense. He had a clear perception of actualities at hand rather than a far-sighted vision of possibilities at a distance. What his instinct or his conscience prompted him to, his courage and resource never failed him to carry through, whether it was a question of personal danger on the battlefield, or of moral responsibility in the taking of momentous decisions. But the ultimate secret of his strength was his deeply-rooted assurance that he was the instrument of the will of God.

135. *The End of Puritan Rule*

By the revised constitution, the Protector was empowered to nominate his successor, and during his last illness Cromwell had so nominated his eldest surviving son, Richard. He was a sensible, well-meaning man of average ability ; but it soon became obvious that something more than this was required to hold the position left vacant by his mighty father. One great change for the worse in the Protector's position was that whereas Oliver's military reputation gave him unquestioned control over the Army, Richard had no pretensions to being a soldier, and had to rely on the support of the generals. The latter began by demanding complete independence of the civilian government. Richard refused, and the matter was closed for the moment, but it was obvious that trouble was brewing.

The new Protector summoned his first Parliament for January, 1659. Amongst the members were a number of out-and-out republicans, such as General Lambert, who had objected to the Protectorate being turned into something like a monarchy after the Humble Petition and Advice. These now began to question the Protector's authority; and when they were out-voted, they made common cause with the dissatisfied officers. The consequence was that the latter compelled the Protector to dissolve his Parliament (April, 1659). A week or two later Richard Cromwell realised that the hostility of the Army made his position impossible. He resigned the Protectorship and retired into obscurity for the rest of his long life (he died in 1714).

The Council of Officers now decided to revive the original Commonwealth at the point where Oliver had broken it off by expelling the " Rump." The surviving members of that body (about fifty in number) were recalled to Westminster in April, but the Generals soon began to resent their subordination to an authority created by themselves, and in August a serious quarrel resulted in the Rump being once more sent packing.

By this action, as matters turned out, the Army chiefs struck the death-blow to their own rule. It had two decisive effects on the situation. (1) In England it caused the Presbyterians— the moderate Puritans, who had always opposed the execution of the King, and whose representatives had been shut out of Parliament by " Pride's Purge " (§ 129) in order that the execu-tion might be carried through—to make common cause with the royalists. They dreaded the rule of the military fanatics with the restraining hand of Cromwell removed ; and they now realised that the only hope of a permanent settlement lay in a restoration of the monarchy. (2) In Scotland, *General Monk*, commander of the army of occupation there, decided that the subjection of the three kingdoms to the rule of a junta of narrow-minded officers was intolerable. He was a professional soldier who had learnt the arts of war on the Continent, and had no religious or political enthusiasms. He had taken service with the Parliament mainly because it seemed to offer the best chance of regular employment. He was inclined to Presbyterianism, and it was with the hearty support (moral and financial) of the Scots that he now led his army into England to rescue both countries from rule by force.

Lambert led such troops as could be spared from the garrison of London to bar his way ; but he soon found himself in difficulties. The feeling in the country was overwhelmingly against the rule of the Army, and now that the dread figure of Cromwell had disappeared, that feeling was no longer afraid to show itself. Monk knew that time was on his side. He prolonged a parley at York until Lambert's forces melted away, owing partly to disaffection in the ranks (for even the Ironsides were affected by the general feeling) and partly to the difficulty of providing for them in a barren countryside with a hostile population. Then he continued his march on London, inundated in his passage through the country by petitions demanding a freely-elected Parliament. Up to this time he had not declared himself in favour of a restoration, but he now realised that public opinion was overwhelmingly in favour of that course, and he determined to get the credit of bringing it about. He recalled the Rump once more, and added to it the Presbyterian members who had been excluded by Colonel Pride. Thus secure of a majority, he caused the House to arrange for a general election, and then dissolve itself. Thus after twenty years was fulfilled the Long Parliament's provision that it could only be dissolved with its own consent.

The new Parliament met in March. As everybody expected, it at once sent to the eldest son of Charles I, in exile in Holland, and invited him to return to his kingdom, upon certain terms which we will discuss in a later chapter. The *Declaration of Breda* duly signed, Charles II was proclaimed King, and the triumph of Puritanism was at an end.

QUESTIONS

(1) *Write a history of the Long Parliament.*
(2) *What made the downfall of Puritanism inevitable ?*

General Test Questions

(1) *Describe the state of religious parties at the accession of James I and the policy of that king towards them.*

(2) *Compare the relations between Crown and Parliament under Elizabeth and James I.*

(3) *How far did religion influence politics under James I and Charles I ?*

(4) *Examine the foreign policy of the first two Stuart kings.*

(5) *Outline the relations of Charles I to his Parliaments.*

(6) *How far did the Parliaments of James I and Charles I try to check the power of the Crown ?*

(7) *Describe the aims and methods of Charles I during the period of his Personal Rule.*

(8) *How far do you consider that the advisers of Charles I were responsible for his downfall ?*

(9) *What were the motives that divided the parties at the outbreak of the Civil War ?*

(10) *Could the Civil War have been avoided ?*

(11) *Which party was really responsible for the outbreak of the Civil War ?*

(12) *Describe the career of the Earl of Strafford.*

(13) *Describe the position of the two sides in the Civil War at the end of 1644. How were those positions changed by the end of the following year ?*

(14) *Give an account of the constitutional experiments tried during the Commonwealth and Protectorate periods.*

(15) *How far was the rise of Cromwell to the Protectorship inevitable, and how far was it of his own seeking ?*

(16) *Describe the policy of Cromwell as to* (a) *foreign affairs,* (b) *religion,* (c) *domestic problems.*

(17) *To what causes do you attribute the Restoration of the Monarchy in* 1660 ?

BOOK IV

The Triumph of Whiggism

(1660–1714)

In this Book we shall see that the Anglican Church and the supremacy of Parliament, which had both suffered eclipse under Cromwell, were restored along with the Monarchy in 1660. The Stuart sovereigns all had a hankering for an absolutist form of monarchy, such as prevailed in nearly all the states of Europe. The struggle between hereditary right and parliamentary power led to the formation of the two political parties which dominated English politics for the next two centuries. In the long run it became evident that Parliament had grown too strong to be overcome.

The Revolution that followed set on a definite and permanent basis the form of constitution towards which the political genius of the nation had been unconsciously tending all through the century : the Constitutional Monarchy, in which hereditary right and parliamentary sanction are combined. England joined in two coalitions against Louis XIV, because he threatened to attack this system in the interests of absolutism as personified by the exiled Stuarts. The country emerged from these wars with greatly enhanced prestige, especially in commercial, financial, naval, and colonial spheres. Finally, the Revolution Settlement was confirmed by the accession of George I ; and with that event our period comes to an end.

THE FALL OF THE STUARTS

Year	Left column	Center	Right column	Year
1660	CHARLES II (§136)			1660
1661	Corporation Act (§139)			1661
1662	Act of Uniformity (§139)	CLARENDON	Royal Society founded (§180) Dunkirk sold (§140)	1662
1663	"Paradise Lost" completed (§177)	(§137)	Carolina founded (§178)	1663
1664	Conventicle Act (§139)			1664
1665	The Great Plague (§140) Five Mile Act (§139)		Lowestoft ✕ (§140)	1665
1666	The Great Fire (§140)		Second Dutch War (§140) The Downs ✕ (§140)	1666
1667			Dutch in Medway ✕ (§140)	1667
1668		THE	Triple Alliance (§142)	1668
1669		CABAL		1669
1670			Treaty of Dover (§143)	1670
1671		(§143)		1671
1672	Stop of the Exchequer (§144) Declaration of Indulgence (§144)		Third Dutch War (§144) Southwold Bay ✕ (§144)	1672
1673	Test Act (§145)		The Texel ✕ (§144)	1673
1674		DANBY		1674
1675		(§146)	2nd. Subsidy Treaty with France (§146)	1675
1676				1676
1677			Princess Mary m. Wm. of Orange (§146)	1677
1678	"Pilgrim's Progress" (§177) Popish Plot (§147)	THREE		1678
1679	Bothwell Brig ✕ (§150) Habeas Corpus (§148)	WHIG PARLIAMENTS		1679
1680	Exclusion Bill (§148)	(§148-9)	Colonisation of Pennsylvania (§178)	1680
1681	"Absolom & Achitophel" (§177) Oxford Parliament (§149)			1681
1682		CHARLES II		1682
1683	Rye House Plot (§150)	TRIUMPHANT		1683
1684		(§150)		1684
1685	JAMES II (§152) Sedgmoor ✕ (§153)		Revocation of Edict of Nantes (§151)	1685
1686		REIGN OF	League of Augsburg (§151)	1686
1687	Newton's "Principia" (§180) Declaration of Indulgence (§155)	JAMES II	Tyrconnel Lord Deputy of Ireland (§162)	1687
1688	The Revolution (§156-7)	(§152-5)	Louis XIV invades Germany (§156)	1688

CHAPTER XXVIII

The Restoration

(1660–1667)

Charles II was greeted with raptures by his people, who saw in him the restorer of the settled and customary modes of life and government. We associate the first seven years of his reign with the rule of Lord Clarendon the architect of the Restoration Settlement, but we shall see that disappointment with the new régime led to the downfall of that statesman.

136. *Charles II*

Never has sovereign been received with more rapturous delight than that which greeted Charles II. The Kentish cliffs were black with spectators when he landed, his road to London was lined, mile after mile, with people from all over the southern counties, and the latter part of the route seemed like a fair-ground, covered with tents and booths. Everywhere houses were gay with bunting, bells rocked the steeples, and wine flowed by the gallon to the health of the prince who was bringing back the reign of peace, freedom, and law.

No doubt many of those who cheered so lustily supposed that the clock had been put back to the days before Parliaments had dared to interfere with the royal authority ; but it gradually became evident that this was impossible—the hands of the clock would not even go back to the situation at the beginning of the Civil War. Enthusiastic legitimists might pretend that Charles II had reigned from the moment when his father's head fell on the scaffold, but all men knew in their hearts that as a matter of sober fact he owed his position to an invitation from Parliament. The situation could never again be what it had been before 1640.

The re-establishment of the monarchy was thus a very critical business, and much depended on the character and outlook of the restored King. On the whole, we may say that Charles might have been less suited by nature for the task than he was. He was thirty years of age, a witty, cool-headed, good-humoured man of the world. He was the complete cynic, with little sense of morality, religion, or honour, and little regard for men's praise or blame so long as he could enjoy life. He had far too keen a sense of humour to believe in " Divine Right " or to pose as " The Lord's Anointed " ; nor had he the least intention of following his father's footsteps as a martyr for that or any other cause. He had spent ten years in poverty and exile, and he intended to take good care not to renew the experience.

The assembly that had invited him back had been summoned by the survivors of the Long Parliament instead of by royal writ. It was therefore not a real Parliament at all, and was usually spoken of as " The Convention." It had been elected under the protection of Monk, and the Presbyterians were strongly represented in it. Thus the Restoration was largely the work of the party which had conducted the war against Charles I without wishing to destroy the Monarchy. Charles II stepped into the place his father would have taken if he had come to terms with the Parliament during his sojourn at Carisbrooke (§ 124). The party vanquished in 1659–60 was not the parliamentary party that had fought the war, but the officers of the New Model who had usurped political power by means of " Pride's Purge." Thus the moderate Puritans who had played a large part in the Restoration felt that their own future was assured ; and the King by his first appointments seemed to recognise their claims. Quite half the members of his Privy Council were Presbyterians, and amongst them were many who had served under Cromwell— notably Monk, who became Duke of Albemarle, and Anthony Ashley Cooper, who became Baron Ashley.

137. *The Convention Parliament*

The chief architect of the Restoration Settlement was Edward Hyde, who now became Lord Chancellor and *Earl of Clarendon.*

In the old days he had supported Hampden ovei Ship Money and Pym over the Impeachment of Strafford, but he had taken the King's side when Parliament split over the Grand Remonstrance (§ 114). He had been the trusted counsellor of Charles I during the war and of Charles II in exile. He was a devoted supporter of the privileges of the Anglican Church, and his general policy was to bring the Monarchy back to the position it had occupied on the day that Charles I left London. He had dropped out of touch with public opinion in England during the ten years he had spent abroad, and in many respects he failed to understand the changed conditions that he came back to. Nevertheless, it was mainly owing to his wisdom and moderation (coupled with the easy-going nature of the King himself) that the Restoration was not followed by any general revenge on the Roundheads. He realised that the first aim of the government must be to make the people of England—even those who had supported the republican governments—feel safe.

In this policy he had the support of the Convention Parliament. It had been intended that this body should be dissolved as soon as the King had had an opportunity to call an official Parliament; but Charles confirmed its authority for the time being, and it continued to sit until the following December. It approved the execution of the regicides—the men who had been directly concerned with the late King's execution; and the bodies of those of them whom death had removed from its power—notably Cromwell and Bradshaw—were disinterred, beheaded, and thrown into dishonoured graves. But these were scapegoats for all the others who had borne arms against Charles I. An *Act of Indemnity and Oblivion* was passed, so complete and sweeping that old cavaliers who had sacrificed their all for their King grumbled that the King's enemies got the indemnity and his friends the oblivion.

From one point of view, all the recent troubles could be traced back to the fatal refusal of the Long Parliament to give the New Model their wages. The Convention took care not to repeat that mistake. One of its first cares was to pay the Army in full and dismiss it. Oliver's old troopers went back into civil life, where they returned to their former avocations or set up in business with their savings.

The Convention next applied itself to the settlement of the land—then the chief source of political power and social position. A large part of the soil had changed hands during the past fifteen years, Church and Crown lands having been sold by the revolutionary governments to relieve the taxes, and private estates sold by individual cavaliers to enable them to meet the fines imposed upon them. These lands had for the most part been bought cheap in a glutted market by Roundheads. Something had to be done to readjust matters ; but what ? Clarendon felt that a dangerous sense of insecurity would be aroused by too great an upheaval in ownership, and members of the Convention were amongst those who had profited by the sales. A compromise was eventually made : the sale of public lands was annulled without compensation to the buyers, while the sale of private lands was confirmed without compensation to the sellers. This was a rough-and-ready settlement which bore very hard on individuals, but it seemed to be the only practical solution of a difficult problem.

The Convention also took up the question of religion. Several conferences of divines met to discuss how the episcopal system of the Anglican Church could be reconciled with Presbyterianism. Clarendon proposed that the decision should be left over to the new Parliament which was to meet early the following year ; and to this course the Convention agreed. After all, the last regular Parliament had taken a very firm stand against the High Church party (§ 114), and they did not see why the next one should not adopt the same attitude. This expectation proved to be one of the most colossal and momentous miscalculations in English history.

138. *Royalism—Within Limits*

Many royalists had been unable to vote at the election of the Convention ; but these disabilities had now been removed, and the General Election of 1661 produced a frantically Cavalier House of Commons. There was at that time no law to compel fresh elections to be held at stated intervals, and Charles II kept this Parliament in being for nearly eighteen years.

The members were full of boisterous delight that the King

should " enjoy his own again " ; but it soon became apparent that what they considered to be his own was a good deal less than his predecessors had enjoyed without question. Parliament felt that it was its own rights as well as the King's that had been restored. They passed a law making it a crime to maintain that it is ever justifiable to take arms against the King ; but they also took ample precaution against the King being ever again able to set up an autocratic government.

They confirmed almost all the restrictions which had been passed in the first year of the Long Parliament ; and they absolutely refused to allow the King to maintain a permanent army. A futile little republican rising at Christmas (1660) gave Charles an excuse to retain a few regiments ; but this was a mere handful compared with the great armies upon which the Continental monarchies had built up their despotisms. It was fortunate for English liberties that the class which most zealously supported the monarchy was the class to which the memory of Cromwell and the Major-Generals was most abhorrent. The instinctive dread of " standing armies " lasted right down to the Napoleonic wars.

Another respect in which the Cavalier Parliament showed that it was not so blindly loyal as to be unforgetful of its own rights was in the settlement of the revenue. It fixed the King's income at just over £1,000,000. This sum was barely enough to pay current expenses in time of peace ; but as the taxes never produced more than about two-thirds of the estimated yield, and Charles had come to England loaded with the debts incurred during his exile, he was always dependent on extra grants from Parliament. No doubt this niggardliness was partly due to the fact that the Land Tax (by which most of the direct revenue was derived) fell on the very class which was most strongly represented in the two Houses of Parliament.

The French Ambassador reported to his master that the restored English monarchy was not really a monarchy at all. In a way he was right. The government of England was very unlike that of France. Louis XIV had had his own " restoration " some ten years before, when the crushing of " The Fronde " had caused the last remnant of political power to be taken from the nobles and the professional classes. What was happening in England was the slow development of a new type of government—the Constitutional Monarchy ; and it was destined to outlast by a great many years the absolutism which to King Louis and his ambassador was the only kind of monarchy worthy the name.

139. " *The Clarendon Code* "

Up to this point the Restoration Settlement had been approved by almost the whole of the nation ; but when the Cavalier Parliament turned its attention to the re-establishment of the Church it showed itself narrow-minded and bigoted.

It began with a *Corporation Act* (1661), which limited municipal corporations to persons who received Holy Communion by the rites of the Church of England. It was these corporations which, in most boroughs, controlled the parliamentary elections, and this measure was designed to give Anglican Churchmen a monopoly of political power.

Next session was passed an *Act of Uniformity* which required all clergymen to declare their " unfeigned consent and assent " to every word of the Prayer Book. Two thousand parsons refused the test and were expelled from their livings.

Many of the dispossessed clergy were supported by their flocks, and continued to hold religious services in private buildings. To put a stop to this, Parliament two years later passed a *Conventicle Act*, by which all religious gatherings save those of the Established Church were punished by imprisonment for the first two offences and transportation for the third.

Lastly, in 1665, when the Plague was raging in London, the Houses (which had taken refuge at Oxford) learnt with dismay that Puritan pastors were tending the wants, physical and spiritual, of the afflicted Londoners, and were regaining all their old influence. They therefore rushed through the *Five Mile Act*, which forbade any clergyman or schoolmaster to come within five miles of a town unless he would make a solemn declaration that he would not " at any time endeavour any alteration in Church or State."

These four Acts are often called " The Clarendon Code," but this is hardly fair to the Lord Chancellor. He was indeed anxious to see the Anglican Church restored to power and privilege ; but the severity of these measures went far beyond his wishes. Nor did the King himself like them. Persecution was altogether foreign to his disposition, and he pointed out to the Houses that they were making him break his promise of a general toleration made at Breda (§ 135). But the members would not listen to him, and his financial needs made it impossible for him to resist them.

In truth, these penal laws were inspired not so much by religious zeal as by the thirst for retaliation. They were the revenge of the Cavaliers for the humiliations and losses they had suffered under Puritan rule. They were also a precaution against any revival of Puritanism as a political power. To a great extent they achieved the object with which they were framed. The Presbyterians were dismayed to find that, so far from any concession being made to their views in the national Church, no distinction was to be made between them and wild Anabaptists. The well-to-do among them—especially those who had become " gentry " by the purchase of Cavalier lands— mostly conformed to the Anglican Church and became the nucleus of the future " Whig Party "—the Low Churchmen who supported toleration for Dissenters. The more stubborn spirits, being ineligible for office in Church and State, and unable to acquire the education to fit themselves for the learned professions, were marked with a badge of social inferiority which they did not outlive for centuries.

140. *The Fall of Clarendon*

Throughout his reign the King's relations with foreign powers were generally connected with his chronic shortness of money. His marriage with Catherine of Braganza, for instance, brought him a handsome dowry, as well as two overseas trading-stations, Tangier and Bombay. A year later he sold Dunkirk, conquered by Cromwell from Spain, to Louis XIV ; and this transaction brought a double profit, since it removed the expense of keeping up a garrison in a perfectly useless possession.

Even in the *Second Dutch War* (1664–7) the chief aim was a commercial advantage that would fill the Treasury. This is not to say that in entering upon it the Government had not the wholehearted support of the nation. It was practically a continuation of the earlier war (§ 128), and the root cause of it was sheer commercial jealousy. English merchants resented the prosperity of Flushing and Amsterdam, which had become the chief centres of East and West India trade, respectively. The earlier stages of the war went on the whole in favour of the English; battles were won off Lowestoft in 1665 and in the Downs in 1666. But then difficulties began to arise. An outbreak of bubonic plague in the summer of 1665 brought business almost to a standstill in London for many months, and a year later a great fire destroyed the whole City from the Tower to Temple Bar. These disasters naturally threw the Government into disorder; and the confusion was worse confounded by the attitude which Parliament now took towards the war. The King was notoriously an evil-liver, and the Commons had reason to believe that a large part of the money they voted for the Navy was spent on the dissipations of the Court. They therefore insisted that arrangements should be made to audit the Government accounts. While these discussions were going on, however, supplies had run so short that the Admiralty were compelled to lay up a large part of the Navy. The Dutch fleet took advantage of this to sail right up the Thames estuary and burn several ships of war as they lay in Chatham dockyard. Peace negotiations had already begun, and the Government now pushed them on. By the *Treaty of Breda* (1667) certain disputed possessions in Asia and Africa fell to Holland, while the Dutch settlements in America were acquired by England. It appeared to contemporaries that the Republic had got the better of the bargain, for colonies in which white men could make permanent homes were then much less prized than ports in which trade could be carried on with native races. Nevertheless, the acquisition of New York (as New Amsterdam was renamed in honour of the King's brother, the head of the Navy) and New Jersey was of great value to England, inasmuch as it gave her undisputed possession of the whole eastern seaboard of North America.

The roar of the Dutch guns in the Medway made a profound impression upon the nation. We may say that it brought to an end the first era of the reign—the era of wholehearted royalism. It was inevitable that a reaction should set in against the extravagant king-worship of 1660 ; but this humiliation greatly intensified it. Men could not but remember that such things had not happened in Oliver's time. London had been visited by the Plague, the Fire and the Dutch in successive years, and people felt that there must be something very wrong somewhere. In such circumstances it is human nature to look for a scapegoat. That unpleasant role fell on this occasion to Lord Clarendon. He was hated by the nobles for his pride (especially after his daughter married the Duke of York, the heir apparent to the throne) ; by the King and the courtiers for his disapproval of their scandalous immorality ; by all who sympathised with the Puritans for the High Church persecution. No such feeling as gratitude ever troubled the King's heart, and he was glad of an opportunity to regain some of his early popularity by so easy a method as the sacrifice of a faithful old servant. Articles of impeachment were prepared against the Chancellor by his enemies, but he escaped this by going into exile, where he spent the last few years of his life in writing the memoirs of the stormy times in which it had been spent.

QUESTIONS

(1) *How far were monarchical, ecclesiastical and parliamentary privileges restored at the accession of Charles II ?*

(2) *The career of Lord Clarendon.*

CHAPTER XXIX

King Charles's "Grand Design"

(1667-1673)

In this chapter we shall see how Charles II made secret plans to turn England into an autocracy, something like that of Louis XIV in France. The course of events went against him, however, and he had too much regard for his own safety to continue with the design when he found public opinion decisively opposed to it.

141. *The French Monarchy*

For the next half-century the history of England is so closely connected with that of France that we must know something of the position there.

The reign of Louis XIV (1643-1714) was the period of the ascendancy of France. From the time when the young king took the government into his own hands (1661) he became the very embodiment of the idea of semi-divine kingship. The position had been created for him by his predecessors on the throne and by the two great cardinals who had ruled the country for the past forty years. There was no Parliament to interfere with his right to make laws and tax his people at his pleasure; the administration, both central and local, was carried on by officials who had no object but to carry out his will; the nobility had become courtiers whose sole ambition was to shine in the reflected glory of his throne; an army of 120,000 troops, commanded by the greatest generals of the age, was by far the most formidable professional fighting force that Europe had seen since the days of the Cæsars. At Versailles he built the most magnificent palace in the world, to be the scene of a

288

splendour which every petty prince in Europe fleeced his subjects to imitate. French fashions in dress and deportment became the models for the civilised world. The French tongue became the universal language of culture and diplomacy. The criticism of Boileau, the tragedies of Racine, the comedies of Molière set new standards in literature.

Louis himself was eminently fitted to play the part for which he was cast. He enjoyed to the full the business of being a king, passing his life in the centre of a blaze of admiration and splendour, always behaving with grace and dignity. Nor did his gifts as *Grand Monarque* stop at mere externals. He was his own prime minister, and worked indefatigably at the business of governing. He knew how to choose able servants, how to support them, and how to gain most of the credit of their achievements. The most famous of his ministers was Colbert, an administrator of extraordinary genius, who encouraged industry and agriculture, husbanded the finances, and built a great navy.

Unfortunately for Europe (and, indeed, in the end for himself) Louis was not content with the magnificent position which he had inherited, but evolved great schemes for territorial expansion. He had little opposition to fear. Spain was still a great power on the map, but her real strength was fast crumbling away through corruption and misgovernment; and Germany was exhausted by the Thirty Years' War. In 1665 died Philip IV of Spain, leaving the crown to a sickly child; and Louis seized this opportunity to make a beginning with his plans. He claimed that by the local laws of inheritance the Spanish Netherlands should pass to his wife, who was a daughter of the late king. His only real argument in support of this claim was the army which in 1667 marched into Flanders under the command of Marshal Turenne. The weak and ill-equipped Spanish garrison was hardly able to make a show of resistance. Europe was greatly alarmed at this revelation of the ambition of the French King.

142. *The Triple Alliance*

The country in which this feeling was strongest was the Dutch Republic. This state was hardly larger than Wales, but it was a hive of industry and wealth, with a teeming population and a world-wide commerce. The government was in the hands of the rich merchants under the leadership of one John de Witt. Great political and military power had formerly been wielded, under the title of " Stadholder," by the very able descendants of William the Silent (§ 58) ; but the merchant-oligarchy had seized every opportunity of pushing this semi-monarchical power into the background. Latterly they had been successful in so doing, owing to the fact that the head of the House of Orange was a mere boy, Prince William Henry. The Dutch Republic, having been founded on a revolt from Spain, had always looked to France for support ; but the seizure of the Netherlands altered the whole outlook. Obviously, it was no longer Spain but France that was to be feared. The Republic began to look round anxiously for an ally to aid them in counteracting this new danger. By a remarkable diplomatic revolution, it found what it was seeking in England, the Power with which it had recently fought two bitter wars !

Sir William Temple, the very able ambassador at the Hague, was the chief figure in this exploit. He had much ado to induce John de Witt to take a step which was bound to give offence to France, nor could English people forget in a moment their old jealousies. But it was obvious, both to Dutch and to English, that if the powerful and ambitious Louis gained possession of the Rhine Delta and the ports of the Spanish Netherlands, France would soon develop into an irresistible commercial rival to them both. Moreover, there was no guarantee that Louis would not next seek to absorb Holland. Yet again, the Great Fire of London had been (quite falsely) ascribed to a papist conspiracy inspired by Louis, and there was a feeling that Protestant states ought to unite against the aggressions of a great Catholic Power. By the terms of the Triple Alliance (as it soon became by the adherence of Sweden) the allies were to join in an attack on France if Louis continued his policy of aggression in the Netherlands. The threat had its effect. Louis was not as yet prepared to undertake a war against such a coalition. He promptly ended the " War of Devolution," as it was called, by a treaty which gave him only a fraction of the claims he had originally made.

143. *The Secret Treaty of Dover*

The Triple Alliance was connected with a remarkable episode in our constitutional history.

Charles II was not a man of principle, but this does not mean that he had no preferences. For instance, while he cared nothing for theories of Divine Right, he chafed at the limitations imposed on him by his position as a constitutional monarch ; and again, although he often scoffed at religion, he always felt an affection for the Catholic Church. He had fallen foul of the Cavalier Parliament partly because of its niggardliness over money, and partly because of its bigoted Anglicanism. There gradually took shape in his mind a plan by which he could gratify all these feelings at once. Suppose King Louis could be induced to pay a subsidy as the price of English support for his schemes of aggrandisement ! That would free him (Charles) from the irksome position of being solely dependent on parliamentary grants, and would enable him to defy the opposition of Parliament to a régime of religious toleration, in which both Catholics and Dissenters would be free from restrictions. Hints of this scheme were dropped by the King to the inner circle of ministers who shared the chief offices of state after the fall of Clarendon. Such inner circles of leading ministers were usually called " cabals " ; but by a curious coincidence the names of the five who were now in power began with letters that made up that word, and they have ever since been known as *The* Cabal. Indeed, the conspiracy against parliamentary government in which they now became involved gave the word such evil associations that it afterwards fell out of use. They were a curiously assorted quintet. Sir Thomas Clifford, a straightforward old cavalier, and Lord Arlington, an adroit politician, were both Catholics ; the Duke of Buckingham was a dissolute boon companion of the King's who, by a curious kink of character, sometimes considered himself an Independent in religion ; Ashley, who had served under Cromwell, was a genuine believer in freedom of opinion ; and the Earl of Lauderdale was a Scottish peer who had formerly been a Covenanter, and was still one at heart. The one point that all these men had in common was that none of them were Anglicans ; hence they were all ready to support the King's plans for granting toleration behind Parliament's back.

The Triple Alliance was accepted by Charles and his Cabal as a screen behind which they could bring into action their very different policy. It had the advantages of being popular, of embroiling Louis XIV with his traditional allies the Dutch, and of teaching him the value of that English support which they were planning to offer him in the near future.

Everything at first went according to plan. Louis was extremely angry with the Dutch, and made up his mind that their resistance must be crushed before he could resume his schemes of expansion. In 1669 Charles calculated that the time had come to broach his scheme to him. The French King welcomed the idea, and secret arrangements were made that, in return for a handsome subsidy, England should join France in attacking and partitioning the Dutch Republic. But the plot went a good deal further than Charles had originally intended. He now undertook to declare himself a Catholic as soon as a suitable moment should arise, and do everything in his power to restore England to the Catholic faith, provided that Louis would support him with money and troops if a revolt broke out in consequence of this action. This arrangement was largely due to the influence of Charles's youngest sister, Henrietta Duchess of Orleans, who was devotedly attached both to the Catholic Church and to her brother. In May, 1670, she came to meet him at Dover, ostensibly on a mere family visit, but really to carry through the final negotiations for the alliance on behalf of King Louis. Only the two Catholic members of the Cabal were in attendance, for the King dared not let the three Protestants know of the Catholic clauses. Of course the others already knew that an agreement was being discussed for a subsidy, a general toleration, and an attack on Holland ; so a sham treaty was prepared and signed by the whole Cabal in 1671, which mentioned these matters alone. Charles was highly amused at having duped so astute a man as Ashley, and to carry the joke a stage further he made him Lord Chancellor and Earl of Shaftesbury. But the man who fooled Shaftesbury was playing a dangerous game—and one that was not likely to last very long.

144. *The Third Dutch War*

Charles had now hired out control over the English Government to the King of France; but the price was not sufficient for his purposes, and he therefore resorted to two other devices—both equally dishonourable—for raising funds. He induced Parliament to make a grant for the support of the Triple Alliance against France, and then immediately prorogued the Houses. He also informed the goldsmiths of London, who at that time acted as bankers and advanced the Government money in anticipation of the taxes, that he could not repay their loans for the present. This *Stoppage of the Exchequer* was a short-sighted trick. It brought ruin to a number of great firms, and injured the Government's credit for years. Still, for the moment Charles could congratulate himself that he was independent of Parliament for a considerable time.

Nevertheless, he and his Cabal were taking a big risk. With funds gained by subservience abroad and trickery at home they were undertaking a war and preparing to undermine the Church without the approval of Parliament or people. They counted on a speedy victory to enable them to claim that they had chastised the insolence in the Medway and had gained valuable ports in Flanders. Buoyed up by these hopes, they made a beginning with the second part of the Dover scheme.* The King issued a *Declaration of Indulgence*, which allowed Protestant Dissenters to worship in places approved by the Government, while Catholics were released from the penalties of the law provided that they held their services in private. The King hoped that the support of Dissenters and Catholics would enable him to override the opposition of the High Church party, and he was not without hopes that a considerable proportion of that party would soon be willing for some sort of reconciliation (on terms) between the Anglican Church and the Pope.

In March, 1672, the third part of the Dover plan was put into action : France and England simultaneously declared war upon Holland. Louis had just previously bribed Sweden into withdrawing from the Triple Alliance, and the little Republic was

---

* *I.e.*, of the scheme that was shared by the whole Cabal. The opportunity for putting into effect the secret Catholic clauses never came, as we shall see.

now completely isolated. When two French armies marched down the banks of the Rhine to invade it by land, while an Anglo-French fleet attacked its coasts, it appeared at first as if resistance would be utterly impossible. The first effect of the danger on the Dutch people was to cause a violent revolution. Frenzied with terror, and believing that they had been betrayed by their rulers, the mob overturned the oligarchy, murdered de Witt, and called on the young *Prince of Orange* to take the position of Stadholder and save the country from its enemies.

Prince William was only twenty-one years of age, but he had an old head on young shoulders. Though his health was always weak, he overcame this disability by the iron determination of his will. Grave, circumspect, never so happy as when grappling with dangers and difficulties, he was as well suited as his rival Louis XIV for the task in life to which his destiny called him. The struggle upon which he now entered on behalf of Dutch liberties against the greed and ambition of the French King was fated to occupy most of his thoughts and energies for the rest of his life. It began under the most desperate conditions. Like their ancestors in the days of the revolt against Spain (§ 58), the people determined to flood their country rather than submit to foreign domination. They pierced the dykes and let in the ocean over the countryside, so that their cities rose like islands out of great stretches of water, and the French attack was held up. This gave the Prince time to organise the defence and to form a coalition with German rulers who feared that they might be the next objects of King Louis' aggression.

Meanwhile the allies had been equally unsuccessful in their naval campaign. The combined fleets had been sought out by de Ruyter in *Southwold Bay* in Suffolk (1672) and so damaged that they were not fit for further service that year. In the following year they made an attack on the *Texel*, the island which commands the entrance to the Zuyder Zee, but de Ruyter again attacked them with inferior forces and compelled them to give up their design.

145. *The Collapse of the Conspiracy*

Thus, by the spring of 1673 Charles found that the unexpected prolongation of the war had upset his plans. He had spent all his money without getting any nearer to the victorious peace on which he depended. He had too much regard for his own safety to try any of his father's devices for raising unauthorised taxes, and his friend Louis had not a franc to spare at this juncture. He therefore bowed to the inevitable and summoned the Parliament again.

The members did not at first attack the war ; what they resented was the Declaration of Indulgence. The King had made a complete miscalculation as to its effects on the public mind. The Anglicans were as determined as ever to maintain the privileged position of the Church, and even the Dissenters were unwilling to accept toleration if the Catholics were to be included in it. A wave of " No Popery " feeling, amounting almost to a panic, spread over the country. Of course nobody knew the whole truth—that Charles had undertaken to restore Catholicism with the aid of foreign troops and money ; but suspicions had been aroused by the recent advancement of many Catholics to posts of responsibility. Any hopes the King might have entertained of saving the Declaration were removed by the action of his Lord Chancellor. Shaftesbury had realised that he had been tricked over the Treaty of Dover, and, boiling with indignation, he took this golden opportunity of revenge. He pronounced the Declaration illegal, and joined the opposition. A few weeks later Arlington was driven into exile by a threat of impeachment for his activity in promoting it. The Cabal was rapidly crumbling away.

Nor was this the end of the King's troubles. Even when he had very reluctantly withdrawn the offending document, Parliament was not satisfied, but pressed on to pass a *Test Act* which made it compulsory for all persons in public service to declare their disbelief in the doctrine of Transubstantiation. A number of Catholics who had hitherto kept their faith secret were thus forced to declare it. Amongst these were Sir Thomas Clifford, who resigned the Lord Treasurership, and the Duke of York, who gave up his post at the Admiralty. It had long been an open secret that the Duke was inclined to Catholicism, and much opposition had been aroused by his recent marriage to a Catholic princess, Mary of Modena, but this public announcement of his conversion gave the nation a very unpleasant shock, and roused the agitation to fever heat.

Parliament next turned its attention to the war. The members had now had time to realise that this was not a struggle for maritime supremacy, but a conspiracy to destroy a Protestant people in conjunction with a great Catholic Power. The House of Commons compelled the King to withdraw from it by the simple expedient of refusing any further grants of money. Thus the whole policy of the Treaty of Dover had fallen into utter ruin.

Questions

(1) *Sketch the history of "The Cabal."*

(2) *Describe the character of "The Cavalier Parliament."*

CHAPTER XXX

The Popish Terror

(1673–1681)

We shall now trace the birth of the Whig and Tory parties, and see how the former took advantage of the national dread of "popery" to overthrow the Cavalier Government. Their triumph was short-lived, however, for the King succeeded in cutting the ground from beneath their feet.

146. *Clarendonism Revived*

The parliamentary explosion which had destroyed the Cabal and the Dover plot taught Charles a lesson which he never forgot. Henceforth he gave up all idea of making England Catholic. He now made a bid to regain the confidence of the Parliament by taking as his chief minister its most influential member. This was Thomas Osborne, later raised to the peerage as *Lord Danby*. Danby was greedy of rank and wealth, but he was a man of principle—a sincere patriot and a sincere Protestant. He was a cavalier of much the same stamp as old Lord Clarendon had been ; and recent events had confirmed his conviction that the only sound basis for government was a strong monarchy linked to a privileged Church. Persecution of Dissent and of Catholicism began again, and to this the King did not trouble to make much resistance ; but with regard to foreign affairs, the line pursued by the Government often wavered in a bewildering way, for Danby was in favour of an alliance with the Dutch against Louis XIV, whereas Charles was still hoping for more French money. Sometimes the King gave way to Danby through easy-going negligence, while Danby sometimes gave way to the King through fear of losing his post. For instance, although the King had 10,000 English troops serving under Louis XIV, he raised another army at home on the pretext that support must be sent to the Dutch. Again, Charles compelled Danby to sign secret treaties whereby Louis obtained promises of English support in return for subsidies ; while Danby induced Charles to allow the marriage of the Princess Mary to the Prince of Orange.

This last event led to very important consequences. The King had no legitimate children, and his brother the Duke of York had only two daughters, by his first marriage with Anne Hyde. These princesses had been brought up as Protestants, and the marriage of one of them to William of Orange—himself a grandson of Charles I—might in the future produce a much-needed Protestant heir to the throne. The King allowed the marriage to go through in order to show Louis (with whom he chanced to be on bad terms at the time) that he had other strings to his bow besides the alliance with France ; but Louis retaliated by supporting the parliamentary opposition with secret bribes in the hope of overthrowing Danby.

The country had recovered somewhat from the fever of fanatical loyalty which had raged when the Cavalier Parliament had been elected. As a matter of fact, the members themselves had cooled a good deal since 1661, and the opposition of " The Country Party " to " The Court Party " was growing stronger year by year ; but there was still much more of the Cavalier spirit about the existing House of Commons than there was likely to be in any new Parliament. The great object of Shaftes-bury (who had now taken the lead in the opposition) was there-fore to find some way of compelling the King to dissolve it, while Danby sought to postpone that event as long as possible. The strength of the opposition lay in the growing unpopularity of the Government with the general public, and the widespread suspicion that the King and his brother were still looking for a chance to introduce a despotic and Catholic government. The possession of office was an immense advantage to Danby in the struggle, for it gave him control over valuable appointments in the service of the Crown, and he could thus hold his majority together by an indirect form of bribery. For some years the minister's position seemed to be impregnable, and the opposition was gnashing its teeth in impotent fury, when an unexpected event changed the whole position.

147. " *The Popish Plot* "

One day as the King was about to take a stroll in St. James's Park he was warned that an attempt on his life was threatened. It appeared that a man named Oates had just arrived from the Continent with information of a Catholic plot to place the Duke of York on the throne. This Oates was a man of infamous character. He had been in turn a Baptist minister, an Anglican clergyman, and an inmate of a Jesuit seminary, and in each position his conduct had led to his being driven away with ignominy. While a pretended convert to Catholicism he had heard something of the plans for the conversion of England. The truth about these plans was enough to give a shock to public opinion, but Oates proceeded to embroider the facts with all sorts of imaginary details, about plots to burn down London, to murder Protestants wholesale, to shoot the King with a silver bullet, to land a French army, and so forth.

At the outset of his campaign of lies, Oates enjoyed two pieces of amazing good luck. Firstly, among the persons whom he denounced as organising the plot was Edmund Coleman, the Duke's secretary. Coleman's rooms were searched, and hidden in the chimney was found some correspondence with Père La Chaise, a priest in high confidence with the King of France, in which plans were discussed for military support for the reconversion campaign. Secondly, Sir Edmund Berry Godfrey, a highly-respected magistrate before whom Oates had made a sworn declaration on the plot, was found murdered in a field near London—slain, it was presumed, by Catholics who feared that he knew too much about their designs.

If the people had been alarmed by the original story of the plot, these confirmations of it sent them mad with fear and fury. The magistrates searched the houses of Catholics, seized their papers, and haled them to prison in scores. London looked like a besieged city, with barricades in the streets, the train-bands marching about, and guns placed at important points.

People went armed with " Protestant flails " to brain Popish assassins.

When Parliament met, Shaftesbury made the most of the situation. It is very unlikely that he really believed Oates' tales, but he pretended he did and fanned the flames of public excitement for his own political ends. King Louis, in order to overthrow Danby, had revealed to the leading members of the opposition that the minister had signed subsidy treaties. This disclosure seemed to the panic-stricken Parliament to be a proof that Charles and Danby had been in league with Louis for the use of troops to subjugate England. An impeachment of the minister was set on foot, and his plea that he had only acted by direct command of the King was brushed aside. To prevent these proceedings from being carried through—when perhaps they might lead to further revelations of his dealings with the French Court—Charles was forced to dissolve Parliament. The opposition had got their way !

Meanwhile, Oates was developing his plot from day to day. Taking advantage of his lucky hit about Coleman, he proceeded to denounce many other Catholics by name. He became the most popular man in the country ; he was granted £1,200 a year, rooms in Whitehall, and a private bodyguard. Other men, jealous of his good fortune, came forward with stories of their own, and a hideous competition in perjury began. Judges and juries were so inflamed with passion and prejudice that they accepted the accusations of these unsavoury blackguards and rejected the evidence of the most respectable witnesses for the Catholics as " tainted." Convictions followed as a matter of course, and scores of perfectly innocent persons were done to death amid the howls and execrations of frenzied mobs. The King was far too shrewd to be taken in by such clumsy impostures, but he had no intention of protecting innocent subjects at the risk of being himself suspected of " popery."

148. *The Exclusion Bill*

The all-important General Election took place early in 1679. Shaftesbury was the first party leader to carry through a political " campaign." He realised that the only way to overcome the power of the Crown was to organise the voting of the classes who distrusted it His headquarters, the famous "Green Ribbon Club," was in Chancery Lane, with branches in most of the larger towns in the provinces.

The new Parliament was as full of anti-Catholic fury as might have been expected. It certainly accomplished one useful piece of legislation—an improved version of the old *Habeas Corpus Act*, which strengthened the safeguards against imprisonment without trial. But apart from this, it devoted itself entirely to heated debates as to the best way of preserving the national liberties and religion against the Duke of York's Franco-Papist designs. Eventually the opposition decided to bring in an *Exclusion Bill* declaring that he could not succeed to the throne. His rights were to pass to the next heir, his daughter the Princess of Orange. The King would have none of this : for once in a way he put his foot down. His whole position depended on maintaining the natural right of inheritance, and when Parliament persisted with the Bill, he dissolved it (July, 1679).

Nevertheless, he could not afford to do without a Parliament for long. He was at the moment on bad terms with Louis XIV (who had helped to precipitate the crisis), and he hoped that a proposal for an alliance with the Dutch and the Hapsburg Powers against France would silence the opposition. Another election was held in January, 1680, but when Charles saw the list of members, he realised that it was not likely to be more reasonable than the last, and he refused to allow it to meet. For the next eight months furious discussions went on over this action. New nicknames for the two parties came into use. Those who petitioned the King to call the Parliament became known as "Petitioners," while those who sent in counter-addresses expressing their abhorrence of the petition were called "Abhorrers." But these names soon changed to others which remained in use for nearly two centuries. The opposition derided those who supported the Catholic Duke by calling them *Tories*, after the name given to a species of Catholic outlaws in Ireland; while the Royalists retaliated by calling the exclusionists *Whigs*, a word hitherto applied to rabid Scottish covenanters who were at that moment in rebellion against the King.

During the whole crisis the King never lost his good humour or his cool common sense. He strolled in the Park and fed the swans and fondled his spaniels as if nothing were amiss. He knew that time was on his side. Sooner or later the nation's mad fit would pass. In the meantime, he sent his unpopular brother over to Brussels, where he would be out of the public eye.

When, in October, 1680, he decided to let the Houses meet, the Commons at once confirmed his unfavourable expectations. The Whig majority would not listen to any talk of a grant for a war with France until the Exclusion Bill had been passed. They now decided to put forward the *Duke of Monmouth* as their candidate for the throne. This was an illegitimate son of the King's, a handsome, charming, but weak and unprincipled young man. The Whigs preferred him to Mary and her husband for several reasons. They did not like foreigners, they feared that William would subordinate English trading interests to Dutch, and they hoped that a king with a weak claim would be a puppet in their hands. They spread a rumour that evidence had been preserved in a black box of the King's marriage with Monmouth's mother, and that he was therefore the true heir.

This second Bill passed the House of Commons, but many prominent Whigs disliked the Monmouth claim ; and when the measure came before the Upper House, Lord Halifax, a very able statesman who had originally been a strong supporter of Shaftesbury, made an impressive speech against it which caused the Peers to reject it. To prevent any further discussion on the subject, the King once more dissolved Parliament.

149. *The Oxford Parliament*

Signs were now appearing that the reign of terror was drawing to an end. Juries were becoming sceptical of Oates' tales and were refusing to convict prisoners on his evidence. At the end of 1680 he succeeded in bringing to the scaffold Lord Stafford, a well-known Catholic peer ; but as the frail and gentle old man passed to his death the crowd expressed their sympathy and their belief in his innocence. A natural reaction always follows such storms of blind and unthinking passion as had recently swept over the land, and to this reaction the Whigs themselves contributed by their tactical mistake in putting forward Monmouth as their candidate for the throne. Nobody of any education or standing believed the story about the black box, and the thought of setting aside the legitimate line of kings in this way disgusted all steady-going, old-fashioned people of both parties. So strong was this feeling that there would probably have been armed resistance if Charles had died, say in 1680, and Monmouth had claimed the throne. And this possibility of civil war was another cogent reason against interfering with the succession. The last war, with its aftermath of military rule, was still fresh in men's memories.

The King felt that the hour for which he had been waiting was at hand. When, early in 1681, his financial needs compelled him to call another Parliament, he summoned it to meet at Oxford, where it would be out of reach of the London mob, which was always ultra-Protestant. But the Houses seemed to be hardly affected by the change of feeling which was taking place in the country. They brought in yet another Exclusion Bill, and they declined to adopt any of the compromises suggested by the King.* They were jubilantly confident that his urgent need for money would soon compel him to give way; and when he summoned them to a special joint session at which he would be present in person, it was generally supposed that he was about to take some such step. What was their stupefaction when they found that it was to announce a dissolution !

Charles had for some time been engaged in secret negotiations with the King of France. Louis was anxious to get England permanently on his side in his European schemes, but knew that this was impossible so long as Whiggish parliaments controlled English policy. He therefore offered Charles a subsidy provided that he would summon no more Parliaments. Charles had waited to see how the session at Oxford would turn out; and he had now decided to give up the parliamentary game and accept the French king's offer.

Shaftesbury made frantic efforts to keep the Houses together

* *E.g.*, that the Prince of Orange should be called over to do the actual work of governing when James became King.

in defiance of the dissolution, but this would have been an act of sheer rebellion. The members had no nerve for such a course. They slipped away to their homes as fast as horses would take them.

150. *The King's Triumph*

The King's action had been well timed. The Popish Plot panic had now completely worked itself out. The Whigs could still have held many of their parliamentary seats in the boroughs, where Dissent was strongest ; but it was only when the Houses were sitting that they could make their voices heard. So long as French subsidies made the King financially independent, opposition was silenced. Nevertheless, Charles was too astute a politician to force the pace : the tide was still flowing in his favour. The Duke of York had returned from Brussels, but was sent off again to Scotland, where he was employed as Lord High Commissioner to punish a rebellion of the Covenanters which had been provoked by persecution by the Anglican Church. The rebels had already been defeated at *Bothwell Brig* by a royal force under Monmouth and Graham of Claverhouse, and York now busied himself with torturing and hanging the survivors.

In 1683 the Whigs made another false move which enabled the King to complete their discomfiture. The leaders of the party, finding themselves powerless to make any headway by constitutional means, began to discuss plans for an insurrection. Their chances of success, always very small, were diminished by the mutual suspicion which prevailed among them. At the end of 1682 Shaftesbury, learning that the Government was about to take action against him, fled to Holland (the country which he had tried to ruin twelve years before), where he died shortly afterwards. Meanwhile, some old Roundheads of humbler station concocted a plot to murder the King and his brother on their way back from Newmarket races. The deed was to be done opposite the *Rye House*, a lonely moated farm on the Newmarket road. The plot was betrayed, and the conspirators were hanged.

The Government determined to take this opportunity to

strike down the whole opposition party once and for all. The aristocratic leaders were all arrested, and one of their number, to save his own life, gave evidence of their recent discussions. It is not certain to this day how far any of them was implicated in the two plots, but a fanatically royalist judge and a packed jury lost no time in condemning them all to death, after a trial in which there was hardly a pretence of fair play to the accused. The most famous of the victims were Lord Russell and Algernon Sidney, who have ever since been regarded as martyrs for the cause of liberty.

The triumph of the King's cause was now complete. The Duke of York came back to London and was reinstated as Lord High Admiral, in defiance of the Test Act. The rank and file of the squires and High Church parsons, whose loyalty had been temporarily checked by the Popish Terror, now swung back to their natural Toryism with redoubled fervour. Every Sunday the extremest doctrines of non-resistance were preached from hundreds of pulpits. Kings, the clergy declared, were the Lord's anointed. Even if a sovereign were as wicked as Nero, to harbour a thought of disobedience to his will was the basest of crimes. The Duke, as the representative of legitimacy, was so much thought of that some people said that the attempt to prevent his accession had made him king while his brother was yet living.

As for Charles, he smiled cynically at all this nonsense, but he enjoyed to the full his final victory in the political game which he had been playing all through his reign. He sauntered on in his care-free way until in February, 1685, he was struck down by apoplexy. On his deathbed his did two highly characteristic things. After a life of shameless immorality and ribald impiety, he was received into the Catholic Church ; and he uttered one of the most famous jokes in history—an apology to the bystanders for being " such an unconscionable time dying."

QUESTIONS

(1) *Trace the relations of England with France under Charles II.*

(2) *Explain the effect of the Popish Plot upon English politics.*

CHAPTER XXXI

The Reign of James II

(1685–1688)

James II came to the throne with every prospect of a successful reign, and he might even have gained toleration for Catholicism if he had not thrown away his chances by the tactless precipitancy and violence with which he set about placing his co-religionists in a position of political supremacy.

151. *An International Event*

The accession of James II was an event of European importance. The coalition organised by William of Orange had prevented Louis XIV from gaining all the objects with which he had attacked the Dutch in 1672 (§ 144), but during the next ten years he had contrived by diplomacy and sudden movements of troops to extend his boundaries eastward without fighting a campaign. Just at this time he began to show himself a militant champion of Catholicism, largely through the influence of the pious Mme. de Maintenon. In 1681 he began a systematic effort to crush Protestantism out of France. By the ordinances known as the *Dragonnades* severe pressure was put on the Huguenots to make them join the Catholic Church. It was foreshadowed that Louis' next war would have a religious aspect—that it would be, in effect, an echo of the Counter-Reformation. Yet at the very moment when he was posing as the defender of Catholic orthodoxy, he was quarrelling with the Pope, for he refused to allow any exception to his authority over every aspect of French life, and he had therefore set up what almost amounted to an independent Gallican Church. The possession of a mighty army made him reckless as to whom he offended.

But at the Hague there was watching and waiting an implacable enemy of all his ways and works. William of Orange was determined that the Balance of Power in Europe should be restored, that Protestantism should not be destroyed, and that the Netherlands should never be absorbed in France. He had desperate difficulties to contend with. Each of the seven little states which composed the United Netherlands (the official name of the Republic) had its own factious oligarchy, jealous in various degrees of his authority as Stadholder ; and to counteract the overwhelming power of France he had to build up a European coalition out of such heterogeneous material as the Empire, the Electorate of Brandenburg, the Kingdom of Spain, and the Papacy.

Thus, for the ten years 1678–88 the air of European politics was full of thunder. Another war was in sight, but nobody knew how or when it would break out. A great deal depended on the attitude of England, for even the high and mighty Louis could not afford to ignore her resources in money and ships. All through the reign of Charles II that attitude had been in doubt. Even when Charles took French money again, after the Oxford Parliament,* the triumphant Tories who dominated Court and Cabinet for the rest of the reign were not all of one mind. Some of them were Protestant supporters of Danby's anti-French policy, while others formed a Catholic pro-French party, under the leadership of the Duke of York. It is thus clear that the sudden accession of that Duke to the throne (Charles was only fifty-five, and of robust constitution) appeared to be a piece of great good fortune for King Louis. With England on his side he had nothing to fear from Prince William's coalition.

152. *Joyous Accession*

James II was fifty-two when he came to the throne. He was in many respects a very different type from his brother. He was

---

* That very year (1681) saw four notable demonstrations of the power of the French monarchy : the defeat of the Whigs in England, the beginning of the Dragonnades, the seizure of Strassbourg, and the publication of the " Four Articles " which offended the Pope.

almost equally licentious and selfish, but he altogether lacked Charles's *bonhomie* and careless good nature. Solemn, slow-witted, obstinate, harsh, and relentless, he was far more conscientious than Charles both in religion and in the business of kingship. Before the passing of the Test Act he had been a highly efficient administrator of the Navy, and he had commanded the fleet (perhaps with more courage than discretion) at the battle of Lowestoft (§ 140).

At his accession he was in a stronger position than any other of the Stuart kings had been. The bulk of the ruling class were devoted to him, he had at his back a regular army of 14,000 men which his brother had gradually collected, and the most powerful monarch in Christendom was his friend and ally. His first actions confirmed the confidence of his supporters. He retained all his brother's ministers in office, he assured the Council that he would always support the existing constitution, both in Church and State, and he at once summoned a Parliament. People might have been less impressed if they had known that he had humbly apologised to Louis XIV for taking this last step ; but on the surface it was an auspicious beginning. Moreover, the Parliament when it met was all that he could have desired. Charles II had taken advantage of his triumph in 1681 to remodel the corporations of many boroughs (including London) in such a way that the Whig influence no longer predominated in them ; and as the parliamentary elections lay largely in the hands of these boroughs a Tory majority was assured. There was no reason why this Parliament should not last all the rest of the reign ; and in any case, it seemed to be only a question of a few years before the Dissenters, the main support of Whiggism, would be crushed out of existence by the renewed pressure of the Clarendon Code.

Parliament began by granting the King a revenue of £2,000,000 for life, and by passing a law which made it High Treason for any member to advocate any alteration in the succession. To be sure, the temperature of the Houses' loyalty fell several degrees when James raised the question of relaxing the penal laws against Catholics ; but the fall was checked almost immediately by the news that rebellions had broken out, in Scotland and in Dorsetshire.

153. *Argyll and Monmouth*

The Netherlands were full of English and Scottish refugees who had fled from the persecution of the triumphant Church-and-State party. Of these " emigrés " the most prominent were the Earl of Argyll and the Duke of Monmouth. Argyll was the head of the great Campbell clan, and his father had been executed soon after the Restoration for his support of the Covenant against Charles I, while he himself had barely escaped from the persecution which followed the more recent rising (§ 150). Monmouth had been sent away in disgrace by his father owing to his connection with the Whig leaders, who were attempting to gain the succession for him. Both these men were assured by their sanguine fellow-exiles that they had only to show themselves in their respective countries to rally thousands to the cause of " the true religion." There was little love lost between the two parties (had not Monmouth commanded the royal forces against the Covenanters at Bothwell Brig ?), but at last it was arranged that two separate expeditions should be fitted out to strike in Scotland and England in quick succession—Argyll in the Western Highlands, where the strength of the Campbells chiefly lay, and Monmouth in the West of England, where he had been received with great acclamations on a previous visit.

Argyll's venture was hopeless from the first. His clan had been cowed by the recent persecution, he was " assisted " by a civilian council of war which destroyed all unity of action, his forces were wearied out with aimless marching and counter-marching, and his supplies fell into the hands of the royal troops. He was captured and executed at Edinburgh, meeting his end with the cheerful fortitude of one who believes that he is a martyr for a sacred cause.

Monmouth came a good deal nearer to success than this. He landed at Lyme Regis in Dorsetshire, and for a week or two his enterprise seemed to be prospering. People were captivated by his handsome face, his gallant bearing, and his winning manners. Moreover, Puritanism was very strong in those parts, both among the farm-folk in the countryside and the wool-manufacturers in the little towns, and these simple folk looked upon the young Duke as a sort of hero-prince who had come to rescue them from the persecution which they were suffering under the Clarendon Code. By the time his force had reached Taunton it was 5,000 strong, and he was proclaimed king there amid great enthusiasm. But his star soon began to wane. He marched to take possession of Bristol, then changed his mind and turned into Wiltshire, then returned to Somerset. Meanwhile the King's forces were fast concentrating in the district. Monmouth's men—armed some with muskets for which they had very little ammunition, and others with scythes tied on poles—made a night attack on the chief body of the royal troops at *Sedgmoor*, but were driven off by the superior discipline and equipment of the regulars. When the latter made a counter-attack, the rustics resisted gallantly for many hours, but at length they broke and fled. Colonel Kirke and his regiment from Tangier distinguished themselves by the ferocity with which they slaughtered the disarmed fugitives, and then hanged them by dozens after the most summary of court-martials. The unhappy Duke tried to escape through the New Forest and take ship back to the Continent ; but search-parties were organised to gain the £5,000 offered for his capture, and he was eventually found, hiding in a ditch, half dead from hunger and fatigue. Parliament had already passed an Act of Attainder against him, and his uncle was not the man to remit the penalty.

Nor was this the end of the tragic story. The gaols of the Assize Towns of the Western Circuit were crowded with prisoners charged with being connected with the rebellion, and the King took care that a suitable judge should be sent down to deal with them. This was Lord Chief Justice Jeffreys. He had already gained the royal favour by his conduct of the trials of the Whigs after the Rye House Plot (§ 150), and by the savage (though not ill-deserved) sentence he had passed upon Titus Oates for perjury.* In Judge Jeffreys an abject desire to curry favour with the Court was combined with an inhuman passion for inflicting suffering on his fellow-creatures. Often under the influence of

---

* Oates was sentenced to pay an enormous fine, to be twice pilloried and flogged through London on two successive days, and to be imprisoned for life. It was probably intended that the flogging should kill him, but he survived it, and early in the next reign was released and given a small pension by the Whigs.

liquor, he would storm at the helpless wretches in the dock, browbeat their witnesses, and silence their counsel. On this famous *Bloody Assize* he began by sentencing an old lady named Alice Lisle to be burned alive for sheltering two fugitives from Sedgmoor, and it was only with great difficulty that he was persuaded to allow her to be beheaded instead. In the course of the next few weeks he sentenced 300 persons to death and 900 to transportation. All that winter the roads of Somerset and Dorset were hideous with the remains of these misguided country-folk rotting on gibbets. On his return to London Jeffreys was rewarded for his zeal with the Lord Chancellorship ; but his barbarities gave a great shock even to the more enthusiastic Tories. Englishmen were not accustomed to that sort of thing.

154. *James Shows His Hand*

But the most serious result of the Western Rebellion for the cause which James had at heart was its effect upon himself. The ease with which it had been suppressed gave him an overweening sense of security, and lured him on to take steps which led to his ruin.

As soon as Parliament met again after the interruption, he informed it point-blank that there were three things on which he had set his heart. He wanted to maintain the army at the strength to which it had recently been raised—some 30,000 men ; and he wanted the repeal of the Habeas Corpus Act and of the Test Act. Unfortunately for him, these were just the things which even the most loyal of Parliaments could not bring itself to grant. When the Houses demurred, he angrily prorogued them, saying that he would have his way—if not with their support, then without it. The fact is, that he and the Tory Party had misjudged each other. The Tories supposed that he meant what he said when he promised to support the Church of England, and he believed that they would consistently carry out their doctrine of Non-resistance.

With the encouragement of the King of France, and under the influence of a Jesuit priest named Petre, he now accelerated the process of converting the country. He claimed that he had the right to " dispense " with any Act of Parliament, and he believed that his army made him independent of public opinion. To overawe the capital, he established a great camp on Hounslow Heath, and this was commanded largely by Catholics in defiance to the Test Act. Then he went on from folly to folly, hacking away at the pillar of Tory support on which his throne rested. He dismissed from the Council Lord Halifax—the man who had procured the rejection of the Exclusion Bill (§ 148)—for opposing the repeal of the Test Act. To gain control over the Church, he set up once more the Court of High Commission which had been abolished in 1641. He appointed Catholics as the heads of Oxford Colleges and turned out the Fellows of Magdalen because they would not elect a particularly disreputable nominee of his as their President ; and he thus antagonised the University which was the very home of the doctrine of Non-resistance. Many a country parson who had hitherto preached that doctrine Sunday after Sunday now began to fear for his vicarage, and many a squire with an estate that had once belonged to a monastery began to wonder how long he would be allowed to keep it. Protestants were turned out, one after another, in Council, Court, the Magistracy and the Services, to make way for Catholics. Most sensational of all was the dismissal of the sons of Clarendon—the second Lord Clarendon, who was Lord Deputy of Ireland, and Lord Rochester, who had been practically Prime Minister. They had supported James through thick and thin, and had gone to unjustifiable lengths in defending his illegalities ; but they drew the line at turning Catholic, and nothing else would satisfy him. The law said that no Catholic could hold office, but the King seemed to intend that no one else should. Most of his co-religionists disliked the policy, for they knew that their fellow-countrymen would never be brought to change their faith by such methods ; and they feared—quite justly, as it turned out—that an anti-Catholic reaction would be aroused, in which their position would be worse than ever. The Pope himself was of that opinion. But James would listen to no counsels of moderation. " I will make no concessions," he would say ; " my father made concessions, and he was beheaded "—·an argument so fatuous that it needs no refutation.

155. *Two Declarations and an Invitation*

Early in 1687 the King decided on a startling change of method. Since 1681 the Court had treated the High Church party as the chief bulwark of the throne. To please it the Dissenters had been persecuted under the Clarendon Code, and the corporations manipulated so that Tories should predominate in them. But that party had now shown that it would not carry Non-resistance so far as to support James in " Romanising " the country. He therefore determined to win the favour of the Dissenters, hoping that they would be glad to purchase toleration for themselves by supporting toleration for Catholics. With this object he issued (April, 1687) a Declaration of Indulgence, which gave freedom of worship to all, and abolished religious tests ; and he followed this up by remodelling the corporations once more, in such a way that Dissenters should have a preponderating voice in the next parliamentary election.

It will be remembered that when Charles II attempted a similar policy in 1672 he was compelled to withdraw his Declaration and admit that it was an illegal use of the " dispensing power " ; but James was a man who could not learn from experience, and he was now surprised to find that the Dissenters were not so easily taken in. They felt that his real aim was to gain their support in the next Parliament for a repeal of the Test Act (which was especially directed against Catholics), and that he would throw them over as soon as they had served his turn. Much as they hated Anglican parsons, they hated Catholic priests far more, and all James's past history was a contradiction of his new pose as a broadminded lover of Toleration. Moreover, only two years before, his close friend and patron, Louis XIV, had taken the final step in his persecution of the Huguenots by revoking the Edict of Nantes. Protestant families were broken up, the men sent to the galleys, the women to convents, and the children to institutions which brought them up with stripes in a faith they had been taught to abhor. By a refinement of cruelty, the victims were not allowed to emigrate, but in spite of this many managed to escape to Protestant countries, and at this moment thousands of them were a living witness to English Protestants of the cruelty of a Catholic king under the influence of Jesuit priests.

Thus the effect of the Declaration was very disappointing to the King, and he had to postpone the summoning of the new Parliament until the following year. In April, 1688, he issued a second Declaration, which he ordered to be read in all churches on two successive Sundays. This was compelling the clergy to be not only the instruments of their own humiliation, but accessories to a breach of the law ; for what was the good of Parliaments passing laws if the King could " dispense " with them in this wholesale way ? There was barely a fortnight before the first Sunday appointed for the reading, but the Archbishop of Canterbury, feeling that the time had come to make a stand, called a meeting of the bishops. Only seven were able to attend, but these drew up a petition to the King begging him to withdraw the order. James was very angry, and he ordered that the bishops should be indicted for publishing a " seditious libel." Their trial was followed with breathless interest, and the verdict of " Not guilty " was received with rapturous enthusiasm. It was an unwonted thing for Presbyterian Londoners to be cheering bishops and pressing round them to ask for blessings. This was the first public expression of feeling about the King's policy, and it should have been a warning to him, especially when the cheers were taken up by the soldiers paraded on Hounslow Heath, as soon as the joyful news reached them.

Still the King pursued his purblind way. He felt just at this moment that he had a special reason to be confident as to the future of his policy, for a son had been born to him while the trial was in progress. Yet by the irony of fate this event was the beginning of the end for him. Thousands of anxious Tories had hitherto consoled themselves with the reflection that they had only to possess their souls in patience until the King died and was succeeded by his Protestant daughter, the Princess of Orange. Now that hope was taken from them and the country was faced with the prospect of a succession of Catholic kings. Something had to be done. On the very night that the bishops were acquitted seven of the leading men in public life, representing both political parties, sent a joint letter to William of

Orange, asking him to come over with an army and save the kingdom from " Popery."

QUESTIONS

(1) *Trace the steps by which James II forfeited the popularity which he had enjoyed at his accession.*

(2) *Compare the characters of Charles II and James II*

CHAPTER XXXII

"The Great and Glorious Revolution"

(1688–1690)

We shall now see how it came about that the situation in European politics gave William first the necessity and then the opportunity of wresting the government of England from James II, how James played into his hands by fleeing the country, and how a new form of government—the Constitutional Monarchy—was establish:d in the persons of William and Mary.

156. *Another European Event*

It is impossible to understand our English Revolution unless we grasp its connection with the politics of Europe as a whole. William of Orange did not come over merely to defend the English constitution, still less from mere ambition to wear the English crown. The passion of his life was resistance to Louis XIV, and he undertook the English adventure solely because he wanted England to be on the right side in the contest. It seemed to be a matter of life and death for the freedom of Europe. The ambitions of Louis had expanded mightily, and he now cherished designs on the throne of Spain (including the Indies) and on the position of the Holy Roman Emperor. If these projects were carried through, this dragonnading despot would be the master of the civilised world, and the absorption of the Netherlands in his vast domains would be a matter of course. William had already formed the League of Augsburg (§ 151) amongst the powers most likely to be attacked, but it was more obvious than ever that everything might depend on the part played by England in the coming struggle.

The Prince of Orange therefore felt that at all costs an Anglo-

French alliance must be prevented. The leaders of the Whig party had long been in correspondence with him ; but he knew all the dangers of an armed invasion, and he would not under- take such a risk so long as (*a*) there was a prospect of a peaceful succession of his wife on the death of James, and (*b*) his coming was desired by only one of the political parties. Then, in June, 1688, came the news of the birth of a son to James and the letter from the representative men (§ 156). These events made him decide to take definite action, but there were still enormous diffi- culties to be overcome. King Louis was well known to be prepar- ing his mighty forces for war, though it was not yet clear against whom they were to be used. William's position as Stadholder did not give him control over the policy of the Republic, and it was very unlikely that the Dutch " Estates " (or Parliament) would denude their country of troops at such a crisis ; yet to attempt armed intervention in England without their support was to invite the fate of Monmouth.

Within a month or two, however, all these difficulties were cleared from the Prince's path by his enemies themselves. Louis heard of the invasion project, and warned the Dutch government that he would consider it an act of war against himself. The effect of this threat was the opposite of what he intended, for it revealed the close connection between himself and James. The Dutch Estates now realised that the dethronement of James would be a severe blow to Louis ; and they agreed to support the Stadholder with men and ships. James, too, found himself in an impossible position, for he was about to call a Parliament, but dared not face it with an admission that he was in close alliance with France. He was therefore driven to deny, with more emphasis than politeness, the existence of any such connection ; and when Louis offered him help against the threatened invasion, he replied with some acerbity that he could take care of himself. Not unnaturally, Louis took offence at this rebuff. He had at the moment urgent need for his army in Germany, to uphold his designs on the Empire, and he thought that a Dutch expedition against England would at once teach James manners and keep William occupied. (Of course, he did not suppose that the invasion would be successful, for James had an army twice as strong as any force that William could bring against him.)

He therefore launched his army across the Rhine, and within a fortnight was far too deeply involved there to be able to do anything for King James. William could now sail without anxiety about the safety of the Dutch Provinces. Thus James's connection with Louis precipitated the invasion, while his petulance prevented that connection from affording him any help in his hour of danger.

157. " A Protestant Wind "

Some days before he sailed, the Prince sent over a declaration to be circulated in England. He mentioned his personal interest in English affairs, especially as the throne was his wife's heritage—for he accepted the story (generally believed in England at the time) that the little Prince of Wales was not the Queen's child, but had been brought to her room " in a warming-pan." He went on to enumerate the grievances which the King had recently inflicted on the country. Finally, he declared that his object in coming was to procure the election of a free Parliament, to which he would refer all questions as to the future government.

On October 21 he set out, intending to land in Yorkshire, but a violent gale drove him back ; and for the next ten days " a Catholic wind " blew from the west and prevented him from getting out of port.   Then on November 1 " a Protestant wind " sprang up from the north-east and carried him down the Channel. His fleet consisted of some 600 transports, carrying about 16,000 troops, escorted by 60 warships. They cast anchor in Torbay, and there he landed on November 5, an anniversary of ill-omen for Catholic England. His troops were of excellent quality. Several battalions had been raised from the English refugees, but most of them consisted of professional soldiers, Dutch, Swedish, and Swiss. They were well armed and equipped, especially in the matter of artillery. The nobles and gentry of the west country soon began to flock in to William's standard (on which was inscribed " A Free Parliament and the Protestant Religion "), but he did not encourage the enlistment of volunteers, who would have been more hindrance than help to his veteran troops.

Meanwhile, King James was wishing he had accepted the French offers of help. He called back the regiments which had been sent to Yorkshire when the landing had been expected there; but it was becoming evident that he could not depend on their loyalty, and that his only reliable troops were the Catholic regiments which had been brought over from Ireland. He appointed Salisbury as the rendezvous for his forces, and thither he himself repaired about the middle of November. The invaders were moving very slowly, for William was anxious not to arouse national feeling against himself by making his expedition appear to be a conquest of England. Soon the King's strength began to melt away. Many prominent people went over to William, and news came that the northern counties had risen in revolt. James decided that it would be wiser to return to London; but this move led to the most notable desertion of all. The brilliant Lord Churchill had always been a favourite with James, who had given him a peerage and made him a General, and his wife was the bosom friend of the Princess Anne. This able but unscruplous man had long been in secret correspondence with William, so as to assure his own future. When the King decided to retreat he made up his mind that the invaders were the winning side, and left the Royal camp to join them. His desertion made a profound impression; but even more distressing news met James on reaching London. The Princess Anne, acting under the influence of Lady Churchill, had also fled. " Heaven help me, my own children desert me ! " exclaimed the unhappy man.

The conviction was now borne in upon him that the game was up, at any rate for the time. He announced that he would call a free Parliament, and entered into negotiations with the Prince; but he secretly informed the French ambassador that this was merely to gain time for the escape of his wife and child. The invading army was drawing steadily nearer to the capital, and after a few days of tension the King's nerve gave way. He slipped off by night to take ship from the Kentish coast. This was exactly what William had hoped, for it would have been very embarrassing for him to have his father-in-law on his hands as a prisoner. Unfortunately some fishermen captured the fugitive, and he had to be brought back to London. Still, every opportunity was given him to renew his flight, and he very obligingly did so. Arrived in Paris, he was received by the French King (a man who found it easier to be generous than to be just) without a reproach for his folly. Louis placed at his disposal a palace at St. Germains, granted him £40,000 a year, and ordered the Court to pay him all the honours due to a reigning sovereign.

158. *The End of Divine Right*

The three months that elapsed between the flight of James and the proclamation of William and Mary are known as " The Interregnum." The Prince was careful to do nothing that could look like usurping authority. He summoned a meeting of such peers and former members of the Commons as were in or near London to decide upon the next step. This body asked him to arrange for a General Election, and meanwhile to carry on the government himself.

Like the Parliament which brought about the Restoration (§ 136), the assembly which carried through the Revolution was not legally a Parliament, not having been summoned by a king ; and it was therefore, like that of 1660, called a " Convention." Its discussions showed that, united as the nation had been in resisting the illegal actions of James II, there were very varied opinions as to what should be done now that he had fled abroad. Each of the plans proposed was open to grave objection. (1) The ultra-Tories were for inviting James back upon certain conditions ; but the drawback to this was that he could not be trusted. No laws could be more explicit than those he had broken wholesale in the past. (2) The ultra-Whigs wanted to take this opportunity of breaking the line of succession altogether, and give the throne to William ; but this would have offended the great bulk of public opinion, which clung to the idea of hereditary monarchy. (3) By way of compromise, it was suggested that James should be still nominally king, while the actual government was entrusted to William with the title of Regent ; but if the royal authority was still exercised in James's name how would it be possible to prevent him from interfering with the government ? (4) Another suggestion was that James's flight should be regarded as an abdication ; in which case the Princess Mary might succeed him as his legal heir—it being taken for granted that the little Prince of Wales was supposititious. She might then give the actual administration over to her husband, perhaps with the title of King-Consort. The difficulty about this was that if Mary died William would be in an impossible position.

It was only the last two proposals that met with much approval, and the debates upon them waxed hot. For a week or two William held his peace ; but when it appeared that a decision might be dangerously delayed he sent for some leading members of the Convention and told them that, without wishing to interfere, he thought they ought to know that for his part he would neither be a regent for James nor a subject of his own wife, much as he esteemed and loved her. If the Convention decided upon either of these schemes, he would cheerfully go back to the Netherlands. Nearly everybody was agreed that his rule was indispensable to England ; and an arrangement was now devised which would at once make him King in his own right and satisfy the desire for hereditary succession. The throne which had been vacated by the flight of James was offered to both husband and wife, to be held by them jointly. Attached to the document which requested them to assume the sovereignty was a *Declaration of Rights* which laid down the conditions under which the offer was made : there was to be no more dispensing with Acts of Parliament, or interference with elections, and so on.

This transaction implied, though it did not express, a new conception of monarchy ; and that conception was the essence of " The English Revolution." The idea of hereditary succession was preserved in the person of Mary, but the idea of Divine Right was abandoned in the person of William. Loyalty to a sovereign who owed his crown to a bargain set forth in a Declaration of Right was a very different feeling from that which had been made into a sort of sacred mystery by the cavaliers.

159. *The Revolution Settlement*

Having been summoned to England by men of all parties, William refused to regard himself as merely "King of the Whigs." He appointed members of both parties impartially to the chief offices of state, while the Treasury and Admiralty he placed under "Boards," as they are to-day. Now that the throne was once more occupied, the elements of the constitution were complete, and the Convention declared itself to be a lawful Parliament. There were many important arrangements to be made for the future government of the country, and to this task the Houses now addressed themselves.

The changed position of the Crown was made definite and permanent by restrictions which were embodied in the law of the land. The Declaration of Rights was now made into a *Bill of Rights*; but experience had shown that such restrictions were of little use unless they were supported by "sanctions," *i.e.* by penalties through which they could be enforced. With this in view, Parliament discontinued the practice of granting the King a regular revenue. A certain fixed income was assured him— "The Civil List"—but this was nothing like enough to make him independent of annual grants; and the King had henceforth to bring evidence before the House of Commons as to the estimated expenditure of government for the ensuing year. This was the origin of the modern Budget, and in effect it compelled the King to summon Parliament every year. This necessity was further emphasised by the Mutiny Act. The prejudice against "standing armies" was as great as ever; but in the face of a possible invasion by Louis XIV (for which he now had a double motive—to restore his friend James and to attack his enemy William) it was impossible at the moment to disband the army. An Act was therefore passed which authorised soldiers being kept under military discipline for the next twelvemonth, in the hope that by the end of that time the danger would have passed. That hope was not fulfilled; from year to year the *Mutiny Act* had to be extended, and the practice has lasted right down to our own day. Another important measure was the *Triennial Act*, which provided for the holding of a General Election every third year. This prevented such anomalies as the first Parliament of Charles II, which remained in existence long after it had ceased to represent public opinion. Lastly, the succession was provided for. When either William or Mary died, the survivor was to reign alone. If they both died without children, the Princess Anne was to succeed.

So far the Houses had shown wisdom and unanimity; but when they came to a settlement of religion, all the old blind passions broke out once more. The King was quite prepared to conform to the Church of England; but this attitude indicated that he cared little for the sacramental distinctions so precious to the High Church Party. He tried to get the Houses to approve of a two-fold scheme for broadening the basis and outlook of the Anglican Church : *Comprehension*, to include moderate nonconformists in the Church; and *Toleration*, to remove all legal distinction between Churchmen and members of other denominations. High Church feeling was too strong for him, however. By the *Toleration Act* Dissenters were permitted to worship without interference; but the Corporation Act (§ 139) was kept in force to prevent their holding any official position. As for the Comprehension Bill, it was rejected altogether.

Many of the High Church clergy went even further in their resistance to William. The attacks of James on the Church had driven them reluctantly to modify their enthusiasm for the doctrine of Divine hereditary Right; but they were opposed to the Revolution. Now that the Catholic danger was removed, their instinct for loyalty to the " legitimate sovereign " had free play once more, and some 600 of them refused to take the oath of allegiance to William and Mary. These *Non-jurors*—amongst whom were most of the bishops who had protested against the Declaration of Indulgence—were expelled from their benefices in January, 1690.

160. *The Character of the Revolution*

The episode which later generations of Whigs called " The Great and Glorious Revolution " did not seem very great or glorious to the men who carried it out. It was enlivened by no days of delirious excitement and enthusiasm such as marked the progress of the French Revolution a century later ; in fact, there was very little enthusiasm of any sort. To the bulk of the nation the whole thing appeared to be a disagreeable necessity. It was carried through with sober common sense by a group of level-headed and practical statesmen, by means of Acts of Parliament passed one by one as the necessity for them arose.

This was in part due to the personality of the new King himself. William III had neither the capacity nor the desire to arouse such heartfelt devotion as Charles I and his sons could always inspire in a large proportion of their subjects. He was a great statesman and an able soldier; he was a man of his word; he was large-minded, and knew when to forget and how to forgive; his courage in danger and constancy in difficulty were of the finest mettle; but he was often harsh and unfeeling, and he had no charm of manner. He cared little for England for her own sake, and was not interested in the settlement of her constitutional problems. All that he cared about was the amount that her resources might contribute to the ultimate defeat of Louis XIV. He was useful to England, and England was going to be useful to him. It was a sound bargain for both, but not a transaction to arouse enthusiasm.

Looking at the matter from a broad point of view, we can see that the Revolution was the nation's final rejection of the policy begun in 1670 at Dover—the policy of a Catholic England in vassalage to France. Charles II had been compelled to abandon it for the time, but there was always a possibility that he might take it up again. Indeed, he actually did so, in part, when he " dished the Whigs " at the Oxford Parliament. So far as the Catholic side of the plan was concerned, Charles realised that discretion was the better part of valour, but his brother was one of those fools who rush in where wiser men fear to tread. His reign had been a reckless attempt to carry through the Dover policy without regard to the consequences; and the consequences had their revenge by leading him straight along the road to St. Germains.

QUESTIONS

(1) *Write a history of the " Dover Policy "* (1668–1688).

(2) *Explain the effect of the Revolution on the English Constitution.*

THE WARS AGAINST "LEGITIMACY"

Year				Year
1688	William lands at Torbay (§157)			1688
1689	Bill of Rights (§159) **WILLIAM** & MARY Act of Toleration (§159)	**A "NON-PARTY MINISTRY"** (§159)	James II in Ireland (§162) England joins Grand Alliance (§163) Killiecrankie ⚔ (§161)	1689
1690			The Boyne ⚔ (§162) Beachy Head ⚔ (§163)	1690
1691			Treaty of Limerick (§162)	1691
1692		**MINISTRY"** (§159)	Massacre of Glencoe (§161) La Hogue ⚔ (§163)	1692
1693	Place Bill rejected (§164)		Neerwinden ⚔ (§165)	1693
1694	Bank of England (§164) **WILLIAM III** Triennial Act (§159)	**THE "WHIG JUNTO"** (§164)		1694
1695			Irish "Penal Code" (§162) Namur ⚔ (§165)	1695
1696				1696
1697			Treaty of Ryswick (§165)	1697
1698	Darien Scheme collapses (§172)	**Tory Reaction setting in** (§167)	1st. Partition Treaty (§166)	1698
1699			2nd. Partition Treaty (§166)	1699
1700			Philip V. King of Spain (§167)	1700
1701	Act of Settlement (§167)		Grand Alliance re-formed (§167)	1701
1702	**ANNE** (§167)	**MARLBOROUGH & GODOLPHIN** (becoming more Whiggish) (§171)	Marlborough in Netherlands (§169)	1702
1703	Scottish Act of Security (§172)		Methuen Treaty (§179)	1703
1704			Blenheim ⚔ (§170) Gibraltar ⚔ (§170) Malaga ⚔ (§170)	1704
1705			Barcelona ⚔ (§170)	1705
1706			Ramillies ⚔ (§170) Turin ⚔ (§170)	1706
1707	Union of England & Scotland (§172)		Almanza ⚔ (§173)	1707
1708		**A (Purely Whig Ministry)**	Oudenarde ⚔ (§173)	1708
1709			Malplaquet ⚔ (§173)	1709
1710	Trial of Sacheverell (§173)			1710
1711	"Conduct of the Allies" (§177) Occasional Conformity Act (§175)	**TORYISM TRIUMPHANT** (§174) (Oxford & Bolingbroke)	Dismissal of Marlborough (§174)	1711
1712	Creation of Tory Peers (§174)			1712
1713			Treaty of Utrecht (§174)	1713
1714	Schism Act (§175) **GEORGE I**			1714

CHAPTER XXXIII

King William's War

(1690–1697)

The Settlement described in the last chapter was for the next few years always in danger of being overturned ; for the exiled King was in constant communication with dissatisfied parties in England. Ireland was almost solidly in his favour ; he had a considerable party in Scotland, and the most powerful monarch in Christendom was his host and supporter. We shall now see how the Revolution survived these manifold dangers.

161. " Bonnie Dundee "

Now that the long-expected European war had begun with the French invasion of Germany (§ 156), William was anxious to get back to play his part in it ; but he could not leave until his authority had been accepted in Scotland and Ireland. In each of these kingaoms—we must never forget that they had separate governments—the events of the past fifty years had aroused religious animosities to such a pitch that the Revolution was bound to meet with resistance.

Let us first consider the situation in Scotland. The Presbyterian Covenanters (§ 111) had successfully resisted the attempt of Charles I to establish the Anglican Church there ; but after the Restoration it had been imposed upon them with more success. In 1678 the Covenanters had been goaded by persecution into open rebellion which had been defeated at Bothwell Brig (§ 150) and repressed with savage cruelty. We have also seen that Argyll's attempt to resist the accession of James II had led to his execution and to renewed severities. Those severities had so far achieved their purpose that Scotland played no part in the movement which led to the Revolution; but the meeting of the Convention in England was followed by a similar event in Scotland. The Edinburgh Convention offered the Scottish crown to William and Mary on condition that the Presbyterian Church was re-established. William made no difficulty about this; but the new régime was resisted by John Graham of Claverhouse, who had been created *Viscount Dundee* by James II for the part he had played in crushing the Covenanters in 1681 (§ 150). To him the Revolution meant the establishment in Church and State of all that he hated most. Betaking himself to the Highlands, he raised a force of clansmen on behalf of James II. These Highlanders cared little who was King of Scotland, nor were they much interested in religious doctrines; the attraction to them of Dundee's call to arms lay mainly in the opportunity to harry the Campbells and to plunder the Lowlands.

The story of the rising is soon told. After some weeks of joyous raiding in the Campbell country, the rebels won a brilliant little victory over a regular army of double their own numbers, just outside the Pass of *Killiecrankie* (1691). For once the disciplined and methodical tactics of European warfare were annihilated by a headlong charge of primitive warriors; but in the course of the action Dundee himself was killed. There was no longer a personality to hold the Highlanders together, and they went off to carry their plunder up to their mountain fastnesses. Their chieftains decided to postpone further action until King James himself should arrive to lead them—which never happened.

A horrible sequel remains to be told. The chiefs gradually became reconciled to the new government, especially when they found that they would be left to carry on their traditional mode of life unmolested. William offered a complete amnesty to all clans whose chiefs had taken an oath of allegiance by January 1, 1692. From feelings of pride the aged head of the Macdonalds of Glencoe left his submission till the last day—and then found that he had applied at the wrong place. While matters were being adjusted, a force of soldiers was sent into Glencoe, ostensibly on a friendly visit, and was hospitably entertained. A week later the soldiers suddenly fell on their hosts by night and slaughtered them without distinction of age or sex. Historians have never determined how far William himself was responsible for this atrocity; but three points are certain: that he knew something about the design; that he inflicted no punishment on those responsible; and that to his cold-blooded nature it hardly seemed a matter to make a fuss about.

162. *The Battle of the Boyne*

In Ireland repeated confiscations of land had divided the inhabitants into two bitterly hostile classes—a small minority of Protestants, English by blood and traditions, and mostly well-to-do; and a large majority of native Catholics, who were for the most part impoverished. The accession of James II led to a dramatic change in the Government. The King appointed as viceroy the *Earl of Tyrconnel*, a violent and reckless Catholic. Catholics were now appointed to all the chief offices of state, and an army was raised, 50,000 strong, in which Protestants were not allowed to serve. To the Protestants, therefore, the news of the Revolution came as a promise of deliverance; but they were a mere handful, and for the time being Tyrconnel's grip over the country was unshaken.

James therefore decided to make Ireland a starting-point for the recovery of England. Louis XIV encouraged the idea, and helped him with officers, munitions and ships. He was received by the native Irish with transports of joy, and at once proceeded to call a Parliament at Dublin. He had intended to conciliate the Protestants, but he found that the Catholics were burning to recover their confiscated property and would give him no support unless he allowed them to do so. The Protestants took to arms, but they were so few that almost the whole country was soon in James's hands. One of the last Protestant strongholds was the town of Derry. Its heroic defence was crowded with romantic incidents, as when the food-ships which London sent to the starving defenders burst the booms which had been placed across the river by the besiegers. In the end the Jacobites (as the supporters of the Stuart cause were beginning to be called, from *Jacobus*, the Latin form of " James ") were compelled to raise the siege.

Still, it was obvious that William would have to take decisive measures if James was to be prevented from making good in Ireland. In June of the next year he therefore went thither himself at the head of a strong and well-equipped army of professional soldiers, English, Dutch, Danish, and Huguenot. Landing at Belfast, he marched southwards to attack Dublin, and the hostile forces came face to face across the River Boyne. There was a marked contrast in their fighting value, for much of the Jacobite army had, through lack of supplies and organisation, degenerated into a plundering rabble. Consequently, the *Battle of the Boyne* (1690) was hardly a battle at all. William's men pushed their way across the river and scattered the opposition after two or three sharp skirmishes. Yet this was, in its consequences, one of the most important victories in modern history ; for had William been defeated or killed (he was twice wounded) it is highly probable that Louis XIV would have conquered Europe and James II have recovered his throne. As it was, the ex-King's nerve failed him once more. He rode headlong to Dublin, took ship for Waterford and sailed thence back to France.

Yet his cause was still far from desperate in Ireland, and his supporters continued to put up a stout resistance. William had to return to England, leaving the rest of the campaign to his second-in-command, a fellow-countryman named Ginkel. It was not until the following year that the Irish were induced to surrender, while they were still in a strong position at Limerick, by the promise of favourable terms. By the *Treaty of Limerick* (1691) those of the Irish troops who wished to do so were allowed to go to France to serve under King Louis, while the Catholics in Ireland were guaranteed the same political and religious freedom that they had enjoyed in the time of Charles II.

Unfortunately, the sequel was even more disgraceful than that which followed the pacification of Scotland. In 1692 the English Parliament, disregarding the terms of the treaty, passed an Act to exclude Catholics from the Irish Parliament ; and the Protestants, who represented little more than a tenth of the population, used their monopoly of power in the Dublin assembly

to perpetuate their supremacy by the *Penal Code*. Catholics
were forbidden to own land or to join the learned professions,
and their priests were banished on pain of death. Thus were
religious feuds fomented, and right down to our own times the
anniversary of the Battle of the Boyne was celebrated by Irish
Protestants as the starting-point of their political ascendancy.
And just as King William was indirectly responsible for the
Massacre of Glencoe, so he was for this far more serious crime.
There is no evidence that he made the least attempt to see that
justice was done or treaty obligations fulfilled.

163. "*The War of the League of Augsburg.*"

During the winter which preceded his Irish campaign,
King William had been forming the " Grand Alliance," pledged
to resist by arms the aggression of Louis XIV. All his con-
summate statesmanship was required to induce the heterogeneous elements of it to co-operate, for they were united by
only one tie—the assurance that if they did not stand together
they would fall victims one by one to the French king.

The war began with French victories both by land and sea.
Louis realised that supreme naval power was needed to deal with
England and Holland, and he therefore concentrated on ship-
building during the winter of 1689-90. The result was the
overthrow of the Anglo-Dutch fleet at the *Battle of Beachy Head*
(June 30, 1690), which gave the French the command of the
Channel. On that same day a French army in the Netherlands
won the battle of Fleurus against the Imperial troops.

This was the situation which brought William back from
Ireland before the fighting there was over. In January, 1691,
he presided at a congress of the Allies at The Hague to concert a
general plan of action. The campaigns that followed were too
indecisive to have much direct bearing on English history, and
we need not follow them in detail. There was much marching
and counter-marching, capturing and recapturing of fortresses ;
and when autumn weather made these occupations unpleasant
both sides suspended them by tacit consent until the following
spring. William had great difficulties to contend with, not

merely in organising the allied forces, but in keeping the Dutch " Estates " and the English Parliament steady in support of the war.

The year 1692 was a critical one for England. Louis determined to distract William's attention from the Continental war by sending an expedition to restore James II. Great preparations were made ; 30,000 picked troops and 500 transports were collected at *La Hogue* in Normandy, and a fleet was sent from Brest to convoy them to the English coast. James prepared a Declaration to the Nation, which showed that he had learnt nothing from his misfortunes, and forgotten none of his old animosities. Queen Mary (who acted as Regent while her husband was campaigning abroad) realised that this document would rally the people to the support of the Government, and took care that it should be widely circulated.

James went to La Hogue to witness the embarkation of the army that was to win back his heritage ; but the process was interrupted by the arrival of the Anglo-Dutch fleet under Admiral Russell. The ex-King assured the French commander Thouville that the English crews were honeycombed with disaffection towards William's government, and would show little fight. Thouville's fleet was much weaker than that of the Allies, but relying on this information he boldly went forth to the attack. The result was that his fleet was crushingly defeated, and when a dozen of his finest ships sought refuge by running aground, they were followed up and burnt to the keels. The luckless James watched from the cliffs his hopes going up in smoke, the fires having been kindled by the navy which in happier days he had done so much to foster.

164. *Party Government*

William always spent in England what may be called the " close season " for war. He found his duties as King exceedingly irksome. He loved fighting for its own sake, and when engaged therein his usual harshness of demeanour gave place to high spirits and good humour. English political life, on the other hand, was just then a particularly ugly business. It is hardly to be wondered at that his preference for his native land increased rather than lessened as time went on; for he spent his summers there in the delights of warfare, while he associated England with winter fogs that aggravated his chronic asthma, and with a group of treacherous politicians. His feelings towards the nation were heartily reciprocated. One abiding cause of his unpopularity was the favour he showed his Dutch friends. It was natural enough, for instance, that he should give his life-long companion Bentinck the Dukedom of Portland and vast estates, but it aroused great jealousy amongst the English nobility. Moreover, very few people appreciated the importance of his struggle against Louis XIV. Now that La Hogue had made the country safe from invasion, it was felt that the lives of English soldiers and the wealth of English tax-payers were being squandered merely in the interests of the Dutch Republic. Many Tories had repented of their action in 1688, and were looking forward to a Restoration, while even among the Whigs there was some anxiety to be on the safe side. There was hardly a man in public life who had not been, at some time or other, in secret correspondence with St. Germains. One of the most shocking cases of this double-dealing was Churchill. It is said that he went so far as to betray naval secrets to James—but with characteristic duplicity contrived that the information should arrive too late to be of use. Even Admiral Russell was in touch with James before he sailed for La Hogue; but when the fleets had once engaged his fighting spirit made him forget everything in his determination to beat the enemy. William knew a good deal of what was going on, but he preferred to live the opposition down rather than take action which might involve most of his ministers.

Several important constitutional developments took shape during these years. The King found that the combination of both parties in the Council worked very badly. The ministers spent most of their time and energy in wrangling, while Parliament was not very ready to vote money to a Government that had no consistent policy. Now that the Commons had gained complete control over taxation, it was important that the Ministry should consist of men whom it trusted. As there was a Whig majority in the existing House, therefore, the King gradually replaced the Tory ministers by Whigs. Not only did he thus ensure parliamentary support, he also gave power to the men who favoured his war-policy, for the leading Whigs had everything to lose by the success of Louis XIV and the return of James II. Thus began the tradition which has since become a constitutional law, that the Cabinet must be chosen from the party that has the support of the House of Commons.

Another important event was negative : the fact that the *Place Bill* (1693) did *not* pass into law. In order to check the power of the Crown to purchase the support of Members of Parliament by appointing them to salaried posts, it was proposed that holders of such posts should be debarred from being members of the House of Commons. The Bill passed both Houses, but was vetoed by the King,* who had no desire to limit his own power of influencing the Commons. There was much to be said in favour of the measure, but if it had passed it would have vitally affected our whole system of government. For one of the most striking differences between the constitution of Britain and that of, say, the United States, is that the members of our Cabinet not only may but *must* also be members of Parliament, where they personally introduce their legislation and defend their conduct of public affairs.

Equally important were the financial steps taken at this time. Governments had long been in the habit of anticipating the revenue by borrowing from merchants, who were repaid when the taxes came in ; and we have seen how the sudden refusal of Charles II in 1672 to pay more than the interest had thrown the City into confusion (§ 144). That was a trick which could not be played twice, but during William's long war the expenditure outstripped the national income year after year, and it became obvious that some permanent arrangements for such borrowings would have to be made. It was fortunate for the King that the party which supported the war was the party which dominated business circles in London ; and these financial experts now devised a scheme to meet the situation. In 1694 Montague, the Whig Chancellor of the Exchequer, arranged with a group of wealthy merchants that they should club together to provide the Government with a loan, of which the principle was not to be

* This was the last occasion on which a King of England has used his power to reject a Bill passed by Parliament.

repayable at any fixed date, but the interest was to be a first charge on the revenue. To compensate the creditors for losing the immediate use of their money, they were granted a Royal Charter which gave them special privileges to act as a bank on a large scale, backed by a Government guarantee. Such was the origin of the *National Debt* and of the *Bank of England*— institutions which proved of enormous advantage to the country in the future development of its commerce.

165. *The Treaty of Ryswick*

In 1695 the waning popularity of the war-policy was revived for a few months by a second threat of invasion from France. The prolonged struggle was bringing Louis XIV to the verge of bankruptcy, and like an exhausted boxer he made a desperate effort to win by a knock-out blow. To prepare the way, the Jacobites hatched a plot to murder William as he crossed the Thames at Richmond for his regular Saturday afternoon hunt in Richmond Forest. The plot was betrayed and the ringleaders executed. Thereupon the invasion scheme was abandoned. Indeed, the British command of the sea robbed it from the first of any real chance of success.

This affair made William himself popular for a little while ; but the effect soon wore off. The death of the Queen in 1694 (which so prostrated the bereaved husband that he was unable to attend to public business for some weeks) left him alone on the throne—an unattractive foreign king waging an expensive foreign war.

Meanwhile, the campaigns in Flanders dragged their slow length along. The oldest regiments in the British army were winning some of their earliest war-honours at Steenkirk and Neerwinden, but there was very little change in the situation from year to year. Almost the only gleam of real success that reached William was the *capture of Namur* in 1696. It has been said of him that he never won a battle and never lost a campaign—that is to say, he failed in his immediate objective, but contrived that the enemy should not derive any ultimate advantage from their successes. His finest trait as a soldier was his constancy in the face of great difficulties and repeated disappointments.

By the end of 1697 the fruitlessness of the struggle was apparent to both sides, and in the following year the *Treaty of Ryswick* was made.   The terms were tantamount to a defeat for Louis, who recognised William as King of England and promised to give no further help to James.   He also surrendered all the conquests he had made since 1672, except Strassbourg, and allowed the Dutch to garrison a number of fortresses in the Spanish Netherlands as a first line of defence against any renewal of his aggressions.

QUESTIONS

(1) *What were the chief dangers to the Revolution Settlement?*

(2) *A character-sketch of William III, as delineated by his career.*

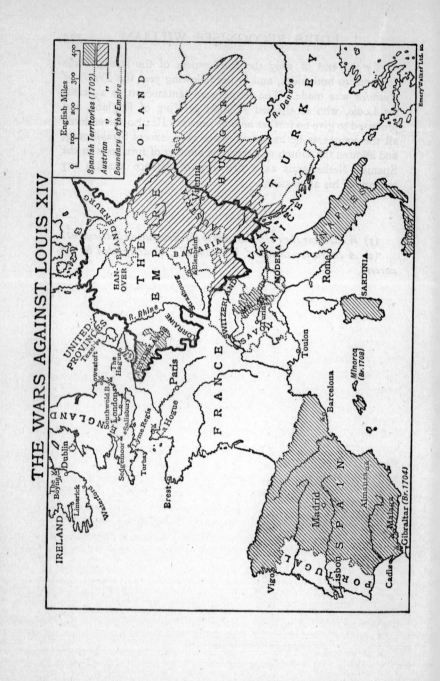

THE WARS AGAINST LOUIS XIV

English Miles
0   100 200 300 400

Spanish Territories (1702).......
Austrian   "   ....
Boundary of the Empire.........

IRELAND
Dublin
Limerick
The Boyne
Waterford

ENGLAND
Southwold B.
Lowestoft
Lr London
Salisbury
Sedgemoor
The Hague
Lyme Regis
Torbay
La Hogue
Brest

HAMBURG
HAN-OVER
HANOVER
UNITED PROVINCES
Texel
NETHERLANDS
Paris
R. Rhine

THE EMPIRE
Strasbourg
LORRAINE
Blenheim
BAVARIA
Vienna
AUSTRIA
STYRIA
R. Danube

POLAND

HUNGARY

TURKEY

FRANCE
Toulon
SWITZERLAND
SAVOY
Turin
MILAN
MODENA
VENICE
Rome

SPAIN
Barcelona
Madrid
Almanza
Malaga
Gibraltar (Br. 1704)
Cadiz
Vigo

PORTUGAL
Lisbon

Minorca (Br. 1708)

NAPLES
SARDINIA
SICILY

Emery Walker Ltd. sc.

CHAPTER XXXIV

The Spanish Succession

(1698–1706)

In this chapter we shall see how William spent his last years in re-forming the Grand Alliance to counteract a renewal of the design of Louis XIV to gain a world-supremacy. William himself died before the war broke out, but Marlborough, his successor in command, succeeded by a series of brilliant exploits in completely defeating the French King.

166. *The Partition Treaties*

King William had now definitely got the better of his great enemy ; yet the three years of life that were left to him were full of anxiety and vexation. The moment the Treaty of Ryswick was signed, Parliament's dread of standing armies returned in full force, and the army was reduced to 7,000 men. Despite the King's almost pathetic appeal, even his Dutch Guards, to whom he and England owed so much, were sent away ; and to add to his chagrin, the " Estates," or Assemblies, of the Dutch Provinces took much the same line.

He had good reason for lamenting the loss of military power at this juncture, for another dangerous storm was looming black in the sky of European politics. King Charles II of Spain, always feeble both in mind and body, was nearing his end. He had no children, and the succession to his throne was in doubt. It was claimed through female descent by three of the reigning families—those of the Emperor, the King of France, and the Elector of Bavaria. We need not discuss the various degrees of validity in their arguments : each candidate was naturally satisfied with his own. The Elector was too weak to have much chance ; and Europe was appalled at the prospect of the overwhelming strength that would be wielded by either of the other potentates if he added to his own dominions the immense empire of Spain.

The only way to avoid a prolonged and terrible war, which would result in the destruction of the Balance of Power which-ever side won, was to agree upon a settlement of the problem beforehand. France had been utterly exhausted by the recent war, and Louis XIV was sincerely desirous of peace—provided the Emperor did not get Spain. He was therefore quite ready to enter into negotiations with William III, the leading spirit among his ex-enemies, for a division of the Spanish heritage among the claimants. Nor was he greedy in making the bargain. By the *First Partition Treaty* (1698) Spanish Italy was to be shared between Bourbon and Hapsburg ; all the rest of the Spanish dominions were to go to the Electoral Prince of Bavaria. But a month or two later that Prince was so disobliging as to die, and the whole question had to be tackled afresh. Louis once more showed himself generous in making concessions. By the *Second Partition Treaty* (1699) it was arranged that the Archduke Charles, the second son of the Emperor, should inherit the whole of the Spanish dominions except a part of northern Italy which went to France.

But here a new difficulty arose : the Spanish government and nation would not tolerate the loss of any part of their empire. The courtiers felt that the best way to prevent this would be to gain the support of a monarch powerful enough to be able to protect them. They therefore induced the dying King of Spain to sign a will bequeathing his entire dominions to Philip, the younger grandson of Louis XIV. If Louis declined to allow Philip to accept, the heritage was to go—still whole and entire, except for Northern Italy—to the Archduke Charles. When, three weeks later, King Charles II died and the will was published, Louis XIV decided to carry it out.

He had been much blamed for this breach of faith ; but it is difficult to see what else he could have done. If he had refused the legacy, it would have passed to the Hapsburgs ; and he would have had to support the Partition Treaty by a war against the Emperor.   Moreover, he would have had to undertake that war single-handed, for neither the English Parliament nor the Dutch Estates took any interest in William's Treaty.

167. *Louis again Plays into William's Hand*

Thus, as a French courtier expressed it, the Pyrenees were abolished. All William's life-work seemed to be undone, and his great enemy more powerful than ever. Moreover, he was tied hand and foot by the constitutions of England and the Netherlands, and in both nations the desire for peace was so strong that William could get no support for his call to arms against Louis. The Tory Party was now gaining the upper hand in Parliament, and the feeling there was entirely against interference in the matter. " It grieves me to the soul," wrote William to Bentinck, " that almost every one here rejoices that France has preferred the Will to the Treaty."

Then, in the course of a few months, the tide of public opinion was turned by the action of King Louis himself. The glorious vista of power which the Spanish Succession opened to him turned his head. He threw to the winds the policy of moderation which he had adopted during the negotiations for the treaties. Since he knew that the other Powers dreaded the connection between France and Spain that would result from his influence over his grandson, his wisest course would have been to avoid anything that might confirm their apprehensions ; but instead of that he went from one act of aggression to another. He alarmed the English and Dutch commercial classes by obtaining for France exclusive trading-rights with the Spanish dominions. He declared that he could not and would not make any promise that Philip should not eventually become King of France as well as of Spain. He displaced the Dutch garrisons in the Barrier Fortresses (§ 165) with his own troops, and held the Dutchmen as hostages till Philip was recognised as ruler of the Spanish Netherlands. These actions convinced even the peace-loving English Parliament that something must be done, and they very reluctantly authorised the King to raise some more troops. But the nation was still very far from being willing

actually to declare war, when a crowning indiscretion on the
French King's part came to William's aid. On the death of
James II in September, 1701, he recognised the ex-king's son as
James III of England, thus treating the Peace of Ryswick as a
" scrap of paper." This action was really no more than a
chivalrous gesture to an orphaned exile, but it led to the ruin of
all his plans.

Only a year before, Parliament had passed an *Act of Settle-
ment* which provided that if (as was almost certain) the Princess
Anne died without children, the Crown should pass to the
Electoral family of Hanover, which was descended from James I.
This expression of the national determination to have no more

THE HANOVERIAN SUCCESSION

JAMES I

CHARLES I   Elizabeth
                                              m.
                                      Elector Palatine

CHARLES II *   Mary   Anne *m.* JAMES II *m.* Mary of   Sophia
          m.   Modena   *m.* Elector of
        William of   Hanover
        Orange   JAMES II   GEORGE I

        WILLIAM III * *m.* MARY * ANNE *

* Died without issue.

Stuarts on the throne had been flouted by Louis XIV, and his
recognition of the Stuart claims seemed like an attempt to
dictate to England, and to imply that, as soon as he found
himself in a position to do so, he would set about placing his
protégé on the English throne. Public opinion was aflame, and
Tories vied with Whigs in urging on a war to chastise the insult.
For almost the first time in his reign William found himself
ardently supported by the English nation, and he eagerly set to
work to re-form the Grand Alliance.

He managed to do so, but it was the last effort of a dying man.
Lung disease had already undermined his strength, and the
broken collar-bone which resulted from a riding accident
merely hastened his end by a few months.

He was succeeded on the throne by his sister-in-law Anne
The change from the able and experienced statesman to this
placid and somewhat stupid lady might have been an
irremediable disaster for the Allies but for the fact that the mind
of the new Queen was completely under the domination of
Lady Marlborough, and that Lady Marlborough's husband was
one of the most brilliant soldier-statesmen that ever lived—
a man comparable to Julius Cæsar and Napoleon Bonaparte.

168. *The Marlboroughs*

The enslavement of Anne to the whims of the imperious
Sarah Churchill had long been a standing joke at the Court.
The story went that the two ladies in their private intercourse
dropped all distinctons of rank and addressed each other as
" Mrs. Morley " and " Mrs. Freeman." Upon this foundation
John Churchill had set out to build his fortunes. Conscious of
commanding ability, and consumed with insatiable ambition for
power and wealth, he was hampered by no scruples as to how he
attained his ends. He and his wife had turned their influence
over the Princess to their own advantage. They had induced
her to desert her father at the critical moment of the Revolution ; they had conducted on her behalf secret correspondence
with St. Germains ; all three had been banished for a time from
the Court in connection with a plot to place the Princess on the
throne. Churchill had won striking success as a subordinate
commander in Ireland and the Netherlands, and had been made
Earl of Marlborough ; but William distrusted him too much to
give him any real responsibility either in the Government or the
Army. Nevertheless, as William lay dying he realised that he
was by far the best man to be his successor in the forthcoming
war, and that with Anne on the throne he would have no motive
to be disloyal to his trust. He therefore expressly designated
him as Captain-General of the forces of the Grand Alliance—
an appointment which the new Queen was delighted to confirm.

Marlborough's chance had come, and he grasped it with
both hands. The task that faced him was one of appalling
difficulty. He had to hold together a coalition, each member
of which had his own ideas and aims ; he had to plan great

campaigns and carry them out with composite forces ; he had to impose his command on dozens of jealous foreign potentates. Over all these difficulties his genius enabled him to triumph. In dealing with the Allies he was aided by his fine presence and handsome face, his winning manners and ready wit, his inexhaustible patience and good humour ; while as a soldier his greatest qualities were the bold imagination with which he conceived far-reaching strategic plans, his mastery of detail, and the unerring skill and nerve with which he seized upon the critical point on the field and the critical moment in the action. In striking contrast to the unlucky William of Orange, it can be said of Marlborough that he never besieged a fortress which he did not take or engaged in a battle which he did not win.

169. " *Malbrouck s'en Va-t-en Guerre* "

When England and Holland declared war on France in April, 1702, the objective before them was to prevent Philip V from inheriting any part of the Spanish dominions except Spain itself. Their prospects were a good deal less promising than they had been at the beginning of the last war. King Louis now controlled the great Spanish Empire, of which his grandson had taken actual possession. It was apparent that the issue would be fought out in the same four theatres of war as before, but the starting-point for the French armies was in each case far in advance of the positions they had occupied during the late war. In the Low Countries, instead of defending the French frontiers, they were in possession of the Spanish Netherlands before they had struck a blow. They no longer had to fight for a footing on the banks of the Rhine, for they could now sweep right into the heart of Germany through the friendly territories of the Elector of Bavaria, whom Louis had bribed into an alliance. The Alps, again, had ceased to be an obstacle, for French troops could occupy the Spanish province of Milan at their will. And whereas the Spaniards had formerly resisted encroachments in the Pyrenees, they now welcomed French support for Philip V, whom they much preferred as their king to the Austrian Archduke. Thus Louis XIV was " the man in possession," and it seemed an impossible task to turn him out.

But there were circumstances, not yet altogether apparent, which were destined as time went on to act decisively in favour of the Alliance. (1) The French nation had hardly even begun to recover from the exhaustion caused by the last war. King Louis might wring the last *sou* out of the wretched peasantry, but he could not take what they had not got. (2) The English Navy could win no brilliant victories, for Louis hardly ventured to challenge it throughout the war ; but sea-power is often most effective when it merely exerts a silent and almost unseen economic pressure on the enemy. Franco-Spanish overseas trade came to a standstill, while English and Dutch commerce throve as never before. (3) Louis himself had lost the energy of youth, and death had removed most of his best counsellors and generals ; yet he now undertook a task beyond the powers of any human being—to carry through a drastic reform of the Spanish administration at the same time that he was directing the operations of war from Versailles. (4) Last, but by no means least, the incalculable human factor : England had in Marlborough the greatest military genius of her history.

In May, 1702, Marlborough crossed to Flanders with an army composed largely of officers and men who had been trained in the wars of William III. The French had already invaded Dutch territory ; but the Allied army under their new commander crossed the River Meuse, and forced the enemy back across the Belgian border, where they remained entrenched in an impregnable position for the next three years. Marlborough's firm and effective dealing with the situation laid the foundation of his military reputation, and gave the Queen an excuse to confer on him a dukedom at the end of the campaign. During that year the fleet, under Sir George Rooke, failed in an attack on Cadiz, but destroyed the Spanish treasure-ships in Vigo Bay ; and its presence in Iberian waters encouraged Portugal to renew the alliance with England which had been first made at the marriage of Charles II with Catherine of Braganza.

For the Grand Alliance the following year (1703) was a disappointing one in Flanders, and a disastrous one in Germany. All Marlborough's movements were subject to the approval of a committee of Dutch civilian " Field Deputies," and by no combination of tact, urgency and banter could they be induced to authorise an attack on the enemy's entrenchments. In Bavaria a great French army under Marshal Villars (the ablest of the French commanders engaged in this war) was preparing for a bold stroke at Vienna, in conjunction with the forces of the Elector and with another French army which was to cross the Alps from Italy. The Emperor was distracted by a revolt of his Hungarian subjects, and it seemed as if nothing could save his capital from capture. Had Villars' scheme succeeded, the war would have been ended at a blow. Fortunately for the Alliance, the Elector insisted upon trying to join forces with the second French army. This move came to nothing, and the whole design had to be postponed until the following year.

170. *The Downfall of Louis XIV*

Marlborough fully realised the gravity of the threat to Vienna, and all the following winter he was in anxious correspondence with Prince Eugene, the commander-in-chief of the Imperial forces, trying to concert a counter-move. The great difficulty was that neither the Dutch nor the English governments would permit him to leave the Netherlands defenceless while he marched his army hundreds of miles away to attack the French in the heart of southern Germany. What would happen to England, Holland, and the Grand Alliance generally, if he were defeated, or even prevented from returning ?

As he could not get the sanction of his governments, he determined to deceive them. He well knew that nothing could justify such an act except overwhelming success ; he was putting his whole career, perhaps his very life, to the hazard. But he weighed the need with the risk, and decided to take his chance. He persuaded the Dutch to let him have a large army of foreign troops in their pay for an attack on the Moselle, and in May, 1704, he reached the neighbourhood of that river with his composite force. Instead of remaining there, however, he pushed on to the Rhine, marched up the river as far as Mainz, and then struck across Germany. He made good his position in Bavaria by the brilliant storming of Donauwerth, and joined forces with Eugene. Then he got into touch with the Franco-Bavarian army, now under Marshal Tallard. Into the details of the *Battle of Blenheim* (August, 1704) it is not our purpose to enter. Suffice it to say that, after a tremendous struggle, in which the Duke displayed the highest ability as a tactician, the French force was broken to pieces, with the loss of 14,000 casualties and 11,000 prisoners, amongst whom was Tallard himself. Vienna was saved ; Bavaria was knocked out of the war ; the French had to withdraw to their own side of the Rhine. The whole position was reversed, and from this time onwards the Allies were always playing a winning game.

In the course of the next two years blow after blow fell upon Louis XIV in each of the other theatres of war. Within a few days of Blenheim a handful of men from Rooke's fleet landed on the neck of land behind *Gibraltar* while the garrison were on the mainland at Mass, and seized the great rock, to be a base for the English Navy in the Mediterranean. A French fleet which attempted to recapture it was defeated by Rooke off *Malaga*. This was not in itself an overwhelming victory ; but as the French never ventured out of their ports again for the rest of the war, it had all the effects of a decisive success, and left the Allies in undisputed command of the sea. Gibraltar has remained a British possession from that day to this.

All through the campaign of 1705 Marlborough was tied up in the Netherlands by the refusal of the Dutch deputies to allow him any freedom of action. Again and again his plans were ruined and his very orders countermanded—vexations which never ruffled the Olympian calm of his demeanour. That year saw marked progress in the Iberian peninsula, however. Lord Galway, with a mixed force of English and Portuguese, advanced into Spain from the west, while in the east a little force under Lord Peterborough captured Barcelona by a recklessly brilliant exploit. In 1706 the Allies gained possession of Madrid itself; and though they were driven out again a few weeks later the fact that they were operating in the very heart of Spain, where a foeman had not been seen for centuries, made a profound impression on Europe.

Greater things still were to follow in 1706. In the Netherlands the Dutch Government decided to allow the Duke a little more latitude, and he was consequently able to win an overwhelming victory over the French at *Ramillies*, where he inflicted losses five times as great as those he suffered. No Englishman has ever gained such an ascendancy over the minds of an enemy as the terrible " Malbrouck " exerted over the minds of the French army, from Marshal Villeroy downwards. During the next few months they surrendered all their chief fortresses one by one, and by the end of the year they had evacuated the Netherlands altogether. Nor was this the end of the Allies' successes, for in September Prince Eugene won a decisive victory at Turin, and the French army were driven out of Italy as well.

The proud Louis was beaten to his knees by this succession of disasters ; and early in 1707 he was forced to sue for peace. But it was in vain that he offered the Allies almost everything that they had been fighting for ; they demanded concessions that he could not possibly make, and the war was resumed. The causes and consequences of this obstinacy we must leave to the next chapter.

QUESTIONS

(1) *Explain how England came to join the Grand Alliance.*
(2) *Account for the defeat of Louis XIV in the War of the Spanish Succession.*

CHAPTER XXXV

A Tory Peace and a Whig Succession

(1706–1714)

After the refusal of peace terms to Louis in 1707 *the tide of the Allies' success slackened, and in the end the French King was able to obtain much better terms than had at one time seemed possible. The triumph of the Tory Party in England contributed much to this result ; but that Party was hindered by internal dissensions from preventing the Hanoverian Succession which led to its downfall.*

171. *The War becomes a Whig War*

The Tory Parliament which had been provoked into war by the aggressions of Louis XIV had never been enthusiastic about it. Wars had to be paid for mainly by increases in the Land Tax, which fell far more heavily on Tory squires than on Whig merchants, and they felt that England had had quite enough of fighting the French on behalf of the Dutch and the Hapsburgs. The Queen herself was much of the same opinion ; it was only the influence of the Duchess of Marlborough that kept her steady in support of the war during the first few years of her reign. We must never forget that the Tory Party was above all things the High Church Party ; they were really far more interested in baiting the Dissenters than in beating the French. They were particularly annoyed that well-to-do Nonconformists were qualifying for office by attending Holy Communion in the Anglican Church two or three times a year. To prevent this evasion of the Clarendon Code, they brought forward an *Occasional Conformity Bill*, which made it a criminal offence for any person who had thus " qualified " to attend a Noncon-

347

formist place of worship afterwards. The measure was only rejected by a small majority in the House of Lords.

Marlborough hated politics and despised politicians, but he had to concern himself with the distasteful subject in order to ensure support for his war. He had hitherto been attached to the Tory Party, but as time went on he fell out more and more with his former political associates. They hindered his recruiting, they cut down his supplies, and they belittled his achievements in the first two campaigns. Their idea of carrying on war on a restricted scale was repugnant to his whole spirit. Nor did they agree with him as to the ultimate object of the war : he was determined that Spain should go to the Archduke Charles, whereas they would have been satisfied to see Philip V King of Spain provided that he would renounce all claim to the throne of France and would throw open his ports to English commerce.

We can now realise what a risk Marlborough was running in undertaking his unauthorised march into Germany. Some of the Tories rejoiced when they heard of it, for they felt that he was certain to fail, and that failure would mean ruin to him and his policy. But he did not fail. On the contrary, he won a victory that dazzled the whole civilised world, and raised him to a pinnacle of international glory and prestige never attained by an Englishman before or since. The nation was intoxicated with delight. The Duke on his return entered London in a procession like a Roman triumph, preceded by hundreds of French standards, the trophies of his victory. He was voted vast wealth, and was presented with the great estate of Woodstock, whereon Blenheim Palace was built for him at a cost to the nation of a quarter of a million. Adored by his country's allies and feared by her enemies, his influence was for the next few years supreme both at the Court and in the Government. He was not in the least vindictive, but his concern for the success of the war made him use his prestige to procure the defeat of Tory candidates in the election of 1705. The Queen, too, could refuse nothing to the glorious husband of her favourite. One by one she replaced the Tories in the Cabinet by Whigs who were wholehearted supporters of the war, until by 1707 it was a purely Whig Ministry, with Marlborough and his relative Godolphin (also an ex-Tory) as its leading spirits. It was this unanimity in the Government that enabled Marlborough to humble King Louis by the crowning victory of Ramillies ; but it turned out eventually to be unfortunate for all concerned that the French King's offer of peace came just at a time when the war-party was in the ascendant in England.

172. *The Union with Scotland*

The most notable legislative achievement of the reign was the abolition of the separate government of Scotland. The connection that began in 1603 had never been popular in either country, and bad feeling had increased rather than diminished throughout the century, as a result of religious differences and commercial jealousies.

The inconvenience of having one king reigning over two countries with separate governments was shown in a striking way over the *Darien Scheme* (1696–98). A group of Scottish merchants determined to start a trading settlement of their own on the isthmus of Panama, and the savings of hundreds of thrifty homes were invested in the enterprise. But it was ill-conceived and ill-managed, and the Spanish Government nipped in the bud the threat to its monopoly of the commerce of Southern and Central America. King William was annoyed with the Scots for embroiling him with an important member of the Grand Alliance, while the Scots were annoyed with him for taking no steps on their behalf. The King realised that the dual system was impossible, and that the only solution was to rule both kingdoms from London. His failing health and his preoccupation with European affairs prevented him from taking the matter up himself, and he left the policy of union as a legacy to his successor.

Proposals were brought forward in the first year of Anne's reign, but they made little progress. The Scots feared to allow their national Presbyterian Church to become subject to a Parliament in which Tory High Churchmen predominated ; while the English had no intention to allowing the Scots to share in the commercial and maritime supremacy which they had just wrested from the Dutch. A year or two later relations were embittered still more. The Scots were very angry that the English Government had arranged the Hanoverian Succession

(§ 167) without consulting them; and in 1704 the Edinburgh Parliament passed the *Act of Security*, which declared that at the death of Anne they would choose a king of their own, and another Act which provided for the formation of a Scottish army.

For a year or two it really seemed as if war was in sight; but the very nearness of such a frightful calamity gave a shock to all sensible men on both sides of the Tweed. It would almost certainly result in England being defeated in her great struggle with the protector of the Stuart cause. There was a considerable Jacobite party in both countries, and the ultimate consequence would almost certainly be a Catholic Stuart King of Scotland—and where would the rights of the Kirk be then? And what a prospect for England—a return to the bad old days of a hostile King of Scotland in alliance with France and cherishing claims to the English throne!

Something had to be done, and at once. English and Scottish commissioners were appointed by the Queen to bring about the only possible safeguard against the danger—a complete fusion of the two governments. Each side had to make great concessions—the Scots to give up their national independence, the English their trade monopoly. It was finally agreed that (*a*) Scotland should keep her own system of law and her own independent Presbyterian Church; (*b*) that Scotsmen should enjoy equal commercial rights with Englishmen; and (*c*) that the Scottish representatives should consist of about 9 per cent. of the Parliament at Westminster, while her contribution to the combined finances should (in view of her comparative poverty) be only $2\frac{1}{2}$ per cent. In March, 1707, the last Scottish Parliament was dissolved at Edinburgh, and on May 1 of the same year the " United Kingdom of Great Britain " came into existence. On the whole, the Scots had the better of the bargain; but it would have been a disastrous source of weakness to England during the next two centuries if she had made enemies of them as she did of the Irish.

173. *Political Upheaval*

When in 1707 the Whig Government refused King Louis' offer to concede all the points that had been the original cause of

the war they committed a crime against peace.   That crime met
with a signal retribution.

Almost from this moment the tide of war began to turn
against the Allies.   Prince Eugene failed in an attack on Toulon,
and the Emperor soon afterwards agreed to an armistice so far
as the Italian theatre of war was concerned.   Charles XII, the
brilliant young warrior-king of Sweden, threatened to invade

THE NETHERLANDS, c. 1702

Germany on behalf of France.   This made the smaller Princes of
the Empire withdraw their contingents from the Imperial Army ;
and their defection led to a French victory on the Upper Rhine
that laid Vienna once more open to attack.   The island of
Minorca was captured by the English fleet ; but on the mainland
of Spain the Allies were decisively defeated by the Duke of
Berwick (the natural son of James II, and one of the ablest
generals of the day) at *Almanza* (1707).   In the Netherlands

Marlborough certainly managed to win a big battle at *Oudenarde* in 1708, but his losses were so severe, and the Dutch were so half-hearted, that he was unable to follow the victory up.

In 1709 Louis again made peace-proposals. This time he offered to abandon all support of Philip V's claim to the Spanish throne and to give the Dutch a line of Barrier Fortresses in the Netherlands ; but still neither the Allies nor the British Government were satisfied. They demanded that Louis should himself send an army to compel his grandson to evacuate Spain. This was more than flesh and blood could stand. The French people were in the last extremity of exhaustion and misery, the peasants dying by thousands of sheer starvation ; but at this outrageous demand they rallied once more round their old king and renewed the struggle. At the battle of *Malplaquet* (September, 1709) the ragged and hungry French army offered such a determined resistance to Marlborough that he suffered 25,000 casualties, including thirteen British generals. The French were compelled to give ground, and the Allies were therefore able to claim a victory, but the great Duke's glory was fading with every battle he fought.

At home in England the nation was growing heartily sick of the Whig leaders and their war, especially as expenses were increasing and successes diminishing year by year. The wave of Toryism which had been gathering during the later years of William III had been thrust back by the war-passion for a time, but it now began to sweep over the country with irresistible force. It was favoured by the situation at the Court. The Queen was a devoted supporter of the Church and of the independent power of the monarchy. She hated being at the mercy of a political clique, above all when it was a Whig clique ; and the Whig party had used their ascendancy to compel her to accept as ministers men whom she disliked and distrusted, such as Sunderland. Moreover, though the faithfullest of friends, she was at last becoming tired of the overbearing tantrums of the Duchess of Marlborough ; and the Tory leaders, realising how much they might gain by this estrangement, contrived that the Queen should find a substitute in a lady of their own persuasion, the mild and amiable Mrs. Abigail Masham. Then Marlborough made matters worse by demanding that he should be made Captain-General for life. He pointed out that this would give renewed confidence to the Allies, who feared that he might be dismissed by a turn of the political wheel at Westminster; but his demand was refused, and it did much to diminish his already waning popularity; for the idea of an ambitious and all-powerful military prince was abhorrent to all classes.

The Whigs felt the ground quaking beneath their feet, and they determined to stop the Tory propaganda which was undermining them. A High Church clergyman named *Sacheverell* preached a violent sermon before the Lord Mayor and Aldermen "On the Perils from False Brethren," in the course of which he attacked the ministers as enemies to Church and Crown. In an ill-advised moment of exasperation, the Government decided to impeach him for libel. At once this hot-headed but otherwise insignificant parson became a figure-head for all the latent anti-war and anti-Whig feeling in the country. So extravagant was the prisoner's popularity that the House of Lords dared not pass a severe sentence upon him—he was merely forbidden to preach for three years. The whole episode gave an immense stimulus to the Tory reaction, and the Queen was emboldened to dismiss her Whig ministers, one by one—including even Marlborough's closest political ally, Godolphin. By the end of the summer of 1710 the complexion of the Government had entirely changed, and a General Election had returned a strong Tory majority to Parliament.

174. *The Peace of Utrecht*

The chief Tory ministers were *Robert Harley* (1661–1724), the Lord Treasurer, and *Henry St. John* (1678–1751), the Secretary of State. Harley had begun his political life as a Whig, and he was always for moderate courses. He had considerable financial ability, and his chief work was to restore order at the Treasury, which had broken down under the prolonged strain of the war. Amongst other devices he raised a loan on terms very similar to those which brought the Bank of England into existence (§ 164); only in this case it was exclusive trading privileges with South America after the war that were promised to subscribers. This was the origin of the famous *South Sea Company*. St. John was a very different type of man. He was little more than

TUDOR T.   N thirty at this time, but he had already made a mark as a brilliant debater. A man of extraordinary political sagacity, he did not believe that Harley's half-measures could be successful in the long run, and was all for bold and adventurous courses.

The Tories were bent on making peace, and they had a very strong case. The Emperor Joseph I (who had succeeded his father, Leopold I, in 1708) had died childless after a very short reign, and his brother—formerly the Archduke Charles—had become the Emperor Charles VI. It seemed absurd that England should go on pouring out blood and gold in order to make him ruler of a two-fold empire that would exceed that of his great ancestor Charles V. Moreover, the Spaniards had shown such a decided preference for Philip V that it was impossible to expel him from the Peninsula. The great obstacle to peace was the greediness of the Allies, each hoping to wring the utmost from the defeat of Louis XIV. St. John therefore opened secret negotiations with France without consulting them. The terms eventually agreed upon were as follows. Philip was to be King of Spain with Spanish America, but was to give up all rights to the French throne. The Emperor was to become the dominant power in Italy by the acquisition of Milan, Naples and Sardinia, and was also to gain the Spanish Netherlands. The Prince of Piedmont was to have Sicily. The Dutch Republic was to be guaranteed against future French aggressions by the possession of six border fortresses in Belgian territory. Britain was assured of naval supremacy in the Mediterranean by the cession of Gibraltar and Minorca, while in America she gained Acadia (henceforth known as Nova Scotia) ; and she was also awarded the Asiento— the sole right of supplying the Spanish colonies with negro slaves. Finally, the Hanoverian Succession was recognised by France, and the Stuart exiles banished to Lorraine.

When these terms were published (November, 1711) there was a tremendous outcry, not only amongst the Allies, who felt that they had been betrayed, but amongst the Opposition in England, who declared that Britain ought to have gained much more from her victories. There was still a small Whig majority in the Lords, and that House refused to approve of the terms as a basis for peace. Thereupon the Ministry induced the Queen to create twelve new Tory peers, and by means of these extra votes the terms were passed. The Government then took the decisive step of dismissing Marlborough from his command, and calling upon him to face charges of accepting bribes from Army contractors and commissions on the payment of subsidies to the Allies. The great Duke had set a fine example to the commanders of his age in his care for the welfare of his men and in his humanity towards the enemy, but he was intensely avaricious, and there is no doubt that he was not altogether innocent of these accusations. It was nevertheless a lamentable end to his career that his coach should have been assailed in the London streets with cries of " Stop thief ! " and that he should have been driven to seek refuge abroad.

Peace had not actually been signed with France, but the Government instructed Marlborough's successor, the Duke of Ormonde, to do as little fighting as possible ; and at a critical moment in the campaign of 1712 the troops (to their own intense disgust) were actually withdrawn from contact with the enemy. The Allies tried to continue, but, deprived of the master mind who had held them together, they were defeated, and compelled to make peace.

The main lines of the Treaty of Utrecht (1713) were those already agreed upon by France and England. On the whole it was a wise and just treaty. Its worst blemish was the abandonment of the Catalans, who had taken arms against Philip V at the instigation of England, and were now left to face his resentment unsupported.

Let us now summarise briefly the results of the war. The French monarchy had recovered in the later stages much of the ground it had lost at first and had put its candidate on the throne of Spain ; but the economic exhaustion of those terrible years set it on the road to the ruin, which overtook it eighty years later. The Hapsburgs gained Italy, but this divided their interests and distracted their attention from the government of the Empire. That venerable institution gradually decayed and was abolished a century later. The only real gainer by the war was England. Her prestige had increased enormously through the financial support she was able to give the Allies and through the genius of Marlborough, and she was henceforth indisputably the leading maritime and commercial power of the world.

175. *The Hanoverian Succession*

The Ministry had hastened on the settlement of Utrecht lest Queen Anne, who was in failing health, should die before the treaty was signed ; for at her death the Act of Settlement would come into force, and George of Hanover (who had now succeeded to the claims of his mother) would probably want to continue the war at the behest of his overlord the Emperor.* Having insured against this danger, the Earl of Oxford (as Harley had recently become) and Viscount Bolingbroke (St. John's new title) began to consider if they could not set the Act of Settlement aside altogether. It would place Britain once more under a foreign king who would embroil her in Continental complications on behalf of his home-land, and it would lead to the reinstatement of the Whigs, the authors of the Revolution and the enemies of France. They had included a guarantee of the Hanoverian Succession in the Treaty of Utrecht so as to make it palatable to the public, but they now opened secret negotiations with the son of James II, who was called " James III " by his supporters and " The Pretender " by his enemies. The essential condition of a restoration, they explained to him, was that he should conform to the Church of England. But to their dismay they found that nothing would shake his adherence to the Catholic faith in which he had been nurtured, nor would he pledge himself to give more than " a reasonable security " for Protestantism. What was to be done next ? Upon this question the Tory leaders quarrelled. Harley was for a reconciliation with the Whigs and for making his peace with the Elector ; but Bolingbroke favoured a bolder plan. He proposed to strengthen the hold of his party on the Government, so that when the critical moment came he would be in a position to enforce reasonable concessions from the Pretender ; or, failing that, to compel the Elector to accept a Tory ministry.

With this in view, he threw in his lot with the Tory squires of the October Club, who wanted to impeach the Whig leaders and persecute Dissenters. They had already managed to pass

---

* The Emperor refused to make peace in 1713 and continued the war alone for another year, when he agreed to the Utrecht terms in the Treaty of Rastadt (1714).

into law their *Occasional Conformity Act*, and he now led them in promoting a *Schism Act* (1714), which forbade any person not licensed by a bishop to teach in any school. The children of Dissenters were to have a Church education or none; Nonconformity was to be cut out at its very roots, and Whiggery was to be deprived of its main support.*

For six months the struggle between the leaders went on. Everything depended on the Queen; and it was always very difficult to get her to take a decisive course upon anything, particularly if it involved dismissing ministers who had served her faithfully. Gradually, however, the active and energetic Bolingbroke gained the upper hand. His advocacy of the Schism Act enabled him to pose as a supporter of High Church; and Anne hated the idea of the Hanoverian Succession. She was half convinced that the death of her children was a punishment of heaven for her desertion of her father in 1689, and it seemed that the best amends she could make would be to bring about the succession of her half-brother—if only he could be persuaded to be reasonable about the Church. At last Bolingbroke had his way. On July 27 his rival was dismissed and he became the undisputed head of the Government. He now pushed on his preparations with frantic haste; but it was too late, for the Queen died barely a week later.

Whigs were still in possession of most of the legal and administrative posts, for which it had been difficult to find Tory substitutes. In the days of their power they had passed an Act which made elaborate arrangements for transferring the government to the Hanoverian on the Queen's death, and these they immediately put into force. Bolingbroke was only half prepared for the crisis, and was powerless to resist these measures. King George I was proclaimed without a sign of opposition.

QUESTIONS.

(1) *How far did the War of the Spanish Succession fulfil the objects with which it had been undertaken by the Allies?*

(2) *Account for the success of the Tories in* 1710 *and for their failure in* 1714.

* These Acts were both repealed early in the next reign.

CHAPTER XXXVI

The Spirit of the Age

(1660–1714)

We must now seek to depict in a few words the spirit—political, philosophical, commercial, and artistic—that manifested itself in the national life and character during this period.

176. The Party Spirit

Perhaps the most notable feature of the period is the shaping of the political parties. In our own days the rise of the Labour Party has somewhat altered the conditions of political life; but until fifty years ago the Liberals and Conservatives were still recognisable as the descendants of the Whigs and Tories who struggled over the Exclusion Bill in the days of Charles II.

Briefly, we may say that the Tories were the party of order and stability, the Whigs the party of liberty and progress. The Tories stood for the prestige of the Monarchy, the Whigs for the privileges of Parliament. The backbone of Toryism was the landed interest—the squires; the backbone of Whiggism was the monied interest—the merchants. The Tories were hand-in-glove with the Established Church, the Whigs with the Dissenters. The Tories were the party of character, the Whigs the party of brains. The main strength of the Tories lay in the countryside, that of the Whigs lay in the towns.

These contrasting characteristics led to sharp divergences of policy on almost every subject of public interest. For instance, the Revolution Settlement, which placed permanent restriction upon the power of the sovereign, was the work of the Whigs. The Stuart dynasty, which had fallen through its leaning towards absolutism, was supported by Louis XIV, whose régime was the archetype of that form of rule. Consequently, the Whigs were the party which wished the country to take an active part in checking the ascendancy of France, while the Tories wanted the country to mind its own affairs and withdraw from foreign entanglements. The French wars were supported by the merchants who profited 'from Army contracts and Government loans. Hence " The City " and all connected with it were always Whig—especially as another Restoration would probably lead to the repudiation of a National Debt incurred to keep the Stuarts off the throne.

The Tories felt that the only class to which it was safe to entrust political power was the landed interest, for they alone had " a stake in the country " and were bound up with its interests ; and they viewed with dismay the growing influence of men whose property consisted merely of goods and chattels, or investments in Government loans. With this in mind, they passed a law in 1714 to disqualify any one from sitting in Parliament unless he held land to the value of at least £300 a year. This Act remained on the Statute Book until 1828, but it hardly ever fulfilled its purpose, for the monied men had little difficulty in evading it. As a matter of fact, most of them invested a part of their capital in land.

It may at first sight seem a contradiction of all this that the nobility who owned the greatest estates were mostly Whigs ; but the explanation is simple. These men had everything to gain from the power of Parliament, inasmuch as they were supreme in it. They sat in the House of Lords themselves, and they exercised the tremendous power of the landlord in many of the boroughs which returned members to the House of Commons.

Nevertheless, the great majority of Englishmen lived in the country, and were subject to the " squirearchy." Consequently, the normal tendency of the nation was towards Toryism. Where the Whigs scored was in their hold over the more intelligent classes of the community, especially the professions ; and this was the strongest factor in their favour when the crisis came in 1714 (§ 180).

177. The " Augustan " Spirit

With the Restoration a new spirit came over English Literature. This may be traced to two influences—the ascendancy of the court of Louis XIV over the mind of Europe, and the reaction from the rigid moral code enforced by the Puritan Republic. " The Saints " had closed the theatres and had forbidden the most harmless pleasures ; and their downfall led to an outbreak of frivolity and licentiousness that found expression particularly in the comedies of such writers as Congreve and Wycherley. But it was the model of Versailles, with its artificiality and sense of " style," that was the most abiding influence. The world of Louis XIV and of his imitators (including the Stuart kings) was a world of gentlemen, and the literature of the period was a literature for gentlemen. Perfection of form became the aim of the writer in verse or prose, rather than the worth of the matter.

There were two notable exceptions to this—two survivals of the lofty spirit and moral earnestness of Puritanism at its best. *John Milton* (1600–1673) had been so closely associated with the Regicides that after the Restoration he was in danger for some time ; and it is said that he owed his pardon to the personal intervention of Charles II. In poverty, blindness, and obscurity he now produced the greatest epic poem in the language, " Paradise Lost," the subject of which is the Fall of Man. A very different type of Puritanism was represented by *John Bunyan* (1628–1688), a Bedfordshire tinker, who was repeatedly imprisoned under the Clarendon Code for unauthorised preaching. In gaol he wrote a number of devotional books, the most famous being " The Pilgrim's Progress," an allegory of human life and salvation—perhaps the most remarkable product of an untutored mind in the whole history of literature.

The verse of the new age found a characteristic form in rhymed couplets, in which the sentence usually closes at the end of the second line. This would have been an intolerable restriction to the untamed and passionate spirit of Shakespeare, but it was admirably suited for didactic and satirical poems, which aim at lucidity, neatness of expression, and epigrammatic wit. The first great master of this form of versification was *John Dryden* (1631–1700) who wrote a "Defence of Dramatic Poetry," in which he deplores Shakespeare's inattention to the rules of composition. His "Absolom and Achitophel" is the most famous satirical poem in the English language. It was written at the crisis of the Exclusion Bill, and attacks Shaftesbury as the evil counsellor who led the King's beloved son into rebellion against his father. It had much effect in turning the current of public feeling in favour of the Court (§ 148).

Dryden's literary successor was *Alexander Pope* (1688–1744), in whom scintillating wit and hard polish of style were carried to the highest pitch of perfection. In his versified "Essay on Criticism" he calls upon poets to return to the Greek and Latin classics for their models. His most famous poem was "The Rape of the Lock," a mock-epic on a trivial incident in fashionable society.

The choice of such subjects as these for poetry suggests that the tone of men's minds was eminently prosaic, and some of the greatest masters of English prose were writing during the latter part of the period. Indeed, the political controversies of Queen Anne's reign were the direct cause of a good deal of it. In those days there were no regular newspapers, and no parliamentary reports. The only means by which the political leaders could reach the public mind was the publication of pamphlets, and each party hired a number of writers. The most famous of those on the Whig side was *Daniel Defoe* (1663–1731), the greatest literary "hack" that ever lived. He could turn his hand to almost any kind of prose-writing that was in demand, and he excelled in half-imaginary memoirs such as "A Journal of the Plague Year," and "Moll Flanders," and "Robinson Crusoe." His "New Way with Dissenters" stung the Tories into punishing him with the pillory when they got into power in 1711. The ablest of the Tory pamphleteers was *Jonathan Swift* (1667–1745), a clergyman who became Dean of St. Patrick's, Dublin. His "Conduct of the Allies" was a most able and persuasive presentation of the case for bringing to an end the War of the Spanish Succession (§ 178), and it powerfully influenced public opinion in that direction.

The reign also saw the beginning of regular journalism:

" The Tatler " (1709–11) and " The Spectator " (1711–12), in which most of the writing came from the pens of Joseph Addison and Richard Steele. These periodicals contained scraps of news, but most of their space was filled by essays on various aspects of contemporary life.

Mention must be made of two men distinguished in other forms of art : *Christopher Wren* (1632–1723), most famous of English architects, who found a unique opportunity for his genius in the rebuilding of London after the Great Fire ; and *Henry Purcell* (1658–1695), the last great English composer for two hundred years.

178. *The Colonising Spirit*

Another striking feature of the period was the growth of the American colonies. The Dutch were the first to appreciate the economic advantage of colonies ; and the important part played by their tiny republic during the seventeenth century was largely due to the wealth they derived from their non-European possessions, especially in Asia. By the middle of the century the rulers of both France and England had learned the lesson. They began to make conscious efforts to extend the settlements which had been made by pioneers in North America, the French going mainly up the St. Lawrence, the English along the eastern seaboard. There was a noteworthy contrast in the methods of the two governments. The French had absolutism in their blood. Louis XIV and Colbert selected the settlers and superintended every detail of their lives in their new homes. The result was that they were never really independent of their Mother Country, and were always a source of expense to it. The English, on the other hand, made little attempt to organise emigration, and left their colonists free to regulate their internal affairs themselves. In the French settlements the King's commands were the only authority, while the English colonies had parliaments of their own almost from the first. Louis was determined to keep Canada strictly Catholic, and forbade the Huguenots to settle there ; whereas the English colonies (at any rate after the middle of the century) enjoyed a degree of religious equality that was unknown even in England. This policy was largely due to the influence of Shaftesbury, who was in many respects a wise and enlightened statesman in the earlier years of his career, before he had given himself over to unscrupulous party tactics. Soon after the Restoration he procured the election of a Council of Colonies, and arranged that the philosopher Locke—the very apostle of political liberty—should be its secretary.

During the latter half of the seventeenth century three important additions were made to the Anglo-American colonies. In 1663 *Carolina* was founded to the south of Virginia, the names of the colony and its capital both being derived from that of the King. We have already mentioned that *New York* (formerly New Amsterdam) was ceded by the Dutch in 1667 (§ 140). The population included more Dutchmen than Englishmen, but they soon realised that they enjoyed far more freedom now than their own government had vouchsafed them, and within a few years they were as good English subjects as any of the other colonists. In 1680 William Penn, a remarkable man who contrived to combine the religion of a Quaker with the life of a courtier, procured an extensive grant of land between New York and Virginia, as payment of a debt owing to his father from the Crown. He here established a new colony, called *Pennsylvania* after himself, which made religious toleration its first principle, and adopted the name Philadelphia (" Brotherly love ") for its chief town.

James II showed some signs of trying to imitate the centralised colonial administration of his patron Louis XIV, but the Revolution checked this course, and gave Locke a further opportunity of organising the relations of the home government to the colonies on liberal lines. Moreover, by making Parliament the supreme factor in the State instead of the King, the Revolution had another effect, hardly apparent at the time, but momentous in the years to come. The Colonists knew and acknowledged the power of the Crown, but they were less ready to submit to the authority of a Parliament in which they were not represented. Thus out of the English Revolution developed, some eighty years later, the American.

179. *The Commercial Spirit*

A very striking feature of the two wars against Louis XIV was the advance of England to the position of chief partner in the Grand Alliance. This advance was due not merely to the fact that William III and Marlborough were the commanders-in-chief, but even more to the fact that the Allies began to look to England as a tower of economic strength. England took up the burden of providing her allies with the " sinews of war," which she bore off and on until the struggle against Napoleon Bonaparte. When we remember what a minor part she had hitherto played in European affairs, this rapid development seems amazing. How did it come about ?

Chiefly because of the growth of manufactures and foreign trade. This growth was partly at the expense of the Dutch, in competition with whom England had advantages both in geographical situation and in natural resources. After the Peace of Utrecht the Netherlands could not keep pace with England's rapid recovery from the strains of war, and they never again became a serious commercial rival. Then again, the Bank of England gave the country a long start in the race for economic leadership ; for upon that foundation was built a banking system far in advance of any other country, and henceforth there was regular machinery for employing English capital in productive enterprise.

It was just at this time that several Englishmen began to study what we to-day call " Political Economy." They looked on it as a branch of the art of government, designed to discover what policy tended most to enrich a country. They adopted what is known as *The Mercantile Theory*. According to this, rulers ought to seek (*a*) to import only from countries that would take our manufactures in exchange, so that we should not have to pay out hard cash ; and (*b*) to trade as little as possible with great powers like France, and as much as possible with small countries like Portugal. It was the Government's duty to carry out this two-fold principle by means of " tariff " regulations—*i.e.* import and export duties. A notable example of the policy was the *Methuen Treaty* (1703) with Portugal, which allowed Portuguese wines to come in cheaper than French wines, while

Portugal gave similar advantages to English woollen goods. This is why in the eighteenth century port replaced claret as the standard drink of the English gentleman.

We can see corollaries of these principles in the treatment of the colonies and of Ireland. The English, like the Dutch, French, and Spanish, looked upon overseas dependencies primarily as a source of profit to the Mother Country. Fresh *Navigation Acts* were passed (1661, 1696, 1706) which compelled the colonists to send their most important products to England, so that (1) London might become the entrepôt of Europe for these wares ; and (2) that the colonists might be compelled to take English manufactures in exchange for them. As for Ireland, the commercial regulations made by the English Parliament strangled the prosperity of that country for a hundred years. The Irish were not allowed to trade freely even with England or the American colonies ; and every form of industry which they took up was starved out of existence. This was a short-sighted policy, for a prosperous Ireland could have imported English goods. But it is only in modern times that we have begun to grasp the fact that the welfare of one country is dependent on that of other countries.

180. *The Scientific Spirit*

In the course of this book we have discussed the deeds of scores of kings, politicians and soldiers, but we have not mentioned the two men of the period whose lives' work most affected the ideas of future generations : Newton and Locke. History deals with men's actions rather than their minds, yet action is the outcome of mind, and no study of the latter half of the seventeenth century would be complete without some knowledge of the contribution of these two thinkers to our civilisation.

We have seen how Bacon, though he made little progress with any particular branch of Natural Philosophy, did much to arouse the scientific spirit (§ 98) in general. During the next few decades such studies became quite a fashionable hobby ; and in 1645 a group of men interested in them began to hold periodical meetings, sometimes at Oxford and sometimes in

London, to discuss the results of their inquiries. Soon after the Restoration, Charles II, himself a dabbler in chemistry, granted the little band a Charter, and it became *The Royal Society*—still the foremost institution of the kind in the world. Among its original members was *Robert Boyle*, an Irishman of aristocratic birth, who investigated the effects of pressure upon gases, and gave his name to the fundamental natural law on the subject.

But the fame of Boyle was soon eclipsed by that of another of the early members of the Society—*Sir Isaac Newton* (1642–1727). Newton became Professor of Mathematics at Cambridge University at the age of twenty-seven, and was for many years Master of Trinity College. His greatness was largely due to his inexhaustible powers of concentrated mental effort. His study of Optics, dealing particularly with the spectrum and the lens, led to the use of refracting telescopes such as are found in all the greatest observatories of to-day. In Dynamics his investigations into the force of Gravity explained the motion of the planets and laid the foundation of modern astronomy ; and in his famous book known as the " Principia " he set forth the laws of motion which constitute the basis of Mechanics. In Pure Mathematics, again, he played a great part in the invention of some of the most valuable instruments with which his successors have worked—notably the Binomial Theorem and the Calculus. Absorbed as he was in these studies, he never became a mere recluse. He played an active part in University life, while as Master of the Mint under William III he greatly assisted the reorganisation of the coinage ; and he was withal the most modest and unassuming of men. In 1703 he became President of the Royal Society, and a few years later he was knighted by Queen Anne.

John Locke (1632–1704) was another thinker whose ideas to-day colour the thoughts of millions who never heard his name. A student of Christchurch, Oxford, his practice as a physician brought him, early in the reign of Charles II, into contact with Shaftesbury, who took him into his household and procured him public employment (§ 178). With the fall of his patron he went into exile, but on his return to England after the Revolution he produced in quick succession three remarkable

books. They were all inspired by the same general principle :
the love of liberty. " The Letter on Toleration " (1689) was an
exposition of *theological* liberalism, in which he argues that
" the power of the civil government relates only to civil affairs,
and hath nothing to do with the world to come." The " Essay
on the Human Understanding " (1690)—his most famous work,
and the starting-point of all philosophy for the next hundred
years—was an exposition of *intellectual* liberalism, in which he
argues that since all knowledge comes through the senses, man
has an inviolable right to follow the findings of experience
so gained. The " Treatise on Civil Government " (1691) was
an exposition of *political* liberalism, starting from the idea that
all government is based on a sort of compact, by which men, in
order to secure peace and order, surrender a part of their natural
right to do as they like to a ruling person or body of persons ;
with the corollary that the powers thus given in trust are forfeited
if that trust is abused. This doctrine was a justification of the
Revolution ; for it implied that the will of the governed is the
basis of all political power. It silently permeated men's minds
all through the following century, and it led (partly through
Rousseau's somewhat mistaken interpretation of it) to the
Revolutions in America and France, with all their incalculable
effects in the modern world.

QUESTIONS

(1) *How far would it be true to say that John Locke was the
typical thinker of the period ?*

(2) *Trace the connection between politics and literature
during this period.*

GENERAL QUESTIONS ON BOOK IV

(1) *Show the importance of the Treaty of Dover as a landmark in this period.*

(2) *What was the origin of the Whig and Tory parties in England ?*

(3) *Explain the importance of " The Popish Plot."*

(4) *How far is it justifiable to ascribe the quarrels between the Stuart kings and their subjects to differences of religion ?*

(5) *What were* (a) *the intentions and* (b) *the results, of the three Declarations of Indulgence during this period ?*

(6) *Summarise English colonisation in America during the seventeenth century.*

(7) *Give reasons for the invitation to William of Orange, and for his acceptance.*

(8) *What difficulties did William III have to face during the first few years of the joint reign ?*

(9) *Write a short history of public finance during this period.*

(10) *Account for the Tories obtaining office in* 1710, *and for the short duration of their power.*

(11) *Trace the development of Party Government during the reigns of William III and Anne.*

(12) *Why did England take part in the Spanish Succession War, what was her share in it, and what did she gain by it ?*

(13) *Why was the Revolution* (1688) *an event of international importance ?*

(14) *Describe the struggle over the Exclusion Bill.*

(15) *How far did Charles II have his own way in public affairs ?*

(16) *What events led up to the Union of Scotland and England ?*

(17) *What was the effect of the Bill of Rights on the English constitution ?*

(18) *Sketch the career of Anthony Ashley Cooper, Earl of Shaftesbury.*

(19) *Write notes on The Schism Act, The Place Bill, The Occasional Conformity Act, The Mutiny Act, The Act of Settlement, The Test Act, The Triennial Act.*

INDEX

THE END